Dark Cognition

GW00778794

Outlining the scientific evidence behind psi research, *Dark Cognition* expertly reveals that such anomalous phenomena clearly exist, highlighting that the prevailing view of consciousness, purely as a phenomenon of the brain, fails to account for the empirical findings.

David Vernon provides essential coverage of information and evidence for a variety of anomalous psi phenomena, calling for a paradigm shift in how we view consciousness: from seeing it as something solely reliant on the brain to something that is enigmatic, fundamental and all pervasive. The book examines the nature of psi research showing that, despite claims to the contrary, it is clearly a scientific endeavour. It explores evidence from telepathy and scopaesthesia, clairvoyance and remote viewing, precognition, psychokinesis, fields of consciousness, energy healing, out of body experiences, near-death experiences and post death phenomena, showing that not only do these phenomena exist, but that they have significant implications for our understanding of consciousness.

Featuring discussion on scientific research methods, reflections on the fields of dark cognition and end-of-chapter questions that encourage critical thinking, this book is an essential text for those interested in parapsychology, consciousness and cognitive psychology.

David Vernon is Senior Lecturer in Psychology at Canterbury Christ Church University. His research interests include a wide range of anomalous phenomena and the implications they have for models/theories of consciousness. His research also encompasses techniques used to enhance human performance and creative problem solving.

"David Vernon's book *Dark Cognition* is an impressive overview of research in parapsychology. There could be no better guide to the basic issues in this field and the scientific literature on these subjects. Not only does Vernon masterfully summarise and discuss what is known, but just as importantly, points out what is not known. The questions at the end of each chapter should lead to many thoughtful discussions. I strongly recommend this book."

—Rupert Sheldrake, PhD, biologist and author of *The Science Delusion*

"*Dark Cognition* is an accurate and comprehensive overview of the scientific evidence, scholarly debates, and implications of psychic phenomena. Anyone interested in this perennially fascinating and controversial topic will benefit by studying David Vernon's book."

—Dean Radin, PhD, Chief Scientist, Institute of Noetic Sciences

"*Dark Cognition* brings together some of the main research areas within the field of parapsychology. The book covers an interesting range of topics, addressing many issues with a seriousness and clarity that makes them accessible to the non-specialist. David Vernon makes a good job of showing how important these findings are for any theory of consciousness."

—Renaud Evrard, Assistant Professor of Psychology, University of Lorraine and President of the Parapsychological Association

Dark Cognition

Evidence for Psi and its Implications for Consciousness

David Vernon

Routledge
Taylor & Francis Group

LONDON AND NEW YORK

First published 2021
by Routledge
2 Park Square, Milton Park, Abingdon, Oxon OX14 4RN

and by Routledge
52 Vanderbilt Avenue, New York, NY 10017

Routledge is an imprint of the Taylor & Francis Group, an informa business

© 2021 David Vernon

British Library Cataloguing-in-Publication Data
A catalogue record for this book is available from the British Library

Library of Congress Cataloging-in-Publication Data
A catalog record has been requested for this book

ISBN: 978-1-138-33101-3 (hbk)
ISBN: 978-1-138-33102-0 (pbk)
ISBN: 978-0-429-44748-8 (ebk)

Typeset in Sabon
by MPS Limited, Dehradun

Close friends are the family we choose.
I dedicate this book to all my chosen family,
with love

∞

Contents

Acknowledgements

Special thanks go to Tammy Dempster for conscientiously reading through every chapter and providing essential corrections, comments and feedback that often helped to make the narrative clearer and more coherent. Thanks to Sabina Hulbert for the continuous support, for making me question my assumptions and ideas, and for always being there. To Kyle Milne and Rosa Ninni for being the most amazing and inspirational friends, and for sharing the journey. It's not over yet. To Greg Fitzgerald for the stimulating coffee house conversations on mind, consciousness, soul and everything in between. Thanks also to Gary O'Mahoney for a lifetime of friendship. We still need to put the world to rights. To Ian Hocking and Dennis Nigbur for the laughter and the music. There is not enough of either in the world and it is nice to think we made some small contribution. To Akira Naito for the friendship, support and inspiration. A heartfelt thank you to Grazyna for being there, listening, offering support, encouragement and words of wisdom. A respectful nod to the memory of James Adamson who inspired me down this road more years ago than I care to remember.

Within the field of psi research, I have been fortunate to meet and be inspired by many of the leading researchers in the field. Special thanks go to Dean Radin, Rupert Sheldrake, Chris Roe, Etzel Cardeña and Renaud Evrard for your time, wisdom, guidance and support. Many thanks to Gary Hewitt, Maria Angela Lippi and Debra Katz and all those who sent me personal accounts of their own psi experiences, only some of which I have been able to include in this book. Thanks also go to my editorial team at Routledge, Cloe Holland and April Peake, for their support, encouragement and flexibility.

The following material appears with permission. The quote from Guy Playfair (2012) which appears in Chapter 3 is reprinted with permission from White Crow Books. Figures 4.1 and 4.2, which appear in Chapter 4, are reprinted with permission from the *Journal of the Society for Psychical Research*. Figure 5.9 in Chapter 5 is reprinted with permission from the *Journal of Scientific Exploration*. The quote from Stephen Braude (2007) in Chapter 6 is reprinted with permission from the University of Chicago Press. Figure 7.1 is reprinted with permission from the *Journal of Scientific Exploration*. The figures in Chapter 7 are reproduced with permissin from the following: Figure 7.2 is reprinted with permission from the journal *Foundations of Physics Letters*, published by Springer. Figure 7.3 is reprinted with permission from the *Journal of Cosmology*. Permission to use Figures 7.4, 7.5, 7.6 and 7.7 was kindly given by Roger Nelson. Finally, the quotes from Sylvia Wright (1999) in Chapter 11 appear with the permission from the *Journal of the Society for Psychical Research*.

Chapter 1

Introduction

Dark cognition

There are many mysteries in the cosmos that are both difficult to comprehend and challenging to explain. For instance, both dark matter and dark energy are believed to be pervasive throughout the cosmos, though have yet to be directly observed. Instead, their presence is implied from a range of scientific observations relating to gravitational effects and the amount of visible matter in the universe (e.g., Wang, Abdalla, Atrio-Barandela, & Pavón, 2016). In a similar way the term *dark cognition* can be used to convey two important points regarding some mysterious aspects of human behaviour and cognition. First, is that scientists have reported a wide range of unusual behavioural and cognitive experiences that challenge current understanding and are, at present, difficult to explain. Over time these experiences have been classified as including, though not limited to, telepathy, clairvoyance, precognition, psychokinesis, energy healing, out of body experiences and various post-death phenomena. Such experiences were originally given the label *psychic phenomena* though this has also changed to include *paranormal phenomena*, as well as *parapsychological, extra-sensory* and *anomalous phenomena*. More recently such experiences have been encapsulated under the more generic and potentially neutral term of *psi* (pronounced 'sigh'), where psi refers to the notion that there is some form of interaction between the individual and the environment, or between one or more individuals, in which it seems that some form of information and/or influence has occurred which cannot be explained in terms of current understanding of the relationship between cause and effect (see, Zahran, 2017). It is important to stress that such behaviours and cognition are not *para*-normal or *extra*-sensory in the sense that they are abnormal or unusual in any way. If real, and as will be shown in the following chapters there is substantial evidence to suggest they are, then such effects are the result of entirely normal human behaviour and cognition. Nevertheless it has been suggested that these various experiences and effects may represent distinct aspects of psi (Rao & Palmer, 1987), much in the same way that human memory is not a single construct but represents a range of distinct processes and systems (e.g., Roediger, Buckner, & McDermott, 1999). However, given the current level of understanding it is too early to reach any firm conclusions regarding this. The second point is that scientists are currently in the dark in terms of precisely what psi-type effects or behaviours represent, why and how they occur. The hope is of course that future research will be able to shed light on our understanding of psi behaviours and cognition, illuminating more precisely what is occurring, why and how. This in turn will likely have significant implications for models and theories of consciousness. Hence, the aim of this book is to highlight some of the evidence for psi, providing a useful resource of current findings in various areas, both to indicate what mysteries remain and to stimulate future researchers. It will also consider what the implications are of such findings for the dominant view of consciousness. However, before outlining which effects and behaviours will be examined in the following chapters it is worth reflecting briefly on how psi research began and how widespread is the belief in such phenomena. This is followed by a brief outline of how mainstream science views psi along with the dominant view of consciousness as a product of brain activity alone.

A brief history

Scientific interest and research in the possible effects of psi was to some extent initiated during the latter part of the nineteenth century when spiritual mediums alleged that they were able to communicate with deceased persons. This led to a growing level of interest by members of the academic community, such as Henry Sidgwick, Frederic Myers and Edmund Gurney, who advocated the need for rigorous empirical scrutiny of such alleged phenomena. This, in turn, led to the establishment in the United Kingdom of the Society for Psychical Research (SPR) in 1882 which had the explicit aim of investigating the various reported phenomena, real or alleged, without prejudice or prepossession whilst adopting the best practices of science and the scientific spirit of enquiry. According to Cardeña (2014) the aim was to move such phenomena from the darkness of the séance room to the hopefully more enlightened surroundings of the modern psychology laboratory. The SPR was not only interested in testing the claims of psi phenomena, it also explored other topics including unconscious cognition, hypnosis and altered states (Cardeña, Lynn, & Krippner, 2017). Similarly, in America the need to establish a scientific organisation led to the founding of the Parapsychological Association (PA) in 1957 which over time became affiliated with the American Association for the Advancement of Science in 1969 (Cardeña, 2014; Irwin, 2007). Both the SPR, which is now over 130 years old, and the PA, which recently celebrated its 60th year, are still going strong. They are both involved in holding regular meetings and organising study days, guest lectures and an annual scientific conference to showcase the most recent research. Alongside these there are several other institutions that pursue both research (e.g., Australian Society for Parapsychology; Institute of Noetic Sciences in USA; Institut Métapsychique International in Paris) and training (e.g., Arthur Findlay College; College of Psychic Studies, both in the UK) of psi-type behaviours. All of which reflects an on-going and extensive interest in the field of psi-type behaviours and effects.

Belief in psi

There may be any number of reasons why psi-based experiences and behaviours should be taken seriously. Perhaps the most obvious is the sheer prevalence of such reported experiences and the level of belief those in the population report. According to Zahran (2017) people have experienced unusual phenomena and believed in them since the 'beginning of recorded history' (p. 34). The validity of such claims is echoed in the surveys carried out across the UK and USA which have repeatedly shown that a large proportion of the population have experienced and believe in such effects. For instance, a Gallup poll reported by Newport and Strausberg (2001) not only showed that the majority of Americans believe in such things but also that there had been a slight increase in the level of such belief since 1990, suggesting that belief in such events/phenomena may be growing. Furthermore, there was a similar increase in the number of reported experiences and the poll also showed that Americans with the highest level of education were *more* likely than others to believe in effects such as the power of the mind to heal the body and telepathy. This high level of belief in psi effects and behaviours is found across societies both geographically and historically, although the content of the beliefs and experiences may vary across cultures. Indeed, a survey in Germany on attitudes towards such phenomena showed that, of those that responded, more than half gave accounts of personal experiences of such unusual events (Knittel & Schetsche, 2005). Furthermore, these experiences can often have dramatic and influential effects on the lives of those that experience them. This may be because they seemingly extend their range of conscious awareness, or offer an alternative view on the nature of consciousness (Cardeña et al., 2017).

Mainstream view of psi

It is difficult to deny the claim that the nature and content of psi-based effects are viewed by many in the mainstream to be at odds with current understanding of science and the world view (Lamont, 2012). Indeed, some view effects such as extra-sensory perception as representing a problematic area of pseudoscience which need to be dealt with by mainstream psychology adopting a more critical model of understanding (Lilienfeld, Lohr, & Morier, 2001). Others have gone so far as to suggest that proponents of psi may be incompetent observers, lack sufficient scepticism or lack the necessary scientific training (Lamont, 2012). A slightly more measured response comes from Hyman (2010) who argued that the limited progress made by the field, in terms of its understanding of the various phenomena under observation, has in turn limited its recognition as a legitimate area of scientific interest.

However, Irwin (2007) has argued that this is a 'misperception' of the field as either unscientific or pseudo-scientific. Indeed, Tart (2009) has argued that the evidence for psi is often irrationally ignored by mainstream scientists and irrationally attacked by ill-informed sceptics. For instance, the research findings from the field tend to be published in selected and/or topic specific journals which have only a limited distribution, readership and impact, and are largely ignored by the mainstream. This, Irwin (2007) points out, means that mainstream awareness regarding the level and quality of evidence from psi research is very limited which in turn weakens the case for the field. Hence, despite the attempts by those conducting psi research to communicate their findings in the form of published peer reviewed scientific journal articles, many have argued that mainstream science simply ignores the field and its findings (e.g., Cardeña, 2018; Luke, 2012; Roe, 2015). There are two lines of enquiry that would seem to support this view. The first examines how many university departments conduct such research and the second asks how much coverage psi receives in mainstream psychology textbooks.

The potential importance of housing the topic within university departments is essential to enable the coverage of the subject to be disseminated to a potentially new generation of students who in time may themselves go on to become the researchers of tomorrow. This is not only an essential component to maintaining the growth of the field but also provides explicit recognition of the area as a legitimate topic of enquiry and research. From an initial survey conducted by Luke (2012), only around four universities in the USA offered some form of teaching in parapsychologically based topics. Luke (2012) has argued that the low offering of such topics suggests a resistance to covering the subject at university level. Indeed Watt (2012) has suggested that the centre of gravity, particularly in terms of the focus on research, has shifted from the USA to Europe. However, Luke (2012) found that of those universities that responded, only six within the UK, out of a total of around 130, taught some combination of parapsychology and/or anomalistic psychology, usually as final year undergraduate options. Such a number certainly seems at the low end given that there are currently over 500 accredited courses on psychology within the UK (British Psychological Society, 2019). This lack of coverage in both the USA and the UK represents a severe limitation to the potential growth of the field in general. It also hinders progress and inhibits recruitment of people to the discipline. Roe (2015) has suggested that this may to an extent be because scientific education is less concerned with encouraging independent critical thinking than in ensuring the incoming students learn and adopt a set of agreed upon practices and approaches to ensure that research work is carried out in the accepted manner. Such a process of socialisation naturally informs the individual in terms of what are and what are not deemed acceptable questions that can be asked and what are acceptable techniques for attempting to find answers. The lack of coverage also gives an implicit indication that the field of psi is somehow outside of the normal mainstream discipline of psychology.

Despite the interest that undergraduate and postgraduate students show in such topics there is also a surprising lack of coverage in key mainstream psychology texts. For example, Roe (2015) surveyed a range of introductory psychology textbooks with the aim of finding out what impression of psi research was presented to undergraduate students within the UK. Roe (2015) found that 50% of the books surveyed made no mention of the field at all and of those that did include some findings related to psi the frame of reference was invariably as a function of distinguishing between myth and reality, with evidence for psi coming under the heading of the former. Furthermore, such texts often presented those studying psi as being distinct from 'scientists' and hence implicitly suggesting that the field is unscientific. Moreover, when there was coverage of psi effects it tended to be overly simplistic and did not provide an accurate picture of the field in general, defaulting to a 'not proven' position. Hence, if the topic is not ignored completely it is often misrepresented, conveying the general view that there is no real evidence here. Such inaccurate information Roe (2015) argues borders on wilful misinformation.

Prevailing view of consciousness

Despite the seemingly obvious implications for human consciousness, mainstream theories tend to deal with the issue of psi by ignoring it and relying on the

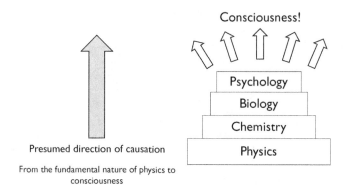

Consciousness!

Psychology

Biology

Chemistry

Physics

Presumed direction of causation

From the fundamental nature of physics to consciousness

Figure 1.1 The direction of causal influence upwards from physics with each realm assumed to deal with mereologically more complicated events, such that causation at the higher levels is derived from or based on events at the lower level(s).

assumption that consciousness is simply an emergent phenomenon of the brain and that all that is required is a better understanding of how the brain works to more fully understand consciousness. However, it should be noted that, at present, there is no single dominant or grand unified theory of human consciousness. Nevertheless, the generally accepted view of consciousness is one that is in-corporated within a view of reality that is referred to as suggesting *upward causation*, whereby physics is thought to represent the basis of reality, upon which chemistry is founded, then biology and then psychology out of which emerges consciousness (see Figure 1.1).

The currently accepted view of mind or consciousness in psychology is one that is encapsulated within the field of scientific materialism. That is, mind or consciousness are simply reliant on and the product of biological brain activity. The notion that *consciousness is the brain and its activity* is often conveyed as an incontrovertible fact that is simply beyond any reasonable doubt (e.g., Beauregard, Trent, & Schwartz, 2018). Essentially this idea suggests that all sensations and perceptions, memories, feelings and emotions are all fundamentally linked to and emergent from the brain. Furthermore, that understanding of these behaviours and states will *only* be available by fully understanding the underlying biological substrate of the brain. Hence, from this it is clear that consciousness resides in the brain and that with the death of the brain consciousness simply ends. Beauregard et al. (2018) have suggested that psychology adopted this view because it sees physics as the fundamental foundation of reality and that in order for psychology to be seen as a legitimate and acceptable science it needed to adopt the same view as its older more well-established cousin. However, this view has a significant impact on the scientific world not least because it represents the established orthodoxy. Furthermore, it is often portrayed as an in-disputable 'fact' that newcomers to the field of science need to learn and accept in order to move on and up.

Given this, a key question the reader should keep in mind prior to and during the examination of the relevant data in the following chapters relates to the implications of such findings for consciousness (see Figure 1.2).

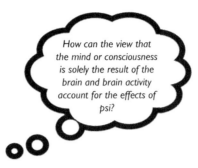

Figure 1.2 A question to keep in mind as you read.

Outline

Each of the following chapters will explore a particular psi-related topic or behaviour. However, given the contentious nature of the field and its findings (e.g., Cardeña, 2014, 2015) chapter 2 begins by providing a brief outline of the nature and processes of the scientific paradigm, distinguishing between ontology and epistemology and identifying the key aspects related to the scientific process (Clough, 2000). Such an exploration needs to include questions such as what should science examine (see, Cardeña, 2015; Saey, 2012), what constitutes evidence, from where and how should it be examined/analysed (e.g., Braude, 2016). It is also worth exploring and clarifying some of the methodological challenges faced by those conducting psi research, such as sampling, participant/experimenter belief, optional stopping effects, issues related to replication, relevance of pre-registration and issues of deception (Hitchman, Pfeuffer, Roe, & Sherwood, 2016; Roe, 2016a, 2016b).

This is followed by an exploration of some of the evidence from a selection of domains within the field of psi. For instance, chapter 3 examines the notion that information can be communicated and/or obtained directly from one mind to another, commonly referred to as telepathy. An associated aspect of this is the notion that individuals often report the idea that they are able to detect when another person is starting at them, something generally referred to as scopaesthesia. The fourth chapter explores the topics of clairvoyance and remote viewing. Clairvoyance refers to the acquisition of information relating to a target person and/or object via non-normal routes. It is distinct from telepathy in the sense that it need not involve another conscious entity. Remote viewing is similar to clairvoyance in the sense that the percipient attempts to obtain information about an item and/or location from a distance via non-ordinary means. However, it is distinct in the sense that the percipient need not enter into an altered state and the procedure may involve pairs of individuals with one acting as a *sender* and the other as a *receiver*. Following this chapter five examines the evidence for precognition, which refers to the notion that behaviour/cognition that occurs now may be influenced by information regarding a future event that is obtained via a non-usual route, prior to the occurrence of the event. Chapter six focuses on research exploring the notion that the conscious human mind may be able to exert a direct influence over a specified target at a distance by thought alone, encapsulated within the term psychokinesis (PK), with fine grained distinctions made between micro PK, macro PK and the direct mental influence on livings systems (DMILS) research. Chapter seven explores the idea that fields of consciousness may exist and can be influenced by global events and the coherent meditative actions of large groups. This is followed by chapter eight which examines the field of energy healing, which refers to the idea that certain individuals are assumed to be able to channel an unknown form of energy, either by thought alone or directed via their hands, into a recipient in an effort to restore that person's health. Chapter nine explores reported out of body experiences, which refers to the idea that an individual allegedly experiences the world or information from a location that is separate from the location of their physical body, and this may or may not involve them viewing their own body. Chapter ten examines evidence suggesting that individuals who had physically died for a short period of time, when resuscitated, report a range of experiences during the time they were thought to be dead. Such near-death experiences are growing increasingly common as resuscitation techniques improve and they provide some interesting insights into the potential nature of consciousness. Chapter eleven takes this idea a step further by examining a range of post-death phenomena. Specifically, it focuses on after death communications, mediumship and electronic voice phenomena. The findings from all three areas have implications for what is commonly referred to as the survival hypothesis. The final chapter reflects back on the evidence covered from the various fields of enquiry and asks how such findings can be accounted for using the current dominant model of human consciousness. However, the fact that the current dominant approach to consciousness fails to provide any sort of coherent account for the findings relating to psi leads to the call for a paradigm shift. This shift requires that consciousness be seen as fundamental.

Useful online resources

The following represent some of the key online resources that provide a useful range of topic information on psi research and effects:

- Society for Psychical Research: https://www.spr.ac.uk/
- Free online psi encyclopaedia: https://www.spr.ac.uk/publicationsrecordings/psi-encyclopedia
- Parapsychological Association: http://www.parapsych.org/
- Institute of Noetic Sciences: http://noetic.org/
- Koestler Parapsychology Unit: https://koestlerunit.wordpress.com/
- Parapsychology Foundation: http://parapsychology.org/

References

Beauregard, M., Trent, N. L., & Schwartz, G. E. (2018). Toward a postmaterialist psychology: Theory, research, and applications. *New Ideas in Psychology, 50,* 21–33. doi: 10.1016/j.newideapsych.2018.02.004.
Braude, S. E. (2016). *Crimes of reason: On mind, nature, and the paranormal.* Boulder, CO: Rowman & Littlefield.

British Psychological Society (2019). Find an accredited course. Retrieved 29/10/2019, from https://www.bps.org.uk/public/become-psychologist/accredited-courses?type=UG.

Cardeña, E. (2014). A call for an open, informed study of all aspects of consciousness. *Frontiers in Human Neuroscience, 8*(17), 1–4. doi: 10.3389/fnhum.2014.00017.

Cardeña, E. (2015). The unbearable fear of psi: On scientific suppression in the 21st century. *Journal of Scientific Exploration, 29*(4), 601–620.

Cardeña, E. (2018). The experimental evidence for parapsychological phenomena: A review. *American Psychologist, 73*(5), 663–677. doi: 10.1037/amp0000236.

Cardeña, E., Lynn, S. J., & Krippner, S. (2017). The psychology of anomalous experience: A rediscovery. *Psychology of Consciousness: Theory, Research and Practice, 4*(1), 4–22. doi: 10.1037/cns0000093.

Clough, M. P. (2000). The nature of science: Understanding how the game of science is played. *The Clearning House: A Journal of Educational Strategies, 74*(1), 13–17.

Hitchman, G. A., Pfeuffer, C. U., Roe, C. A., & Sherwood, S. J. (2016). The effects of experimenter-participant interaction qualities in a goal-oriented nonintentional precognition task. *Journal of Parapsychology, 80*(1), 45–69.

Hyman, R. (2010). The demise of parapsychology, 1850–2009. *The Skeptic, 22*(2), 17–20.

Irwin, H. J. (2007). Science, nonscience and rejected knowledge: The case of parapsychology. *Australian Journal of Parapsychology, 7*(1), 8–32.

Knittel, I., & Schetsche, M. (2005). Everyday miracles: Results of a representative survey in Germany. *European Journal of Parapsychology, 20*(1), 3–21.

Lamont, P. (2012). The making of extraordinary psychological phenomena. *Journal of the History of Behavioral Sciences, 48*(1), 1–15. doi: 10.1002/jhbs.21516.

Lilienfeld, S. O., Lohr, J. M., & Morier, D. (2001). The teaching of courses in the science and pseudoscience of psychology: Useful resources. *Teaching of Psychology, 28*(3), 182–191.

Luke, D. (2012). Parapsychology and anomalistic psychology in the UK: A brief review. *Mindfield: The Bulletin of the Parapsychological Association, 4*(2), 59–63.

Newport, F., & Strausberg, M. (2001). Americans' belief in psychic and paranormal phenomena is up over last decade. Retrieved 11/06/2018, from http://news.gallup.com/poll/4483/americans-belief-psychic-paranormal-phenomena-over-last-decade.aspx.

Rao, K. R., & Palmer, J. (1987). The anomaly called psi: Recent research and criticism. *Behavioral and Brain Sciences, 10*(4), 539–551.

Roe, C. A. (2015). What are psychology students told about the current state of parapsychology? *Mindfield, 7*(3), 86–91.

Roe, C. A. (2016a). Is inconsistency our only consistent outcome? *Mindfield, 8*(2), 70–75.

Roe, C. A. (2016b). The problem of fraud in parapsychology. *Mindfield, 8*(1), 8–17.

Roediger, H. L., Buckner, R. L., & McDermott, K. B. (1999). Components of processing. In J. K. Foster & M. Jelicic (Eds.), *Memory: Systems, process or function?* (pp. 31–65). Oxford: University Press.

Saey, T. H. (2012). Designer flu: How scientists made a killer virus airborne – and who should know. *Science News, 181*(11), 20–25.

Tart, C. T. (2009). *The end of materialism: How evidence of the paranormal is bringing science and spirit together.* New York: New Harbinger.

Wang, B., Abdalla, E., Atrio-Barandela, F., & Pavón, D. (2016). Dark matter and dark energy interactions: Theoretical challenges, cosmological implications and observational signatures. *Reports on Progress in Physics, 79*(9), 096901. doi: 10.1088/0034-4885/79/9/096901.

Watt, C. (2012). Integration or independence? *Journal of Parapsychology, 76*, 63–64.

Zahran, S. K. (2017). What is psi? From anti-parapsychology to psi as a next scientific revolution: Theoretical reviews and hypothesized vision. *American Journal of Applied Psychology, 5*(2), 33–44. doi: 10.12691-ajap-5-2-1.

Chapter 2

Psi as science

When examining any type of research and in particular those findings argued to be based on psi, as they are distinctly unusual by nature, it is imperative to have a clear understanding of the nature of science and the scientific process as well as some of the methodological challenges faced by those conducting research in this area. This is also important because it can help to address some of the critical claims often levelled at psi research (e.g., Helfand, 2011; Hyman, 2010; Shermer, 1997; Smith, 2010, see Table 2.1).

Reading through the criticisms shown in Table 2.1 raises a number of questions regarding the scientific nature of psi research. First, is the question of whether psi research is scientific and whether its findings represent an assault on science. To help understand these issues the chapter begins by outlining the nature of science, explaining both the paradigm and the process. Second, is the presumption that psi research requires some form of extraordinary evidence. This raises a number of issues, including how evidence is obtained, what processes can be used to discriminate between types of evidence and whether there is a need for such evidence to be extraordinary. The chapter examines these points by exploring the nature of evidence from anecdote to experimental, highlighting the use of Occam's razor as a discriminatory tool and exploring the concept of extraordinary evidence. Finally, there are the claims of experimenter effects, inconsistent findings, poor replication, possible fraud and the file drawer effect. These claims are often grouped under the heading of methodological issues with an assumption that they relate specifically to psi research alone, the implication being that the field of psi research lacks a robust methodological approach which in turn raises doubts regarding any findings. However, whilst these do represent methodological challenges they are in no

Table 2.1 A selection of critical claims levelled at psi and psi research

Critical claims
• Psi research is not really science.
• The findings of psi research are an assault on science and rationality.
• The extraordinary claims of psi require extraordinary evidence.
• The results of psi are simply due to experimenter effects.
• Psi research fails to produce consistent, independent replications.
• Evidence for psi is likely the result of fraud or a file drawer effect.

way unique to psi research. A brief examination of each claim will help to make this clear.

The nature of science

It is worth stating at the outset that science plays a key role in many aspects of modern society. At a very basic level science is used to shed light on the nature of reality, showing us that the world is round rather than flat and that it orbits the sun as one of many planets in a single system that is part of a larger galaxy. Science also plays an important role in medicine helping to keep people healthy; engineers use science to construct buildings that are safer in an earthquake; and science has played a central role in the increasing globalisation of communication around the world. In general, when conducting science, the researchers or scientists use a shared set of rules, beliefs, concepts and practices, usually referred to as a paradigm, to examine the various aspects of reality (Kuhn, 1970, 1974). A simple way of thinking about the notion of a paradigm is as a pair of epistemological glasses.

Epistemological glasses

Knowledge and understanding within science can often be viewed as an episte-mological perspective within science that is attempting to explain the ontological reality. The distinction between ontology and epistemology may seem somewhat abstract but a useful way to think about such concepts is to understand that *ontology* refers to what is, or what things really are, as in the nature of reality, whereas *epistemology* represents a way of knowing about this reality. In the same way a short-sighted person may put on a pair of glasses to see the world around them scientists use a particular *epistemological paradigm* in order to make sense of reality. Hence, a scientific paradigm can be thought of as a pair of epistemological glasses allowing, or enabling, the scientist to view and understand the underlying reality (see Figure 2.1). Importantly, as with all glasses, such a paradigm may bring some aspects of the underlying reality into a sharper focus whilst ignoring or ex-cluding other parts.

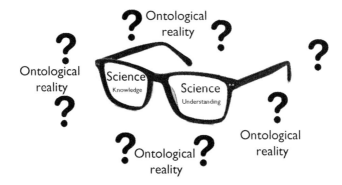

Figure 2.1 A pair of epistemological glasses representing the scientific paradigm which is used to expand knowledge and understanding of the underlying ontological reality.

Paradigms of science

There may be different scientific paradigms in use and the paradigms themselves can also change over time. Hence, there is no such thing as a universal ahistorical scientific method or paradigm (see, Clough, 2000). It is more often the case that scientists will use the method they perceive of as best suited for gaining insight into the research question/problem they are interested in. Nevertheless, the most dominant paradigm which is usually taught in schools and universities and is most commonly referred to in science texts is the hypothetico-deductive approach (Gravetter & Forzano, 2009). Here the idea is that the experimenter/researcher develops a hypothesis based on prior research or directly from a theory and then tests this hypothesis experimentally, usually to obtain some quantitative measure or data, to see if the theory holds up. If it does the theory expands to encapsulate this new information and if not, the theory may need to be modified. In severe cases if the observed findings do not support the theory it may be that it needs to be adapted or discarded. An alternative approach that is growing in popularity is the *inductive approach*, which is often seen as a form of reasoning that is based on individual circumstances and may take a more qualitative approach (Howitt, 2013). It is not the case that one approach is better than another but rather by combining information and understanding obtained from different methods it may be possible to gain a more comprehensive understanding of the process and or issue as well as avoid any potential pitfalls that may emerge when using only one approach.

According to Gravetter and Forzano (2009) there are three key principles that form the foundation of the hypothetico-deductive approach: that it is empirical, public and objective. By empirical they mean that answers are obtained to questions by making systematic and clearly defined observations and/or measurements. In a sense the observations are there to provide an empirical test of the ideas and/or theories. The idea that the scientific paradigm is public revolves around the notion that observations and findings are made available to others to view and evaluate. Such a process forms a key part of the peer-review process that is a central tenant of publishing scientific journal articles. The final point is that the scientific paradigm is objective in the sense that observations made and/or measurements taken are not in any way influenced by the biases or beliefs of the individuals making them. However, it should be noted that not everyone agrees with the notion that science and/or scientists are purely objective (see, Hodson, 1985; Ryan & Aikenhead, 1992). Some have argued that science, whilst attempting to maintain an air of objectivity, is in fact subjective in the sense that it is influenced by theory which is the product of human imagination, society, culture and creativity (Abd-El-Khalick, Bell, & Lederman, 1997). There are also suggestions that experimenters may unconsciously influence the outcome of research (see *Experimenter effect* below) or that the beliefs of those taking part may influence the results (e.g., Palmer, 1997; White, 1977). Hence, it is important to realise that whilst science *aims* to be empirical, public and objective it is essentially a human endeavour and humans are apt to bias and may hold particular sets of beliefs, whether they are scientists or not. As such, the aim is for scientists to be aware of such influences and attempt to reduce them as much as possible in order to obtain as clear and unbiased an outcome as possible.

Thus, as is clearly evident from the literature showing that those conducting psi research rely on empirical observations and/or measurements, make their methods and findings public and attempt to remain as objective as possible, they are working within a scientific paradigm and hence are conducting scientific research. As such, psi research is unequivocally science. However, is it possible that the findings of such research represent an assault on science and/or rationality? According to Sheldrake (2012) such a view would be more *scientistic* than *scientific* as it suggests both a greater certainty and understanding of the nature of reality than is currently known and somewhat misleadingly implies that science is an end point, or *outcome*, when in fact it is a *process* of achieving that outcome.

Science as a process

Those unfamiliar with science often make the mistake of thinking that it will *prove* something to be *true* or not. Words such as '*prove*' and '*true*' are too heavily loaded and suggest a finality that fails to take note of the fact that science is a process rather than an outcome. 'Proof' represents a binary notion (i.e., proved/not) that may exist within the field of mathematics and logic, but only because these are both closed systems. Furthermore, proof suggests a finality in the sense that once it has been shown to be true it remains that way, whereas science attempts to understand the nature of reality as it exists and deals with evidence, not proof. Hence, scientific knowledge and understanding is tentative, meaning it is subject to change and not final. The currently accepted theory of a particular phenomenon is simply the best explanation for it from among the alternatives available based on current evidence. The challenges associated with this approach can often be seen in mainstream media when they criticise scientists for changing their mind about a particular finding or effect. However, this preference for a rigidity in thinking shows a fundamental lack of understanding about the nature of science as a process. Rather than remaining dogmatically attached to a single theory or idea that no longer stands up against the evidence it is essential that scientists update their views and theories, which may necessitate what Kuhn (1970) referred to as a paradigm shift in knowledge and understanding. A brief look at some of the historical shifts in scientific understanding, such as the importance of hand washing to reduce germ transfer (Semmelweis, 1850), black holes in the cosmos (Chandrasekhar, 1930), continental drift (Wegener, 1915) and neurogenesis (Nottebohm, 1989), to name only a few, clearly shows the importance of updating the way people think about things. Thus, scientists changing their minds is simply a reflection of the nature of the process of science. Indeed, the notion that science does *not* do certainty is a reality that many scientists think is fundamental (e.g., Rovelli, 2011; Sheldrake, 2012). Hence, new findings that are difficult to account for using current theories and understanding in no way can be conceived of as an assault *on* science. Rather, such new and challenging ideas simply reflect the unfolding process of science in action.

Scientific evidence

Given that psi research is clearly scientific and that the findings reflect the nature of science as a process the next issue is the call for such findings to be based on extraordinary evidence (e.g., Shermer, 1997). This raises a number of questions including what types of evidence are available/acceptable, how are decisions made between competing views and what constitutes extraordinary evidence. There are many ways to obtain evidence and it should not be surprising that researchers have suggested that collecting evidence using different methods from a variety of sources is likely to provide a better assessment of the effect in question (e.g., Moralejo, Ogunremi, & Dunn, 2017). The most common sources of evidence include testimonials/anecdotal evidence, case studies and experimental evidence.

Testimonial/anecdotal evidence

Testimonials are popular and can be persuasive if they are thought to be from credible sources. However, testimonials and anecdotes need to be treated with caution as their accuracy can be influenced by various psychological factors (Smith, 2010). For example, memories are not perfect copies of what happened – as can clearly be seen from the plethora of research on the accuracy problems of eyewitness testimony (e.g., Toglia, Read, Ross, & Lindsay, 2007). Hence, an individual's recall of a particular event may not be as accurate as they think. As such, testimonials and anecdotes are often viewed rather negatively as they can be prone to contamination, bias, selective attention, influenced by prior beliefs and may suffer distortions over time (French & Stone, 2014; Smith, 2010). Furthermore, a key problem with anecdotal evidence is that it is invariably not gathered under controlled circumstances (Graziano & Raulin, 2004). Nevertheless, testimonials and anecdotal evidence can often be a good starting point for a more thorough investigation (see, Bradley, 1992). For instance, anecdotes can be investigated or checked and tested.

Case study

It has been suggested that a case study can provide valuable information helping scientists to achieve a level of competence and understanding that simply would not be possible by relying on the use of context independent facts and rules (Flyvberg, 2006). A case study or report often involves an intensive examination of a specific issue and/or individual or event (Leary, 2004). Within psychology they have been used extensively and with good effect particularly in clinical cases of noteworthy pathology (e.g., Cytowic, 2002; Sacks, 1985). Indeed, it has been suggested that more discoveries have emerged from using case studies than from relying on statistical analysis of large samples (Kuper & Kuper, 1985). A case study may involve a single person, representing a typical individual or one that deviates in a particular way from the norm, an event, an organisation or even a community (Janis, 1982). Typically, the interested researcher brings together the data to create a narrative of the issue, event or individual. This data can come from a variety of sources such as observation, interview, questionnaire, archival records and eyewitness testimony. This information is then examined and an interpretation offered to explain the underlying event, issue or why the particular individual behaved as they did. According to Leary (2004) the case study method has at least four uses:

1   It can be a rich source of ideas and insights – especially in the early stages of an investigation of a topic issue.
2   It can be used to describe a rare phenomenon.

3   It can be used to explore and understand the lives of notable individuals.
4   It can provide rich and illustrative examples of more general principles.

As such, a case study that demonstrates a new and unusual finding may encourage scientists to reconsider the area and in such a way case studies may help advance understanding of science and knowledge (see, Shaughnessy, Zechmeister, & Zechmeister, 2006). Indeed, Flyvberg (2006) argues that a discipline without a generous range of case studies 'is a discipline without systematic production of exemplars' (p. 242).

Both personal testimonials and case studies are often viewed as providing a qualitative view of the topic which may help to provide a richer level of detail that may be overlooked when relying only on quantitative data (Howitt, 2013). Indeed, examination of psi research shows that it has a rich history of evidence based on testimonials and case studies (e.g., Alvarado, 2017; Wehrstein, 2019).

Experimental evidence

Experimental evidence has the element of control at its heart. It is where participants are recruited and randomly allocated to the various conditions, usually blind as to the aims of the study to reduce or eliminate bias and responder effects, where one of the conditions may act as the control condition and the other the intervention or experimental condition. The participants' performance and/or behaviour are then compared on one or more dependent measure, such as response time, accuracy, physiological arousal and so forth. The key aim here is that this type of research allows the researcher more control over the situation in an attempt to reduce or eliminate potentially confounding variables. Such control is also used to more precisely and systematically manipulate relevant variables. By conducting research in this tightly controlled manner scientists are able to draw causal inferences, usually based on inferential statistics, from the data they obtain. Nevertheless, observations obtained from a laboratory under tightly controlled conditions are often seen as representing one end of a spectrum of research approaches with naturalistic observations at the other end, leading to claims that highly controlled experimental research may lack ecological or external validity (e.g., B. E. Roe & Just, 2009). Indeed, there is often a perceived 'trade-off' between the level of experimental control and the level of external validity (Shaughnessy et al., 2006).

A method that represents a quasi-experimental approach involves the collection of information regarding different variables in order to measure them and the possible relationship between them. This survey method is very common and includes opinion polls, market research, evaluations and government census (see, Haslam & McGarty, 2014). This approach allows the researcher some degree of control over what variables may be included in the survey but often with less control over who completes it, what their motivation may be and whether their beliefs and/or biases influence their responses. It also restricts the researcher's interpretations to that of associations or relationships and not causation.

As can be seen from the above there are many sources of potential evidence, though some have suggested that experimental evidence is seen as more persuasive and credible than testimonials and anecdotal reports (Hornikx, 2005). However, it should be noted that not all topics lend themselves to the randomly allocated controlled designs often incorporated in experimental research. For instance, research on near-death experiences (NDE) represents an intriguing area of psi but is not easily amenable to such experimental approaches. Nevertheless, there is good evidence that psi research is based to a large extent on the use and findings from experimental research. For example, in their compendium Parker and Brusewitz (2003) show that psi research has made good use of a wide variety of experimental evidence. Hence, psi research, like many other fields of scientific enquiry, has incorporated evidence from a variety of sources using multiple approaches, an approach which has been argued will likely provide a more coherent picture of any emerging phenomenon (e.g., Gravetter & Forzano, 2009; Haslam & McGarty, 2014; Howitt, 2013). However, when faced with the challenging findings from psi research the principle of Occam's razor is often invoked as a mechanism to adopt a simpler alternative explanation (French & Stone, 2014; Smith, 2010).

Occam's razor vs Occam's broom

Occam's razor is the idea that all things being equal the objective scientist accepts the simplest explanation possible, sometimes referred to as not multiplying up complexities. In essence it means that science, whilst not denying the possible existence of psi effects and/or a supernatural world containing various deities, works to focus on the natural world. As such, the explanations of science must be couched in terms of natural expression without the need to fall back on supernatural ones. Most people should be familiar with the concept of Occam's razor or the principle of parsimony. However, Occam's broom is a somewhat more recent conceit, attributable to Sydney Brenner, and embodies the principle whereby *inconvenient facts* are swept under the carpet in the interests of a clear interpretation of a messy reality (Robertson, 2009). From this it is possible to see that there is an inherent conservatism implicit in the use of Occam's razor as it implies that current understanding, views and thinking be given preference and are accepted in the face of unusual views. Palmer (1987) refers to this as the *coherence principle* where the more parsimonious view that should be accepted is the one that is consistent with current and/or established ways of thinking. When applied to scientific research Palmer (1987) argues it leads to a circular logic that increases the probability of Type II errors (i.e., rejecting valid findings). Furthermore, whilst it does make sense to veer towards the more conservative explanation of an effect it is important to be aware that such views and theories are based upon current interpretations of available data by human scientists who are just as apt to bias and favour when developing and maintaining their own ideas. Indeed, Alters (1997, p. 41) points out that 'abandoning cherished knowledge that has been falsified usually occurs with reluctance'. Given this preference for preserving current views and ideas it is unsurprising that some call on psi research to provide extraordinary evidence to support such unusual findings (French & Stone, 2014; Smith, 2010).

Extraordinary evidence

The idea here is that the claims related to psi phenomena are so unusual, or extraordinary, that even if they were to occur they would require 'extraordinary' evidence to support them (Shermer, 1997). Unfortunately, as Murdie (2015) points out this expression is used more as a convenient *sound bite* rather than operating as a principle for discerning possible differences in the types of evidence available. This becomes clear when attempts are made to define and/or decide what constitutes extraordinary evidence. For instance, what may seem extraordinary to one person may seem quite ordinary to another. Furthermore, even if a researcher were to claim that their evidence of psi is extraordinary there is no agreed upon and meaningful way in which such a claim could be assessed. The call for extraordinary evidence is also problematic as it would suggest that evidence supporting any psi-type effect would need to be directly proportional to the intrinsic belief individuals have regarding how congruent such phenomena may be with current understanding. The more closely it fits with current knowledge and understanding the less 'extraordinary' the evidential requirement and the more unusual the more 'extraordinary' the evidence required. There is also the implication of a *double standard* here with psi research essentially, by its very nature, being unusual and as such the idea is that it needs to be held to a higher level of account than more usual/mainstream research. There can be no doubt that it is incumbent upon those in the field of psi research to provide clear evidence to support any claims made. However, there is no such thing as extraordinary evidence. Hence, it should be the case that the claims of psi rest on their supporting evidence and not on an ambiguous interpretation of whether a particular individual thinks such evidence is exceptional or not. Thus, the call for extraordinary evidence is nothing more than a diversion as there is simply evidence and more evidence.

Methodological issues

The final part of this chapter focuses on some of the key methodological issues that have been assumed to be particularly problematic for psi research. This includes the idea that any effects found are the result of the experimenter, or that when effects do emerge they are often inconsistent and do not replicate. Then, there is the possibility that evidence of psi is the result of fraud and/or deception. Finally, there is the possibility that the file drawer effect leads to a biased view of any positive findings.

Experimenter effects

It has been suggested that some psi researchers, or laboratories, consistently obtain positive results whereas others continuously fail to find any positive evidence and show only chance effects. This differential performance is encapsulated within the *experimenter effect* and is something that all fields of scientific enquiry have to deal with, not only those focusing on psi. According to White (1976, p. 335) the effect describes the 'response of subjects to the needs and wishes of the experimenter or to factors in the experimental situation'. The terms *psi-conducive* and *psi-inhibitory* have also been used to apply to both participants and experimenters who produce differential results in psi research (Thalbourne, 2003). The experimenter effect has long been an issue in the sciences and taken to its extreme undermines the notion of objective verification without influence.

The evidence for experimenter effects is both controversial and inconsistent. Possibly the most well-known study directly examining the effect of experimenter on psi behaviour was undertaken by Wiseman and Schlitz (1997, 1999). In a series of studies using a standard staring detection paradigm, where individuals aim to identify whether they are being stared at or not, both Wiseman who is a prominent sceptic and Schlitz a proponent of psi collaborated to run sessions using the same equipment and participant pool. The conducted studies replicated earlier patterns they had found independently, with Schlitz's participants scoring significantly better than Wiseman's (see, Wiseman & Schlitz, 1997, 1999). Others have also shown that the experimenter's belief in psi can influence the outcome of scores when measuring participant belief in psi (Watt & Ramakers, 2003; Watt & Wiseman, 2002). M. Smith (2003) also found that those researchers who reported having more psychic experiences themselves considered themselves as more successful at testing for psi. However, not all attempts to elicit this effect have been successful. For instance, re-search attempting to influence psi performance by having the experimenter make psi-supportive or psi-unsupportive suggestions found this had no impact on performance (Watt & Baker, 2002). Also, attempts to replicate the experimenter effect using the standard staring-type paradigm failed to show any evidence of psi or any differential effects as a function of experimenter (Schlitz, Wiseman, Watt, & Radin, 2006).

One possible explanation of the experimenter effect is that the experimenter's per-sonality, behaviour and/or enthusiasm may indirectly influence the results of the study by motivating participants or providing them with clues that provide further in-formation about the nature of the study and about the experimenter's hopes or ex-pectations. These *demand characteristics* may affect the subsequent behaviour of the participants and thus the results of the study itself (Harris & Rosenthal, 1985; Rosenthal & Jacobson, 1966; see also White, 1977). For example, in terms of their communication skills, there is some evidence that, at least in a non-experimental context, psi-conducive and psi-inhibitory experimenters differ in how their body lan-guage is perceived by observers. For instance, Schmeidler and Maher (1981) videotaped researchers as they gave talks and fielded questions at an academic conference and found that psi-conducive experimenters were considered to be, *inter alia*, more flexible, enthusiastic, friendly, likeable and warm, and less tense, irritable and cold. Alongside these potential personality differences, it has been suggested that the belief of the ex-perimenter may influence the outcome. For instance, when M. D. Smith (2003) sur-veyed researchers who had produced at least one positive finding he found a clear positive association between the researcher's belief in psi-type effects and their ability to elicit such effects in the laboratory. A further possibility is that it is the experience of the experimenter, in particular when that experience has been associated with positive outcomes, that can influence participant performance. For example, in a combined psi and psychokinesis task researchers found that participant performance was sig-nificantly better when they were initially briefed by a more experienced experimenter (C. A. Roe, Davey, & Stevens, 2006).

A slightly different view is that it is not simply, or solely, the experimenter's person-ality, behaviour or expectations but rather something about the *interaction* between the experimenter and the participant that leads to the success or not of psi-based tasks. For instance, Honorton, Ramsey and Cabibbo (1975) had two experimenters who interacted either in a positive manner in which time was taken to establish rapport with the par-ticipant or in a negative manner (i.e., abrupt, formal and unfriendly) in which they went quickly into the task. They found that the positive interaction produced a significantly higher psi score than the negative interaction. However, when Schneider, Binder and Walach (2000) manipulated the experimenter-participant interactions so that for half the participants the experimenter attempted to create a psi-conducive atmosphere and for the other half the experimenter remained neutral they found no difference in psi performance. More recently, Hitchman, Pfeuffer, Roe and Sherwood (2016) examined the influence of experimenter-participant interactions on a precognition task and found positive interactions were associated with positive precognitive scores. However, further analysis showed that this was only true for the female experimenter and not the male experimenter despite the fact that participants were both female and male. Hence, the interaction between experimenter and participant may be important but it may also be influenced by other factors such as the complexity of the task and gender. As such, it is imperative that future researchers ensure they clearly and precisely document and outline the type and nature of any experimenter-participant interactions.

A final alternative considered here is the suggestion that the experimenter's own psi ability may be responsible for the outcome of their experiment (Parker & Millar, 2014). Given that most if not all experimenters are intensely involved and interested in their research and in particular the outcome, the idea is that they use their own psi ability to influence either the participants taking part or the results more directly. As the experimenters are invariably highly motivated to find their predicted effect or result the suggestion is that this motivated attitude leads them to unconsciously, or unintentionally, use psi to influence the outcome, though it should be noted that this line of reasoning would apply to all experimenters conducting all types of research. As such, it may be that some experimenters are psi-conducive whilst others are psi-inhibitory. However, this idea is not supported by clear and consistent findings, and may be influenced by a range of factors. It should also be pointed out that these factors may interact and/or combine to influence both an experimenter and a participant. Importantly, if such factors do influence the outcome of an experiment they are likely to do so for *all types* of experiment where the researcher has a vested interest in the outcome, which is most if not all research. Hence, this is not a valid criticism of psi research alone but simply a reflection of any science that involves human researchers with vested interests and motivations.

Inconsistent results

It is true that some of the findings from psi research are not always consistent. However, this claim is not unique to psi research but is reflected in much of psychological research where the outcome is reliant upon individual performance. A good example is creativity, which has been shown to be heavily reliant upon the differences in individual ability (e.g., Choi, 2004; Woodman & Schoenfeldt, 1989). Hence, the type of individuals that form the basis of any case study and/or experimental work may have a large impact on the outcome of that work. The difficulty is that along with the unknown nature of psi it is not clear whether psi, like many other human behaviours and attributes, is more of a *capacity* in the sense that all people are endowed with the capacity to exhibit psi-type behaviours, or whether it is more of an *ability* such that some talented people may have more of it than others.

Without a clear understanding of the nature of psi the most common approach adopted in research is simply to use an *unselective method* whereby the researcher recruits and tests anyone that is both available and willing to participate. A strength of this approach is that there are many more of these type of people willing to participate in research, and in fact much of experimental psi, and mainstream psychological research, utilises such *opportunity* or *convenience sampling* (e.g., Bornstein, Jager, & Putnick, 2013; Farrokhi & Mahoudi-Hamidabad, 2012). Another strength is that this makes the findings easier to generalise to the population as a whole as there is nothing unique or distinct about this sample. However, such an approach does have some limitations. For example, if one were to go out into the nearest town and offer a large financial reward to anyone conveniently available who could jump over a horizontal bar held at a height of 1.2 metres, or 5 feet, it is very likely no one would be able to achieve the task and the experimenter could easily walk away convinced that jumping over a bar at a height of 1.2 metres is quite impossible. In fact the current world record stands at 2.45 metres (held by Javier Sotomayor from Cuba), which is double this height. The point is that the selection of individuals who either become the focus of a case study and/or are invited to take part in experimental studies is very likely to play a key role in whether any effects emerge or not.

Braude (2016) has suggested that psi may operate in a way that is similar to other natural abilities and skills. If correct this would mean that it would likely be as variable as any other natural human ability, such as the ability to run fast, jump high, be creative and so on. This is important as it has interesting and influential implications. For instance, if psi is an ability, much like any other human ability, then it would make sense to argue that:

- Not everyone is psychic.
- Some people are more psychic than others.
- Not all psychics are psychic in the same way.

If this is the case, then it would make sense for experimental research to selectively recruit and test those who have *clearly exhibited* psi-type abilities as opposed to randomly testing a convenient sample of the population in the hope of finding people who can complete the task. This debate is sometimes couched in terms of an *elitist* versus a *universalist* approach (see, Braude, 2016) and is not new as Haraldsson (1970) has shown that selectively recruiting promising candidates can be an effective method for eliciting precognitive effects. Furthermore, a meta-analysis of precognition utilising forced-choice experiments reported significantly larger effects for those individuals *pre-selected* on the basis of prior test performance (Honorton & Ferrari, 1989). Hence, whilst the findings of psi are sometimes inconsistent this is not unique to psi research and may simply reflect the differential ability of those taking part. As such, it may be more fruitful for future researchers to selectively recruit participants based *both* on belief and prior ability, ensuring the ability is consistent with one under focus as Braude (2016) quite reasonably points out psi abilities are likely to be 'as idiosyncratic and variable as any other ability' (p. 147).

Replication issues

Replication sits at the heart of the scientific process and no phenomenon or finding is generally accepted as real without being replicated, ideally by others not involved in the original research. Here we will consider some of the key issues regarding replication such as why do it, is it even possible, what if any are the various types of replication and whether a failure to replicate is something specific to the field of psi research.

Replication – what is it and why do it?

One of the main corrective processes in the scientific method is whether others not involved in the original finding/study can sufficiently replicate the original finding (see, Judson, 2004). Replication is a way to ensure any original finding is not simply a one-off anomaly in the data, but a reliable and robust effect. According to Schmidt (2009) it is one of the most important tools for the verification of evidence within the empirical sciences. O'Hear (1989) has also argued that replication of observations, findings and data by others is a key feature underpinning the objectivity of science. Hence, replication is seen as a 'crucial aspect of the objectivity and openness of science' (C. A. Roe, 2016a, p. 71). According to Schmidt (2009), there are at least two good reasons why replications should be conducted:

- First: they help to establish stability in our knowledge and understanding by differentiating between supported (i.e., replicated) and unsupported claims.
- Second: they are useful for helping to establish norms which enable us to differentiate between scientific and unscientific claims.

It was recognised early on that for the field of psi research to progress, a repeatable experimental paradigm would need to be identified that would allow independent replication of statistically significant results (Puthoff & Targ, 1976). Unfortunately this has yet to be established and a common criticism levelled at the field of psi research is that it has yet to show a clear and robust effect that can be replicated on demand (Milton & Wiseman, 1999; Stokes, 2015). For instance, Hyman (2010) has argued that lack of replication is the Achilles' heel in psi research. He points out that if the data are elusive and incapable of being replicated then they can safely be ignored. Others agree, stating that psi research has yet to demonstrate a repeatable effect (e.g., Alcock, 2010; Novella, 2012). These are valid criticisms regarding the failure of psi research to produce clear, consistent and repeatable findings. However, it is worth considering whether replication on demand is always possible.

Replication – is it always possible?

C. A. Roe (2016a) argues that it is naive to think that *replication on demand* is always possible given what is currently known about the various factors that can and do influence study outcomes. For example, changes in the sample size can directly influence study power and the sampling error which in turn influence the likelihood of capturing an effect again. Furthermore, there may be many aspects of human behaviour that do not easily replicate on demand (see, Braude, 2016). Simply placing a participant in a lab-based setting and asking them to be 'creative' or 'make you laugh' are unlikely to elicit promising results. This does not mean that individuals cannot be creative and/or exhibit a sense of humour, simply that such behaviours often require a specific context. For example, most people would agree with the notion that dreaming is not only possible but also that it occurs relatively frequently. However, asking participants to have a particular dream and/or alter their dreams in some way would not only be very demanding but also extremely difficult to assess. There are few people, without long training, who can 'dream on demand' and fewer still are likely to be able to influence and/or control the nature of such dreams. Furthermore, it is only with the advent of recent technological advances that investigations into the nature of dreaming have even been possible (e.g., Cipolli, Ferrara, De Gennaro, & Plazzi, 2017). The point is, that no matter what sort of process or function psi is, or may be, it is likely to function in a manner similar to the many other skills and attributes that individuals possess (Braude, 2016). As such, it will likely be influenced, or mediated, by situation variables, context and other physical and psychological circumstances much as other aspects of human behaviour are. It is important to stress here that this is not an attempt to suggest that psi should not be held up to the methodological gold standard of replication, simply that such variability in potential performance needs to be considered in the same way that such variability would be taken into account for other less anomalous psychological processes.

Replication – types

In general, replication is seen as a way of repeating an experimental procedure with the aim of establishing a consistent and robust outcome. However, a distinction is often made between a *direct replication* and a *conceptual replication* (Schmidt, 2009).

Direct replication is the repetition of an experimental procedure to as exact a degree as possible. This means that, as far as possible, the same equipment, material, stimuli, design and statistical analysis should be used. According to Simons (2014) direct replication by multiple researchers provides the best possible evidence for the reliability of an effect. In particular, those effects seen as fragile or influenced by potential moderators are the effects most in need of such replication. Such replication provides support for the original findings and confidence that the original findings were not simply the result of a convergence of unknown factors. Direct replications are also seen by some as providing a greater level of confirmatory power as it need not be assumed that the same phenomenon is being tested (see, Simons, 2014). However, despite the fact that replication sits at the heart of the scientific process direct replications are not encouraged in mainstream psychology as it is exceedingly difficult for such replications to be published. For instance, a survey of social science journal editors, who often act as the gatekeepers to publication, found that 94% would either discourage or reject replication studies. This is because replications are often seen as not 'newsworthy' or not 'new' and hence represent a waste of time and/or resources (see, Neuliep & Crandall, 1993). Such a view may seem odd given the notion that a new and/or unusual finding or idea may stand or fall on the ability of others to replicate it and show it to be robust. Furthermore, as Heraclitus once said 'no man ever steps in the same river twice'. That is to say that many psychological phenomena may rely on culture, language, socially primed knowledge and ideas, the meaning of questions and phrases and an ever-shifting experience of participant populations making direct replications difficult if not impossible (see, Crandall & Sherman, 2016). Hence, rather than rely *only* on direct replications many utilise conceptual replications.

A conceptual replication involves the use of different methods to repeat the test of a hypothesis or experimental result (Crandall & Sherman, 2016; Schmidt, 2009). Hence, a conceptual replication often involves an attempt to test the same fundamental idea behind the original study, but the operationalisations of the phenomena, the independent and dependent variables, the type and design of the study, and the participant population may all differ. However, Schmidt (2009) points out that this approach comes with its own set of challenges. For instance, conceptual replication only holds if the different methods used are measuring the same phenomenon. Conceptual replications can also be 'unreplicated'. That is, a study that follows up a conceptual replication of an original finding could show that the conceptual replication was in fact measuring something else. Hence, the conceptual replication has now been unreplicated. Conceptual replications can also exacerbate confirmation bias. For instance, if a researcher finds a similar psi effect using a different method they may claim to have conceptually replicated the original finding. However, if the researcher does not find the same effect using a different method they cannot claim to have falsified the original findings. This is because they may have used a different method and/or different measures to test for the psi effect. This reveals an element of bias. Finally, there is concern that conceptual replication may substitute and devalue direct replication, particularly as scientific journals seem reluctant to publish direct replications in favour of conceptual ones (for a discussion of this see, Zwaan, Etz, Lucas, & Donnellan, 2018).

Overall, whilst some suggest direct replication is more stringent and powerful (Simons, 2014), others argue in favour of conceptual replications (Crandall & Sherman, 2016; Stroebe & Strack, 2014). It is likely that a combination of *both* would prove the most useful.

Replication – failures

It is certainly true that many have expressed disappointment that psi research has yet to establish a repeatable experiment (e.g., Beloff, 1985; Utts, 1991). However, some have argued that strict replication is uncommon in many areas of science and that psi research should not be singled out on this basis (Honorton, 1985; Rao, 1985). Nevertheless, there are two points worth considering here. First, does the failure to replicate mean that an original finding is no longer noteworthy? Second, is the difficulty or lack of replication for psi-type effects something that is unique to this field alone?

An implicit assumption contained within the concept of replication is that if an original study were to show a significant effect of psi but a follow-up study fails to show the same or similar effects then the initial result was probably an error and/or due to chance. However, Utts (1991) has noted that replications are directly influenced by their 'power' and sample size, issues which are rarely given much thought. Interestingly, Utts (1991) has demonstrated that an experimenter who may not have access to large samples and as a consequence runs many smaller sized studies can produce an effect that may be equivalent to another experimenter who runs fewer studies with a much larger sample. Utts (1991) suggests that such misconceptions about the nature of statistical power and the usefulness of effect sizes are often responsible for claims that a particular psi effect has failed to replicate. She argues that it would be more appropriate to compare effect sizes over time for similar studies to see if the effect is consistent or not. Interestingly, when researchers did this for psi-based effects in forced-choice paradigms across a period of 70 years they found relatively stable effects (see, Storm, Tressoldi, & Di Risio, 2012).

A second point, often made by critics of psi-type phenomena (e.g., Wagenmakers, Wetzels, Borsboom, Kievit, & van der Maas, 2015) is that the failure or difficulty in replicating findings is something specific to psi-based effects. However, this is simply not the case (see, Ioannidis, 2005). For instance, a joint attempt to explore and replicate the top 100 studies published in three mainstream psychology journals for 2008 showed that 65% of the original studies failed to replicate (Collaboration, 2015). Furthermore, similar problems have been highlighted in other areas of science. For example, attempts to replicate a series of studies focusing on cancer research found that just over 88% failed to replicate (Begley & Ellis, 2012), and similar doubts have been cast on the findings within the field of neuroscience (e.g., Button et al., 2013; Hong, Yoo, Wager, & Woo, 2019). The reasons for such replication failures may be many and varied. Nevertheless, a key point to note here is that the field of psi research is in no way unique in its attempts to deal with problematic replications.

Deception and/or fraud

It is possible that those who claim to have experienced a paranormal event or some form of psi-based phenomena have been deceived. Indeed, phenomena related to the early séance work thought by many to be showing genuine evidence of psi-based events later turned out to be produced by deliberate trickery (see, Brandon, 1983; French & Stone, 2014; Hansen, Utts, & Markwick, 1992). Beyond the realms of séance work some have even gone so far as to suggest that the evidence of psi conforms 'to the pattern that would be expected if a small minority of psi researchers has engaged in fraud' (Stokes, 2015, p. 42). As such, it is important to examine whether deception or fraud is possible and if so what evidence is there that it takes place, and if it occurs whether it does so at a rate that is comparable to other fields of scientific enquiry?

Is deception/fraud possible?

A classic study referred to as 'Project Alpha' is perhaps the most notable case of trickery and deception (see, Randi, 1983; Smith, 2010; Thalbourne, 1995). Randi selected two magicians and sent them to the McDonnell Laboratory for Psychical Research with the instruction that they were to claim possession of psychic powers. For a number of years, the two magicians fooled a large number of scientists in a range of experiments involving spoon bending, identification of pictures in sealed envelopes, rotating a paper propeller isolated inside a glass dome and creating pictures on a film inside a camera. They did all this using nothing more than standard magician's tricks. To make matters worse when Randi wrote to the director of the facility to point out possible ways that people could be tricked, even offering himself as a consultant witness for free, the lab director refused the offer of help claiming he was quite capable of detecting deception. Unfortunately, when all was later revealed, it did not reflect well on the lab and it eventually closed. Hence, this is a good example of how it is possible to deceive professional researchers. Nevertheless, clear evidence that such deception or fraud occurs can be difficult to obtain.

Evidence of fraud

Evidence of fraud and/or deception is difficult to obtain and any findings are necessarily biased as they rely only on the events that have been uncovered. Nevertheless, there have been some reported cases of fraud, for instance, the case of Walter Levy who was one of the early researchers at the Rhine research lab involved in exploring animal psi. Levy created a host of automatic tests designed to elicit psi-type effects from gerbils, rats and chick embryos. Unfortunately for Levy his research colleagues became suspicious about the amount of time he spent around the equipment and when they attempted to replicate his findings without his knowledge were only able to produce random results where Levy's data showed a deviation in the predicted direction. When Rhine, who was the head of the research lab, was informed of this he confronted Levy who then admitted to having falsified the data (see, Kennedy, 2012, 2017). To his credit Rhine (1974) wrote about this in a subsequent issue of the *Journal of Parapsychology* noting that this deception had cast a shadow of doubt over all work involving Levy. A second generally accepted case of fraud was perpetrated by Samuel G. Soal whose findings were initially seen as providing good evidence of psi. However, he was later accused by a co-worker of altering his data and subsequent re-analysis of his data suggested strong evidence of manipulation (see, Markwick, 1978). Once again it is important to note that it was a co-worker who initially raised the alarm regarding the veracity of Soal's work. Hence, it is not simply the case that *all* those conducting research into psi are guilty of fraud. Furthermore, the notion that such early problematic case studies naturally means that all subsequent cases *must be* fraud has also been challenged (see, C. A. Roe, 2016b). Indeed, C. A. Roe (2016b) goes on to argue that there is no compelling case for the idea that experimenter fraud is prevalent or commonplace in psi research.

There are inherent difficulties in clearly identifying whether fraud and/or deception has taken place in any realm of psychological research. However, whilst it is possible, there is no evidence that the findings of psi research are the result of such malpractice. Indeed, psi researchers have led the field of social science research practice by allowing others to scrutinise *beforehand* the planned methodology of their research along with any proposed analyses. In addition, such researchers often make any subsequent raw data from their research free and openly available to others to scrutinise (e.g., Koestler Parapsychology Unit; Psi Open Data). This use of pre-registration and open data sharing represents a methodological gold standard for research practice and one that many other areas of psychological research would do well to adopt.

File drawer effect

A final criticism often levelled at the findings reported from psi research is that they may represent a biased sample of the total number of research projects conducted. This bias could be influenced by the tendency for journals to only publish studies with statistically significant results and/or the possibility that researchers may 'file away' inexplicable or unfavourable results (Rotton, Foos, Van Meek, & Levitt, 1995). Hence, by focusing only on the known published data it is possible that a biased conclusion could be reached, which over-estimates the effect of any finding as these may not include the non-significant unpublished research, which is left, or hidden away, in a file drawer. Indeed, when authors of mainstream science articles were surveyed about their publishing practices it was found that around 15% of the work they produced was not put forward for publication, as the results were not significant and/or they were difficult to interpret (Rotton et al., 1995). However, C. A. Roe (2016b) has suggested that the 'file drawer' argument fails to stand up to close inspection when examining the field of psi research for a number of reasons. First, the field of psi research, unlike many other areas of mainstream science, accepts and publishes replication studies even when they produce null results (e.g., Vernon, 2017a; Vernon, 2017b). Hence, the field of psi research can be seen to lead the way in terms of publication practice. Second, such a view fails to consider the possibility of a *reverse file drawer effect* where sceptics of psi do not publish findings that are supportive of psi. Third is the argument that the field has only a small number of active researchers making it more likely that they will present their findings at conferences/ workshops irrespective of whether they support psi effects or not. This also has implications for the *failsafe N* often used in meta-analyses.

A meta-analysis refers to a statistical technique used to examine a collection of individual results/studies for the purpose of integrating the findings and providing a clear overview of any evident effects (Mullen, 1989). However, the file drawer problem can be particularly problematic for meta-analyses as they are often reliant on peer reviewed published results that are available. As such, Rosenthal (1979) proposed that it is possible to calculate a failsafe number of missing studies averaging a z-value of zero (i.e., they are not significant) that, if they were added to the combined effect size from a meta-analysis, would reduce the overall effect size to one that is statistically insignificant (see also, Rosenberg, 2005). The idea here is that if the calculation of the failsafe N indicates that only a relatively small number of non-significant studies would need to be retained in the file drawer to reduce an overall effect from significant to not significant then the possibility of a selective bias in the publication of positive results becomes a plausible interpretation. However, if the number of studies assumed to lay in the file drawer needs to be very large in order to counterbalance the positive results of a meta-analysis then this may be an unreasonable interpretation. It should be noted that not all agree with Rosenthal's (1979) approach, in particular the criteria used to decide what is a small or large number of studies, which led some to suggest that it may be prone to misinterpretation (Rothstein, Sutton, & Borenstein, 2006). Nevertheless, a meta-analysis of precognition effects carried out by Honorton and Ferrari (1989) estimated that 46 null effect studies would be needed to reduce the observed effects below statistical significance. More recently a meta-analysis of psi effects using forced-choice paradigms by Storm, Tressoldi and Di Risio (2012) suggested that over 500 unpublished papers with overall non-significant results would be needed to reduce their reported positive finding to a chance result. Such findings lend weight to the idea that the reported positive effects for psi effects are not the result of a file drawer problem.

Overview

There are no entry criteria for what can be examined scientifically. For science and scientific understanding to progress there must be an open, critical and respectful debate that considers the evidence thoroughly and remains open minded to the notion of change. It is clear that science is a process that utilises a variety of procedures to inform understanding and answer questions. Given that psi research utilises these procedures it is clearly working within a scientific paradigm and as such should be considered a scientific endeavour. Few would disagree with the notion that the findings from psi research represent a challenge to current scientific knowledge and understanding. However, such new and challenging ideas cannot be conceived of as an assault on science but simply represent the on-going process of scientific enquiry engaging with and working to understand new aspects of the underlying reality. Whilst there is some consensus that experimental evidence may be viewed as more robust and persuasive this does not negate the influence and importance of anecdotal evidence and case studies, both of which can represent useful starting points. Furthermore, it is important to keep in mind that a critical review of any evidence requires a balance to be maintained between a conservative reliance on current understanding and a liberal acceptance of alternative new ideas. Nevertheless, calls for 'extraordinary' evidence are quite simply a distraction when what is needed is clear, consistent and coherent evidence from multiple sources. The methodological challenges faced by those conducting psi research are certainly real but are in no way unique to the field of psi alone. The influence of an experimenter can emerge whenever an experimenter is involved in research. The lack of consistent replicable results, the challenges associated with fraud and deception, and possible file drawer effects are issues faced by all those participating in research. None of these single out psi research as unique in facing them. In fact, the field of psi research has often led the way in terms of transparent publication practices and the incorporation of pre-registration and open data repositories. This in no way negates the necessity for psi research to be held up to the highest and most rigorous scientific standards, simply that attempts to dismiss the findings from psi research *en masse* based on these issues does not stand up to any level of scrutiny.

Reflective questions

Some questions that may prove helpful when reflecting on the material covered in this chapter.

- Once a scientific theory has been developed can it ever change, if so why?
- Is there a difference between scientific theory and scientific law? What examples can you think of?
- What use, if any, are case reports of single psi-based phenomena?
- Should only experimental research be considered as providing evidence?
- Is there such a thing as 'exceptional evidence' and if so what would it be?
- Is it possible to eliminate the influence of the experimenter from the research?
- Have you ever experienced a psychic phenomenon or event? Would you consider this as sufficient evidence, why?
- What are the advantages and disadvantages of convenience sampling?

- What is meant by replication and is it even possible?
- What is meant by the file drawer effect?
- What would convince you of the possibility that psi is real?

References

Abd-El-Khalick, F., Bell, R. L., & Lederman, N. G. (1997). The nature of science and instructional practice: Making the unnatural natural. *Science Education, 82*(4), 417–436.

Alcock, J. E. (2010). Attributions about impossible things. In S. Krippner & H. L. Friedman (Eds.), *Debating psychic experience: Human potential or human illusion?* (pp. 29–41). Santa Barbara, CA: Praeger.

Alters, B. J. (1997). Whose nature of science? *Journal of Research in Science Teaching, 34,* 39–55. doi: 10.1002/1098-2736/34.

Alvarado, C. S. (2017). Telepathy, mediumship, and psychology: Psychical research at the international congresses of psychology 1889–1905. *Journal of Scientific Exploration, 31*(2), 255–292.

Begley, C. G., & Ellis, L. M. (2012). Raise the standards for preclinical cancer research. *Nature, 483,* 531–533. doi: 10.1038/483531a.

Beloff, J. (1985). What is your counter-explanation? A plea to skeptics to think again. In P. A. Kurtz (Ed.), *A skeptic's handbook of parapsychology* (pp. 359–377). Buffalo, NY: Prometheus.

Bornstein, M. H., Jager, J., & Putnick, D. L. (2013). Sampling in developmental science: Situations, shortcomings, solutions, and standards. *Developmental Review, 33*(4), 357–370.

Bradley, C. P. (1992). Turning anecdotes into data – the critical incident technique. *Family Practice, 9*(1), 98–103.

Brandon, R. (1983). *The spiritualists: The passion for the occult in the nineteenth and twentieth centuries.* London: Weidenfeld and Nicholson.

Braude, S. E. (2016). *Crimes of reason: On mind, nature, and the paranormal.* Boulder, CO: Rowman & Littlefield.

Button, K. S., Ioannidis, J. P. A., Mokrysz, C., Nosek, B. A., Flint, J., Robinson, E. S. J., & Munafo, M. R. (2013). Power failure: why small sample size undermines the reliabilty of neuroscience. *Nature Reviews Neuroscience, 14,* 365–376. doi: 10.1038/nrn3475.

Chandrasekhar, S. (1930). XXVII. The Ionization-formula and the sew statistics. *The London, Edinburgh, and Dublin Philosophical Magazine and Journal of Science, 9*(56), 292–299. doi: 10.1080/14786443008565002.

Choi, J. N. (2004). Individual and contextual predictors of creative performance: The mediating role of psychological processes. *Creativity Research Journal, 16*(2), 187–199. doi: 10.1080/10400419.2004.9651452.

Cipolli, C., Ferrara, M., De Gennaro, L., & Plazzi, G. (2017). Beyond the neuropsychology of dreaming: Insights into the neural basis of dreaming with new techniques of sleep recording and analysis. *Sleep Medicine Reviews, 35,* 8–20. doi: 10.1016/j.smrv.2016.07.005.

Clough, M. P. (2000). The nature of science: Understanding how the game of science is played. *The Clearing House: A Journal of Educational Strategies, 74*(1), 13–17.

Collaboration, O. S. (2015). Estimating the reproducibility of psychological science. *Science, 349*(6251), aac4716. doi: 10.1126/science.aac4716.

Crandall, C. S., & Sherman, J. W. (2016). On the scientific superiority of conceptual replications for scientific progress. *Journal of Experimental Social Psychology, 66,* 93–99. doi: 10.1016/j.jesp.2015.10.002.

Cytowic, R. E. (2002). *Synaesthesia: A union of the senses.* Cambridge: MIT Press.

Farrokhi, F., & Mahoudi-Hamidabad, A. (2012). Rethinking convenience sampling: Defining quality criteria. *Theory and Practice in Language Studies*, 2(4), 784–792. doi: 10.4304/tpls. 2.4.784-792.

Flyvberg, B. (2006). Five misunderstandings about case-study research. *Qualitative Inquiry*, 12(2), 219–245. doi: 10.1177/1077800405284363.

French, C. C., & Stone, A. (2014). *Anomalistic psychology: Exploring paranormal belief and experience*. Hampshire, UK: Palgrave Macmillan.

Gravetter, F. J., & Forzano, L. B. (2009). *Research methods for the behavioural sciences*. Belmont: Wadsworth, Cengage Learning.

Graziano, A. M., & Raulin, M. L. (2004). *Research methods: A process of inquiry* (5 edn). Boston, MA: Allyn and Bacon.

Hansen, G. P., Utts, J., & Markwick, B. (1992). Critique of the PEAR remote-viewing experiments. *Journal of Parapsychology*, 56, 97–113.

Haraldsson, E. (1970). Subject selection in a machine test precognition test. *Journal of Parapsychology*, 34(3), 182–191.

Harris, M. J., & Rosenthal, R. (1985). Mediation of interpersonal expectancies effects: 31 meta-analyses. *Psychological Bulletin*, 97, 363–386.

Haslam, S., & McGarty, C. (2014). *Research methods and statistics in psychology*. London: Sage.

Helfand, D. (2011). ESP, and the assult on rationality. Retrieved 07/09/2018, from https://www.nytimes.com/roomfordebate/2011/01/06/the-esp-study-when-science-goes-psychic/esp-and-the-assault-on-rationality.

Hitchman, G. A., Pfeuffer, C. U., Roe, C. A., & Sherwood, S. J. (2016). The effects of experimenter-participant interaction qualities in a goal-oriented nonintentional precognition task. *Journal of Parapsychology*, 80(1), 45–69.

Hodson, D. (1985). Philosophy of science, science and science education. *Studies in Science Education*, 12(1), 25–57. doi: 10.1080/03057268508559922.

Hong, Y. W., Yoo, Y., Wager, T., & Woo, C. (2019). False-positive neuroimaging: Undisclosed flexibility in testing spatial hypotheses allows presenting anything as a replicated finding. *bioRxiv*, 514521. doi: 10.1101/514521.

Honorton, C. (1985). Meta-analysis of psi Ganzfeld research. *Journal of Parapsychology*, 49, 51–91.

Honorton, C., & Ferrari, D. C. (1989). Future telling: A meta-analysis of forced-choice precognition experiments, 1935–1987. *Journal of Parapsychology*, 53, 281–308.

Honorton, C., Ramsey, M., & Cabibbo, C. (1975). Experimenter effects in extrasensory perception. *Journal of the American Society for Psychical Research*, 69, 135–149.

Hornikx, J. (2005). A review of experimental research on the relative persuasiveness of anecdotal, statistical, causal, and expert evidence. *Studies in Communication Science*, 5(1), 205–216.

Howitt, D. (2013). *Introduction to qualitative methods in psychology* (2nd edn). London: Pearson.

Hyman, R. (2010). The demise of parapsychology, 1850–2009. *The Skeptic*, 22(2), 17–20.

Ioannidis, J. P. A. (2005). Why most published research findings are false. *PLoS Medicine*, 2(8), e124. doi: 10.1371/journal.pmed.0020124.

Janis, I. L. (1982). *Groupthink: Psychological studies of policy decisions and fiascos*. Boston: Houghton Mifflin.

Judson, H. F. (2004). *The great betrayal: Fraud in science*. London: Harcourt.

Kennedy, J. E. (2012). The easily tested ideas have been tried, now engage the phenomena. *Journal of Parapsychology*, 76, 28–30.

Kennedy, J. E. (2017). Experimenter fraud: What are appropriate methodological standards? *Journal of Parapsychology*, 81(1), 63–72.

Kuhn, T. S. (1970). *The structure of scientific revolutions*. Chicago, IL: University of Chicago Press.

Kuhn, T. S. (1974). *The essential tension: Selected studies in scientific tradition and change*. Chicago, IL: University of Chicago Press.

Kuper, A., & Kuper, J. (1985). *The social science encyclopaedia*. London: Routledge & Kegan Paul.

Leary, M. R. (2004). *Introduction to behavioral research methods*. New York: Pearson.

Markwick, B. (1978). The Soal-Goldney experiments with Basil Shackelton: New evidence of data manipulation. *Proceedings of the Society for Psychical Research*, 56, 250–277.

Milton, J., & Wiseman, R. (1999). Does psi exist? Lack of replication of an anomalous process of information transfer. *Psychological Bulletin*, 125(4), 387–391.

Moralejo, D., Ogunremi, T., & Dunn, K. (2017). Critical appraisal toolkit (CAT) for assessing multiple types of evidence. *Canada Communicable Disease Report*, 43(9), 176–191.

Mullen, B. (1989). *Advanced BASIC meta-analysis*. Hillsdale, NJ: Erlbaumm.

Murdie, A. (2015). *Extraordinary evidence versus similar fact evidence: Proving the occurance of psi outside the laboratory*. Paper presented at the 39th SPR International Annual Conference, University of Greenwich.

Neuliep, J. W., & Crandall, R. (1993). Reviewer bias against replication research. *Journal of Social Behaviour and Personality*, 9(6), 22–29.

Nottebohm, F. (1989). From bird song to neurogenesis. *Scientific American*, 260(2), 74–79.

Novella, S. (2012). *Your deceptive mind: a scientific guide to critical thinking skills*. The Great Courses. Available at: www.thegreatcourses.co.uk

O'Hear, A. (1989). *An introduction to the philosophy of science*. Oxford, UK: OUP.

Palmer, J. (1987). Dulling Occam's razor: The role of coherence in assessing scientific knowledge claims. *European Journal of Parapsychology*, 7, 73–82.

Palmer, J. (1997). The challenge of experimenter psi. *European Journal of Parapsychology*, 13, 110–125.

Parker, A., & Brusewitz, G. (2003). A compendium of the evidence for psi. *European Journal of Parapsychology*, 18, 33–52.

Parker, A., & Millar, B. (2014). Revealing psi secrets: Successful experimenters seem to succeed by using their own psi. *Journal of Parapsychology*, 78(1), 39–55.

Puthoff, H. E., & Targ, R. (1976). A perception channel for information transfer over kilometer distances: Historical perspective and recent research. *Proceedings of the IEEE*, 64(3), 329–354.

Randi, J. (1983). The project alpha experiment: Part 1. The first two years. *Skeptical Inquirer*, 7(4), 24–33.

Rao, K. R. (1985). Replication in conventional and controversial sciences. In B. Shapin & L. Coly (Eds.), *The repeatability problem in parapsychology* (pp. 22–41). New York: Parapsychology Foundation.

Rhine, J. B. (1974). Comments: 'Security versus deception in parapsychology'. *Journal of Parapsychology*, 38(1), 99–121.

Robertson, M. (2009). Ockham's boom: a new series. *Journal of Biology*, 8(9), 79. doi: 10.1186/jbiol187

Roe, B. E., & Just, D. R. (2009). Internal and external validity in economics research: Tradeoffs between experiments, field experiments, natural experiments and field data. *American Journal of Agricultural Economics*, 19(5), 1266–1271. doi: 10.1111/j.1467-8276.2009.01295

Roe, C. A. (2016a). Is inconsistency our only consistent outcome? *Mindfield*, 8(2), 70–75.

Roe, C. A. (2016b). The problem of fraud in parapsychology. *Mindfield*, 8(1), 8–17.

Roe, C. A., Davey, R., & Stevens, P. (2006). Experimenter effects in laboratory tests of ESP and PK using a common protocol. *Journal of Scientific Exploration*, 20(2), 239–253.

Rosenberg, M. S. (2005). The file-drawer problem revisited: A general weighted method for calculating fail-safe number in meta-analysis. *Evoluion*, *59*(2), 464–468.

Rosenthal, R. (1979). The file drawer problem and tolerance for null results. *Psychological Bulletin*, *86*(3), 638–641. doi: 10.1037/0033-2909.86.3.638

Rosenthal, R., & Jacobson, L. (1966). Teachers' expectancies: Determinants of pupils' IQ gains. *Psychological Reports*, *19*(1), 115–118.

Rothstein, H. R., Sutton, A. J., & Borenstein, M. (2006). *Publication bias in meta-analysis: Prevention, assessment and adjustments*. London: John Wiley & Sons.

Rotton, J., Foos, P. W., Van Meek, L., & Levitt, M. (1995). Publication practices and the file drawer problem: A survey of published authors. *Journal of Social Behavior and Personality*, *10*(1), 1–13.

Rovelli, C. (2011). *The first scientist: Anaximander and his legacy*. Yardley, PA: Westholme Publishing.

Ryan, A. G., & Aikenhead, G. S. (1992). Students' preconceptions about the epistemology of science. *Science Education*, *76*(6), 559–580. doi: 10.1002/sce.3730760602.

Sacks, O. (1985). *The man who mistook his wife for a hat*. London: Duckworth.

Schlitz, M., Wiseman, R., Watt, C., & Radin, D. (2006). Of two minds: sceptic-proponent collaboration within parapsychology. *British Journal of Psychology.*, *97*, 313–322. doi: 10. 1348/000712605X80704.

Schmeidler, G. R., & Maher, M. (1981). Psi-conducive and psi-inhibitory experimenters – reply. *Journal of the American Society for Psychical Research*, *75*(4), 364–365.

Schmidt, S. (2009). Shall we really do it again? The powerful concept of replication is neglected in the social sciences. *Review of General Psychology*, *13*(2), 90–100. doi: 10.1037/a0015108.

Schneider, R., Binder, M., & Walach, H. (2000). Examining the role of the neutral versus personal experimenter-participant interaction: An EDA-DMILS experiment. *Journal of Parapsychology*, *64*(2), 182–195.

Semmelweis, I. (1850). The etiology, concept, and prophylaxis of childbed fever. In C. Buck, A. Llopis, E. Najera, & M. Terris (Eds.), *The challenge of epidemiology: Issues and selected readings* (pp. 46–59). Washington: Pan American Health Organisation. (Reprinted from 1988.)

Shaughnessy, J. J., Zechmeister, E. B., & Zechmeister, J. S. (2006). *Research methods in psychology* (*7th edn*). New York: McGraw-Hill.

Sheldrake, R. (2012). *The science delusion*. London: Coronet.

Shermer, M. (1997). *Why people believe weird things: Pseudoscience, superstition, and other confusions of our time*. New York: A. W. H. Freeman.

Simons, D. J. (2014). The value of direct replication. *Perspectives on Psychological Science*, *9*(1), 76–80. doi: 10.1177/1745691613514755.

Smith, J. C. (2010). *Pseudoscience and extraordinary claims of the paranormal*. West Sussex: Wiley & Sons Ltd.

Smith, M. (2003). The psychology of the 'psi-conducive' experimenter: Personality, attitudes toward psi, and personal psi experience. *Journal of Parapsychology*, *67*, 117–128.

Smith, M. D. (2003). The role of the experimenter in parapsychological research. *Journal of Consciousness Studies*, *10*(6–7), 69–84.

Stokes, D. M. (2015). The case against psi. In E. Cardena, J. Palmer, & D. Marcusson-Clavertz (Eds.), *Parapsychology: A handbook for the 21st century* (pp. 42–48). Jefferson, NC: McFarland & Company.

Storm, L., Tressoldi, P., & Di Risio, L. (2012). Meta-analysis of ESP studies, 1987–2010: Assessing the success of the forced-choice design in parapsychology. *Journal of Parapsychology*, *76*(2), 243–273.

Stroebe, W., & Strack, F. (2014). The alleged crisis and the illusion of exact replication. *Perspectives on Psychological Science*, *9*(1), 59–71. doi: 10.1177/1745691613514450.

Thalbourne, M. A. (1995). Further studies of the measurement and correlates of belief in the paranormal. *Journal of the American Society for Psychical Research*, 89(3), 233–247.

Thalbourne, M. A. (2003). *A glossary of terms used in parapsychology*. Charlottesville, VA: Puente.

Toglia, M. P., Read, J. D., Ross, D. F., & Lindsay, R. C. L. (Eds.) (2007). *The handbook of eyewitness psychology* (Vol. 1: Memory for events). Mahwah, NJ: Lawrence Erlbaum Associates Inc.

Utts, J. (1991). Replication and meta-analysis in parapsychology. *Statistical Science*, 6(4), 363–378.

Vernon, D. (2017a). Attempting to elicit a precall effect using emotive images and participants with high levels of belief in psi. *Journal of Consciousness Studies*, 24(11–12), 216–237.

Vernon, D. (2017b). Exploring precall using arousing images and utilising a memory recall practise task on-line. *Journal of the Society for Psychical Research*, 81(2), 65–79.

Wagenmakers, E. J., Wetzels, R., Borsboom, D., Kievit, R., & van der Maas, H. L. (2015). A skeptical eye on psi. In E. C. May & S. B. Marwaha (Eds.), *Extrasensory perception: Support, skepticism, and science* (pp. 153–176). Denver, CO: Praeger.

Watt, C., & Baker, I. S. (2002). Remote facilitation of attention focusing with psi-supportive versus psi-unsupportive experimenter suggestions. *Journal of Parapsychology*, 66, 151–168.

Watt, C., & Ramakers, P. (2003). Experimenter effects with a remote facilitation of attention focusing task: a study with multiple believer and disbeliever experimenters. *The Journal of Parapsychology*, 67(1), 99–116.

Watt, C., & Wiseman, R. (2002). Experimenter differences in cognitive correlates of paranormal belief, and in psi. *Journal of Parapsychology*, 66, 371–385.

Wegener, A. (1915). *Die entstehung de kontinente und ozeane (The origin of continents and oceans)*. Braunschweig, Germany: Vieweg.

Wehrstein, K. S. (2019). An adult reincarnation case with multiple solved-lives: Recalling Wilhelm Emmerich. *Journal of the Society for Psychical Research*, 83(1), 1–17.

White, R. A. (1976). The limits of experimenter influence on psi test results: Can any be set? *Journal of the American Society for Psychical Research*, 70, 333–369.

White, R. A. (1977). The influence of the experimenter motivation, attitudes and methods of handling subjects in psi test results. In B. B. Wolman (Ed.), *Handbook of parapsychology* (pp. 273–304). New York, NY: Van Nostrand Reinhold.

Wiseman, R., & Schlitz, M. (1997). Experimenter effects and the remote detection of staring. *Journal of Parapsychology*, 61, 197–207.

Wiseman, R., & Schlitz, M. (1999). *Replication of experimenter effect and the remote detection of staring*. Paper presented at the Proceedings of Presented Papers: The Parapsychological Association 42nd Annual Convention, Stanford University, Palo Alto, CA.

Woodman, R. W., & Schoenfeldt, L. F. (1989). Individual differences in creativity: An interactionist perspective. In J. A. Glover, R. R. Ronning, & C. R. Reynolds (Eds.), *Handbook of creativity* (pp. 77–91). Boston, MA: Springer.

Zwaan, R., Etz, A., Lucas, R., & Donnellan, M. (2018). Making replication mainstream. *Behavioral and Brain Sciences*, 41, e120. doi: 10.1017/S0140525X17001972.

Chapter 3

Telepathy and scopaesthesia

This chapter focuses on two aspects of direct mental communication. The first is telepathy and the second is scopaesthesia. The chapter begins by briefly outlining the nature of telepathy and explores the main paradigms that have been used to examine potential telepathic effects. This ranges from the more spontaneously reported cases of crisis telepathy to the influence on various aspects of a receiver's physiology. The second part focuses on scopaesthesia, more commonly referred to as the feeling associated with an awareness of being stared at. Here the chapter examines evidence from the three main paradigms of direct staring, remote staring and physiological responses to staring. The chapter ends by examining some of the factors that have been suggested to influence such mind-to-mind communications.

Telepathy

Telepathy refers to a broad range of effects and can be defined in different ways, which often reflect the nature of the behaviour under scrutiny as well as the paradigm used to elicit such behaviour (see Figure 3.1).

For instance, at a specific level it can refer to a form of mental communication, with target information transferred directly from one mind to another, encapsulated in the term *mental telepathy*. Such telepathic processes have also been referred to as *thought transference, mental suggestion* and *mind reading* (Alvarado, 2017). At a broader level, telepathy has been used to refer to the notion that one mind, or conscious individual, may acquire information relating to the thoughts, feelings and/or intentions of another conscious being from a distance via a non-usual route (Sheldrake, 2015). It is not clear at present whether these different aspects of telepathy represent distinct underlying processes or simply reflect the particular aspect of psi under observation at that moment in time. Nevertheless, telepathy as a topic, which hints at some form of mind-to-mind communication, has long been viewed as a challenging and problematic topic, in part due to its early association with spiritualism which has a chequered past (see, Moore, 1938), and because such mind-to-mind communication represents a challenge to currently understood mechanisms of cause and effect (Beloff & Henry, 2005; Cardeña, Marcusson-Clavertz, & Palmer, 2015). However, according to Palmer (1979) the reported feeling of receiving information from the mind of another person is one of the most commonly reported psi experiences. This common belief is likely to be influenced by the many anecdotal accounts reported of such behaviours occurring during, or as a result of, a crisis (Playfair, 1999, 2012; Sheldrake, 2002).

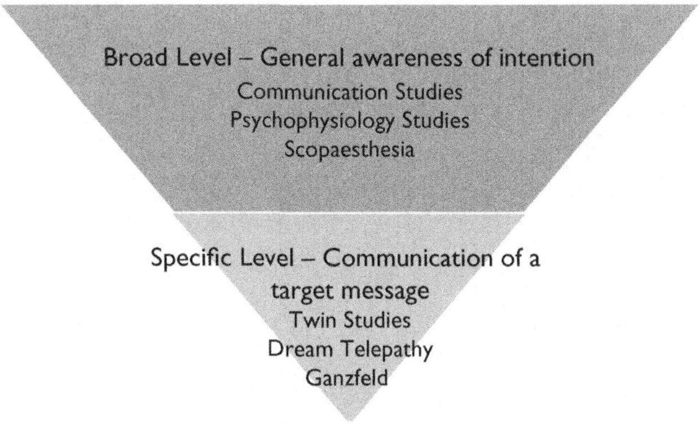

Figure 3.1 Possible definitions of telepathy as a function of the broad or specific level of focus along with identified research paradigms.

Crisis telepathy

This type of telepathy refers to the notion that one individual may experience a strong feeling that someone close to them is in danger. According to Playfair (1999) there are many anecdotal accounts of crisis telepathy which involve highly emotional states usually associated with death, an accident or an illness. Such cases have also been found to occur in situations where no prior cause or expectation of danger would be expected (see, Watt, 2005). For instance, the early work of L. E. Rhine (1953) focused on what she referred to as '*call cases*'. This involved an individual allegedly hearing the call of a loved one, who would be some distance away. The individual in question would later find out that the loved one was in distress or danger at the time of the alleged call. However, it was later noted that the 'caller' or 'agent' did not always call to the individual who heard the call (see, L. E. Rhine, 1956). Hence, it was suggested that it need not always be the case that one person 'calls out' to another but it could be that the 'receiver' is actively seeking out information about the agent. Others have reported cases where one twin suffers the physical pain of the other twin when involved in an accident, or feels the pain of their distant twin when they undergoes an operation (Playfair, 1999, 2012). Sheldrake (2002) has also suggested that mothers of newborn infants reportedly know when their baby needs them even when they are out of sight/hearing, often by feeling the 'milk let down' reflex that would normally occur in response to hearing a baby cry. Such a possible telepathic link between a mother and her child would have strong evolutionary advantages, making survival of the baby more likely.

However, as with all anecdotal accounts there is the possibility that such information may be misreported, and/or not accurately accounted for in a precise manner. The individuals in question are likely to be distracted by the emotional impact of the situation and rarely, if ever, make clear documentation of such feelings and thoughts at the time. It may also be the result of suggestion or expectation if one twin knows the other is about to undergo an operation they may attempt to feel some of the pain. It could even be that they view such feelings as a representation of the

closeness of their bond. Mainstream psychology has also suggested that such anecdotal accounts may be more readily explained in terms of the clustering illusion
(Gilovich, Vallone, & Tversky, 1985), availability error (Tversky & Kahneman,
1973) and confirmation bias (Wason, 1960). Indeed, it is very likely that these effects
may account for some of the anecdotal accounts reported. However, it is important
not to throw the baby out with the bathwater. Hence, whilst it is important to interpret anecdotal accounts with caution this does not mean they should be completely
ignored. Playfair (1999) argues that even when such notions as faulty memory,
bias and coincidence are accounted for, telepathy is still worth studying in controlled
lab-based research.

Early lab studies of telepathy

Credit should be given to J. B. Rhine (1947) who pioneered the examination of
telepathy in laboratory controlled conditions using a set of specific cards, called *Zener
cards,* that displayed one of five different symbols (see Figure 3.2). The symbols included a circle, a cross, three wavy-lines, a square and a star. Each standard pack
would contain 25 cards, with five of each symbol, and as such participants would be
expected to correctly 'guess' an average of five out of the 25.

Going through the whole pack of 25 cards would constitute a *run* and an experiment could consist of many runs. During each run the experimenter would select
a card from the deck, hold it in such a way that the participant could not see it, look
at it and hold its image in their mind. The participant would then be required to
identify the target card. The experimenter would note this response down and then
place the card face-down and select another. If the participant correctly identified the
target card this was referred to as a *hit*, and an incorrect call was a *miss*. This work is
often identified as *'forced choice'* research as each participant is forced to choose
between 1 of 5 possibilities. Hence mean chance expected (MCE) performance would
be 5 out of 25. Thus, by having the participant complete a number of runs their
performance could be compared to MCE and a statistical analysis conducted to see if
their performance differed.

Over time Rhine worked to tighten his experimental procedure to control for
possible sources of sensory leakage. These included using cards with no markings
on the rear as well as not allowing the participant to see or hear the experimenter.
Since then others have modified and/or adopted similar approaches using, for example, drawings of a clock face with the hour hand pointing to one of the 12 hours
(see, Fisk & Mitchell, 1953) as well as the inclusion of a random event generator to

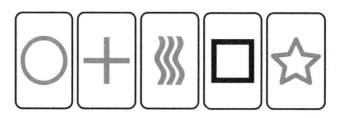

Figure 3.2 Examples of classic Zener cards.

select the target (H. Schmidt, 1970). Early research using this type of approach seemed to produce some encouraging results, particularly when the *sender* and *receiver* were in different locations (e.g., J. B. Rhine & Pratt, 1954; Rýzl & Pratt, 1962). However, in one instance researchers suggested that a particularly successful participant may have been able to identify the cards from a fleeting visual image that they then attempted to interpret (see, Kelly, Kanthamani, Child, & Young, 1975). These early positive findings led many others to try to replicate the effects using the card guessing technique developed by Rhine and his colleagues. However, though some success was evident many found that the hoped for positive results failed to emerge and this seems to have led to a loss of interest (see, Mauskopf & McVaugh, 1980).

Since this early work a range of paradigms have been developed each focusing on a distinct way to elicit and assess potential telepathic responses. The dominant paradigms focusing on the transfer of a target message include twin telepathy, dream telepathy, the ganzfeld paradigm and more recently the use of immersive virtual reality (IVR), whereas research focusing on broader issues of telepathic awareness of intention or shared responses has examined communication paradigms and a range of autonomic physiological responses.

Twin telepathy

There is an enduring and popular belief that a special emotional bond exists between twins, in particular identical twins, due to their shared genetic heritage (see, Nash & Buzby, 1965; Playfair, 1999, 2012). Indeed, survey research has suggested that twins experience more frequent telepathic events than non-twins and that identical twins report having such experiences more often than fraternal twins (Brusewitz, Cherkas, Harris, & Parker, 2014). Identical twins also report a greater level of 'connectedness' with their twin (see Box 3.1) compared to fraternal twins (A. Parker & Jensen, 2013), and a higher number of shared dreams (Playfair, 2017).

Box 3.1 Twin telepathy

Playfair describes an event regarding two twins, Noel and Christopher:

> Noel had a toothache and Christopher was found at the same time weeping in pain in another part of the school, and quite ignorant of his twin's distress or the cause of his personal suffering.
>
> (excerpt from Playfair, 2012, p. 78, with permission)

These reported links between the pairs would seemingly make them ideal candidates to test for the telepathic transfer of information. Such a paradigm would invariably test pairs of twins physically separated/isolated, with one acting as the *sender* and the other as the *receiver*. The role of the sender would be to focus on a selected target and attempt to 'send' this to their twin. After the completion of a set number of trials they would then swap roles and repeat the procedure.

However, despite the seemingly robust reports suggesting a strong link between twins, early research into twin telepathy failed to elicit any significant positive effects (see, Kubis & Rouke, 1937; Rogers, 1960). However, Playfair (1999, 2012) did note that the research by Kubis and Rouke (1937) was primarily involved in testing how similar each of the responses from the twins was to that of a third person, not whether there was any evidence of thought transference between them. Furthermore, there was some suggestive evidence that one pair did go on to produce higher than chance scores on a card guessing scenario. Charlesworth (1974) used a modified paradigm, which involved twins attempting to communicate telepathically via their dreams. This involved one twin attempting to insert a target image into the dream of the other twin. Somewhat counterintuitively, Charlesworth (1974) found that fraternal twins scored significantly higher than identical twins. However, this was put down to the fraternal twins being more extroverted than their identical counterparts.

Some intriguing results were reported by Robichon (1989) who found that identical twins can produce remarkable evidence for telepathy given the appropriate conditions. This involved testing a single pair of identical twins using a standard set of Zener cards which produced some suggestive results (e.g., mean score of 80.66%), particularly in one set of trials where the twins turned up for testing after having consumed alcohol at a local bar. However, the target selection method was less than ideal with one twin shuffling the pack of cards before simply picking out a target and it is also possible that the outcome may have been influenced by experimenter effects. Nevertheless, when reviewing this research Playfair (1999) pointed out that future researchers may want to examine the potential influence of alcohol on telepathic performance. More recently, A. Parker (2010) examined twin telepathy using 14 pairs of identical twins, with one acting as the sender and the other as receiver. In this instance the receiver remained in a relaxed state whilst the sender viewed a randomly selected film clip. Throughout this time the receiver was instructed to provide a continuous verbalisation of any internal imagery that occurred. At the end of a trial the receiver was shown four film clips (one target and three decoys) and asked to rank them from 1 (closest) to 4 in terms of how close they were to the information received. The results were encouraging with a reported hit rate of 35.7% when MCE was 25%. However, this difference was not statistically significant, possibly due to a lack of power, and as such needs to be interpreted with caution.

These results may seem disappointing but would be consistent with the claims of those that argue there is no clear evidence of mental communication between twins (see, Segal, 2017). Indeed, others have suggested that the reported similarities in thinking and decision making processes between twins is simply the result of a shared genetic and social history, an effect referred to as *thought concordance* (Blackmore & Chamberlain, 1993). Blackmore and Chamberlain (1993) tested the idea of thought concordance in twins by asking one twin to simply choose a picture and draw whatever they liked whilst the other twin was asked to draw whatever came to mind. Hence, there was no conscious effort made by either twin to communicate information. They compared this to a second condition that specifically tested for telepathy by requiring one twin to send selected target information to the other receiving twin. According to Blackmore and Chamberlain (1993) the pattern of results clearly favoured the former task suggesting a high level of thought concordance between the twins and not telepathy. Playfair (1999) admits that thought concordance between twins may play a role in their responses particularly when given the task of thinking of a specific image or number but would not necessarily account for results based on the random selection of a target image from a large pool. He also argues that the research focusing on thought concordance is limited as the data is based on only three pairs of twins, that there were no selection criteria and that the setting may not have been psi-conducive (see, Playfair, 2012).

Hence, it may be that twins are no better able to discern a telepathic link or message, should one exist, than non-twins. However, it is also clear that only a limited amount of research has been conducted in this area which led Playfair (2002, p. 97) to suggest that twin telepathy 'has never been adequately investigated'.

Dream telepathy

Research focusing on telepathic effects in dreams comes almost entirely from a programme carried out at the Maimonides Medical Centre in Brooklyn, New York. This lab was established in the early 1960s and ran 11 separate studies examining dream telepathy until it later closed in 1978 (Krippner, 1993). A key assumption of this type of research is that psi-type experiences, in this particular instance telepathy, are more likely to occur during sleep, in particular when the individual is dreaming. Indeed, early researchers suggested that as much as 65% of spontaneous cases of psi occur during the dream state (see, L. E. Rhine, 1981). To some extent this is based on the notion that altered states of consciousness may be psi-conducive (e.g., Roe, Jones, & Maddern, 2007). Others however have suggested that the transitional state between wakefulness and sleep, usually referred to as the hypnogogic state, may be more conducive for telepathic communication than during sleep per se (e.g., Braud, 2003).

As with most telepathy type studies the procedure for a dream telepathy paradigm involves a *sender* and a *receiver*. The specific target would be selected from a large pool of possible options on the basis of, for example, emotional intensity, vividness or colour, and placed in a sealed envelope prior to the start of the trial. The envelope containing the target would then be given to the sender who would reside in a separate room from the receiver eliminating any possible normal contact or sensory leakage. The receiver would reside in a sleep lab and be attached to various monitors providing a readout of brainwave and/or heart rate activity, with the aim of sleeping and if possible dreaming of the target. When the receiver enters a particular sleep state such as REM sleep, which is indicative of dreaming (Hobson, 2009), a signal would be passed to the sender indicating that they should open the sealed envelope and focus on the selected target with the intention of sending it to the receiver. Meanwhile an experimenter would continuously monitor the physiology of the receiver and once the REM phase had ended the experimenter would wake the receiver via an intercom and ask them to describe their dreams. The verbalised response would be recorded and later transcribed. In some situations, the sender may also have had heard the receiver's verbalisation of the target via an intercom to help focus and/or reinforce the strategy used. Once the trial is completed the receiver would be encouraged to return to sleep and the process repeated throughout the night for each REM phase. In the morning the receiver would be shown a selection of between 8–12 images, one of which was the target and the others decoys. The receiver would usually rank each of the images according to the fit with their dreams. The target sets could also be sent along with transcripts of the receiver's dreams to an external judge blind to the various conditions who would be required to make similar ranking judgements. If a target was ranked in the top half of the target set it was scored a *binary hit*, if not it was classified as a *binary miss*. The aim was to test whether the hit rate would exceed MCE.

An early review of the dream telepathy research from the Maimonides lab produced an overall hit rate that was 'significant beyond the 0.0001 level' (Child, 1985, p. 1221). However, not everyone agreed with the view that Maimonides produced such seemingly incontrovertible evidence. Clemmer (1986), for instance, suggested that possible experimenter fraud may have influenced the findings and that the case for dream telepathy remained unclear and that researchers should not 'devote any more time to such research' (p. 1174). This was later refuted by Child (1986) who argued that Clemmer had misrepresented the findings, often failing to examine the data and relying on biased and/or misleading secondary sources. This sentiment has been echoed by others who point out that no plausible mechanism for fraud has yet been put forward that could account for all the data (Sherwood & Roe, 2003). Indeed, a review of the dream telepathy work conducted at the Maimonides centre and afterwards showed that correct target material was identified more frequently than would be expected by chance alone (see e.g., Sherwood & Roe, 2003). This was despite the fact that much of the post-Maimonides research utilised different procedures, such as not monitoring the physiology of the sender, allowing them to sleep in their homes rather than at a designated sleep lab, which in turn means it was often not possible to synchronise sending with the various phases of REM sleep, along with differences in the precise judging procedure and the lack of pre-screening procedures to identify potentially gifted participants (see, Roe, Sherwood, Farrell, Savva, & Baker, 2007). These changes in the procedure may have influenced the outcome which is why at times the data may have been inconsistent (Sherwood & Roe, 2003, 2013). However, it should be noted that the paradigm developed at Maimonides represents something of an ideal. Such research is logistically intensive, requiring experienced research staff, equipment and sufficient funding, all points which would likely influence possible follow-up studies and potential replications. Indeed, reviews of the dream telepathy studies conducted over time have shown that the Maimonides studies were more successful than those coming after (Sherwood & Roe, 2013), though a direct comparison of scores between these data sets showed no significant difference (Storm & Rock, 2015). Nevertheless, a recent meta-analysis focusing on dream-based telepathy studies from 1966 to 2016 reported results at a rate beyond that expected by chance alone (Storm et al., 2017). However, it has been suggested that certain statistical decisions used in the process of this meta-analysis could have inflated the overall effect size and that when the data is re-analysed weighting the effects by sample size the overall effect is substantially reduced (Howard, 2017). This led Howard (2017) to suggest that future researchers should focus on ensuring sufficiently large sample sizes in their research.

Hence, it is clear that findings in this area remain contentious. Nevertheless, the positive findings from dream telepathy research has led many to suggest that the paradigm is worthy of further study.

Ganzfeld

The German term *ganzfeld* refers to the 'whole field' and is used to identify a procedure in psi research that is thought to improve the signal to noise ratio by reducing sensory input in the receiver. To some extent this is based on the assumption that psi effects or signals may be weak and transient and as such may be easily overshadowed by the internal somatic and the externally generated physical and sensory stimulation (Honorton, 1977). Honorton (1985) has also suggested that ancient texts describing the psychic experiences of adepts (i.e., those highly skilled) suggest that a psi-conducive state requires a quiet and relaxed mind with an inward focus. It is also thought that the ganzfeld procedure can induce an altered state of consciousness (Wackermann, Putz, & Allefeld, 2008). As such, the ganzfeld technique provides a useful approach to eliciting psi effects.

Typical of most telepathy paradigms the ganzfeld procedure involves both a *sender* and a *receiver* separated into different rooms and generally consists of three main stages: the preparation stage, the sending stage and the judging stage. In the preparation stage the receiver goes through a relaxation process which may involve sitting or reclining in a comfortable chair with halved ping-pong balls over the eyes, having a red light shone on them. They would also wear a set of headphones through which white or pink noise (static) is played. This puts the receiver into a state of mild sensory deprivation. In the sending stage a target item would be identified and given to the sender. In the early ganzfeld research this target selection process was often conducted using a manual randomisation and/or selection process. However, this was subsequently criticised as lacking adequate methodological rigour (see, Bem & Honorton, 1994; Honorton et al., 1990; Hyman & Honorton, 1986) and led to the use of automatic computerised software to select targets and record responses (Goulding, Westerlund, Parker, & Wackermann, 2004). The task of the sender is to then concentrate on the target item and mentally send this information to the receiver. The receiver will then verbalise aloud their impressions describing what they can see. This information may or may not be fed back to the sender over a one-way audio link in an attempt to provide them with feedback in terms of how accurate the link and information may be. The verbalised impressions given by the receiver, or *mentations*, may also be recorded and used during the judging procedure. The final judging stage may or may not include external judges blind to the various conditions (see e.g., Milton, 1997; Milton, 1999). For instance, a common approach would be to remove the receiver from the ganzfeld state and give them a set of possible targets, from which they select the one that most resembled the images/information they received. During this target identification process they may listen to their own recorded mentations during the trials in an attempt to identify any degree of correspondence between each potential target and their mentation at the time. If, for instance, they are shown four clips or images consisting of one target and three decoys their ability to correctly identify the target is compared to MCE (i.e., 25%) in order to ascertain if anything unusual has occurred. Alongside this, judging may involve independent arbiters not involved in the study and blind to the various conditions. These judges will be given a transcript of the receiver's mentations along with the same selection of images and asked to rank or identify the one they think most closely matches the verbalisations. Irrespective

of the specific judging procedure the claim is that if the overall hit rate is significantly above chance then this represents evidence for telepathy.

Many claim that the ganzfeld paradigm represents the most effective and reliable
design for eliciting telepathic effects (e.g., Bem & Honorton, 1994; Honorton et al.,
1990; A. Parker, 2000; Schlitz & Radin, 2003) with some suggesting that it may be
wasting valuable resources to continue looking for proof oriented effects rather
than shift the focus to more process oriented effects (Utts, 1995). However, perhaps
unsurprisingly, not all agree. For instance, Wackermann et al. (2008) pointed out
that the problem with suggesting that the ganzfeld procedure produces a psi-
conducive state is that this term is simply too vague to be usefully meaningful.
However, over time a growing database of reported findings is suggestive of
something unusual occurring.

For instance, early research on telepathy using the ganzfeld procedure showed
some intriguing results that significantly exceeded those expected by chance (i.e.,
37% compared to chance of 25%) but were called into question as the studies lacked
sufficient methodological rigour (see, Honorton, 1985; Hyman, 1985; Hyman &
Honorton, 1986). This led to cautious conclusions that awaited 'the outcome of
future experiments conducted by a broader range of investigators and according to
more stringent standards' (Hyman & Honorton, 1986, p. 351). Since then researchers have argued that these more stringent standards have been met and that the
data from ganzfeld research still shows robust positive effect sizes (Bem & Honorton,
1994). For instance, Honorton et al. (1990) reported hit rates of 34% which were
significantly above chance. Since then others have conducted reviews and/or meta-
analyses of the many research studies showing overall hit rates significantly above
those of MCE. For example, Parker (2000) reported on a series of five ganzfeld
studies showing a mean hit rate of 36% when chance expectation would suggest
20%. Similarly, a meta-analysis of 30 ganzfeld studies by Storm, Tressoldi and Di
Risio (2010) reported from 1997 to 2008 found a hit rate of 32.2% when chance
expectations would be 25%. Even attempts to examine telepathy using a modified
ganzfeld procedure that did not disclose to the participants in question that the study
was potentially testing for telepathy produced an average hit rate of 32.5% which
exceeded MCE (Putz, Gabler, & Wackermann, 2007). More recently, a review of 59
ganzfeld studies showed a combined hit rate of 30% which is significantly above the
MCE of 25% (Williams, 2011, see Figure 3.3).

However, others have argued that the results of the ganzfeld paradigm need to
be interpreted with caution as they could potentially be explained by sensory leakage
(Wiseman, Smith, & Kornbrot, 1996). For instance, they point out that when the
receiver is listening back to their own mentations the experimenter may point out
potential correspondences between their voiced thoughts and a possible target.
Hence, the experimenter may consciously or unconsciously cue the receiver as to
which was the correct target particularly if they had at any time during any of the
trials heard any noise and/or comments made by the sender which could cue them as
to what the target was. This sort of noise leakage could be a potential problem with
serious consequences. It is difficult to know the possible extent of this as senders were
not monitored or recorded during the sessions. Nevertheless, it is possible that a
sender may make more noise when viewing a dynamic target which would account
for the finding that dynamic targets are associated with higher hit rates. Furthermore,

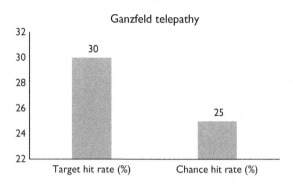

Figure 3.3 Mean hit rate for targets (left) compared to chance (right) from 59 ganzfeld studies (adapted from Williams, 2011).

when Milton and Wiseman (1999) conducted their own meta-analysis of 30 ganzfeld studies they found no clear evidence for telepathy. This they argued casts serious doubt on the field and on the effectiveness of the ganzfeld procedure to elicit clear replicable effects. However, a re-examination of the data used by Milton and Wiseman (1999) showed a strong confirmation of the original ganzfeld effect with the effect sizes correlating with the degree to which the research adhered to the standard ganzfeld procedure (see, Bem, Palmer, & Broughton, 2001).

There does seem to be some agreement in the literature that the more closely subsequent studies followed the classic ganzfeld procedure the more they were able to elicit comparable effects of telepathy (Bem et al., 2001; Palmer, 2003; Williams, 2011). Hence, while there is variability in terms of the results of the ganzfeld research this is in part due to the heterogeneity of the studies. At present it is not entirely clear precisely what these factors are, though they are likely to include the personality of the participants, the target, the type of experimenter and how the effect is analysed (see, Palmer 2003; Williams, 2011). However, given the wide-ranging reports of positive effects it is unsurprising that claims have been made regarding anomalies in the ganzfeld database that present a challenge to normal plausible explanations (Palmer, 2003).

Immersive virtual reality

The use of immersive virtual reality (IVR) settings is a more recent development based in part on the technological developments in computing. The idea here is to give more consideration to the nature and setting of the way the target is 'experienced' by the sender. It is often the case that target materials are visual in nature and the sender is generally required to simply focus on the target with the intention of sending information regarding the target to the receiver. However, it has been suggested that multi-sensory targets that encourage a greater level of processing may help to elicit stronger telepathic responses (Delanoy, 1989), with research also suggesting that colourful dynamic targets may be preferred (Honorton et al., 1990; Watt, 1996). As such, in an effort to provide more dynamic, colourful and potentially life-like targets that allow real-time interaction researchers have begun, albeit in a limited way, to utilise IVR in a telepathic setting (Murray, Howard, Wilde, Fox, & Simmonds-Moore, 2007).

The suggestion is that the IVR environment, similar to the ganzfeld procedure, helps to reduce awareness of reality and dampen the level of sensory input. In addition, the IVR setting can enable *both* the sender and the receiver to simultaneously experience the same environment together without any need or scope for them to interact. This would help to keep potential sensory leakage to a minimum. By sharing the environment it may be possible to facilitate the acts of both sending and receiving, particularly if the receiver includes in their representation of the target the wider surrounding context.

This idea was tested by Murray et al. (2007) who had both sender and receiver interact with a target pool of objects simultaneously in the same virtual environment. The aim was that this simultaneous interaction would facilitate any potential telepathy effects. Unfortunately, they found no evidence of telepathy occurring between pairs of participants placed in IVR environments. Nevertheless, they offered a range of reasons as to why such a null result may have occurred, including the lack of any relaxation period, the use of an opportunity sample and very short duration trials. As such, the use of IVR to examine potential telepathic effects is both novel and in its infancy. Moreover, this area is likely to expand and develop as the technology supporting it continues to develop. Hence, it represents an area that is ripe for future researchers to modify and develop.

Communication

As mentioned above telepathy can refer to the specific transmission of a message from a sender to a receiver or that the receiver is able to pick up on the more generic feelings or intentions of the sender. For instance, there are many anecdotal reports of individuals claiming to think about a particular person they may not have seen for some time just prior to receiving some form of communication from them. This next section examines these aspects of telepathy via communication.

Telephone

According to Sheldrake and Smart (2003a) *telephone telepathy* represents the most common type of telepathy. This is where one person may be thinking of someone they have not seen for some time when for no discernible reason they receive a phone call from that person, alternatively, when receiving a phone call, and before looking to see who it is or answering it, reportedly knowing whom it is from. Indeed, respondents to a survey asking such questions in Europe and America found that 92% of those that responded reported experiencing such feelings (Brown & Sheldrake, 2001). Furthermore, surveys show that more women than men reportedly claim to have experienced such experiences (Sheldrake & Smart, 2003a, 2003b).

Such reports could of course simply represent coincidence or highlight a chance occurrence that confirms a biased interpretation. There may be many times when a person thinks of an old friend or acquaintance that they have not seen for some time, and receives no phone call and as such does not give it much thought. It is the chance coming together of such thoughts along with a phone call that can mislead people to think that this is indicative of something unusual. They simply fail to remember the many times they have thought about this person and not received a call. These chance coincidences and selective memory give the illusion that something more is happening. An alternative possibility is that the person who receives the call is intimately related with the caller and as such may know their routine to such an extent that receiving a call from them at a particular time is highly likely. For instance, thinking about a spouse and then receiving a phone call from that person during a lunchtime period may not be unusual as such calls may occur often. As such, it is difficult to provide a clear account of such anecdotal reports as people generally do not note down each time they think of a person who either does or does not subsequently contact them.

Nevertheless, Sheldrake and Smart (2003a, 2003b) attempted to test such ideas of chance and unconscious telepathy by developing a procedure in which a participant receives a telephone call from one of four possible callers. The receiver would know who all the callers are, they may be friends or family members for example, but not which one will be calling at any specific time. Hence, the caller would be selected at random by the experimenter and then call the receiver. However, before the receiver picks up the phone and/or looks to see who is calling on the caller ID, they has to say aloud who they think the caller is. Such a procedure by chance would suggest that performance should be correct at a rate of 25% of the time and as such it is possible to test whether responses exceed this. When Sheldrake and Smart (2003a) used this procedure, they found an overall hit rate of 40% which was significantly above that expected by chance alone (see, Figure 3.4).

They argued that the results could not be accounted for in terms of optional stopping effects, whereby low hit rates may have led some participants to give up and drop out, or by sensory leakage in terms of hints given by a caller about whether they may call again. They followed this up with a second study that continuously filmed participants prior to and during each trial to ensure that they adhered to the procedure (Sheldrake & Smart, 2003b). This required the receiving participants to name the potential caller out loud to a camera prior to answering the telephone. Again, Sheldrake and Smart (2003b) found the number of correctly identified trials, at 45.5%, was significantly higher than chance. Interestingly, in both studies they found

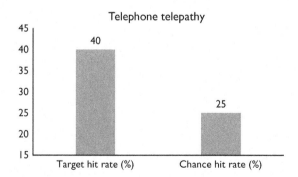

Figure 3.4 Mean percentage hit rate for targets (left) compared to chance (right) across all trials of a telephone telepathy study (adapted from Sheldrake & Smart, 2003a).

that these highly successful identification rates were for the familiar callers not when the caller was a stranger. However, it should be noted that attempts to replicate the effect of telephone telepathy using people that were either known or unknown to the receiver failed to show any significant effects (S. Schmidt, Muller, & Walach, 2004). Schmidt et al. (2004) noted that the failure to elicit an effect could have been the result of methodological differences. Indeed, in a series of follow-up studies they found that pre-selecting a participant that had scored above chance in prior trials did lead to hit rates above chance (S. Schmidt, Erath, Ivanova, & Walach, 2009). Such findings suggest that the effect may not be as widespread as people often believe but may rely to a great extent on a few high performing individuals.

More recent attempts to examine this effect utilised a more automated set up involving a computer selecting individuals to call a receiver on their mobile phone and enabling researchers to automatically collect responses from the receivers via direct input on their phones (Sheldrake, Smart, & Avraamides, 2015). Such an approach cut down on the possibility of sensory leakage or potential cheating. Nevertheless, the overall results showed that with tests using three possible callers the receivers were able to correctly identify them at a rate of 41.8% which was significantly above that expected by chance (i.e., 33.3%) and those using two callers showed a hit rate of 55.2%, which was again above chance. These telephone telepathy effects have also been replicated by others (see, Lobach & Bierman, 2004).

SMS/text

A recent development of this type of paradigm has been to try to see if it is possible that a person can correctly classify the identity of a person sending them a text message. In a typical study there may be several potential 'senders' located at various distances from the receiver. The experimenter then uses a pre-set procedure to randomly select one of the senders to send a brief text message to the receiver. As soon as the text message arrives at the receiver's phone they must guess the identity of the sender before checking. Sheldrake and Beharee (2009) used this type of procedure to test whether participants could identify which one of four possible senders had sent them a text message. In an interesting twist two of the senders in this instance were computers, generating text messages on demand. Across 6000 trials they found the hit rate of the receivers correctly identifying the sender was significantly above chance. Unfortunately, when the high scorers were re-tested in a follow-up task their performance returned to mean chance levels. Nevertheless, use of a modified procedure which varied the delay between the sending of a text and the requirement for the receiver to respond led to hit rates which significantly exceeded those of chance (Sheldrake, Avraamides, & Novak, 2009).

Email

Similar to the telephone telepathy procedure here four potential emailers are identified, who are ideally known friends or family members of the receiver, and one is randomly selected to send an email to a receiver housed in a separate room or building. Prior to the email being sent the receiver would be required to identify who they think the email that they are *about to receive* will be from. Sheldrake and Smart

(2005) found that people's level of accuracy significantly exceeded that of chance (see Figure 3.5). In a second experiment they selectively recruited participants who had performed well (i.e., >50%) in the first experiment and then filmed them throughout to ensure that they followed the procedure. Again, they found that the receivers were able to identify the potential emailers at a rate of 47%, which significantly exceeded chance. This led them to conclude that in the absence of any normal sensory communication it is possible for people to tell when they are about to receive an email and from whom. Interestingly, a follow-up study that utilised a more automatic online procedure, involving a computer to randomly select participants and required an input response from the receiver prior to delivering the email message, again found results at 41.8% that were above chance level (Sheldrake & Avraamides, 2009).

Overall, the results of communication telepathy via phone, SMS and email are encouraging and offer a potentially fruitful area for future researchers to explore.

Physiology

Though not strictly telepathy in the sense that a target image or word is sent from one individual to another this research has focused on potential changes in the physiology of a receiver when a distant sender is stimulated in some way. For instance, exposing a sender to specific visual stimuli or startling them with a loud unexpected noise are all known to elicit distinct and particular changes in the sender's physiology (see e.g., Andreassi, 2000). However, the question addressed here is whether an induced change in the physiology of one person (i.e., the sender) will make itself evident in the physiology of a distant receiver. As such, researchers may focus on trying to identify possible correlations in the electroencephalographic (EEG) activity of the brains of both sender and receiver whilst they are spatially separated (see e.g., Ambach, 2008). Such possibilities are interesting for a number of reasons. First, they provide clear and objective measures of changes in physiology that, if found, should be possible to replicate. Second, such changes invariably occur without the receiver becoming consciously aware of them. Hence, this represents an implicit or non-conscious measure of psi-based behaviour. To date, potential changes have been reported in electrocortical brain activity as measured by the

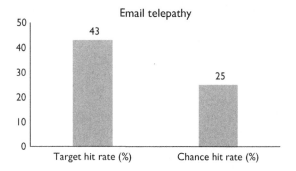

Figure 3.5 Mean percentage hit rate for email targets (left) compared to chance (right) across unfilmed trials (adapted from Sheldrake & Smart, 2005).

EEG, changes in brain-based blood flow, as measured by functional magnetic resonance imaging (fMRI) techniques, and changes in autonomic arousal measures such as galvanic skin response and heart rate.

EEG

Examining brainwave activity via the EEG is a complex and challenging process and it is possible to elicit many different types of changes in the EEG (see, Andreassi, 2000). For example, changes may occur in the amplitude or power of one of the main spectral frequencies, such as alpha (8–12Hz) or beta (12–25Hz), or in a specific event-related potential (ERP) or the coherence, or correlation, of brainwave activity across different regions. Possibly one of the first attempts to examine potential telepathic communication between the brains of two physically separated individuals was conducted by Duane and Behrendt (1965). They examined this by inducing changes in the alpha spectral frequency of one individual to see if similar effects would emerge in the brain of the distant receiver. They used pairs of twins as participants but found that only two out of the 15 pairs showed any evidence of a change in their EEG in line with expectations.

Others have focused on eliciting changes in EEG event-related potentials that are evoked by visual (i.e., VEP) or auditory (i.e., AEP) stimuli. In part this may be because such signals can evoke clear and consistent changes in the EEG of the stimulated individual (i.e., sender). However, early attempts to use a visual flicker method to invoke a VEP showed inconsistent changes in the alpha activity of the non-stimulated receiver (Puthoff & Targ, 1976). A modified paradigm which subsequently had the two individuals (i.e., sender and receiver) spend time together prior to the EEG recording with the aim of achieving a bond between them did show that visual flashes to the sender evoked changes in the EEG of a distant receiver (Grinberg-Zylberbaum, Delaflor, Attie, & Goswami, 1994). Grinberg-Zylerbaum et al. (1994) referred to this as evidence for a *transferred potential* that could be seen as a mechanism for possibly supporting telepathy. Unfortunately, it was later shown that such correlated changes in brain activity could have occurred spontaneously due to the large autocorrelations that occur in the brain naturally (see e.g., May, Spottiswoode, & Faith, 2000; Wackermann, Seiter, Keibel, & Walach, 2003). Nevertheless, on-going attempts to examine the potential changes in the EEG of a receiver when a distant sender is stimulated have continued to produce intriguing effects. For instance, Standish, Kozak, Johnson and Richards (2004) examined ERPs from the occipital region of the cortex in sender–receiver pairs of participants separated by 10 metres. Each trial involved the sender being presented with visual stimulation whilst the receiver simply relaxed. When stimulated the sender was told to attempt to send a thought and/or image to the receiver whilst the receiver was told to remain open to receiving such information. These sender–receiver pairs knew each other well and claimed to have had prior experience of being emotionally and psychologically connected to one another. Overall, Standish et al. (2004) found significant changes in the EEG during the flickering condition but not during the static control condition. This led them to suggest that stimulation of the brain of one member of the pair could be detected in the brain of the non-stimulated receiver when located at a distance. Others have also reported changes in the EEG of a non-stimulated receiver when a distant sender is exposed to visual flashes (e.g., Kittenis, Caryl, & Stevens, 2004; Radin, 2004a).

An alternative approach is to attempt to induce changes in brainwave activity of the sender by exposing them to a complex magnetic field (Persinger, Koren, & Tsang, 2003). This magnetic field, usually produced by a toroid device held near or worn on the head, can elicit clear changes in the EEG of the person exposed to such energy (i.e., the sender). As with other approaches the question is whether such induced changes in the EEG of the sender will be evident in the EEG of a distant receiver. One such study reporting on a pair of siblings, one of whom was exposed to a complex magnetic field for 5 minutes, showed changes in the low level theta (4–8Hz) brainwave activity of the non-stimulated sibling housed at a distance (Persinger et al., 2003; Persinger, Saroka, Mulligan, & Murphy, 2010). This induced effect has also been reported for pairs of strangers that met and remained in close proximity to one another for one-hour twice a week over a four-week period (Persinger, Tsang, Booth, & Koren, 2008). This has led to claims that it is possible to generate correlations in the brain activity of separated individuals even at a distance of thousands of kilometres (Rouleau et al., 2015; Scott et al., 2015).

However, it should be noted that such positive effects have not always been found, or have only been found in a sub-set of those taking part (e.g., Sabell, Clarke, & Fenwick, 2001; Standish, Johnson, Kozak, & Richards, 2003) and that there are many methodological differences that occur across the various studies that could potentially influence the outcome. These include, but are not limited to, the type of stimuli used to induce a physiological response, the specific psychophysiological measure obtained, the location of the change on the scalp, the relationship between the sender–receiver pairs as well as their experience with relaxation/meditation techniques (see, Radin & Pierce, 2015; Wackermann, 2008). Such a lack of consistency led Wackermann (2008, p. 151) to suggest that 'it is highly doubtful there is anything such as a real effect'. However, a recent review by Giroldini and Pederzoli (2018) exploring the possible interaction between isolated pairs of individuals examined changes in brainwave activity as evident in the EEG. It was often the case that these individuals knew each other well and that the changes in EEG were more evident in the sender who was exposed to the various stimuli than the receiver who was not stimulated. Nevertheless, they concluded that the effect, whilst weak, was evident in the EEG of the receiver and is indicative of information transfer between spatially separated individuals outside of any normal means of communication.

fMRI

Researchers have also utilised functional magnetic resonance imaging (fMRI) to measure changes in blood flow in the cortex of a receiver when the brain of a distant sender is stimulated (Richards, Kozak, Johnson, & Standish, 2005; Standish et al., 2003). For instance, Standish et al. (2003) found that stimulation of the visual cortex of a sender elicited increased levels of blood oxygenation in the visual processing regions of the brain of the receiver. Importantly, there was no evidence of any such signal in the brain of the receiver when the sender was not stimulated. Furthermore, they found that this effect was not evident when the sender–receiver roles were reversed. This led them to suggest that transmission of a signal in one direction does not ensure or predict transmission in the other direction, though they did conclude that the pattern of brain activity evident in the receiver suggested that they had 'processed' a signal from the sender. More recently Karavasilis et al. (2017) tested for such changes in the brains of twins. During the procedure, one twin was exposed to emotionally arousing images and sounds whilst the other twin housed 25 metres away underwent an fMRI recording. Despite the fact that neither of the twins were aware of the experimental procedure and its aim to test for possible correlated brain activity, Karavasilis et al. (2017) found a clear correlation between the exposure of emotive stimuli in one twin and a cortical response in the other twin. They concluded that this showed a clear connection between pairs of identical twins.

Autonomic response

Others have examined physiological changes in autonomic responses such as galvanic skin response, blood pressure and heart rate activity when one of a pair of individuals is presented with a mild shock or a surprising stimulus (Jensen & Parker, 2012; A. Parker & Jensen, 2013). For instance, Jensen and Parker (2012) examined the potential physiological connections between pairs of twins who were physically separated by 100 metres. During this time one of the twins (the sender) would be stimulated or shocked in a specific way and the physiology of the other twin measured to see if any change could be elicited. Unfortunately, they found no clear evidence of any physiological connectedness between the twins. However, they did point out that there were a number of methodological problems that may have influenced this outcome. For example, when the experimenter carried in a bucket of cold water, used to immerse the sender's foot and elicit a mild shock, the twin in question could hear experimenter and bucket approach. This would likely lead to an expectation effect, reducing any possible shock response to the stimulus which in turn could reduce the potential transference of a signal. Nevertheless, they did find that one pair of twins seemed to exhibit a possible telepathic link with three out of five trials in which one twin was startled producing physiological changes in the non-startled twin. They attempted to account for this by pointing out that this pair of twins had the closest reported embryonic background with both sharing the same placenta and amniotic sacs, generally referred to as mono-amniotic twins. Hence, they suggested that future researchers should obtain records of the embryonic background of the twins and prioritise those who are classified as monoamniotic.

A follow-up study by A. Parker and Jensen (2013) tested four sets of identical twins assessing a range of physiological measures including electrodermal activity (EDA), pulse rate, blood pressure and heart rate. Their procedure involved exposing one twin to randomly selected material that would either produce a shock or surprise response while measuring the physiology of the remaining twin located in a distant room. An external expert, blind to the aims of the study, judged the physiological recordings with the aim of correctly identifying the time window during which the twin acting as *sender* would be viewing the target material. They found a marginal effect, but this seemed to be largely due to the outstanding performance of one set of twins, who were the youngest in the sample, which could be taken to indicate that some individuals may be more psychic than others (see, Braude, 2016).

Overall, the data from physiological studies of telepathy are intriguing but inconsistent. As noted above this type of paradigm is not assessing telepathy in the sense of a specific message transferred from a sender to a receiver. It is also important to point out that there are many methodological challenges faced when recording and analysing such physiological data. Nevertheless, the findings from both the EEG and fMRI research paradigms are suggestive of potential links between individuals physically separated. Hence, this certainly represents a potentially fruitful area for future researchers to examine as it may help to uncover and/or identify a potential mechanism for possible telepathic communication.

Scopaesthesia

The second part of this chapter examines another area of alleged mind-to-mind communication that is widely reported: that of scopaesthesia, or more generally an awareness or sense that one is being watched or stared at by someone (Braud, Shafer, & Andrews, 1993b; Sheldrake, 2005a, 2005b, 2015). This is not a recent phenomenon as one of the earliest studies to examine the level of belief in scopaesthesia polled a group of American students and found that, of those that responded, 77% reported that they believed they could tell when a person was staring at them (Coover, 1917). More recent surveys have shown similar levels of belief, with between 70% and 90% of the population reporting that they believe they can sense when someone is staring at them (Braud et al., 1993b; Sheldrake, 2003). However, belief levels in scopaesthesia have also been shown to decrease as barriers between the individuals in question increase and may also be mediated by levels of self-consciousness and social anxiety (I. S. Baker, 2015). According to Sheldrake (2015) these experiences are more commonly reported when people felt themselves being stared at by strangers in public places and also when people felt vulnerable rather than secure. The precise motives for this alleged effect are unclear but have been suggested to include sexual attraction, anger and affection (Sheldrake, 2003). Furthermore, it has also been suggested that people can feel when animals are staring at them (see e.g., Sheldrake, 2015). The three main paradigms used to examine this effect are direct staring, remote staring and physiological changes.

Direct staring

Direct staring paradigms generally involve individuals working in pairs with one acting as the *starer* and the other as the *staree*. The staree may sit either in the same room or in a separate room viewed via a one-way window facing away from the starer. The starer then conducts a sequence of trials during which they randomly stare, or not, at the back of the neck of the staree. In each trial the staree will be required to respond to the question of whether the starer was or was not staring at them. The question is whether the staree can identify whether they were being stared at a rate above chance (i.e., 50%: see, Radin, 2004b; Sheldrake, 1999, 2008; Sheldrake, Overby, & Beeharee, 2008).

The notion of such remote gaze detection gained popularity in the 1990s via exposure in science-based magazines and television. Throughout this time many thousands of trials were run producing some remarkably consistent results. Typically, the reported hit rate was around 55% when a hit rate of 50% (see, Figure 3.6) would be expected by chance alone (see, Sheldrake, 1999, 2000, 2003, 2005a, 2005b). Such positive hit rates

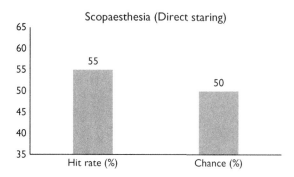

Figure 3.6 Mean percentage hit rate for detecting direct staring (left) compared to chance (right) expectations (adapted from Sheldrake, 1999).

have been reported across different countries (Sheldrake, 1998), when the procedure has been run online (Sheldrake et al., 2008) and remained consistent when attempts were made to eliminate any possible contaminating cues such as smell and sound (see, Sheldrake, 2005a, 2005b). Interestingly a large set of trials run as part of a science experiment in Amsterdam not only showed significant effects but found that children under the age of 9 were more sensitive to such effects (see Sheldrake, 2003).

Not everyone however has been able to elicit such positive effects. The early work of Coover (1917) found no support for such claims. More recently R. Baker (2000) stared at people through a one-way mirror and found that they were no better than chance at identifying when they were being stared at. However, Sheldrake (2005a) has suggested that such null results were more likely due to the ambiguous methodology used. Indeed, a meta-analysis conducted by S. Schmidt, Schneider, Utts and Walach (2004) reported that whilst there was a small but significant effect the effect size was inversely related to the quality of the study. As such, the better quality and more tightly controlled studies produced less of an effect. Hence, their conclusion that more quality research is needed in this area.

Remote staring

Closed circuit television (CCTV) cameras are a feature of modern life and appear in shopping centres, town centres and many other areas to provide various services with surveillance options. According to Sheldrake (2015) interviews of those who use CCTV as part of their job has shown that most believe that people could sense when they were being watched. This would suggest that people may be able to detect when they are being stared at or watched from a distance even when the staring/watching is not direct. However, the evidence for this is both mixed and inconsistent. For instance, a remote staring study carried out by Wiseman and Schlitz (1997) showed that the positive effects were influenced by the belief of the experimenter. In this case Schlitz, a psi proponent, obtained significant effects whereas Wiseman, the sceptic, did not. Others have also failed to find effects of remote staring detection and suggest that performance may be more usefully accounted for in terms of implicit learning of non-random sequences (Colwell, Schroder, & Sladen, 2000). However, the notion of implicit learning was not specifically tested for and when Sheldrake (2015) later requested access to the raw data to examine this idea he reports that they 'refused to supply the data' (p. 359). As such, Sheldrake (2015) argues that the idea of implicit learning is not fully supported by the data and cannot account for all the data, particularly when using computerised randomisation procedures (see also, Sheldrake, 2008).

Staring and physiology

Research has shown that when stared at the staree will exhibit a physiological response (Helminen, Kaasinen, & Hietanen, 2011). Hence, a question posed within this framework is whether such a physiological effect can be detected when the staree is not aware or cannot see the starer. This is thought to be a more robust measure of the effect because it is not under volitional control of the staree and given the autonomic nature of the responses may be influenced more unconsciously (Muller, Schmidt, & Walach, 2009). It is also thought to be less susceptible to the potential influence of sensory leakage.

Research has produced some interesting effects when focusing on the potential changes in skin conductance level (SCL) as a function of being stared at. For instance, Schlitz and LaBerge (1997) had pairs of participants work together in separate locations, with the starer observing the staree via a video monitor. At randomly allocated times the starer would focus on the staree. During these periods Schlitz and LaBerge (1997) found that SCL levels in the staree increased compared to the no-stare trials. This in turn led to research focusing on the use of EDA along with CCTV systems to allow the starer and staree to be completely separated and often located in different rooms. Such research is collectively referred to as EDA-CCTV research (see, I. S. Baker, 2005). Using this type of remote staring procedure some researchers have found that the EDA levels of those being stared at becomes significantly more activated during the staring condition compared to the no-staring condition (Braud et al., 1993b). However, again, others have found no clear effects of staring on physiological measures (Muller et al., 2009). Indeed, a recent attempt to examine the potential electrocortical correlates of being stared at to ascertain whether there is any evidence of specific brain activity during the process of remote staring detection failed to show any positive effects (I. S. Baker & Stevens, 2013).

A meta-analysis of fifteen remote staring experiments conducted between 1989 and 1998 showed a significantly positive effect in that people were more accurate than chance (S. Schmidt, Schneider, et al., 2004). Interestingly there was no association between the quality of the reported study and the effect size. This would suggest that the reported effects are not an artefact of poor-quality studies. Indeed, Schmidt et al. (2004, p. 245) argue that this provides clear evidence 'of a remote staring effect'.

Overall, the effects of being stared at are interesting but inconsistent. There may be clear reasons why such inconsistencies arise. For example, as mentioned above the belief of the experimenter has been shown to influence the outcome. However, it should be noted that this may not simply reflect the 'belief' of the individual in question but also their 'ability' to stare. It could be that some people are simply better starers than others. It has also been suggested that the 'quality of the starer's attention is important in determining the nature of the experimental outcome' (Braud, Shafer, & Andrews, 1993a, p. 405). In particular the starer's mental strategy during the non-staring periods may be important (Muller et al., 2009). That is, it may be important to distract the starer during periods of non-staring as they may still be thinking about the target participant and simply thinking about the staree may be sufficient to reduce any possible difference between staring and no-staring conditions. Hence, distracting the starer with a demanding cognitive task during the non-stare trials could help to tease apart any potential differences. Despite the effects reported the different camps come to unsurprisingly distinct conclusions. On the one hand the sceptics reach the conclusion that 'there is no convincing evidence of the ability to detect if one is being stared at' (French & Stone, 2014, p. 229), whereas proponents argue that 'the commonness of the sense of being stared at in everyday life, together with the positive results from numerous experiments, makes it very probable that this is a real ability' (Sheldrake, 2015, p. 360).

Mediating factors

A number of variables have been suggested to influence or mediate the potential effects of telepathy; these include the specific target used, the distance between the sender and the receiver, their emotional closeness and levels of belief, as well as some general behavioural characteristics and the earth's geomagnetic field.

Target

Research examining potential telepathic effects has suggested that using dynamic video clips with accompanying sound may lead to better results compared to the use of silent stationary pictures (Honorton et al., 1990). Others have also agreed that films that show dramatic changes (A. Parker, 2000) or targets that are rich in emotional detail and are dynamic in nature may be more psi-conducive (Bem & Honorton, 1994; Sherwood & Roe, 2003). However, the evidence is not consistent, as some have found that static targets led to higher hit rates compared to dynamic ones in a telepathy experiment (Lantz, Luke, & May, 1994). The researchers suggested that this may be because it is easier to focus on the content of a static image whereas the changing scenes within a dynamic target may make this more difficult to focus on and/or more difficult to receive. Such findings are likely influenced by the precise nature of the task as well as the particular paradigm used. For example, May, Spottiswoode and James (1994) found that dynamic targets were better than static ones, but only when using a free response task. Furthermore, a meta-analysis by Storm et al. (2017) found no difference in the reported hit rate between dynamic and static targets within dream telepathy paradigms.

Distance

Within mainstream signal communications there is an effect referred to as the inverse square law. This is where the intensity of a signal is inversely proportional to the square of its distance from the physical source. Hence, the further away the receiver is from the source the weaker the signal, something many individuals have experienced when far away from a telecommunications mast making it difficult for them to obtain a signal on their mobile phone.

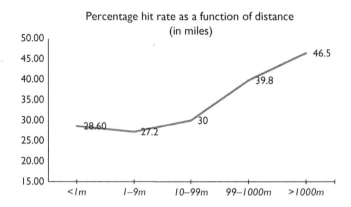

Figure 3.7 Percentage hit rate as a function of distance as measured in miles (adapted from Sheldrake & Lambert, 2007).

However, contrary to this, when Sheldrake and Lambert (2007) conducted an automated telepathy study they found that as distance between participants increased so did the hit rate (see, Figure 3.7). Others testing for telephone telepathy also found no decline in the reported effect as the distance between the caller and receiver increased (Sheldrake & Smart, 2003a, 2003b), with a similar pattern found for research focusing on email telepathy (Sheldrake & Smart, 2005). Such findings are interesting as they would suggest that whatever mechanism is supporting such communications it is not adversely influenced by the distance between those attempting to communicate. It also opens up the possibility of conducting studies across large distances which would eliminate any possibility of sensory leakage or cues.

Feedback

In general, though not in every case, the sender and/or receiver may receive feedback in terms of the accuracy of their hit rate. An assumption here is that if the receiver does well and is given clear feedback they may be able to discern how such decisions are made and learn to improve them. The flip side of this is that if feedback shows performance to be either at chance or lower it can lead to a lack of interest and motivation. For instance, Parker (2000) found higher hit rates when the receiver's auditory mentations of the possible target were monitored by the sender. Such feedback may help the sender to focus and refine their thinking styles. However, this is not a consistent effect and many have shown that providing immediate feedback does not influence performance (e.g., Sheldrake, 2008; Sheldrake & Beharee, 2016).

Belief and ability

The positive association between belief in psi and performance is still debated, especially given the on-going discussions about whether such beliefs represent psychological traits or states (e.g., Irwin, Marks, & Geiser, 2018). However, it has been suggested that such belief directly influences motivation, which in turn leads to better performance. Alternatively, it could be that those with low levels of belief simply perform much worse than chance (see, Bem & Honorton, 1994). Nevertheless, examination of successes in the ganzfeld paradigm showed a higher hit rate for participants that had higher levels of belief in psi and had reported some psi-type experiences (A Parker, Frederiksen, & Johansson, 1997), though others have found effects even when participants are not selected for their belief (Putz et al., 2007). Contradictory findings have also been reported based on the belief levels of the experimenters (Lobach & Bierman, 2004; Wiseman & Schlitz, 1997). In terms of ability a review of the dream based telepathy research showed that those studies to elicit the largest telepathic effects involved the use of gifted individuals that had been previously selected based on their ability (Sherwood & Roe, 2003). However, this need not be the case for telepathy assessed using other paradigms.

Behavioural characteristics

Honorton et al. (1990) report a significant positive association between extroversion and hit rates found in the ganzfeld studies, suggesting that extroverts may be better suited to this because they exhibit lower levels of cortical arousal than introverts, or that they respond favourably to novel stimuli (see Bem & Honorton, 1994). For instance, in a ganzfeld setting the sensory deprivation may starve the extrovert of stimuli which leads them to become highly sensitive to potentially weak incoming psi signals. Others have found associations between performance on telepathy studies and participants classified as *Feeling-Perceiving* or *Intuitive-Feeling-Perceiving*, on measures of personality (Honorton, 1997; Palmer, 1998). Davis (1991) suggested that such aspects of personality were indicative of a right hemisphere dominance. However, when Alexander and Broughton (2001) tested this idea they found no evidence that right hemisphere dominance was associated with more accurate performance. It has also been suggested that those reporting better performance are identified as creative in terms of exhibiting either musical talent or artistic skill (Radin, McAlpine, & Cunningham, 1994). Such artistic individuals, with more divergent thinking styles, may be more receptive to imagery and/or information as well less constrained in reporting such information, both of which may influence the potential hit rates (Bem & Honorton, 1994).

Emotional closeness

Given the fact that telepathy is based on the presumed communication between two, or more, individuals it has been suggested that the emotional closeness of the two could help establish a bond between the sender and receiver which in turn would facilitate the emergence of psi (Schouten, 1982). For instance, Broughton and Alexander (1997) found that using parent-child and sibling combinations as senders and receivers in a ganzfeld telepathy study produced unusually high hit rates. However, the number of participant pairs was too small to draw any firm conclusions. Sheldrake and Smart (2003a, 2003b) also reported higher hit rates of telephone telepathy for sender–receiver pairings that shared some emotional bond compared to when the callers were strangers (see Figure 3.8). A review and meta-analysis of results using the ganzfeld paradigm also showed a significantly higher hit rate when the

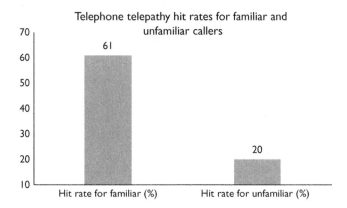

Figure 3.8 Percentage hit rate in a telephone telepathy study as a function of whether the caller was known and familiar (left) or unknown and unfamiliar (right) (adapted from Sheldrake & Smart, 2003b).

sender–receiver parings were friends compared to when they were assigned by the laboratory (Bem & Honorton, 1994). Such findings are consistent with the claims that those who experience telepathy mainly do so with familiar people such as friends, siblings and parents (e.g., Schouten, 1982; Sheldrake 2002, 2003). Moreover, it would suggest that telepathy based research should pre-screen individuals and ensure that both sender and receiver have a close bond.

Geomagnetic field fluctuations

All humans on the planet are immersed within the earth's *geomagnetic field* (GMF) and it has been suggested that telepathic performance may be related to fluctuations in GMF intensity (Persinger, 1988). For instance, periods of lower GMF activity have been associated with greater levels of accuracy in dream trials (Dalton, Steinkamp, & Sherwood, 1999; Krippner & Persinger, 1996). Others have also found that telepathic performance was better when GMF activity was lower, but only for those participants classified as non-creative. For the creative participants the opposite pattern emerged (Radin et al., 1994). However, some have suggested that the influence of GMF on psi may be mediated by the rotation of the earth with respect to the stars, which is evident in *Local Sidereal Time* (LST: Ryan, 2008; Spottiswoode, 1997). For instance, Spottiswoode (1997) reported a significant correlation between the accuracy of telepathic responses and the geomagnetic index. In particular, he found a large increase in the magnitude of the correlation occurring between 11.00 and 14.00 hours LST. This led Spottiswoode (1997) to suggest that what seems to be occurring is that psi improves as LST nears 13.00 hours. Furthermore, it would indicate that attempts to elicit psi effects outside of this time range may fail to identify significant results. It is not yet clear why, or how, the earth's GMF could influence psi. Persinger and Koren (2001) have suggested that such experiences may be related to temporal lobe disturbances; however, this does not explain why local electromagnetic fields cause such effects and/or influence behaviour. Indeed, Adair (1991) argues that the earth's magnetic field is not sufficiently strong enough to produce any physiological changes in the human body. It is possible that humans may be particularly sensitive to the earth's GMF, however this is a speculative idea. Spottiswoode (1997) has suggested that rather than fluctuations in the magnetic field causing the changes in psi it is more likely that psi effects are being mediated by some other parameter associated with the GMF changes. Nevertheless, Radin et al. (1994) suggest that it is worth monitoring the GMF as this may help to illuminate the possible mechanisms of telepathy.

Overview

The initial part of this chapter examined telepathy, which represents a form of direct mind-to-mind communication whereby a receiver may be able to identify specific information from a distant sender or exhibit a physiological response when the sender is stimulated. There are anecdotal accounts of crisis telepathy occurring when one individual is either in danger or suffers some accidental trauma. Such early accounts led to the development of a range of paradigms designed to elicit telepathic responses between individuals. The initial work using card guessing showed interesting results but also suffered from a number of methodological criticisms and over time this approach has been used less frequently. Given the strong emotional empathic bond reported between twins some researchers have assessed their telepathic ability. However, the evidence for twin telepathy is limited at best, though this may be due to a lack of thorough investigation. Nevertheless, research focusing on dream telepathy, in particular the Maimonides studies, produced hit rates beyond the expectations of chance and is sufficiently suggestive to warrant further research. In addition, the ganzfeld paradigm has produced results that exceed chance expectations which is clearly suggestive of an anomalous effect. The more recent use of IVR is interesting but the potential of such a procedure is largely unexplored at present making it difficult to reach any firm conclusions. However, the data from communication telepathy studies using telephones, text messages and email are reasonably robust and certainly suggestive. The implicit and objective measures taken from physiological telepathy studies are again interesting, in particular the use of visual evoked potentials and changes in blood flow as measured by fMRI. Such research is necessarily resource intensive but may provide good objective evidence of telepathic links as well as highlighting potential mechanisms for the shared/transferred target information. The second part of the chapter examined scopaesthesia, which represents another form of mind-to-mind communication more commonly referred to as the feeling of being stared at. This has been examined directly, remotely and again by looking for possible changes in physiology of the individual stared at. Again, the evidence was not always consistent but is sufficiently robust to encourage more research be done. For instance, the positive effects reported with younger children would suggest that, if set up as a game, this could prove a fruitful avenue for research. Furthermore, the physiological changes evident when an individual is stared at without their knowledge also represents an intriguing avenue for further investigation. Finally, the chapter examined a number of variables that have been suggested to positively influence telepathic or scopaesthesic performance. This included the richness of the target, the distance between the sender and receiver, whether feedback is given or not, the belief levels of those taking part in the study, certain behavioural characteristics, the emotional closeness of the pairs and possible fluctuations in the earth's geomagnetic field.

Reflective questions

Some questions that may prove helpful when reflecting on the material covered in this chapter.

- What is telepathy?
- Have you ever experienced a telepathic communication?
- What do you think would be the best way to measure telepathy?
- What variables have been shown to influence telepathic ability?
- What is scopaesthesia?
- Have you ever had the feeling someone was staring at you?
- What evidence would convince you that telepathic communication or scopaesthesia exist?
- Are there any moral or ethical issues that arise from such findings?

References

Adair, R. K. (1991). Constraints on biological effects of weak extremely-low-frequency electromagnetic fields. *Physical Review A*, *43*(2), 1039.

Alexander, C. H., & Broughton, R. S. (2001). Cerebral hemisphere dominance and ESP performance in the autoganzfeld. *Journal of Parapsychology*, *65*(4), 397–416.

Alvarado, C. S. (2017). Telepathy, mediumship, and psychology: Psychical research at the international congresses of psychology 1889–1905. *Journal of Scientific Exploration*, *31*(2), 255–292.

Ambach, W. (2008). Correlations between the EEGs of two spatially separated subjects – a replication study. *European Journal of Parapsychology.*, *23*(2), 131–147.

Andreassi, J. L. (2000). *Psychophysiology: Human behaviour and physiological response* (4 edn). Mahwah, NJ: Lawrence Erlbaum.

Baker, I. S. (2005). Nomenclature and methodology. *Journal of Consciousness Studies*, *12*, 56–63.

Baker, I. S. (2015). The relationship of the feeling of being watched to paranoia, self-consciousness, and social anxiety. *Journal of Parapsychology*, *79*(2), 203–218.

Baker, I. S., & Stevens, P. (2013). An anomaly of an anomaly: Investigating the cortical electrophysiology of remote staring detection. *The Journal of Parapsychology*, *77*(1), 107–122.

Baker, R. (2000). Can we tell when someone is staring at us from behind? *Skeptical Inquirer*, 34–40.

Beloff, J., & Henry, J. (2005). Extrasensory perception. In J. Henry (Ed.), *Parapsychology: Research on exceptional experiences* (pp. 99–107). Hove, East Sussex: Routledge.

Bem, D. J., & Honorton, C. (1994). Does psi exist? Replicable evidence for an anomalous process of information transfer. *Psychological Bulletin*, *115*, 4–18.

Bem, D. J., Palmer, J., & Broughton, R. S. (2001). Updating the Ganzfeld database: Is it a victim of its own success? *Journal of Parapsychology*, *65*, 207–218.

Blackmore, S., & Chamberlain, F. (1993). ESP and thought concordance in twins: A method of comparison. *Journal of the Society for Psychical Research*, *59*(831), 89–96.

Braud, W. (2003). *Distant mental influence: Its contributions to science, healing, and human interactions*. Charlottesville, VA: Hampton Roads.

Braud, W., Shafer, D., & Andrews, S. (1993a). Further studies of autonomic detection of remote staring: Replication, new control procedures, and personality correlates. *Journal of Parapsychology, 57*(4), 391–409.

Braud, W., Shafer, D., & Andrews, S. (1993b). Reactions to an unseen gaze (remote attention): A review, with new data on autonomic staring detection. *Journal of Parapsychology, 57*(4), 372–390.

Braude, S. E. (2016). *Crimes of reason: On mind, nature, and the paranormal*. Boulder, CO: Rowman & Littlefield.

Broughton, R. S., & Alexander, C. N. (1997). Autoganzfeld II: An attempted replication of the PRL ganzfeld research. *Journal of Parapsychology, 61*(3), 209–226.

Brown, D. J., & Sheldrake, R. (2001). The anticipation of telephone calls: A survey in California. *Journal of Parapsychology, 65*(2), 145–156.

Brusewitz, G., Cherkas, L., Harris, J., & Parker, A. (2014). Exceptional experiences amongst twins. *Journal of the Society for Psychical Research, 77*, 220–234.

Cardeña, E., Marcusson-Clavertz, D., & Palmer, J. (2015). Reintroducing parapsychology. In E. Cardeña, J. Palmer & D. Marcusson-Clavertz (Eds.), *Parapsychology: A handbook for the 21st century* (pp. 1–11). Jefferson, NC: McFarland & Company, Inc.

Charlesworth, E. A. (1974). Psi and the imaginary dream. *Research in Parapsychology*, 85–89.

Child, I. L. (1985). Psychology and anomalous observations: The question of ESP in dreams. *American Psychologist, 40*(11), 1219–1230.

Child, I. L. (1986). Reply to Clemmer. *American Psychologist, 41*(10), 1174–1175.

Clemmer, E. J. (1986). Not so anomalous observations question ESP in dreams. *American Psychologist, 41*(10), 1173–1174.

Colwell, J., Schroder, S., & Sladen, D. (2000). The ability to detect unseen staring: A literature review and empirical tests. *British Journal of Psychology, 91*(1), 71–85. doi: 10.1348/000712600161682.

Coover, J. E. (1917). *Experiments in psychic research: Monographs no. 1*. Stanford, CA: Stanford University.

Dalton, K., Steinkamp, F., & Sherwood, S. J. (1999). A dream GESP experiment using dynamic targets and consensus vote. *Journal of the American Society for Psychical Research, 93*, 145–166.

Davis, S. (1991). *Why the MBTI is a brain dominance instrument*. Paper presented at the Ninth biennial international conference of the Association for Psychological Type, Richmond.

Delanoy, D. (1989). Approaches to the target: A time for reevaluation. In L. A. Henkel & J. Palmer (Eds.), *Research in parapsychology* (pp. 89–92). Metuchen, NJ: Scarecrow Press.

Duane, T. D., & Behrendt, T. (1965). Extrasensory electroencephalographic induction between identical twins. *Science, 150*(3694), 367. doi: 10.1126/science.150.3694.367.

Fisk, G., & Mitchell, A. (1953). ESP experiments with clock cards: A new technique with differential scoring. *Journal of the Society for Psychical Research, 37*, 1–14.

French, C. C., & Stone, A. (2014). *Anomalistic psychology: Exploring paranormal belief and experience*. Hampshire, UK: Palgrave Macmillan.

Gilovich, T., Vallone, R., & Tversky, A. (1985). The hot hand in basketball: On the misperception of random sequences. *Cognitive Psychology, 17*(3), 295–314.

Giroldini, W., & Pederzoli, L. (2018). Brain-to-brain interaction at a distance based on EEG analysis. *Journal of Consciousnes Exploration & Research, 9*(6), 501–513.

Goulding, A., Westerlund, J., Parker, A., & Wackermann, J. (2004). The first digital autoganzfeld study using a real-time judging procedure. *European Journal of Parapsychology, 19*, 66–97.

Grinberg-Zylberbaum, J., Delaflor, M., Attie, L., & Goswami, A. (1994). The Einstein–Podolsky–Rosen paradox in the brain: The transferred potential. *Physics Essays*, 7(4), 422–428.

Helminen, T. M., Kaasinen, S. M., & Hietanen, J. K. (2011). Eye contact and arousal: The effects of stimulus duration. *Biological Psychology*, 88(1), 124–130.

Hobson, J. A. (2009). REM sleep and dreaming: Towards a theory of protoconsciousness. *Nature Reviews Neuroscience*, 10(11), 803–813.

Honorton, C. (1977). Psi and internal attention states. In B. Wolman (Ed.), *Handbook of parapsychology* (pp. 435–472). New York: Van Nostrand Reinhold.

Honorton, C. (1985). Meta-analysis of psi Ganzfeld research. *Journal of Parapsychology*, 49, 51–91.

Honorton, C. (1997). The ganzfeld novice: Four predictors of initial ESP performance. *The Journal of Parapsychology*, 61(2), 143–158.

Honorton, C., Berger, R. E., Varvoglis, M., Quant, M., Derr, P., Schechter, E. I., & Ferrari, D. C. (1990). Psi communication in the ganzfeld: Experiments with an automated testing system and a comparison with a meta-analysis of earlier studies. *Journal of Parapsychology*, 54(2), 99–139.

Howard, M. C. (2017). A meta-reanalysis of dream-ESP studies: Comment on Storm et al. (2017). *International Journal of Dream Research*, 11(2), 224–229.

Hyman, R. (1985). The ganzfeld psi experiment: A critical appraisal. *Journal of Parapsychology*, 49, 3–49.

Hyman, R., & Honorton, C. (1986). A joint communiqué: The psi ganzfeld controversy. *The Journal of Parapsychology*, 50(4), 351–364.

Irwin, H. J., Marks, A. D., & Geiser, C. (2018). Belief in the paranormal: A state, or a trait? 1. *The Journal of Parapsychology*, 82(1), 24–40.

Jensen, C., & Parker, A. (2012). Entangled in the womb? A pilot study on the possible physiological connectedness between identical twins with different embryonic backgrounds. *Explore*, 8(6), 339–347. doi: 10.1016/j.explore.2012.08.001.

Karavasilis, E., Christidi, F., Platoni, K., Ferentinos, P., Kelekis, N. L., & Efstathopoulos, E. P. (2017). Functional MRI study to examine possible emotional connectedness in identical twins: A case study. *EXPLORE*, 14(1), 86–91. doi: 10.1016/j.explore.2017.06.008.

Kelly, E. F., Kanthamani, H., Child, I. L., & Young, F. W. (1975). On the relation between visual and ESP confusion structures in an exceptional ESP subject. *Journal of the American Society for Psychical Research*, 69(1), 1–31.

Kittenis, M., Caryl, P., & Stevens, P. (2004). *Distant psychophysiological interaction effects between related and unrelated participants*. Paper presented at the Proceedings of the Parapsychological Association Convention.

Krippner, S. (1993). The Maimonides ESP-dream studies. *The Journal of Parapsychology*, 57(1), 39–55.

Krippner, S., & Persinger, M. A. (1996). Evidence for enhanced congruence between dreams and distant target material during periods of decreased geomagnetic activity. *Journal of Scientific Exploration*, 10(4), 487–493.

Kubis, J. F., & Rouke, F. L. (1937). An experimental investigation of telepathic phenomena in twins. *Journal of Parapsychology*, 1(3), 163–171.

Lantz, N. D., Luke, W. L. W., & May, E. (1994). Target and sender dependencies in anomalous cognition experiments. *Journal of Parapsychology*, 58(3), 285–302.

Lobach, E., & Bierman, D. J. (2004). *Who's calling at this hour? Local sidereal time and telephone telepathy*. Paper presented at the Proceedings of Parapsychology Association Annual Convention, Vienna.

Mauskopf, S. H., & McVaugh, M. R. (1980). *The elusive science: Origins of experimental psychical research*. Baltimore, MD: Johns Hopkins University Press.

May, E. C., Spottiswoode, S. J. P., & Faith, L. V. (2000). The correlation of the gradient of Shannon entropy and anomalous cognition: Toward an AC sensory system. *Journal of Scientific Exploration*, 14(1), 53–72.

May, E. C., Spottiswoode, S. J. P., & James, C. L. (1994). Managing the targetpool bandwidth: Noise reduction for anomalous cognition experiments. *Journal of Parapsychology*, 58, 303–313.

Milton, J. (1997). Meta-analysis of free-response ESP studies without altered states of consciousness. *Journal of Parapsychology*, 61, 279–319.

Milton, J. (1999). Should ganzfeld research continue to be crucial in the search for a replicable psi effect? Part I. Discussion paper and introduction to an electronic-mail discussion. *Journal of Parapsychology*, 63(4), 309–333.

Milton, J., & Wiseman, R. (1999). A meta-analysis of mass media tests of extrasensory perception. *British Journal of Psychology*, 90, 235–240.

Moore, J. T. (1938). Is there anything to mental telepathy? *Peabody Journal of Education*, 15(4), 186–198.

Muller, S., Schmidt, S., & Walach, H. (2009). The feeling of being stared at: A parapsychology classic with a facelift. *European Journal of Parapsychology*, 24(2), 117–138.

Murray, C. D., Howard, T., Wilde, D. J., Fox, J., & Simmonds-Moore, C. (2007). Testing for telepathy using an immersive virtual environment. *Journal of Parapsychology*, 71, 105–123.

Nash, C., & Buzby, D. E. (1965). Extrasensory perception of identical and fraternal twins. *The Journal of Heredity*, 2, 52–54.

Palmer, J. (1979). A community mail survey of psychic experiences. *Journal of the American Society for Psychical Research*, 73, 221–251.

Palmer, J. (1998). Correlates of ESP magnitude and direction in the FRNM manual ganzfeld database. *The Journal of Parapsychology*, 62(2), 111.

Palmer, J. (2003). ESP in the ganzfeld: Analysis of a debate. *Journal of Consciousness Studies*, 10(6/7), 51–68.

Parker, A. (2000). A review of the Ganzfeld work at Gothenburg University. *Journal of the Society for Psychical Research*, 64, 1–15.

Parker, A. (2010). A ganzfeld study using identical twins. *Journal of the Society for Psychical Research*, 73, 118–126.

Parker, A., Frederiksen, A., & Johansson, H. (1997). Towards specifying the recipe for success with the ganzfeld. *European Journal of Parapsychology*, 13, 15–27.

Parker, A., & Jensen, C. (2013). Further possible physiological connectedness between identical twins: The London study. *Explore*, 9(1), 26–31. doi: 10.1016/j.explore.2012.10.001.

Persinger, M. A. (1988). Increased geomagnetic activity and the occurrence of bereavement hallucinations: Evidence for melatonin-mediated microseizuring in the temporal lobe? *Neuroscience Letters*, 88(3), 271–274.

Persinger, M. A., & Koren, S. A. (2001). Predicting the characteristics of haunt phenomena from geomagnetic factors and brain sensitivity: evidence from field and experimental studies. In J. Houran & R. Lange (Eds.), *Hauntings and poltergeists: Multidisciplinary perspectives* (pp. 179–194). Jefferson, NC: McFarland.

Persinger, M. A., Koren, S. A., & Tsang, E. W. (2003). Enhanced power within a specific band of theta activity in one person while another receives circumcerebral pulsed magnetic fields: A mechanism for cognitive influence at a distance? *Perceptual and Motor Skills*, 97, 877–894.

Persinger, M. A., Saroka, K., Mulligan, B. P., & Murphy, T. R. (2010). Experimental elicitation of an out of body experience and concomitant cross-hemispheric electroencephalographic coherence. *NeuroQuantology*, 8(4), 466–477. doi: 10.14704/nq.2010.8.4.302.

Persinger, M. A., Tsang, E. W., Booth, J. N., & Koren, S. A. (2008). Enhance power within predicted narrow band of theta activity during stimulation of another by cerebral weak magnetic fields after weekly spatial proximity: Evidence for macroscopic quantum entanglement? *NeuroQuantology*, 6(1), 7–21.

Playfair, G. L. (1999). Identical twins and telepathy. *Journal of the Society for Psychical Research*, 63(854), 86–98.

Playfair, G. L. (2002). *Twin telepathy: The psychic connection*. London: Vega.

Playfair, G. L. (2012). *Twin telepathy*. Guildford: White Crow Books.

Playfair, G. L. (2017). Monozygotic twins and macro-entanglement. *Journal of Nonlocality*, 5(1), 1–10.

Puthoff, H. E., & Targ, R. (1976). A perception channel for information transfer over kilometer distances: Historical perspective and recent research. *Proceedings of the IEEE*, 64(3), 329–354.

Putz, P., Gabler, M., & Wackermann, J. (2007). An experiment with covert ganzfeld telepathy. *European Journal of Parapsychology*, 22(1), 49–72.

Radin, D. (2004a). Event-related electroencephalographic correlations between isolated human subjects. *Journal of Alternative and Complementary Medicine*, 10(2), 315–323.

Radin, D. (2004b). The feeling of being stared at: An analysis and replication. *Journal of the Society for Psychical Research*, 68, 245–252.

Radin, D., McAlpine, S., & Cunningham, S. (1994). Geomagnetism and psi in the ganzfeld. *Journal of the Society for Psychical Research*, 59, 352–363.

Radin, D., & Pierce, A. (2015). Psi and psychophysiology. In E. Cardeña, J. Palmer, & D. Marcusson-Clavertz (Eds.), *Parapsychology: A handbook for the 21st century* (pp. 230–243). Jefferson, NC: McFarland & Co Inc.

Rhine, J. B. (1947). *The reach of the mind*. New York: William Sloane Associates.

Rhine, J. B., & Pratt, J. G. (1954). A review of the Pearce-Pratt distance series of ESP tests. *Journal of Parapsychology*, 18, 165–177.

Rhine, L. E. (1953). The relation of experience to associated event in spontaneous ESP. *The Journal of Parapsychology*, 17(3), 187–209.

Rhine, L. E. (1956). The relationship of agent and percipient in spontaneous telepathy. *The Journal of Parapsychology*, 20(1), 1–32.

Rhine, L. E. (1981). *The invisible picture: A study of psychic experiences*. Jefferson, NC: McFarland.

Richards, T. L., Kozak, L., Johnson, L. C., & Standish, L. J. (2005). Replicable functional magnetic resonance imaging evidence of correlated brain signals between physically and sensory isolated subjects. *Journal of Alternative & Complementary Medicine: Research on Paradigm, Practice, and Policy*, 11(6), 955–963.

Robichon, F. (1989). Contribution à l'étude du phénomène télépathique avec des individus liés par la condition biologique de gémellité monozygote. *Revue française de psychotronique*, 2(1), 19–35.

Roe, C. A., Jones, L., & Maddern, C. (2007). A preliminary test of the 'Four-Factor Model' using a dream ESP protocol. *Journal of the Society for Psychical Research*, 71(886), 35–42.

Roe, C. A., Sherwood, S. J., Farrell, L., Savva, L., & Baker, I. S. (2007). Assessing the roles of sender and experimenter in dream ESP research. *European Journal of Parapsychology*, 22(2), 175–192.

Rogers, W. C. (1960). A study of like pattern formations in twins. *Journal of Parapsychology*, 24(1), 69.

Rouleau, N., Tessaro, L. W., Saroka, K. S., Scott, M. A., Lehman, B. S., Juden-Kelly, L. M., & Persinger, M. A. (2015). Experimental evidence of superposition and superimposition of cerebral activity within pairs of human brains separated by 6,000 km: Central role of the parahippocampal regions. *NeuroQuantology*, 13(4), 397–407. doi: 10.14704/nq.2015.13.4.891.

Ryan, A. (2008). New insights into the links between ESP and geomagnetic activity. *Journal of Scientific Exploration*, *22*(3), 335–358.

Rýzl, M., & Pratt, J. (1962). Confirmation of ESP performance in a hypnotically prepared subject. *The Journal of Parapsychology*, *26*(4), 237.

Sabell, A., Clarke, C., & Fenwick, P. (2001). *Inter-subject EEG correlations at a distance – the transferred potential*. Paper presented at the Proceedings of the 44th Annual Convention of the Parapsychological Association.

Schlitz, M., & LaBerge, S. (1997). Covert observation increases skin conductance in subjects unaware of when they are being observed: a replication. *The Journal of Parapsychology*, *61*(3), 185–196.

Schlitz, M., & Radin, D. (2003). Non-sensory access to information: The ganzfeld studies. In W. B. Jonas & C. C. Crawford (Eds.), *Healing, intention and energy medicine: Science, research methods and clinical implications* (pp. 75–82). Edinburgh, UK: Churchill Livingstone.

Schmidt, H. (1970). A quantum mechanical random number generator for psi tests. *Journal of Parapsychology*, *34*, 219–224.

Schmidt, S., Erath, D., Ivanova, V., & Walach, H. (2009). Do you know who is calling? Experiments on anomalous cognition in phone call receivers. *The Open Psychology Journal*, *2*(1), 12–18. doi: 10.2174/1874350100902010012.

Schmidt, S., Muller, S., & Walach, H. (2004). *Do you know who is on the phone? Replication of an experiment on telephone telepathy*. Paper presented at the The Parapsychological Association Convention.

Schmidt, S., Schneider, R., Utts, J., & Walach, H. (2004). Distant intentionality and the feeling of being stared at: Two meta-analyses. *British Journal of Psychology*, *95*(2), 235–247.

Schouten, S. A. (1982). Analysing spontaneous cases: A replication based on the Rhine collection. *European Journal of Parapsychology*, *4*(2), 113–158.

Scott, M. A., Rouleau, N., Lehman, B. S., Tessaro, L. W., Juden-Kelly, L. M., Saroka, K. S., & Persinger, M. A. (2015). Experimental production of excess correlation across the atlantic ocean of right hemispheric theta-gamma power between subject pairs sharing circumcerebral rotating magnetic fields (Part I). *Journal of Consciousness Exploration & Research*, *6*(9), 658–684.

Segal, N. L. (2017). *Twin mythconceptions: False beliefs, fables, and facts about twins.* Cambridge, MA: Academic Press.

Sheldrake, R. (1998). The sense of being stared at: Experiments in schools. *Journal of the Society for Psychical Research*, *62*, 311–323.

Sheldrake, R. (1999). The sense of being stared at confirmed by simple experiments. *Biology Forum*, *92*, 53–76.

Sheldrake, R. (2000). The sense of being stared at does not depend on known sensory clues. *Biology Forum*, *93*, 209–224.

Sheldrake, R. (2002). Apparent telepathy between babies and nursing mothers: A survey. *Journal of the Society for Psychical Research*, *66*(3), 181–185.

Sheldrake, R. (2003). *The sense of being stared at, and other aspects of the extended mind.* New York: Crown.

Sheldrake, R. (2005a). The sense of being stared at. Part 1: Is it real or illusory? *Journal of Consciousness Studies*, *12*(6), 10–31.

Sheldrake, R. (2005b). The sense of being stared at. Part 2: Its implications for theories of vision. *Journal of Consciousness Studies*, *12*(6), 32–49.

Sheldrake, R. (2008). The sense of being stared at: Do hit rates improve as test go on? *Journal of the Society for Psychical Research*, *72*(891), 98–106.

Sheldrake, R. (2015). Psi in everyday life. In E. Cardeña, J. Palmer, & D. Marcusson-Clavertz (Eds.), *Parapsychology: A handbook for the 21st century* (pp. 350–363). Jefferson, NC: McFarland & Company Inc.

Sheldrake, R., & Avraamides, L. (2009). An automated test for telepathy in connection with emails. *Journal of Scientific Exploration, 23*(1), 29–36.

Sheldrake, R., Avraamides, L., & Novak, M. (2009). Sensing the sending of SMS messages: An automated test. *EXPLORE, 5*(5), 272–276. doi: 10.1016/j.explore.2009.06.004.

Sheldrake, R., & Beharee, A. (2009). A rapid online telepathy test. *Psychological Reports, 104*(3), 957–970.

Sheldrake, R., & Beharee, A. (2016). Is joint attention detectable at a distance? Three automated, internet-based tests. *Explore, 12*(1), 34–41. doi: 10.1016/j.explore.2015.10.006.

Sheldrake, R., & Lambert, M. (2007). An automated online telepathy test. *Journal of Scientific Exploration, 21*(3), 511–522.

Sheldrake, R., Overby, C., & Beeharee, A. (2008). The sense of being stared at: An automated test on the internet. *Journal of the Society for Psychical Research, 72*(891), 86–97.

Sheldrake, R., & Smart, P. (2003a). Experimental tests for telephone telepathy. *Journal of the Society for Psychical Research, 67*, 184–199.

Sheldrake, R., & Smart, P. (2003b). Videotaped experiments on telephone telepathy. *Journal of Parapsychology, 67*, 187–206.

Sheldrake, R., & Smart, P. (2005). Testing for telepathy in connection with e-mails. *Perceptual and Motor Skills, 101*, 771–786.

Sheldrake, R., Smart, P., & Avraamides, L. (2015). Automated tests for telephone telepathy using mobile phones. *Explore, 11*(4), 310–319. doi: 10.1016/j.explore.2015.04.001.

Sherwood, S. J., & Roe, C. A. (2003). A review of the dream ESP studies conducted since the Maimonides dream ESP programme. *Journal of Consciousness Studies, 10*(6–7), 85–109.

Sherwood, S. J., & Roe, C. A. (2013). An updated review of dream ESP studies conducted since the Maimonides dream ESP program. In S. Krippner, A. J. Rock, J. Beischel, H. L. Friedman, & C. L. Fracasso (Eds.), *Advances in Parapsychological Research 9* (pp. 38–81). Jefferson, NC: McFarland.

Spottiswoode, J. P. (1997). Geomagnetic fluctuations and free response anomalous cognition: New understanding. *Journal of Parapsychology, 61*, 3–12.

Standish, L. J., Johnson, L. C., Kozak, L., & Richards, T. (2003). Evidence of correlated functional magnetic resonance imaging signals between distant human brains. *Alternative Therapies in Health and Medicine, 9*(1), 122–128.

Standish, L. J., Kozak, L., Johnson, L. C., & Richards, T. (2004). Electroencephalographic evidence of correlated event-related signals between the brains of spatially and sensory isolated human subjects. *The Journal of Alternative and Complementary Medicine, 10*(2), 307–314.

Storm, L., & Rock, A. J. (2015). Dreaming of psi: A narrative review and meta-analysis of dream-ESP studies at the Maimonides dream laboratory and beyond. In J. A. Davies & D. B. Pitchford (Eds.), *Stanley Krippner: A life of dreams, myths, and visions: Essays on his contributions and influence* (pp. 117–138). New York: University Professors Press.

Storm, L., Sherwood, S. J., Roe, C. A., Tressoldi, P., Rock, A. J., & Di Risio, L. (2017). On the correspondence between dream content and target material under laboratory conditions: A meta-analysis of dream-ESP studies, 1966–2016. *International Journal of Dream Research, 10*(2), 120–140.

Storm, L., Tressoldi, P. E., & Di Risio, L. (2010). Meta-analysis of free-response studies, 1992–2008: Assessing the noise reduction model in parapsychology. *Psychological Bulletin, 136*(4), 471–485. doi: 10.1037/a0019457.

Tversky, A., & Kahneman, D. (1973). Availability: A heuristic for judging frequency and probability. *Cognitive Psychology, 5*(2), 207–232.

Utts, J. (1995). An assessment of the evidence for psychic functioning. *Journal of Parapsychology*, 59(4), 289–321.

Wackermann, J. (2008). Dyadic EEG correlations re-examined: A commentary on the replication study by W. Ambach. *European Journal of Parapsychology*, 23, 147–153.

Wackermann, J., Putz, P., & Allefeld, C. (2008). Ganzfeld-induced hallucinatory experience, its phenomenology and cerebral electrophysiology. *Cortex*, 44, 1364–1378. doi: 10/1016/j.cortex.2007.05.003.

Wackermann, J., Seiter, C., Keibel, H., & Walach, H. (2003). Correlations between brain electrical activities of two spatially separated human subjects. *Neuroscience Letters*, 336, 60–64.

Wason, P. C. (1960). On the failure to eliminate hypotheses in a conceptual task. *Quarterly Journal of Experimental Psychology*, 12(3), 129–140.

Watt, C. (1996). What makes a good psi target? *The Journal of Parapsychology*, 60(1), 25–41.

Watt, C. (2005). Psychological factors. In J. Henry (Ed.), *Parapsychology: Research on exceptional experiences* (pp. 64–79). Hove, East Sussex: Routledge.

Williams, B. J. (2011). Revisiting the ganzfeld ESP debate: A basic review and assessment. *Journal of Scientific Exploration*, 25(4), 639–661.

Wiseman, R., & Schlitz, M. (1997). Experimenter effects and the remote detection of staring. *Journal of Parapsychology*, 61, 197–207.

Wiseman, R., Smith, M. D., & Kornbrot, D. (1996). Exploring possible sender-to-experimenter acoustic leakage in the PRL autoganzfeld experiments. *Journal of Parapsychology*, 60, 97–128.

Chapter 4

Clairvoyance and remote viewing

Imagine a scenario whereby an individual can accurately identify, or *see*, a distant target location or object simply by focusing their mind in a particular way. Such a skill could prove useful in a range of situations, not simply when attempting to locate a lost set of keys. It also raises interesting moral issues of privacy or the possible lack of it. This chapter explores two areas of psi that suggest an individual may be able to obtain information about a distant target without the need for a sender or other conscious mind. These are the areas of *clairvoyance* and *remote viewing*. These two aspects of psi are natural bedfellows in the sense that both rely on *seeing* or *sensing* a distant target. The first part of the chapter begins by defining clairvoyance and exploring how it may be distinct from other aspects of psi such as telepathy. It then explores the main paradigms used to test for clairvoyance, from forced-choice tests to recording physiological responses. The chapter then examines the evidence for clairvoyance and notes some of factors that have been shown to mediate performance. The second section of the chapter examines the concept of remote viewing. This involves a definition of what remote viewing is and a brief explanation of the various types of remote viewing. This is followed by a brief outline of one of the most well-known projects in the field, project Stargate. The chapter then examines evidence for the main types of remote viewing, which includes associative remote viewing, and ends by exploring some of the mediating factors suggested to influence performance.

Clairvoyance

The word clairvoyance stems from the French words *clair*, referring to 'clear', and *voir*, which means 'to see'. Hence, it is a way of seeing clearly. Within the field of psi research it refers to the acquisition of information relating to a target object or event via non-usual routes. The generally accepted definition is one that involves an individual receiving, seeing or obtaining some direct perception of information about an object, place or event not known by others (Sherwood, Dalton, Steinkamp, & Watt, 2000; Targ & Tart, 1985). Some have also referred to this as a form of *direct knowing* (Braud, 1992). Whilst the meaning of the word clairvoyance primarily relates to vision it is generally used to refer to all types of information received or obtained from any of the senses, though others have suggested terms such as *clairaudience* to refer to hearing messages (Ashby, 1972), *clairempathy* for an ability to feel the emotional state of a distant other, or *claircognisance* to refer to the more generic ability to know something without the usual routes of sensory exposure, processing or reasoning (see, Wahbeh, McDermott, & Sagher, 2018).

Clairvoyance as a distinct aspect of psi

A key difference between clairvoyance and telepathy is that the former only involves a target item, object or place whereas the latter generally involves another conscious entity acting as a sender. For instance, when attempting to clairvoyantly *see* a target telepathy can be excluded because the experimenter or others involved in the study may not know the identity of the target at the time the clairvoyant call is made. There have also been suggestions that clairvoyance can be distinguished from telepathy by using a computer to generate the targets and then destroying the information regarding the sequence of presentations before anyone has seen the data (Palmer, 2015; Targ & Tart, 1985).

Psychologists and researchers have long debated the similarities and differences between clairvoyance and other aspects of psi such as telepathy or precognition (see, Rhine, 1945; Targ & Tart, 1985). For instance, it may be that clairvoyance represents a wider more generic extra-sensory perceptual (GESP) ability, which could include precognition (Rhine, 1945). However, current understanding of these processes makes it difficult to draw any firm conclusions. For example, on the one hand it could be that clairvoyance and precognition are distinct as the latter may require additional processing associated with accessing remote unseen information which is then used to extrapolate about possible future events (Steinkamp, Milton, & Morris, 1998). If this is the case then Steinkamp et al. (1998) argue that the effect size for clairvoyance may be greater than precognition. In contrast, if clairvoyance is similar to precognition in the sense that it involves pre-calling the feedback of the target identity which is generally given at a later date then the effect sizes of these processes would be expected to be similar (Steinkamp et al., 1998). Unfortunately, the data is far from consistent. Of the studies that have directly compared effect sizes of clairvoyance with precognition, Tart (1983) reported stronger effects for clairvoyance whereas many others have found no clear difference in effect size between these two aspects of psi (Sartori, Massacessi, Martinelli, & Tressoldi, 2004; Steinkamp et al., 1998; Storm et al., 2017). As such it may not be possible to completely rule out the potential influence of telepathy and/or precognition when measuring clairvoyance. Furthermore, it may be that such processes provide an auxiliary means of supporting clairvoyance.

Testing for clairvoyance

Attempts to elicit or test for clairvoyance have utilised a range of paradigms over time. The most common of these are those that have relied on either forced-choice or free responses, including dream and physiological paradigms.

In a forced-choice design, participants attempt to see a distant object, or target from a specific set of possible targets, such as one of four pictures. Classic examples are the Zener type cards that are also used in other paradigms. Here the percipient would attempt to see, or guess, the order of the symbols in a complete shuffled deck before they are turned over, or by guessing the identity of one randomly picked card at a time. Sometimes a deck of cards, usually though not always Zener type cards, would be shuffled and placed face down on a desk and the percipient would then be required to write down their clairvoyant guesses for each card prior to looking through them. This type of procedure has been referred to as the *down through* technique (Child & Kelly, 1973). Some have also used pages with visual representations of the 12 hours around a clock face (e.g., 3 o'clock) which would be sealed in an envelope before asking the percipient to clairvoyantly see the target and note it down (Schmeidler, 1985). Others have utilised a free-response approach where the percipient is encouraged to give as many detailed responses in various ways as they wish (see, Milton & Wiseman, 1997). This allows for an unconstrained level of responses, similar to that seen in ganzfeld research.

Given the suggestion that the dream state is thought to be conducive to psi (Braud, 1977) some have attempted to elicit or assess potential clairvoyant abilities when the percipient is asleep and dreaming. For instance, a clairvoyant dream paradigm may involve the use of a computer to randomly select and play images or video clips at certain points throughout the night whilst the percipient sleeps at home (Dalton, Steinkamp, & Sherwood, 1999; Sherwood et al., 2000). The following day the percipient will be presented with a set of images or clips, which includes the target along with a number of decoys. Their task is to rank the stimuli from 1 to 4 with 1 denoting the greatest correspondence between the information and their dream. A rank of 1 given to the target represents a *hit* otherwise the trial would be scored a *miss*. This allows for the hit rate to be compared to MCE.

There have also been attempts to examine potential clairvoyant effects by monitoring changes in physiology (e.g., Beloff, 1974). For example, this type of procedure would involve presenting participants with a range of stimuli, such as images of landscapes, plants and flowers. During this presentation phase their heart rate physiology would be recorded. Once all images had been presented the participant would be required to clairvoyantly identify which of the images represented the target. The question the researchers then ask is whether the participant's physiology was in any way different when the target image was shown compared to non-target images (Sartori et al., 2004). A significant difference in the participant's physiology when viewing target versus non-target images would be an indication of some form of clairvoyance.

Evidence for clairvoyance

Reviewing the evidence for clairvoyance suggests some intriguing effects have emerged though not always consistently. For instance, early work utilising forced-choice card guessing paradigms reportedly found evidence of clairvoyance (Jephson, 1928; Nash, 1985; Soal & Goldney, 1943). However, some of these findings were later questioned by Markwick (1985) and others reported ambiguous results that were not clearly indicative of clairvoyance (Child & Kelly, 1973). Nevertheless, when Braud (1977) gave a group of students an exam with the question paper stapled to an envelope that contained answers to certain questions he found their performance was significantly better on the questions for which the hidden correct answers were supplied without their knowledge. Braud (1975) referred to this as a form of unconscious clairvoyance. Schmeidler (1985) also reported evidence of clairvoyance when participants were more accurate than chance at guessing a sealed target image of a clock face, particularly when they were told not to think too hard about their guesses. However, when Schmeidler (1985) ran a second series of studies to explore this issue no significant effects emerged, making such support limited at best. Nevertheless, attempts to assess clairvoyance using dream-based paradigms have produced some encouraging results. For instance, a dream clairvoyant study conducted by Dalton et al. (1999) reported a hit rate of 46.8% when 25% would be expected by chance. However, others have not found dream clairvoyance to elicit any strong effects (Harley, 1989).

An early review of the evidence for clairvoyance conducted by Targ and Tart (1985) suggested that the overall hit rates obtained by those conducting research into clairvoyance were significantly above chance. This positive overview has been echoed by those conducting meta-analyses which suggests that the evidence, though weak, is clearly suggestive of an anomalous effect and is not an artefact of poor methodology or design (Storm, 2006; Storm, Tressoldi & Di Risio, 2012).

Mediating factors

Several factors have been suggested to influence or mediate the accuracy of clairvoyant perceptions including the use of feedback, the ability of the percipient, the emotionality of the target and the judging procedure.

Feedback

In general, a clairvoyant paradigm requires a percipient attempting to *see* a remote target object or location and once the individual has made their guess they may then be given feedback regarding how accurate, or not, such a guess turned out to be. It has been suggested that providing feedback in such a situation can be helpful for improving such psi abilities or performance (Targ & Tart, 1985) though some have found that providing feedback makes no difference (Bierman et al., 1984; Steinkamp et al., 1998). However, this may be because the influence of feedback is not a simple one but may interact with the individual percipient's belief about its use. For instance, Targ and Tart (1985) conducted an experiment testing for what they referred to as 'pure clairvoyance' using a number guessing test automatically presented and scored by computer. For half of these trials the computer provided feedback on the accuracy of the guess. Interestingly, they found that feedback on the accuracy of each trial did not enhance clairvoyant performance. However, they did find that the feedback interacted with the percipient's *belief* about such feedback. That is, if a percipient thought feedback would help then that seemed to be the case. If however, a percipient believed that feedback was not essential then performance was better in the no-feedback condition. Hence, it may not simply be a case of providing feedback leading to better performance per se, but that the level of feedback may interact with the beliefs held by those taking part.

Psi ability

As noted by Braude (2016) if psi is real then it is likely to exhibit itself like other aspects of behaviour. That is, some individuals may be better at psi tasks than others and some may be better at certain psi tasks compared to other psi tasks. Hence, by comparing performance of those opportunity sampled, that is simply available at the time of testing, to those with extensive experience in psi testing, previous psi experience and/or well-established records of performance in psi-based tasks it may be possible to ascertain whether such natural ability influences performance. For example, early work by Schmidt (1969) showed that carefully selecting those who showed both a special interest in psi and some prior ability led to better psi performance on later tasks. Targ and Tart (1985) also compared the clairvoyant performance of an opportunity sampled group to a pre-selected one with psi experience and found that those in the pre-selected group showed significant evidence of clairvoyance whilst the opportunity sampled group did not. Such findings suggest that pre-selecting individuals based on experience and/or ability is likely to lead to more effective results.

Targets

It has long been suggested that dynamic multi-sensory targets may be more effective at eliciting a psi-based effect (Delanoy, 1989); however, the evidence is not consistent. For example, participants have been shown to perform more successfully with emotive targets compared to neutral targets. More specifically, using emotionally negative video clips produced a greater clairvoyant effect than using either positive or neutral clips (Sherwood et al., 2000). Hence, the level of emotional arousal and the valence of this arousal may be important. Such a pattern could be explained by taking an evolutionary stance as the negative stimuli may be better at evoking psi effects as there may be a survival benefit incurred from awareness of such potential threats or danger. Such a view would also account for the anecdotal descriptions of clairvoyance that often involve emotionally close people and negative life events. However, not all have found such clear associations between the emotionality of the target and success on clairvoyance trials. For instance, when Roe, Sherwood, Luke and Farrell (2002) examined clairvoyant performance as a function of the emotive aspects of the target they found no clear evidence of any relationship. However, they did note that this non-significant effect could be the result of a small sample being unduly influenced by potential outlying scores. Nevertheless, others have also found that the target type had no influence on the outcome of clairvoyance studies (Storm et al., 2017; Storm, Tressoldi, & Di Risio, 2012).

Judging

It may seem obvious to point out that the way clairvoyant scores are judged could influence the outcome in terms of identifying hits or misses, but that does seem to be the case. This could be the range of scores used to rank the potential target items as well as the number of individuals involved in such rankings. For example, in a standard forced-choice paradigm once the percipient has made their clairvoyant guess they may be presented with a set of four items, one of which is the target and the other three acting as decoys. The percipient is then required to view the items and rank order them in terms of how closely they match the clairvoyant guess, from 1 (i.e., highest correspondence) to 4 (i.e., lowest). Kanthamani and Khilji (1990) have argued that having the percipients rank potential targets from 1 to 4 is a superior measure compared to rating them from 0 (i.e., lowest correspondence) to 99, with 99 indicating almost exact likeness between the clairvoyant perception and the target. Others have suggested that using multiple individuals to rank the trials as either a hit or a miss can also influence the outcome. Such a *consensus judgement* procedure may involve combining the responses from several individuals into a single judgement about whether the trial is a hit or a miss. For instance, using a consensus type approach has been suggested to yield a higher number compared to individual judgements (Roe et al., 2002; Sherwood et al., 2000). Sherwood et al. (2000) found that only when a group consensus procedure was used to identify the possible target was there any evidence of dream-based clairvoyance. Furthermore, they reported that whilst this was significant the effect size when using two judges was slightly smaller than a previous study that had utilised three judges. Sherwood et al. (2000) suggest that this could be interpreted to indicate that the accuracy of the judging procedure improves as the number of judges also increases. They further suggest that consensus judging techniques may be more sensitive than individual judgements. However, they also admit that having multiple judgements made for each trial could produce a stacking effect where more than one call may be made per trial which in turn could increase the probability of obtaining a hit. Hence, not only the use of a consensus approach but also the number of judges that take part in such discussions may influence the outcome.

Remote viewing

The term *remote viewing* was coined by Targ and Puthoff (1974) and refers to a paradigm that is conceptually similar to that used to examine clairvoyance. It usually involves a participant, the *remote viewer* or *percipient* remaining in a set location, usually a lab or room, with an experimenter whilst a confederate may need to go outside and visit a location. It is similar to clairvoyant research in the sense that the receiver attempts to obtain information about a distant event and/or location. However, it is distinct in the sense that the remote viewer is fully awake, not undergoing any form of sensory deprivation whilst attempting to *see* what the confederate sees (see, P. H. Smith, 2017; Targ, 2019). It is also distinct from clairvoyance in the sense that part of the aim is for the remote viewer to describe the surrounding geographical location and context of the distant confederate and not simply focus on a specific set target (see Figure 4.1). The precise target location may be a randomly selected site, such as a nearby bridge, church, or other building or the confederate may be free to select a target site of their choosing (see, Dunne & Jahn, 2003; Hansen, Utts, & Markwick, 1992; Puthoff & Targ, 1976; Targ & Puthoff, 1974). The targets do not have to be buildings, they can also be open spaces but it has been suggested that it may be easier for a remote viewer to focus on specific details of a building whereas an open space is more generic and may be difficult to identify. Variations of this included using more than one sender, such that a group simultaneously try to telepathically transmit information about the target location. Or the remote viewer may simply be given a set of map co-ordinates and asked to describe what is at that location. Other names that have in the past been used to describe seemingly similar processes include autoscopy and travelling clairvoyance (see, Puthoff & Targ, 1976).

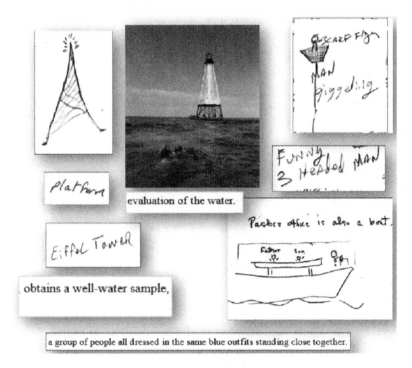

Figure 4.1 Target image (top centre) and words/sketches from Sublime Group of Remote Viewers (from Katz et al., 2019, p. 77, with permission).

Types of remote viewing

There are several types of remote viewing (RV) that have been developed over time and it is not always clear how distinct these are. For instance there is an *outbound protocol,* as well as controlled or *coordinate RV, precognitive RV, extended RV* and *associative RV, or ARV* (Graff & Cyrus, 2017; Katz, Smith, Bulgatz, Graf, & Lane, 2019; Lee, 2008; McMoneagle, 1997; P. H. Smith, 2017). The typical *outbound protocol* would involve someone travelling out to a randomly selected site. This would have involved the creation of a target pool of local sites all reachable within a pre-set timespan, of for example 30 minutes. The individual travelling to the site, the *outbounder,* would be requested to arrive at the target site within the allotted time and remain there for a set period making observations of the surrounding area. Meanwhile, the remote viewer back in the lab would attempt to visualise or experience the target and describe any sensory impressions received during this time in a free-response stream of consciousness form, and these verbalisations would be recorded and coded (see Figure 4.2; Dunne & Jahn, 2003). The percipient may also be required to draw a sketch of their perceptions regarding the target location. The percipient can also at a later stage visit the site to assess their own impressions and degree of match between their verbalisations and the target site. A *coordinate RV* paradigm would be similar except in this instance the remote viewer would simply be given a set of map co-ordinates as the target (Lee, 2008). The typical RV paradigm

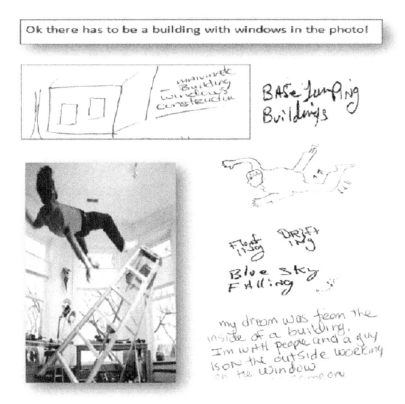

Figure 4.2 Target image (bottom left) and excerpts from remote viewer's transcripts (from Katz et al., 2019, p. 78, with permission).

has also been extended to include a *precognitive* component which involves the remote viewer attempting to describe the location of a remote target location where a confederate will be at a specified *future* time (Puthoff & Targ, 1976). This also includes perceptions and mentations made by the remote viewer *before* the target is selected, see Box 4.1 (Graff & Cyrus, 2017; Dunne & Jahn, 2003). According to McMoneagle (2000) *extended RV* uses meditative methods to help the percipient reach a semi-trance like state which is thought to help establish a connection with the target. The percipient then reports whatever is being seen, felt, heard or experienced.

Finally, there is *associative remote viewing* (ARV). According to Schwartz (2014) the original idea for ARV was based on the premise that an individual target could be used to identify or denote a specific course of action. He also notes that the idea of ARV is a popular one given its aim at potentially making money. Others have also agreed with the notion that finding a practical application for a psi effect or behaviour will likely increase the level of interest and research (Dunne & Jahn, 2003; C. C. Smith, Laham, & Moddel, 2014).

Box 4.1   Precognitive remote viewing

I direct myself to move into the future and imagine I'm looking at the photo that will be sent to me on my computer screen, or printed out and hanging on my wall, and then just wait for impressions to arrive in the form of visuals, words, thoughts and feelings that were not there before. Or, I'll pretend I'm moving into the actual scene that is displayed within the parameters of the future photo, moving my awareness either to ground level, up above looking down, or looking through the lens of the camera or the eyes of the photographer, prompting myself to see what he is seeing. Or, I may just write the command: 'describe what is most important about the future feedback photo' and trace these words with my pen or finger, while just relaxing. When an image enters my mind I'll sketch this, then touch the sketch to stimulate further impressions and sensations. As soon as I receive the feedback photo, I will compare this to my written transcript, to complete the feedback loop.

(from remote viewer DK, with permission)

In ARV there is an element of precognition as the target is usually associated with some form of *future* activity or outcome such as stock market prices, sporting outcomes or lottery numbers (Katz et al., 2019; Schwartz, 2014). Here, the remote viewer will be tasked with attempting to *view* a target image that will be associated with a *future* outcome. For example, in a horse race with five entrants each horse would be associated with a distinct target image. The remote viewer will then be tasked with describing the target image that they will see in the future that is linked to the horse that wins the race. Some have suggested that such a paradigm could be used as a way for psi researchers to fund themselves (Schwartz, 2014). However, it has also been pointed out that such a protocol is challenging and may be difficult to sustain over a long period of time due to psychological and emotional reasons (Schwartz, 2014). Such remote viewing paradigms have not only been used within the field of psi research but have also been adopted to some extent by *futurists* who aim to provide accurate scenario developments of specific outcomes (Lee, 2008) or visualise potential future patterns in business (Markley, 2008).

Project Stargate

No examination of the field of remote viewing would be complete without a brief mention of the remarkable project *Stargate*. Sadly, there is so much written about this that it is beyond the scope of a single chapter to provide a full summary hence interested readers are encouraged to read the recent comprehensive summaries by May and Marwaha (2018a, 2018b).

Project Stargate was initially set up in the early 1970s and funded by the United States government in response to claims that the Soviet Union was undertaking psi-based research, with an emphasis on information capture and infiltration. Hence, at the time there were concerns that the USA might be either falling behind in the psi application stakes and/or that the Soviet Union was leading the way in psi-based military applications (see e.g., May & Marwaha, 2018a, 2018b; McMoneagle, 2002; McMoneagle & May, 2004; Wiseman & Milton, 1998). Much of the early work was reliant on two allegedly gifted remote viewers, Ingo Swann and Pat Price (see, Schoch & Yonavjak, 2008). Their work allegedly involved them attempting to obtain information about Soviet military sites using RV. In one instance the CIA are alleged to have provided map co-ordinates for an unidentified Russian facility in Semipalantinsk. According to Schoch and Yonavjak (2008), Price was able to accurately describe the facility and the work carried out there despite the fact that he was at the Stanford Research Institute (SRI) over nine thousand miles from the target site. However, not all of Price's RV attempts were successful and he also reported much information that turned out to be inaccurate. In another example Swann was asked to remotely view Jupiter which resulted in him reporting a ring around the planet, which at the time was thought to be an error or a possible description of nearby Saturn. However, when the NASA Pioneer 10 probe visited Jupiter in 1973 it identified a ring system (Schoch & Yonavjak, 2008).

Unfortunately, due to the political climate at the time the CIA decided to officially terminate the programme in 1975. Nevertheless, the programme did continue with funding provided by other interested government agencies such as the Defence Intelligence Agency (DIA) and the US Air Force. In 1990 the programme moved to the Science Applications International Corporation (SAIC). The alleged goal of this programme was to train people in psychic spying in order to obtain military information not available via the usual channels of communication. Government participation in such research became public knowledge in 1995 following a freedom of information act at which time it was decided to terminate the programme (see, Schoch & Yonavjak, 2008).

As part of a review initiated by the CIA, two experts external to the project were required to examine the evidence for RV; they were Professor Utts and Professor Hyman. Utts (1995) produced a review of the work carried out at the SRI and SAIC which reported an overall effect size of 0.22. These findings led her to argue that the effects found were 'far beyond what is expected by chance' (p. 289) and that it could be concluded that psi 'has been well established' (p. 289). Whilst Hyman (1995) agreed with the results, he disagreed with the conclusion. He argued that whilst the results cannot easily be dismissed as due to chance or statistical anomalies, because all possible alternative explanations for non-psi-based functioning had not been examined and eliminated, a psi-based alternative could not be accepted. The discussions and controversy over these results continue. For instance, a later re-evaluation of one of the studies suggested that some critical information was missing (Wiseman & Milton, 1998). This included, for instance, whether anyone who knew the identity of the target interacted in any way with those who judged the outcomes. Furthermore, procedural details originally reported may have been incorrect, whilst discussion about the assertion that such details could have accounted for the pattern of effects found did not lead to a clear conclusion (see, Wiseman & Milton, 1999).

According to J. C. Smith (2010) the project was abandoned in 1995 after '24 years of fruitless research' (p. 252) after it had allegedly cost approximately $20 million. Others take issue with this and argue that the project was consistently funded over time *because* it managed to produce successful results (McMoneagle & May, 2004). Some have also suggested that government agencies may have terminated the funding and programme in order to take it *underground* and away from media exposure. Such an idea may seem more at home in the various conspiracy novels that abound but there does seem to have been legitimate concern that if such an effect became publicly recognised as possible and/or interesting it could pose serious challenges to intelligence based agencies (Schoch & Yonavjak, 2008).

Evidence

The early reports examining the effectiveness of RV generally produced positive results (e.g., Bisaha & Dunne, 1976; Dunne & Bisaha, 1979). For instance, in one series of precognitive remote viewing trials the percipient was asked to describe the location of an agent 5,000 miles away and 24 hours in the future. At the appropriate time the agent was asked to concentrate on their surroundings at the target time and location and take a photograph to be later compared with the percipient's descriptions. Bisaha and Dunne (1976) reported that the results were statistically significant suggesting positive evidence of precognitive remote viewing (see also, Dunne & Bisaha, 1979). An early review summarising the results of over 50 experiments by Puthoff and Targ (1976) proposed that the effect is real and people are capable of accurately viewing target material located at a distance. They argued that the robustness of the effects produced across the large number of empirical studies provides substantial support for the notion that humans can perceive complex remote stimuli. Others who reviewed the evidence came to similar conclusions, arguing that the results were so overwhelming that some explanation other than chance would be needed to account for the data (May et al., 1988; Puthoff, 1996; Schmeidler, 1994; Targ, 1996).

However, some have suggested that the RV data may be limited by certain methodological weaknesses (e.g., French & Stone, 2014; Hansen et al., 1992; Lee, 2008; Milton, 1997; Wiseman & Milton, 1998). For example, it was suggested that in some cases the list of targets was not randomly presented to the judges which could have influenced their decisions. Lee (2008) also pointed out that transcripts or output from a remote viewing session can at times be vague and may be subject to personal interpretation. Furthermore, Wiseman and Milton (1998) point out that possible clues in the transcripts could have provided cues to the correct target position in the sequence of potential targets. Whilst these would indeed represent potential methodological flaws, it should be noted that there is *no evidence* that such factors *did* influence the outcome. Nevertheless, a recent attempt to utilise Twitter to invite members of the public to use RV to identify a pre-specified location failed to elicit any evidence of remote viewing over a four day period (Wiseman & Watt, 2010). On each of the four days Wiseman sent out a tweet from one of five possible locations in Edinburgh and invited people to send in their thoughts and impressions. Judges were then given the target location along with four other decoy locations and using the impressions from the public attempted to identify the correct target. No hits were recorded. Thus, in this instance, there was no evidence for remote viewing. However, it should be noted that there are many methodological problems associated with relying on members of the public to simply tweet a response without giving it any/much thought. Furthermore, this is a very different scenario from the more standard RV procedure whereby a viewer would spend time and effort focusing on and trying to *see* the target rather than simply guessing (see, May & Marwaha, 2018a, 2018b).

Despite the claims regarding potential methodological weaknesses, when Kennedy (1979) recalculated the probabilities correcting for series dependence the significance of the remote viewing tests was reduced but not eliminated, suggesting that any effects found cannot have been the result of methodological problems alone. More recently, Dunne and Jahn (2003) presented a comprehensive examination of the RV data across a 25 year period, taking into account the various methods used to score trials, and argued that the overall results are still significantly above what would be expected by chance alone. They concluded that many of these studies demonstrate a sufficient degree of anomalous information acquisition to justify continued exploration of this process to gain a fuller understanding. Finally, a recent review of the evidence for remote viewing by Tressoldi (2011) that utilised both frequentist and Bayesian statistical approaches also concluded that clear evidence exists for non-local communication. Hence, the results from RV studies are certainly intriguing and worthy of continued exploration. This is particularly true for the area of associative remote viewing (ARV), given its financial and applied potential.

Evidence for ARV

Given that ARV aims to use remote viewing techniques to identify the outcome of a specific *future* event, many have suggested that if this can be clearly demonstrated the field of psi research may be able to fund itself and many others with a vested interest in various future outcomes will be quick to take notice (Bierman & Rabeyron, 2013; Katz et al., 2019). To date ARV has been used in order to predict US presidential election outcomes (Katz & Bulgatz, 2013) and stock market fluctuations (Katz, Grgic, & Fendley, 2018; C. C. Smith et al., 2014), as well as the outcome of sporting events (Katz et al., 2019). Given the potential financial gain it should not be surprising that the field of ARV has its own organisation which provides in-house training and access to various resources including annual conferences (see https://www.irva.org/).

Some have suggested that ARV is primarily useful when there is a limited number of possible future outcomes, such as deciding whether a certain investment will make money or lose money within a set timeframe (Lee, 2008). Certainly, one of the most well-known studies was set up to use ARV to forecast the price of silver over a series of one-week periods. The procedure used four possible outcomes, which were classified according to the monetary change in silver values from 'up a little', 'up a lot', 'down a little' and 'down a lot' (Harary & Targ, 1985; Targ, 2012). These four outcomes were each represented by distinct target images such as a light bulb, a flower, a book and a stuffed toy animal. The procedure involved one of the experimenters contacting the RV each week to get their impressions of the object 'associated' with the future outcome of silver, i.e., the change in value. Based on this, silver futures contracts were either bought or sold. Of the nine forecasts performed in the study all were correct and a sum of $120,000 was earned. The story even made the front page of the Wall Street Journal. However, an attempt to repeat the feat in the following year failed. Targ (2008) believes this was due to pressure to perform as many as two trials a week, which affected the feedback to the viewer, and also because the team had lost its 'spiritual focus' with a shift in emphasis to making a financial gain. Nevertheless, Targ, Katra, Brown and Wiegand (1995) completed a further study using a modified protocol and again they found that 11 out of the 12 predictions were in the right direction when attempting to predict the outcome of the silvers market. Others have also reported some success in using ARV to make financial gains. For instance, a long-term ARV study that covered 13 years of stock market trades reported a success rate of 60% and yielded a profit of over $100,000 (Kolodziejzyk, 2012). More recently C. C. Smith et al. (2014) reported on a class based exercise carried out using ten inexperienced remote viewers to predict the movement, either up or down, of the Dow Jones Industrial Average. Out of seven trials seven correct guesses were made and relevant trades were conducted. It was recorded that on an initial investment of $10, 000 they gained $16,000. Such findings are encouraging and these positive effects were supported in a review of 17 studies by Bierman and Rabeyron (2013) who found a mean scoring rate of 63% success where 50% would be expected by chance alone.

However, not everyone has been successful when attempting to use ARV to identify possible future outcomes. For example, attempts to use ARV to make accurate predictions regarding US presidential elections proved ambiguous. Katz, Bulgatz and McLaughlin-Walter (2017) used ARV to predict the outcome of the 2016 US presidential elections and found no clear evidence as viewers 'failed to describe the assigned feedback photo associated with Donald Trump' (p. 13). Another attempt involved recruiting more than 60 remote viewers to make a range of predictions over a 14-month period with the aim of using ARV as an investment tool to enhance a for-profit scheme focused on trading on the Foreign Exchange (FOREX) currency market in the USA (Katz et al., 2018). Though the project began with over $40,000 to invest with the stated goal of 'creating wealth' (p. 27) most of this was lost over the course of the study. To some extent they suggest that the increasing stress associated with the continuing loss of the original fund may have exacerbated the miss rate, along with an over-complex procedure and a heavy workload of over two hundred predictions in a single year. They suggested that this may simply have been a case of making too many predictions in too short a time span, a point made earlier by Targ (2012). Hence, it is not yet clear whether ARV could be used as a means of financially supported psi-based research. Nevertheless, there is some agreement in the literature that ARV shows promise as a potential practical application and that the current findings warrant more in-depth research and further development in an attempt to yield more consistent and repeatable results (C. C. Smith et al., 2014).

Mediating factors

A number of factors have been put forward as potentially influencing the outcome of remote viewing research studies. These include the experience or training of the remote viewers, the type of target, the type of feedback and the use of a single versus multiple group of viewers or agents.

Experience/training

It certainly seems to be the case that much of the early work was reliant on a limited number of possibly gifted individuals, such as Ingo Swann, Joe McMoneagle, Pat Price and Hella Hamid (Schwartz, 2014; May & Marwaha, 2018a). This raises the issue of whether remote viewing is something only those gifted individuals can do or whether it is something everyone may be able to do, with sufficient time and/or training.

McMoneagle (1997), for example, argued that RV is something that is a basic innate ability in everyone and that it can be refined and developed with training. This view echoes earlier claims by Puthoff and Targ (1976; Targ, 2004) that individuals can learn and/or be trained to remotely view material where such training can assist in the accuracy of their attempts. However, not everyone agrees with such a view; Schwartz (2014) for instance, has suggested that it is 'easier to find than train good remote viewers' (p. 12). Nevertheless, encouraging results have been found using both trained and untrained viewers. For instance, when Dunne and Bisaha (1979) examined remote viewing they used two inexperienced female participants, the only proviso being that they held a positive attitude to the idea of RV. Despite the lack of training Dunne and Bisaha (1979) found clear evidence of accurate, above chance, remote viewing. Others have produced successful results using novice remote viewers (e.g., Carpenter, 2010; C. C. Smith et al., 2014). However, Puthoff and Targ (1976) have suggested that rather than thinking that inexperienced participants cannot do this it may simply be that their ability and the results they achieve are just more sporadic and less consistent. There does seem to be some support for this idea as when Mumford, Rose and Goslin (1995) reviewed a selection of remote viewing studies from 1983 to 1989 they found that the effect sizes reported for novice percipients was significantly lower than that for the more experienced remote viewers. This is consistent with others who have argued that the more experienced remote viewers are able to exhibit more robust results (McMoneagle & May, 2004). Lee (2008) has also suggested that this may account for the poor results based on opportunity sampling approaches. However, it is also worth noting that such outcomes may also be influenced by the experience of the percipient in terms of their interactions with the experimenter. For instance, a meta-analysis by Milton (1997) noted that in much of the work reported by Targ and Puthoff the experimenters went to a great deal of trouble to ensure that the percipients felt relaxed and at ease and that the setting in general was one of supportive attention with the aim/hope of producing a favourable outcome.

Targets

Over time a wide variety of target types have been utilised. This has included, but is not limited to, 1mm micro-dots, books, key-rings, aluminium cans, pictures and re-mote outdoor geographical locations (Milton, 1997; Schwartz, 2014; Targ & Puthoff, 1974). Schwartz (2014) argued that such a range suggests that the size of the target may not matter. Others have noted that targets that have a clear shape, form and colour are more easily identified by a potential remote viewer than the target's function or other analytical information (Targ & Katra, 1999). A meta-analysis of

78 free-response type studies found that target objects and geographical locations were associated with better performance (Milton, 1997). It may be that such targets have a greater perceptual richness which in turn makes it easier to transmit or remotely view. There is also some consistency in the literature suggesting that targets that are dynamic and have an emotional impact, or that are associated with high numinousity ratings are more easily identified (Krippner, Saunders, Morgan, & Quan, 2018; May, Spottiswoode, & James, 1994; Watt, 1996). Interestingly the data is less consistent regarding the number of possible targets. On the one hand using a limited range of possible targets, such as a binary outcome, has been suggested to reduce the overall variability and lead to improved accuracy (Smith et al., 2014), whilst others have suggested that a more open free response approach, in which the percipient attempts to describe a potential target, was more successful than those paradigms using a forced-choice approach, which required the participant to select a single target from a small set of possibilities (Schwartz, 2014). Though most agree that targets that fail to engage and/or are uninteresting are more difficult and may lead to a higher drop-out rate (Krippner et al., 2018).

Distance and shielding

In physics there is a clear understanding of the relationship between the intensity of a signal and the distance it has travelled, encapsulated within the inverse-square law. This states that any specified physical quantity or intensity is inversely proportional to the square of the distance from the source of that physical quantity (Brown, 2013), something most people are naturally aware of when they are far from a mast and the signal for their mobile phone is poor. Hence, the question here is whether increasing the distance between a remote viewer and their target reduces the accuracy of the process. The literature is reasonably consistent in suggesting that the distance between RV and target has little or no impact (Dunne & Jahn, 2003; Puthoff & Targ, 1976). That is, the signal, or ability of the percipient does not seem to deteriorate as distance to the remote target increases (Jahn & Dunne, 2005; Targ, 1996). For instance, when reviewing the literature Dunne and Jahn (2003) identified variations in distance from under one mile up to an excess of several thousand miles. Furthermore, they found no clear relationship between the effect size of RV and the distance between the percipient and the agent. The fact that distance does not seem to reduce or limit the strength of the RV effect has important implications for its application and for theoretical understanding of the processes involved.

The second issue is whether it is possible to shield the remote viewer and/or the target in such a way that the percipient is unable to remotely view the target. Some early work regarding the potential mechanisms for RV suggested that it may be mediated by, and/or based on, extremely low frequency (ELF) waves that occur in nature (see, Persinger, 1975). However, Schwartz (2014) has argued that deep dive experiments involving submarines going deep beneath the ocean produced RV results that cannot be accounted for in terms of ELF waves. Furthermore, attempts to shield the viewer have been shown to have little or no impact. For instance, Targ and Puthoff (1974) report on participants who were isolated in a shielded room. The room provided both visual and acoustic isolation by means of a steel double-walled construction with a locked door and a one-way audio link running from inside out to record the percipient's responses. Such an approach aimed to eliminate any possible sensory leakage. Nevertheless, despite such precautions they still found evidence of remote viewing (see also Schwartz, 2014). Targ (1996) also reported that RV was not affected by electromagnetic shielding around the percipient. As such, it seems that screening and shielding have little or no impact on remote viewing. This has important implications in terms of trying to understand the potential mechanisms.

Feedback

It may be that providing feedback regarding the accuracy of a possible target could improve performance in multiple ways. First, it could help the remote viewer identify what processes and procedures did and did not lead to a positive outcome. Second, by providing accurate information about the target in the future the percipient may also be able to use precognitive remote viewing to access and utilise such information. Such speculations would suggest that providing feedback would be associated with improved performance. However, when testing for this by manipulating the intensity of the feedback provided May, Lantz and Piantineda (2000) found no clear evidence of a positive relationship between feedback and performance. One suggestion put forward by May et al. (2000) based on this finding was that the accuracy of remote viewing would not seem to rely on the need to obtain feedback of the target at some future date, which implies that it may be based more on a real time effect. Others disagree, suggesting that the more significant and emotional the feedback event is the more likely it is that the remote viewer can tap into the feedback event rather than the prediction event (Schwartz, 2007). Therefore, increasing the emotional and perceptual significance of the feedback event may lead to an increase in the likelihood of the percipient remotely perceiving that event, leading to a positive outcome. Hence, at present the precise influence of feedback on RV is not clear.

Single vs multiple

There are two related issues here. The first is whether having one or more senders or agents would be more effective. The second, related, point is whether having one or more remote viewers would be better. For example, if a single agent were to visit a remote site and attempt to *send* information to the RV relating to that site then it may make sense to think that multiple agents visiting the same site and attempting to relay such information would make for a stronger signal, which in turn may lead to more robust RV effects. Such an idea is based on what Rogo (1986) termed the *committee effect*. The idea here is that a group of individuals all aiming to achieve the same outcome may be able to elicit a more consistent and robust psi effect. Hence a group may be able to produce a stronger RV effect and do so more consistently than an individual. This idea was tested by Storm (2003) who compared the RV effects when one agent was used compared to three agents. Whilst he did find some evidence of RV, above that expected by chance, he also found that performance of the three agents did not lead to a more robust effect compared to a single agent alone.

However, Storm (2003) did point out that using more than one agent could also result in more noise, resulting in a jumble of ideas and images from multiple agents, which in turn could reduce or overshadow the signal. It should also be noted that not all agree with the need or requirement of using a sender or agent. Indeed, Schwartz (2014) has suggested that an agent/sender is not necessary for high quality remote viewing to occur.

In terms of using multiple RVs the aim would be to produce a majority or consensus view which may improve the signal to noise ratio (Carpenter, 2010; Smith et al., 2014). For instance, Smith et al. (2014) have suggested that having multiple remote viewers and taking a majority view utilises what they refer to as a built-in error correction aspect, making it more likely to identify the correct target. Carpenter (2010) also points out that the use of such averaged responses is commonplace in other disciplines where measurements with imperfect reliability must be used. He furthermore argues that use of such majority decisions can improve the success rates if the individuals in question successfully predict at above chance rates, or show a persistent tendency to correctly remotely view the target.

Overview

Both clairvoyance and remote viewing refer to the notion that an individual may be able to acquire information, or *see* a distant target, via a non-usual route. Both also include information from all senses alongside vision. Clairvoyance is distinct in the sense that it need only involve the percipient attempting to view the target. There is no need for anyone else to be involved, whereas remote viewing may involve the use of an agent who visits a specific location before attempting to relay this information. Attempts to elicit, or test for clairvoyance, have utilised a range of paradigms including forced-choice selections and unconstrained free responses. There have also been attempts to elicit clairvoyant effects whilst the percipient is asleep and dreaming and monitor for unconscious clairvoyant responses by examining changes in physiology. It would be fair to say that the evidence for clairvoyance, across the various paradigms, is both intriguing and encouraging. Effects across a range of studies have been reported though not always consistently and the effects are generally weak. Providing feedback may facilitate the clairvoyant effect provided the percipient believes that this will aid their performance. Clairvoyant performance may also be improved by carefully selecting individuals with a clear interest in psi and some prior experience or ability. There are also suggestions that using targets that contain dynamic multi-sensory information, ideally of an emotionally negative valence, may also aid performance. The use of a consensus approach to judging the outcomes which includes multiple judges may also help. With regards to remote viewing a number of paradigms have been developed over time. These include standard or controlled, precognitive, extended and associative remote viewing. It is not that one approach is better than another and it is not clear at present whether they all tap the same processes and/or skill set. It is more that each procedure reflects an attempt to remote view a target under different circumstances, whether this be at a distant location, at a distant time or associated with a distinct outcome. The findings from project Stargate are a rich source of insights and revelations, not least because it shows evidence of a government willing to fund a psi project for many years. Some have argued this was a waste of tax payers' money whilst others have argued that such funding only continued because the project produced useful results. The evidence for RV is certainly encouraging and raises a number of profound questions about the nature of such experiences. The possibility that ordinary individuals can obtain information about distant events or locations via non-normal routes, even when such target events or locations have yet to be selected, challenges some of the most fundamental premises of the prevailing view of science. Given the practical applications and potential financial gains linked with ARV this is certainly an area worth exploring further, although a focus on making money and the potential stress and pressure to make such gains may act as a natural limiting factor. Similar to clairvoyance the findings from remote viewing are more robust when based on viewers with experience, though it may be possible, over time, to train such skills. Also, targets that are perceptually rich in detail, dynamic and contain emotive content tend to be easier to remotely view. Interestingly remote viewing does not seem to be hindered by the distance between the viewer and the target and whether the target is shielded or not. Furthermore, providing feedback regarding the target does not seem to enhance the outcome. Finally, using multiple remote viewers and taking a consensus approach may help to reduce errors and enhance the accuracy of such attempts.

Reflective questions

Some questions that may prove helpful when reflecting on the material covered in this chapter.

- Do you think clairvoyance is a distinct aspect of psi?
- What do you think are the similarities and differences between clairvoyance and RV?
- What do you think would be the best way to test for clairvoyance or RV?
- What factors influence the accuracy of clairvoyance and RV?
- Do you think both clairvoyance and RV are influenced by the same factors?
- If you could remotely view a target what would it be and why?
- Are there any ethical and/or moral issues associated with RV?
- Should ARV be used to facilitate the outcome of sensitive/difficult decisions?

References

Ashby, R. (1972). *The guidebook for the study of psychical research*. London: Rider & Co.
Beloff, J. (1974). ESP: The search for a physiological index. *Journal of the Society for Psychical Research*, 47(761), 403–420.
Bierman, D. J., Berendsen, J., Koenen, C., Kuipers, C., Louman, J., & Maisson, F. (1984). The effects of ganzfeld stimulation and feedback in a clairvoyance task. In R. A. White & R. S. Broughton (Eds.), *Research in parapsychology* (p. 14). Metuchen, NJ: Scarecrow.
Bierman, D. J., & Rabeyron, T. (2013). *Can psi research sponsor itself? Simulations and results of an automated ARV-casino experiment*. Paper presented at the 56th Annual Convention of the Parapsychological Association in Viterbo, Italy, August.

Bisaha, J., & Dunne, B. (1976). Precognitive remote viewing in the Chicago area: A replication of the Stanford experiment. *Research in Parapsychology*, 84–86.

Braud, W. (1977). Long-distance dream and presleep telepathy. In J. D. Morris, W. G. Roll, & R. L. Morris (Eds.), *Research in parapsychology 1976* (pp. 154–155). Metuchen, NJ: Scarecrow Press.

Braud, W. (1992). Human interconnectedness. *ReVision*, 14(3), 140–148.

Braude, S. E. (2016). *Crimes of reason: On mind, nature, and the paranormal*. Boulder, CO: Rowman & Littlefield.

Brown, R. G. (2013). *Introductory physics I: Elementary mechanics*. Durham, NC: Duke University.

Carpenter, J. (2010). Laboratory psi effects may be put to practical use: Two pilot studies. *Journal of Scientific Exploration*, 24(4), 667–690.

Child, I. L., & Kelly, E. F. (1973). ESP with unbalanced decks: A study of the process in an exceptional subject. *The Journal of Parapsychology*, 37(4), 278–297.

Dalton, K., Steinkamp, F., & Sherwood, S. J. (1999). A dream GESP experiment using dynamic targets and consensus vote. *Journal of the American Society for Psychical Research*, 93, 145–166.

Delanoy, D. (1989). Approaches to the target: A time for reevaluation. In L. A. Henkel & J. Palmer (Eds.), *Research in parapsychology* (pp. 89–92). Metuchen, NJ: Scarecrow Press.

Dunne, B. J., & Bisaha, J. P. (1979). Precognitive remote viewing in the Chicago area: A replication of the Stanford experiment. *Journal of Parapsychology*, 43, 17–30.

Dunne, B. J., & Jahn, R. G. (2003). Information and uncertainty in remote perception research. *Journal of Scientific Exploration*, 17(2), 207–241.

French, C. C., & Stone, A. (2014). *Anomalistic psychology: Exploring paranormal belief and experience*. Hampshire, UK: Palgrave Macmillan.

Graff, D. E., & Cyrus, P. S. (2017). *Perceiving the future news: Evidence for retrocausation*. Paper presented at the American Institute of Physics.

Hansen, G. P., Utts, J., & Markwick, B. (1992). Crtique of the PEAR remote-viewing experiments. *Journal of Parapsychology*, 56, 97–113.

Harary, K., & Targ, R. (1985). A new approach to forecasting commodity futures. *Psi Research*, 4(3–4), 79–88.

Harley, T. A. (1989). Psi missing in a dream clairvoyance experiment. *Journal of the Society for Psychical Research*, 56(817), 1–7.

Hyman, R. (1995). Evaluation of the program on anomalous mental phenomena. *Journal of Parapsychology*, 59, 321–352.

Jahn, R. G., & Dunne, B. J. (2005). The PEAR proposition. *Journal of Scientific Exploration*, 19(2), 195–245.

Jephson, I. (1928). Evidence for clairvoyance in card-guessing. *Proceedings of the Society for Psychical Research*, 38, 223–268.

Kanthamani, H., & Khilji, A. (1990). *An experiment in ganzfeld and dreams: A confirmatory study*. Paper presented at the 33rd Annual Convention of the Parapsychological Association, Chevy Chase, MD.

Katz, D., & Bulgatz, M. (2013). Remote viewers predict the outcome of the 2012 presidential election. *Aperture*, 23, 46–51.

Katz, D., Bulgatz, M., & McLaughlin-Walter, N. (2017). Predicting the 2016 US Presidential election: Using a double blind associative remote viewing protocol. *Eight Martini's Remote Viewing Magazine*, 15, 4–14.

Katz, D., Grgic, I., & Fendley, T. W. (2018). An ethnographic assessment of project firefly: A yearlong endeavor to create wealth by predicting FOREX currency moves with associative remote viewing. *Journal of Scientific Exploration*, 32(1), 27–60.

Katz, D., Smith, N., Bulgatz, M., Graf, D., & Lane, J. (2019). The associative remote dreaming experiment: A novel approach to predicting future outcomes of sporting events. *Journal of the Society for Psychical Research*, 83(2), 65–84.

Kennedy, J. E. (1979). Methodological problems in free-response ESP experiments. *Journal of the American Society for Psychical Research*, 73(1), 1–15.

Kolodziejzyk, G. (2012). Greg Kolodziejzyk's 13-year associative remote viewing experimental results. *Journal of Parapsychology*, 76, 349–367.

Krippner, S., Saunders, D. T., Morgan, A., & Quan, A. (2018). Remote viewing of concealed target pictures under light and dark conditions. *Explore*, 1–11. doi: 10.1016/j.explore.2018. 07.001.

Lee, J. H. (2008). From my perspective: Remote viewing as applied to future studies. *Technological Forecasting and Social Change*, 75, 142–153.

Markley, O. W. (2008). Mental time travel: A practical business and personal research tool for looking ahead. *Futures*, 40, 17–24.

Markwick, B. (1985). The establishment of data manipulation in the Soal-Shackleton experiments. In P. A. Kurtz (Ed.), *A sceptics handbook of parapsychology* (pp. 287–312). Buffalo, NY: Prometheus.

May, E. C., Lantz, N. D., & Piantineda, T. (2000). Feedback considerations in anomalous cognition experiments. In E. C. May & S. B. Marwaha (Eds.), *Anomalous cognition: Remote viewing research and theory* (pp. 104–117). Jefferson, NC: McFarland & Company, Inc.

May, E. C., & Marwaha, S. B. (2018a). *The star gate archives: Reports of the United States governments sponsored psi progam, 1972–1995. Volume 1: Remote viewing 1972–1984.* Jefferson, NC: McFarland.

May, E. C., & Marwaha, S. B. (2018b). *The star gate archives: Reports of the United States governments sponsored psi progam, 1972–1995. Volume 2: Remote viewing 1985–1995.* Jefferson, NC: McFarland.

May, E. C., Spottiswoode, S. J. P., & James, C. L. (1994). Managing the targetpool bandwidth: Noise reduction for anomalous cognition experiments. *Journal of Parapsychology*, 58, 303–313.

May, E. C., Utts, J., Trask, V., Luke, W., Frivold, T., & Humphrey, B. (1988). Review of the psychoenergetic research conducted at SRI International (1973–1988) *SRI International Technical Report, March 1989.*

McMoneagle, J. (1997). *Mind trek.* Charlottesville, VA: Hampton Roads Publishing.

McMoneagle, J. (2000). *Remote viewing secrets: A handbook.* Charlottesville, VA: Hampton Roads Publishing Company.

McMoneagle, J. (2002). *The stargate chronicles: Memoirs of a psychic spy.* Charlottesville, VA: Hampton Roads Publishing Company, Inc.

McMoneagle, J., & May, E. C. (2004). *The possible role of intention, attention and expectation in remote viewing.* Paper presented at the The Parapsychological Association Convention., Vienna, Austria.

Milton, J. (1997). Meta-analysis of free-response ESP studies without altered states of consciousness. *Journal of Parapsychology*, 61, 279–319.

Milton, J., & Wiseman, R. (1997). *Guidelines for extrasensory perception research* (Vol. 2). Hatfield,UK: University of Hertfordshire Press.

Mumford, M. D., Rose, A. M., & Goslin, D. (1995). *An evaluation of remote viewing: research and applications.* The American Institutes for Research Report.

Nash, C. B. (1985). Clairvoyant determination of the most frequent of five cards. *Journal of the Society for Psychical Research*, 53, 26–30.

Palmer, J. (2015). Experimental methods in anomalous cognition and anomalous perturbation research. In E. Cardena, J. Palmer, & D. Marcusson-Clavertz (Eds.), *Parapsychology: A handbook for the 21st century* (pp. 49–62). Jefferson, NC: McFarland & Co.

Persinger, M. A. (1975). Geophysical models for parapsychological experiences. *Psychoenergetic Systems*, *1*(2), 63–74.

Puthoff, H. E. (1996). CIA-initiated remote viewing program at Stanford Research Institute. *Journal of Scientific Exploration*, *10*(1), 63–76.

Puthoff, H. E., & Targ, R. (1976). A perception channel for information transfer over kilometer distances: Historical perspective and recent research. *Proceedings of the IEEE*, *64*(3), 329–354.

Rhine, J. B. (1945). Telepathy and clairvoyance reconsidered. *The Journal of Parapsychology*, *9*(3), 176–193.

Roe, C. A., Sherwood, S. J., Luke, D., & Farrell, L. (2002). An exploratory investigation of dream GESP using consensus judging and dynamic targets. *Journal of the Society for Psychical Research*, *66*(869), 225–238.

Rogo, D. S. (1986). *Mind over matter: The case for psychokinesis: How the human mind can manipulate the physical world*. London: Aquarian Press.

Sartori, L., Massacesi, S., Martinelli, M., & Tressoldi, P. E. (2004). Physiological correlates of ESP: Heart rate differences between targets and nontargets. *The Journal of Parapsychology*, *68*(2), 351–360.

Schmeidler, G. R. (1985). Field and stream: Background stimuli and the flow of ESP responses. *Journal of the American Society for Psychical Research*, *79*(1), 13–26.

Schmeidler, G. R. (1994). ESP experiments 1978–1992: The glass is half full. *Advances in Parapsychological Research*, *7*, 104–197.

Schmidt, H. (1969). Clairvoyance tests with a machine. *The Journal of Parapsychology*, *33*(4), 300–306.

Schoch, R. M., & Yonavjak, L. (2008). *The parapsychology revolution: A concise anthology of paranormal and psychical research*. New York, NY: Tarcher/Penguin.

Schwartz, S. A. (2007). *Opening to the infinite: The art and science of nonlocal awareness*. Buda, TX: Nemoseen Media.

Schwartz, S. A. (2014). Through time and space: The evidence for remote viewing. In D. Broderick & B. Groetzel (Eds.), *The evidence for psi*. New York: McFarland.

Sherwood, S. J., Dalton, K., Steinkamp, F., & Watt, C. (2000). Dream clairvoyance study II using dynamic video-clips: Investigation of consensus voting judging procedures and target emotionality. *Dreaming*, *10*(4), 221–236.

Smith, C. C., Laham, D., & Moddel, G. (2014). Stock market prediction using associative remote viewing by inexperineced remote viewers. *Journal of Scientific Exploration*, *28*(1), 7–16.

Smith, J. C. (2010). *Pseudoscience and extraordinary claims of the paranormal*. West Sussex: Wiley & Sons Ltd.

Smith, P. H. (2017). *The essential guide to remote viewing*. Cedar City, UT: Intentional Press.

Soal, S. G., & Goldney, K. M. (1943). Experiments in precognitive telepathy. *Proceedings of the Society for Psychical Research*, *47*, 21–150.

Steinkamp, F., Milton, J., & Morris, R. L. (1998). A meta-analysis of forced-choice experiments comparing clairvoyance and precognition. *Journal of Parapsychology*, *62*, 193–218.

Storm, L. (2003). Remote viewing by committee: RV using a multiple agent/multiple percipient design. *Journal of Parapsychology*, *67*(2), 325–342.

Storm, L. (2006). Meta-analysis in parapsychology: II. Psi domains other than ganzfeld. *Australian Journal of Parapsychology*, *6*(2), 135–155.

Storm, L., Sherwood, S. J., Roe, C. A., Tressoldi, P., Rock, A. J., & Di Risio, L. (2017). On the correspondence between dream content and target material under laboratory conditions: A meta-analysis of dream-ESP studies, 1966–2016. *International Journal of Dream Research*, *10*(2), 120–140.

Storm, L., Tressoldi, P., & Di Risio, L. (2012). Meta-analysis of ESP studies, 1987–2010: Assessing the success of the forced-choice design in parapsychology. *Journal of Parapsychology*, 76(2), 243–273.

Targ, R. (1996). Remote viewing at Stanford Research Institute in the 1970s: A memoir. *Journal of Scientific Exploration*, 10(1), 77–88.

Targ, R. (2004). *Limitless mind: A guide to remote viewing and transformations of consciousness*. Novato, CA: New World Library.

Targ, R. (2008). *Do you see what I see: Memoirs of a blind biker – Lasers and love, ESP and the CIA, and the meaning of life*. London: Hampton Roads.

Targ, R. (2012). *The reality of ESP: A physicist's proof of psychic abilities*. Wheaton, IL: Quest Books.

Targ, R. (2019). What do we know about psi? The first decade of remote-viewing research and operations at Stanford Research Institute. *Journal of Scientific Exploration*, 33(4), 569–592. doi: 10.31275/2019/1669.

Targ, R., & Katra, J. (1999). *Miracles of mind: Exploring nonlocal consciousness and spritual healing*. Novato, CA: New World Library.

Targ, R., Katra, J., Brown, D., & Wiegand, W. (1995). Viewing the future: A pilot study with an error-detecting protocol. *Journal of Scientific Exploration*, 9(3), 67–80.

Targ, R., & Puthoff, H. E. (1974). Information transmission under conditions of sensory shielding. *Nature*, 251, 602–607.

Targ, R., & Tart, C. T. (1985). Pure clairvoyance and the necessity of feedback. *Journal of the American Society for Psychical Research*, 79(4), 485–492.

Tart, C. T. (1983). Information acquisition rates in forced-choice ESP experiments: Precognition does not work as well as present-time ESP. *Journal of the American Society for Psychical Research*, 77, 293–311.

Tressoldi, P. (2011). Extraordinary claims require extraordinary evidence: The case of non-local perception, a classical and Bayesian review of the evidence. *Frontiers in Psychology*, 2(117), 1–5. doi: 10.3389/fpsyg.2011.00117.

Utts, J. (1995). An assessment of the evidence for psychic functioning. *Journal of Parapsychology*, 59(4), 289–321.

Wahbeh, H., McDermott, K., & Sagher, A. (2018). Dissociative symptoms and anomalous information reception. *Activitas Nervosa Superior*, 60(3–4), 75–85.

Watt, C. (1996). What makes a good psi target? *The Journal of Parapsychology*, 60(1), 25–41.

Wiseman, R., & Milton, J. (1998). Experiment one of the SAIC remote viewing program: A critical re-evaluation. *Journal of Parapsychology*, 62(4), 297–308.

Wiseman, R., & Milton, J. (1999). Experiment one of the SAIC remote viewing program: A critical re-evaluation: Reply to May. *Journal of Parapsychology*, 63(1), 3–14.

Wiseman, R., & Watt, C. (2010). Twitter as a new research tool: A mass participation test of remote viewing. *European Journal of Parapsychology*, 25, 89–100.

Chapter 5

Precognition

Imagine a situation where an individual could train themselves to unconsciously prefer and select the correct winning numbers of the next lottery. Alternatively, where technology monitoring subtle changes in physiology provides the individual with a warning of something that is *about to* happen. This chapter explores research suggesting that such ideas may be more than wishful thinking; they may be examples of precognition. The chapter begins by defining what precognition is and briefly examines the suggestion that it may be the only form of psi. This is followed by an exploration of some of the key experimental research on precognition using explicit, implicit, physiological, dream and animal paradigms to elicit and examine such effects. The chapter will then briefly examine some of the more prominent factors that have been proposed to influence or mediate precognitive performance. The chapter ends by briefly outlining some of the theories that have been put forward to account for precognition.

Precognition

Precognition is generally taken to refer to the ability to obtain information about a future event, or predict a future event, using information that is obtained via a non-usual route, prior to the occurrence of the event (see e.g., Bierman & Bijl, 2014; Franklin, Baumgart, & Schooler, 2014; Honorton & Ferrari, 1989; Marwaha & May, 2016). According to Radin (2017), this can take the form of insights, premonitions or presentiments regarding future possibilities. See the example in Box 5.1.

The individual's experience outlined in Box 5.1 could be taken to suggest that they became aware of an event that was about to happen in the very near future. Alternatively, they could simply have noted the environmental cues (i.e., children playing ball) and unconsciously mapped out a range of potential scenarios regarding what could happen in the next few minutes. The idea that it was simply an unconscious response to environmental cues certainly makes it easier to explain than the notion that the individual caught a glimpse of a future event. Nevertheless, according to Franklin et al. (2014) claims of precognition have been made throughout time. Indeed there is a long history of research focusing on precognition and its effects (e.g., J. B. Rhine, 1947; L. E. Rhine, 1955). However, the basis of precognition is both counterintuitive and paradoxical in terms of everyday understanding of the nature of cause and effect. For instance, a key aspect of everyday experience is the nature of

---

Box 5.1   A precognitive premonition?

This occurred some time ago but the memory of it remains fresh in my mind. I was doing a lot of martial arts training at the time – I don't know if that's relevant – but I was walking along the street with a friend and noticed up ahead some children playing ball against a wall. The only way I can explain it is there was a certainty that just came to me that the ball they were playing with would somehow come flying towards me and that I would knock the ball away with my hand.

It almost felt as if I were being told what would happen and what I would do about it. I've gone over it many times in my head and I know that seeing children playing with a ball could have given me a cue, but this was absolutely different. Anyway, after about a minute or so as we walked passed the children the ball did come towards me and I did bat it away with my hand – I would just say that I don't recall seeing the ball or making any conscious move regarding knocking the ball away. It just happened. I was stunned when it happened exactly the way I thought it would.

As I say, I've reflected back on it many times because it was so odd. Not just the event but the absolute feeling of clarity and certainty about what was going to happen. I am convinced that … somehow, I saw a flash of the future.

(from EHW with permission)

---

causality, which tells us that the cause–effect order is sacrosanct (Radin, 2017). That is, time moves inexorably forwards from past to present to future. Such a principle may seem self-evident from an everyday perspective. The milk does not separate from the coffee, the eggs do not unscramble themselves. There is also the paradoxical example of an individual having a precognitive premonition about an impending journey that ends in disaster which leads the individual to change their travel plans and cancel the journey. However, if the individual cancels the journey how can they then obtain a premonition about it beforehand, given that the journey now does not take place? Such questions are certainly challenging and some have suggested that precognition provides a glimpse into *probable* future information and not certain future events (Radin, 1997). It is interesting to note that from those responding to a recent survey over half reported premonitions of future events that they claim later occurred and 45% changed travel plans as a result of an 'intuitive' sense that something might occur (Mack & Powell, 2005).

Despite the counterintuitive nature of precognition much of what occurs in science can seem at odds with common sense. For instance, the quantum measurement problem, quantum entanglement and the notion of non-locality are just some examples of counterintuitive findings (see e.g., Briggs, Butterfield, & Zeilinger, 2013). Radin (2017) has suggested that this opens the door to thinking about such unorthodox events. Sheehan (2015) agrees, pointing out that both time and consciousness are neither adequately defined nor understood. Furthermore, it is well known that the fundamental equations of physics are time symmetrical. That is, they possess time-forward and time-reversed solutions. Some have even suggested that the notion of retrocausality could be essential for understanding quantum mechanics (Sutherland, 2017). Hence, the notion that information may travel both forwards and backwards in time does not contravene current understanding of the nature of reality (Sheehan, 2006, 2015).

It is possible that some may argue that the notion of precognition negates free will. For example, in order for precognition to occur the future must already exist in which case any decision made in the present is irrelevant. Marwaha and May (2016) disagree and note that what an individual does in the present *may* or *may not* be influenced by what occurs in the future and hence free will to select a preferred course of action remains open. They also point out that there may be more than one possible outcome to any event. Interestingly, it has been argued that this process (assuming it is a transfer of information over time) cannot influence the past (Marwaha & May, 2016). According to such views the present *may* be influenced by potential future events but the past remains closed.

Precognition as the only form of psi

Previous chapters have raised the issue of whether and how distinct telepathy and clairvoyance may be. In a similar vein, some have suggested that precognition is the main, or only form of psi and may account for both telepathy and clairvoyance as well as possibly micro-psychokinesis (Marwaha & May, 2016). The suggestion here is that in each of these paradigms there is an initial time when the receiver, viewer or participant does not know what the target is and then a later time, usually when the particular trial has ended, when the participant is shown the target. Hence, Marwaha and May (2016) suggest that rather than thinking of these as separate processes they may all be tapping the same underlying process which involves precognition. They also suggest that micro-psychokinesis could be accounted for precognitively by the participant gaining some precognitive insight about when to begin the trial which would coincide with a change in the output from the target device. Such ideas are interesting and suggest that each of the various paradigms used may in fact be measuring distinct aspects of the same underlying generic anomalous psi behaviour. However, the evidence for this is scant at present. For instance, an early meta-analysis by Milton (1997) comparing the effect sizes of precognition to both telepathy and clairvoyance showed that the former produced larger effect sizes than the latter, which is suggestive of distinct underlying processes. In contrast, others have found no clear evidence of a difference in the effect size of precognition and clairvoyance (Steinkamp, Milton, & Morris, 1998; Storm, Tressoldi, & Di Risio, 2012).

Experimental research

The focus on experimental research should not be taken to indicate that those in the field either deny or ignore the more spontaneous experiences reported by those who claim to have had precognitive insights or premonitions. It is simply the case that such events are often random, difficult to control for and difficult to assess. Hence, a range

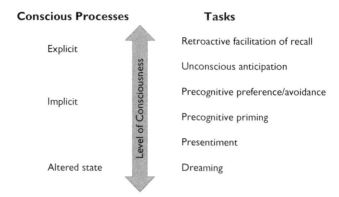

Figure 5.1 The levels of conscious processing on the left along with the various tasks designed to elicit and/or measure precognition on the right.

of experimental procedures have been developed in an attempt to elicit and measure precognitive processes that rely on explicit, implicit or altered states of conscious processing (see Figure 5.1).

The distinction between explicit and implicit processing/tasks has a long history in mainstream cognitive psychology and as such the findings from this field may help to inform understanding regarding precognition. For instance, explicit tasks require participants to intentionally or consciously retrieve information from memory. In contrast, implicit tasks are usually assessed via non-conscious procedures such as preference or priming tasks. Here the individual will be asked to perform a task that makes no reference to any prior learning episode. This distinction between explicit and implicit is not precise and has at times referred to both the level of conscious processing involved as well as the type of task used (Roediger, Buckner, & McDermott, 1999). Furthermore, when used to assess possible precognitive effects it should be noted that it is not clear at present whether such differences are manifestations of a single underlying precognitive phenomenon measured using different tasks, or whether there are distinct types of precognitive processes. To an extent this is similar to the debate in mainstream cognitive psychology regarding the distinction between explicit and implicit memory in terms of separate memory systems or distinct memory processes (Roediger et al., 1999; Schacter & Tulving, 1994). Nevertheless, across these levels of conscious effort, from explicit to altered states, a variety of paradigms have been developed to elicit and assess possible precognitive effects. These include, but are not limited to, retroactive facilitation, unconscious anticipation, precognitive preference, precognitive priming, presentiment and dream precognition. Evidence from each of these areas will be explored briefly followed by some intriguing effects from non-human animal studies.

Retroactive facilitation

No one would be surprised by the claim that after the initial exposure to any new material repeated practice would lead to benefits in encoding and enhance later recall

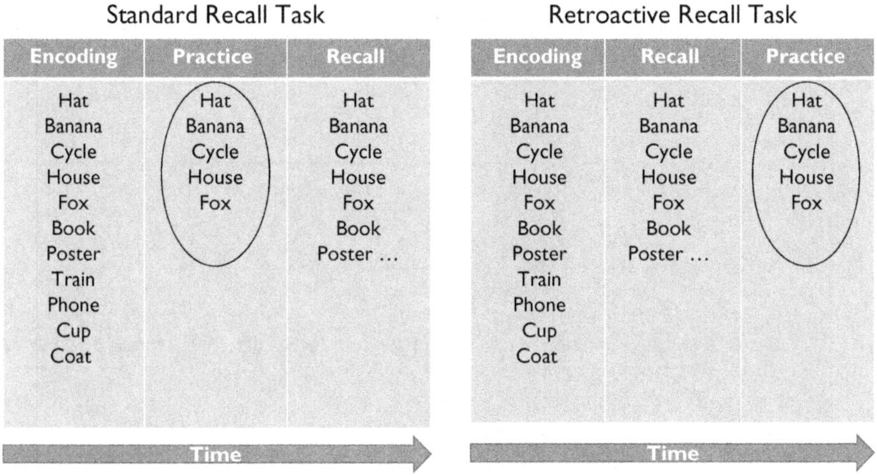

Figure 5.2 An outline of a standard memory recall paradigm on the left with an intervening practice session and a retroactive facilitation paradigm on the right with a post-test practice session.

(Brown & Craik, 2000). Retroactive facilitation is similar to this in the sense that repeated practice facilitates, or improves, performance. However, it is distinct in the sense that the practice comes *after* the recall test rather than before it, as can be seen in the visual outline in Figure 5.2. It should be noted that the individual participating in such a task would not be aware of which, if any, of the stimuli would be repeated in the future. Hence, whilst the recall task itself may rely predominantly on explicit processes the precognitive effect may still be influencing performance unconsciously.

The task is to explicitly recall the target material, words, images, sounds, etc. with the idea that practice occurring *after* the recall test will have a retroactive, or reverse time, influence such that the material that is practised in the future will be recalled more accurately. This paradigm was made popular by Bem (2011) in his attempts to use a standard psychology task that contained a small modification to the sequence of events that could be easily analysed and replicated by others. Bem (2011) originally reported significant retroactive effects for two tasks focusing on word recall (experiment 8 and 9). Since then others have replicated such retroactive effects (Bierman & Bijl, 2014; Subbotsky, 2013; Vernon, 2015, 2018). For instance, Vernon (2018) found that future practice was associated with a significant improvement in the prior recall of arousing images (see Figure 5.3).

Research has also shown that not only can future practice benefit present accuracy levels but it can also improve speed of responses. For instance, Bierman and Bijl (2014) examined the possible effects of retroactive facilitation on a standard Go/NoGo task. This is where an individual is presented with a selection of stimuli and told to either respond (i.e., Go) or not respond (i.e., NoGo). They found that future practice was associated with participants responding approximately 2% faster in the present. This led them to conclude that the data provided evidence of a clear link between present behaviour and future random conditions. Such findings, perhaps unsurprisingly, caused quite a stir within the scientific community and attracted

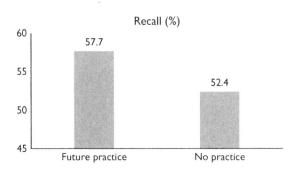

Figure 5.3 Percentage recall of images that *will be* practised in the future (left) compared to those not practised (right) in the future (adapted from Vernon, 2018).

strong criticism regarding the use of inferential statistics and possible questionable research practices (Wagenmakers, Wetzels, Borsboom, & van der Maas, 2011). However, it should be noted that no evidence has yet been seen to support such ideas. Nevertheless, others attempting to replicate these retroactive effects have not always been successful (Baruš & Rabier, 2014; Galak, LeBouf, Nelson, & Simmons, 2012; Ritchie, Wiseman, & French, 2012; Vernon, 2017a, 2017b). For instance, Baruš and Rabier (2014) presented participants with 48 nouns, one at a time, and then required the participants to recall as many of the nouns as they could before asking them to rehearse a sub-set of 24 of the nouns. They found that level of recall for words practised in the future was no different from those not practised (see Figure 5.4).

This pattern of responses led Baruš and Rabier (2014) to conclude that there was no support for the retroactive influence on word recall. Such inconsistent findings are usually interpreted in one of two ways; either no effect was found because none exists or no effect was found in this particular study due to some specific aspect of the method and/or procedure (Baruš & Rabier, 2014). For instance, Vernon (2017b) failed to find evidence of retroactive facilitation effect on prior recall using arousing images and a participant sample specifically selected to include those with high levels of belief in psi. However, this study was conducted online which could have led to reduced levels of participant motivation, as well as a reduced focus of attention or

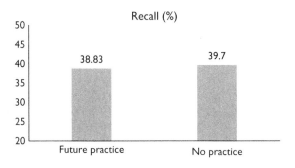

Figure 5.4 Percentage recall of word nouns that *will be* practised in the future (left) compared to those not practised (right) in the future (adapted from Baruš & Rabier 2014).

general involvement of the participants. Indeed, Galak et al. (2012) admit that online studies run the risk of involving many more distractions than a typical lab-based study which could impact on the attention of the participants and negatively influence their performance. Alternatively, it may be, as Ritchie et al. (2012) point out, that such retroactive effects are genuine but problematic to replicate given the elusive nature of psi. Nevertheless, the findings are certainly suggestive, potentially easy to replicate in a typical lab and as such are worthy of further exploration.

Unexplained anticipation

Here the idea is that an individual is able to precognitively guess correctly, or at a level beyond that of chance, something that is about to happen. This could involve pressing one of a number of buttons to indicate which of a set of lights will come on (Haraldsson, 1970; Schmidt, 1969). For example, the individual may be seated in front of a *button box* that contains four separate buttons, each of which corresponds to a light. The individual is required to guess precognitively which lamp will light next by pressing the corresponding button. Once the button has been pressed, a random event generator then selects a lamp to light. Schmidt (1969) was one of the early pioneers of such a method and reported significant effects in two experiments where participants were required to guess which of four lamps would light up next by pressing the corresponding button. Unfortunately, a follow-up study by Haraldsson (1970) failed to find a similar effect when testing individuals based on opportunity sampling. However, when he identified the best performers from this group and re-tested them he did find significant evidence of unconscious anticipation. This suggests that pre-selection of participants based on prior ability and experience would be a good idea when testing for precognition.

Precognitive preference/avoidance

Here the aim is to examine whether participants are able to precognitively prefer a positive or arousing image and/or avoid a negative or noxious image. The use of this paradigm to examine potential precognitive effects was popularised by Bem (2011). For instance, in a precognitive preference task the participant may be shown a screen with an image of two sets of curtains side by side, behind one of which is the target. If it is a preference task then participants will be required to press one button to select the set of curtains (i.e., Left vs. Right) that is hiding the target image. In Figure 5.5 this would mean selecting the curtains on the right. If participants are able to do this at a rate that is statistically greater than chance (i.e., 50%) then they are deemed to be showing a precognitive preference. In general, the task emphasises the need for participants to respond as quickly as possible to ensure that the task relies on/incorporates more implicit processing. Bem (2011) reported that when erotic pictures were used participants correctly selected them at a rate of 53.1% which was significantly above chance at 50%. This positive precognitive preference effect is something that has been replicated by some (Luke, Delanoy, & Sherwood, 2008; Luke, Roe, & Davison, 2008) but not others (Hitchman, Pfeuffer, Roe, & Sherwood, 2016; Hitchman, Sherwood, & Roe, 2015). The inconsistent effects may, to some extent, be the result of differences in the method or procedure. For example, research

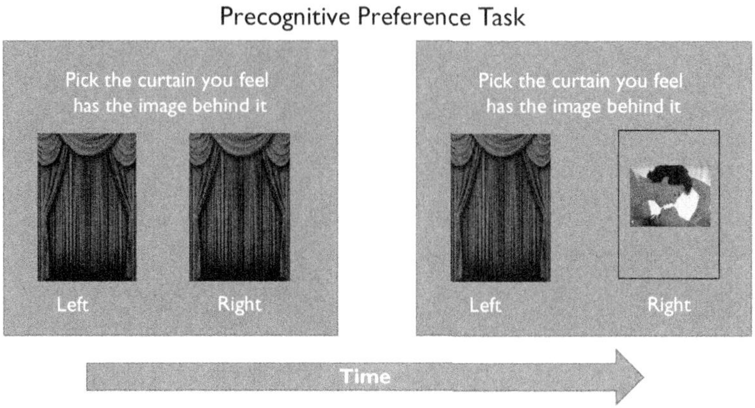

Precognitive Preference Task

Figure 5.5 The stages of a precognitive preference task with an erotic/arousing image as the target hidden behind the right-hand curtain.

has shown that the task elicits more robust precognitive effects when using erotic images as the target (Bem, 2011; Bem, Tressoldi, Rabeyron, & Duggan, 2015).

Maier et al. (2014) modified and extended this task by requiring participants to simultaneously press two keys on a standard keyboard rather than one. Each key was randomly associated with either a positive or a negative masked picture that would appear *after* the key press. The rationale for this was that, if a participant was able to unconsciously access future information, they would press the key associated with the positive image prior to (i.e., faster) the key associated with the negative image. In this way it was thought that the participants would be able to use precognition to view positive images and avoid being exposed to negative ones. Indeed, Maier et al. (2014) found that participants were able to avoid the negative stimuli at a level significantly greater than chance. They then replicated this in a second experiment using a larger sample size, in a third experiment using an even larger sample and running the study online, and again in a fourth study that utilised a more sophisticated randomisation procedure. They argued that across all these studies the effect was small but the avoidance of negativity was nevertheless 'significant overall and therefore can be considered to be a substantial effect' (Maier et al., 2014, p. 19). Hence, they concluded that they had found reliable evidence for a form of precognitive avoidance of negative stimuli.

Precognitive priming

Priming refers to the notion that the simple repetition of a stimulus influences performance, in terms of both speed and accuracy, even when conscious recall or recollection of any prior exposure to the stimulus is not required (see e.g., Ratcliff & McKoon, 2000). Such priming can simply be by repetition, usually referred to as a repetition priming effect, or the simple exposure to a target stimulus, referred to as a mere exposure effect. These paradigms have been adopted or modified to elicit and assess precognition by reversing the order of events (Bem, 2011; Vernon, 2015). For example, a repetition

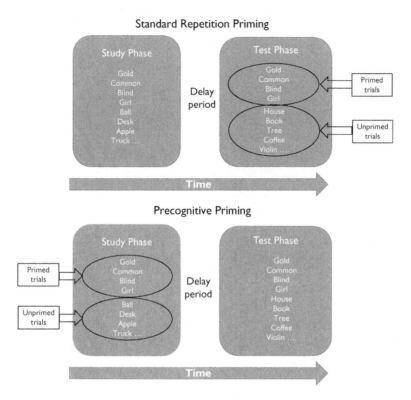

Figure 5.6 A standard repetition priming paradigm (above) with both primed and unprimed trials identified in the test phase, and a precognitive priming paradigm (below) with both primed and unprimed trials identified in the initial study phase.

priming effect is generally examined in a procedure that contains two phases referred to as the *study phase* followed after a variable delay by the *test phase*. The idea is that the participant may be exposed to stimuli in the study phase and required to respond to it, for example by simply naming the word or object. Later, after a specific delay, in the test phase they will again be exposed to a range of stimuli, some from the previous study phase (i.e., primed) and some *new* (i.e., unprimed) not seen before words/objects (see Figure 5.6).

The task for the individual in the test phase will be to simply name the word as quickly and as accurately as possible. This can be done without needing to think back to the earlier study phase; however, participants will generally be faster and more accurate to respond to those words that they were exposed to previously. A key aspect of this repetition priming effect is that it is preserved in those exhibiting amnesia and has been suggested to be underpinned by either a separate memory system or distinct types of processing (e.g., Schacter & Tulving, 1994). The notion that such a paradigm could be used to examine and/or elicit precognitive effects was largely promoted by Bem (2011). The general idea is that rather than examine performance on the primed trials in the test phase researchers examine participants' responses to the trials in the study phase that *will* be repeated (i.e., primed) in the *later* test phase.

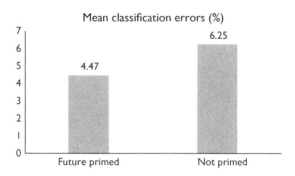

Figure 5.7 Percentage of errors for items primed in the future (left) compared to those not primed (right) (adapted from Vernon, 2015).

For instance, Vernon (2015) examined precognition using just such a modified repetition priming paradigm which required participants to complete a functional classification task. He found that when the target words were primed in the future participants were significantly more accurate (i.e., made fewer errors) in the present (see Figure 5.7). Interestingly, this was only found when the primes were repeated four times in the future and not simply shown once. This would suggest that multiple future repetitions may be required to elicit robust precognitive priming effects.

Precognitive priming can also be examined using a reversed mere exposure effect procedure. The mere exposure effect is a long known standard psychological finding demonstrating that the *mere exposure* to a stimuli can lead individuals to prefer that stimuli, even when presented subliminally (Zajonc, 1968). In fact, stimuli perceived without consciousness awareness can often produce substantially larger effects than when they are consciously perceived (Bornstein, 1989). Hence, exposure to a particular stimulus would generally lead an individual to *prefer* that stimuli compared to one not shown. Bem (2011) took this approach and simply reversed the order of the exposure. That is, he presented participants with two stimuli on screen side by side and asked them to identify the one they preferred. After they had identified the preferred item the computer would randomly select one of the images to be repeatedly flashed up on screen. The rationale was that if participants preferred the image that *would be* flashed on the screen in the future this would demonstrate a precognitive priming effect. When testing this, Bem (2011) found that participants selected the target image that would be flashed on screen in the future significantly more (53.1%) than chance (i.e., 50%). This, he argued, provided evidence of a precognitive mere exposure effect which he then replicated using erotic images (Bem, 2011, experiment 6). A similar pattern of effects was reported by Savva, Child and Smith (2004) when testing individuals with high self-reported levels of fear of spiders and using images of spiders. An attempt by Parker and Sjoden (2010) to demonstrate such precognitive priming using negative and neutral images was only partially successful in that only those who showed a typical mere exposure effect also showed evidence of a precognitive mere exposure effect. This may have implications in terms of trying to understand the underlying mechanisms suggesting that the processes involved in the standard mere exposure effect may also be required to elicit the precognitive effect.

However, not everyone has managed to find evidence of precognitive priming (Traxler, Foss, Podali, & Zirnstein, 2012). For instance, in a standard reading task Traxler et al. (2012) compared the reading speed of one group who read the same piece of text twice to another group who read two separate pieces of text. The rationale was that the group reading the same piece of text twice should show a precognitive priming effect whereby their reading speed the first time around should be faster than those who do not get to read the same text a second time. Unfortunately, they found that reading the text in the future had no impact on reading speed in the present. In fact, they found that those who did read the same text in the future were marginally slower compared to those that did not. This led them to conclude that information that does not exist in the mind at the time of testing cannot influence performance, even if such information is obtained later. Once again, there are methodological differences in this task that may account for the findings, or lack of them. For example, it was a 'self-paced' reading task and as such there was no time pressure on the participants to read at a fast rate. The researchers also told participants that they should 'read in a manner that would enable them to answer comprehensive questions' (p. 1368). As such, the participants could have been focusing more attention on comprehension compared to reading speed. It would be interesting to see if the same pattern of results emerged if participants were told to read the text as fast as they can but ensuring a sufficient level of comprehension to answer some questions.

Overall, the evidence for precognition using explicit and implicit measures has produced some interesting findings. Attempts to gain an overview by reviewing the data and conducting meta-analyses have shown small but reliable effects for precognition (e.g., Honorton & Ferrari, 1989; Steinkamp et al., 1998; Storm et al., 2012). Interestingly the meta-analyses reported by Storm et al. (2012) showed that as the quality of the studies improved over time with additional safeguards the effect size also increased. The most recent meta-analysis examined over 90 studies from various laboratories and again found significantly reliable effects of precognition for implicit tasks, but not when assessed by explicit tasks (Bem et al., 2015).

Presentiment

It has long been known that exposing an individual to an unexpected stimulus, such as a loud noise, or emotive image, can evoke an autonomic response which can be seen by changes in their physiology (Andreassi, 2000). For example, a loud unexpected noise may lead to an increase in heart rate along with changes in electrodermal activity (EDA), subjectively experienced as a beating heart and sweaty palms. Such changes in arousal can be measured in the skin conductance response (SCR) or skin conductance level (SCL; Andreassi, 2000). From a precognitive perspective the idea is to look for and measure such changes *prior* to the exposure of any unexpected or emotive stimuli. These physiological changes occurring prior to the stimuli have been referred to as *presentiment* effects (Bierman & Radin, 1997), *predictive anticipatory activity* (Mossbridge, Tressoldi, Utts, Ives, & Radin, 2014) and *anomalous anticipatory effects* (Kittenis, 2018).

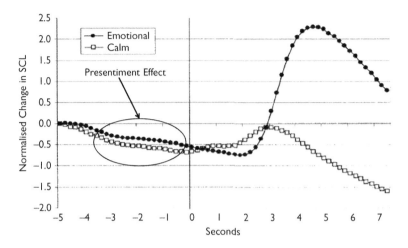

Figure 5.8 Evidence of a presentiment effect, indicated by the higher skin conductance levels (SCL) in response to emotional images compared to calm images *prior* to their exposure at time 0 (from Radin, 2004, p. 259, with permission).

The procedure for assessing presentiment does not require a behavioural response but rather relies on changes in physiology to unknown future stimuli. For instance, a participant may view or be exposed to a range of stimuli that are fully randomised whilst their physiological data are continuously recorded. In general, the prediction is that a participant's physiology will respond in a manner that is congruent with a *future* stimulus. Hence, for example, if seeing an emotive image leads to an increase in arousal evident by higher levels of skin conductance, the presentiment prediction is that such a difference in arousal would be evident *just prior* to the exposure of the stimulus. Thus, just before an individual is exposed to an arousing and/or stimulating image their physiology would be expected to respond. Evidence of this would be seen in higher skin conductance levels (i.e., greater levels of arousal) for emotive images compared to neutral calm images just before the images are shown on screen (see Figure 5.8).

According to Mossbridge et al. (2014), such presentiment effects are indicative of an unconscious physiological response to a future event. Such a response, they suggest, may provide an evolutionary advantage to the organism allowing it to mobilise and respond to future events in less time. Indeed, since these effects were first reported a large number of studies have reported presentiment effects evident in physiological changes or responses prior to the exposure of a particular stimulus. This has included presentiment changes in skin conductance levels (Bierman & Radin, 1997; May, Paulinyi, & Vassy, 2005; Spottiswoode & May, 2003) or other aspects of EDA (Radin, 1997, 2004), brain function as measured by changes in electrocortical activity (Baumgart, Franklin, Jimbo, Su, & Schooler, 2017; Kittenis, 2018; Radin, Vieten, Michel, & Delorme, 2011), as well as changes in blood flow (Bierman & Scholte, 2002) and changes in heart rate (McCraty, Atkinson, & Bradley, 2004). For example, Bierman and Scholte (2002) found an increase in brain activity just prior to the appearance of emotive images that could not be the result of simply guessing.

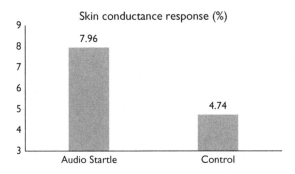

Figure 5.9 Percentage of skin conductance responses (SCR) occurring just *prior* to audio startle (left) and control (right) trials (adapted from Spottiswoode & May, 2003).

Interestingly they found a gender effect such that male participants showed the presentiment effect prior to erotic stimuli whereas female participants showed the effect prior to both erotic and violent stimuli. Radin and Borges (2009) also found presentiment effects when looking at eye movements prior to exposing participants to either an emotive stimulus or a neutral one. They reported that pupillary dilation and spontaneous eye blinking were significantly higher prior to emotive stimuli compared to calm controls. Interestingly they found that such effects were more robust for females compared to males. Spottiswoode and May (2003) also found evidence of a presentiment effect when using an audio startle stimulus, which was a 1 second burst of white noise at 97 decibels. Here participants were randomly presented with either an audio startle sound or no sound, as a control. They found a significantly higher level of SCRs prior to the audio startle trials compared to the non-startle control trials (see Figure 5.9).

May and colleagues went on to replicate this effect and ruled out a number of potential artefacts that may have influenced the data (May et al., 2005). However, they did suggest that a possible alternative may be that the experimenter utilises a form of psi to set up and initiate the trials to exhibit the effect. Though they admit that such an idea is speculative, it could account for trials that are not randomly presented.

It should be noted however that not everyone has been able to elicit such presentiment effects (Schönwetter, Ambach, & Vaitl, 2011). For instance, Siller, Ambach and Vaitl (2015) examined a range of physiological measures including EDA, respiration and heart rate variability (HRV) and found no evidence of presentiment effects. However, the design of their study was very different from the more typical presentiment studies utilised by Radin and colleagues and involved participants carrying out a mock theft and then being interviewed about the items they had taken. The participants were instructed to lie during this phase and the assumption was that physiological responses should have been evident when they were asked about items they had stolen compared to items not stolen. Broughton (2004), however, utilised a paradigm that was similar to other presentiment research measuring changes in SCR levels to emotionally arousing stimuli and found no evidence of a presentiment effect. Nevertheless, Broughton (2004) did point out that the lack of a presentiment effect could have been due to insufficient contrast between the emotive stimuli and the control stimuli. This would certainly be consistent with others who have only found precognitive effects for highly emotive stimuli (e.g., Maier et al., 2014).

The positive findings outlined above would strongly support the notion that presentiment effects are real. However, as the researchers themselves suggest, it is possible that these effects could more easily be accounted for by a subtle but ordinary form of activity (Spottiswoode & May, 2003). For instance, the effect may have occurred because of some form of cueing, that is, subtle cues may have occurred that would inform the participant that the next trial contains a target stimulus. Alternatively, it could be the result of expectation, that is, the participant shows a physiological change over time as expectation of a possible target builds up, or it may have been due to programming errors, or even fraud. However, researchers are aware of these possibilities and many have examined their data for any evidence of such alternative explanations. For instance, Bierman and Scholte (2002) argued that the differences they find between the presentiment effects that occur as a function of erotic and violent stimuli would argue against simple expectation or cue-based effects. Furthermore, others reporting positive presentiment effects have specifically examined their data to ascertain whether such effects could be the result of expectation, sensory cues, hardware or software artefacts, inappropriate analysis or fraud, and find no evidence to support such ideas (Mossbridge et al., 2014; Radin, 2004; Spottiswoode & May, 2003). Moreover, if presentiment effects were the result of an order effect then a negative correlation between study effect size and number of trials would be expected. When trial data was examined with this idea in mind no such relationship was found (Mossbridge & Radin, 2018; Mossbridge et al., 2014). Mossbridge and Radin (2018) also point out that an over-concerned focus on possible Type I errors could lead to an inflated Type II error rate. This could mean rejecting effects that are in fact real, which they argue is just as serious a problem. To help deal with this they recommend that all future studies pre-register their experiments and predictions/hypotheses in advance with one of the online data sharing sites (e.g., Psi Open Data or Koestler Parapsychology Unit).

Overall, the findings from presentiment studies have led Radin (2004) to argue that there is clear evidence of a small but robust form of precognition evident in the human autonomic nervous system. Such a view is supported by meta-analyses all showing significant evidence of a presentiment effect using both frequentist and Bayesian analyses (Duggan & Tressoldi, 2018; Mossbridge, Tressoldi, & Utts, 2012; Tressoldi, 2011). These positive effects have led some to suggest that the focus of research should shift away from concentrating on evidence-based research to exploring the potential applications of such effects. Indeed, some have suggested that such presentiment effects could be harnessed via computerised applications to avoid possible accidents when driving or in the military where quickly taking cover in advance of an explosion could be life-saving (Duma, Mento, Manari, Martinelli, & Tressoldi, 2017; Khoshnoud, de Silva, & Esat, 2015; Mossbridge et al., 2014). For example, Duma et al. (2017) recorded participants' brain activity via EEG whilst they watched a driving simulation exercise that had two possible random endings. The first was a crash scenario in which the video simulated a crash with a car coming in the opposite direction. The second contained no crash and simply ended with the cue 'Journey terminated without accidents' (p. 4). The researchers found that analysis of participants' EEG showed greater negativity occurring in the fronto-central regions approximately 1000ms prior to the car crash occurring in the former trials. This led them to suggest that the brain may be able to predict future random events. Such a process, they argue, would allow for more adaptive and efficient behaviour and from an evolutionary point of view could aid in the likelihood of survival. They take this idea a step further and speculate that in future, cars, among other machines, may be linked more intimately with the brain of the driver and if such presentiment effects are able to be extracted from the brain prior to the event occurring it could have dramatic safety implications. For example, software linked to the physiology of the driver could provide feedback when such presentiment effects occur, providing a potential warning of possible forthcoming danger and/or engaging an automatic safety override.

Dream precognition

Dreaming about future events has been suggested to occur quite frequently with surveys showing up to 38% of those responding indicating that they have experienced at least one precognitive dream (Haraldsson, 1985; Thalbourne, 1994) and this prevalence rate rises to over 50% when student populations are sampled (Schredl, 2009), with women more likely to believe in the reality of precognitive dreams and report them (Valasek & Watt, 2015). However, running a sleep lab with all the equipment and research staff usually involved is both expensive and logistically intensive. A more realistic and potentially useful procedure is to allow the dreamer to sleep at home as normal and attempt to dream of a particular target that they *will* be shown at a later date. Upon waking in the morning, the dreamer may be required to transcribe the content of their dreams and then later attempt to match them to the target. If matched this would be scored as a hit, if not it would be a miss. This approach is often referred to as a *dream diary* procedure (Schredl, Götz, & Ehrhardt-Knutsen, 2010; Watt, Valasek, & Donald, 2015). In an initial pilot study, Schredl et al. (2010) asked participants to dream about a short film they would see later (i.e., the target) and keep a dream diary for that week. At the end of the week, participants were randomly allocated to either Group A or Group B, and each group viewed a different film. The film shown to Group A was labelled Film A; and Group B's film was labelled Film B. Rather than provide a narrative description of their dreams participants were given response sheets which contained a number of randomly ordered categories (e.g., sword fighting, Buddhism) along with positive (e.g., happiness, feeling at ease) and negative (e.g., being trapped, anxiety) emotions and asked to indicate which of the categories they felt most applied to their dreams. The rationale for this was that if participants' dreams contained any precognitive insights of the future target film then Group A would select more categories and emotive content related to Film A compared to Film B, and Group B would report more content consistent with Film B than Film A. Using the responses Schredl et al. (2010) were able to accurately predict which of the two films the participants were later shown. This led them to conclude that precognition was evident in the dreams of the participants in the seven days prior to seeing the target film. A similar pattern of precognitive dreaming was reported by Watt (2014) who conducted an online dream precognition study which required participants to dream each night of a target video clip that they would be shown later. Following their dream collection period participants were required to send transcripts of their dreams to a blind external judge who viewed the transcript along with the target video and three decoys. The judge ranked how similar the transcript was to each video using a ranking system from 1 (most similar) to 4 (least similar). If a rank of 1 was given to the designated target this was considered a 'hit'. Watt (2014) found that the dream precognition hit rate was significantly higher than would be expected by chance. Initially this led her to argue that the data supported the idea that dream precognition could occur. However, a post hoc analysis showed that there seemed to be nothing distinctly unique about the video clips that were classified as hits compared to misses, which was taken to indicate that the effect could have been due to some other non-specific factor. Furthermore, attempts to replicate the effects using participants who reported prior precognitive dream experience failed to elicit any effect (Watt, Vuillaume, & Wiseman, 2015). However, there were methodological differences in the way dream content was captured and the identification of targets which may have influenced the outcome. As such, future research may more fruitfully adopt a methodology that more closely mirrors that of Schredl et al. (2010).

Non-human animal precognition

In principle, if precognitive effects are real there is no reason to suspect they should be limited to humans. It may well be the case that all conscious living organisms are able to exhibit them. If so, the expectation would be that non-human animals could also produce a physiological and/or behavioural response to a target stimulus prior to it appearing. The literature on precognition by non-human animals is scant but has provided some intriguing findings. For instance, Alvarez (2010) presented Bengalese finches with either a video clip that contained the image of a slowly crawling snake appearing at random times (i.e., target) or a clip that did not contain the snake (i.e., control) and compared the finches' displays of alarm at time points *prior* to the target appearing. He argued that, given the snake was a natural predator, the birds would be expected to exhibit physiological and behavioural characteristics of alarm and that these could be assessed for possible presentiment effects by examining the alarm rates *prior to* image exposure. When this was done Alvarez (2010) found that the birds produced significantly more alarm type reactions, up to 9 seconds before the image of the snake appeared (see Figure 5.10).

Such data clearly shows that the birds exhibited a greater number of alarm responses prior to the target appearing which is suggestive of precognition. Alvarez (2010) points out that the ability of any species to anticipate the presence of a predator would increase their chances of survival and hence confer an evolutionary benefit that could be favoured by natural selection processes. A similar pattern was also reported by Alvarez (2016) when he examined the behaviour of planarian worms that were exposed to random audio startle stimuli. When exposing the worms to either an audio startle or silent control trial he found that the worms produced significantly more head movements, indicative of distress, prior to the startle trial. The results, he suggested, demonstrate that planarian worms are, to a limited extent, able to anticipate future events.

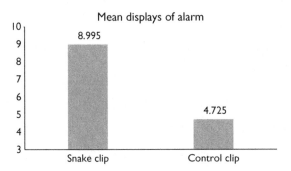

Figure 5.10 The mean number of Bengalese finches' displays of alarm prior to a target video clip containing a snake (left) and a control clip (right) when no snake was evident (adapted from Alvarez, 2010).

These findings from non-human animals show that precognitive effects are not limited to humans. They also counter the idea that the effects are simply the result of an expectation effect. It is unlikely that either the birds or worms used in these studies had much of a conscious understanding of what was occurring and as such their level of expectation of a target stimulus occurring is unlikely to account for the pattern seen in the data.

Mediating factors

The aim of understanding which factors influence precognitive performance would be to ensure that future research consider such points in order to elicit the most robust effects possible. However, the findings are ambiguous and may be influenced by a range of other additional factors such as the explicit or implicit nature of the task as well as the range of alternative responses allowed or required. For instance, a recent meta-analysis exploring potential factors that may be associated with more robust performance on forced-choice precognition tasks found six key aspects (Zdrenka & Wilson, 2017). There was a small but significant relationship between precognitive performance and greater belief in luck, belief in psi, openness to experience, perceptual defensiveness (i.e., greater awareness of surroundings) and extraversion. With a small negative relationship between better precognitive performance and the view that time is more fixed than dynamic. Zdrenka and Wilson (2017, p. 23) suggest that what underlies these various factors is the idea of remaining 'open minded, curious, social and intuitive'.

Others have suggested that there are benefits to selectively recruiting individuals with prior experience and/or prior test performance (Haraldsson, 1970; Honorton & Ferrari, 1989; Schmidt, 1969). Bierman and Bijl (2014) have also suggested that thinking style could influence precognitive performance. To test this idea they compared the precognitive effects of *intuitive* versus *rationale* thinkers. Thinking style was measured using the Human Information Processing (HIP) survey (Taggart & Torrance, 1984). This is claimed to assess processing preference in terms of favouring the left hemisphere, right hemisphere, or adopting a more integrative approach and using both. Bierman and Bijl (2014) found evidence of a precognitive priming effect when asking participants to select a shape that would *later* be identified as a target. Interestingly they found this effect only for those in the group who were identified as *intuitive* thinkers. Those identified as *rational* thinkers did not show any precognitive effects. The researchers argued that this may be because rational thinkers adopt a rigid style of information processing which could hamper potential psi effects, whereas the intuitive thinker remains more open and flexible which would allow psi to reveal itself. Others have found that precognitive effects tend to be more robust when the delay between the precognitive test and the future exposure is shorter (Honorton & Ferrari, 1989; Mossbridge et al., 2014; Steinkamp et al., 1998). This would suggest that such precognitive effects may be short lived. However, it may be that multiple repetitions of the target stimulus in the future could offset such declining effects. In terms of the specific targets used there is some evidence to suggest that using images that have a high emotional content may be better at eliciting pre-cognitive effects (Bierman & Scholte, 2002; Lobach, 2009; Maier et al., 2014; Radin, 2004). Though it should be noted that precognitive effects have been reported with a wide range of stimuli including words (Radin & May, 2001; Vernon, 2015), sounds (Spottiswoode & May, 2003) and even found in games (Franklin & Schooler, 2011; Vernon & Ivencevic, 2018). In terms of providing feedback to participants regarding the outcome of their trials the findings are mixed. Some suggest that providing feedback can facilitate precognition (Honorton & Ferrari, 1989; Stenikamp, et al., 1998), whilst others have found robust effects without providing any feedback (Bem, 2011; Vernon, 2018). In addition, claims suggesting that the provision of a reward may facilitate precognition have gained little empirical support (Luke & Morin, 2014; Luke, Roe, et al., 2008; Vernon, 2018). Finally, some have found gender effects but only when using emotive images (Bierman & Scholte, 2002), or focusing on particular eye movements (Radin & Borges, 2009). Hence, any effect of gender may interact with both the nature of the task and the stimuli used.

Theories of precognition

The final section of the chapter focuses on some of the theories or models that have been put forward to account for precognition. For example, one intriguing idea is that an individual's conscious experience may be delayed by a second or more relative to external time and it is this reception of delayed or filtered information that accounts for the seeming precognitive effects. There is certainly support from mainstream neuroscience that the brain can exhibit changes in neural activity a few seconds before a consciously induced movement occurs (Bode et al., 2011). However, when Mossbridge et al. (2014) examined this idea they argued that such changes in neural activity and/or physiology would be expected to occur prior to all events, not only those that contain a precognitive target. In addition, they suggest that the different order of events that can occur within a precognitive paradigm make it difficult for this idea to explain presentiment responses. Other proposals put forward to specifically account for precognition include the multiphasic model of precognition and the consciousness induced restoration of time symmetry approach, both of which share certain similarities with a block universe model. At present, such models represent more a set of speculative ideas about why and how precognitive effects may occur rather than offering a detailed explanation. However, this should not be seen as problematic given our limited understanding of the nature of psi, as well as that of time and consciousness. Furthermore, attempts to model the findings of precognition may help to stimulate debate and uncover new ways to explore the phenomenon and as such should be encouraged.

Multiphasic model of precognition (MMPC)

According to Marwaha and May (2016) the problem of precognition can be separated into one relating to the physics domain and one relating to the neuroscience domain. From the physics perspective, the question they focus on is how information is transferred from the future back in time to the present. In essence, they attempt to identify the energy carrier of any future signal. Given the time symmetric equations of physics they suggest that entropy may be what provides the arrow of time (Greene, 2011). Entropy is a measure of randomness or disorder and a fundamental aspect of time is that entropy always increases. Hence, they suggest that the link between time and entropy may be reflected by a link between entropy and precognition. In essence, they propose that changes in entropy unfold over time providing a plausible candidate carrier for precognitive information. From a neuroscience perspective the question they focus on is how such information could be transduced from *entropic energy* to neural energy that could then be decoded and processed by the brain. They propose that this may be underpinned by cortical hyperconnectivity of the sort seen in individuals who exhibit synaesthesia. Synaesthesia represents an idiosyncratic variation in brain organisation whichh means the individual blends sensory experiences across modalities (Kolb, Whishaw, & Teskey, 2016). For example, a person may hear colours, feel sounds or taste shapes (Cytowic, 2002). Such multi-sensory experiences are thought to be the result of increased or hyper-connectivity between the various sensory regions of the brain. In a similar way, Marwaha and May (2016) suggest that individuals with what they refer to as cortical hyperconnectivity may be more sensitive to the environment and able to pick up information from the entropic energy, even at an unconscious level. This information would then be processed and could then possibly influence physiological responses and behaviour. Hence, the model would suggest that precognitive ability, much like synaesthesia, would be more of an inherent ability as opposed to one that could be trained. Furthermore, the model would suggest that a synaesthete, with good implicit learning skills, should exhibit stronger precognitive effects compared to a non-synaesthete. Such ideas are both interesting and speculative though it can be hoped that they may stimulate future researchers.

Consciousness induced restoration of time symmetry (CIRTS)

According to the CIRTS model time symmetry is intrinsic in all physical systems (Bierman, 2010; Bierman & Bijl, 2014). This means that, given a specific initial condition, solving the equations of time generally results in two identical solutions, one in which time can be shown to move forward and one in which time moves backward. Given that such time symmetry is fundamental some have argued that psi phenomena are both natural and should be expected as part of everyday physics

(Bierman, 1988; De Beauregard, 1998). The fundamental assumption of CIRTS is that the brain, as a self-conscious organism, represents a special system that 'restores time symmetry' and in doing so allows the future to occur. According to Bierman (2010), the consciousness-sustaining brain can partially restore the break in time symmetry, thus allowing for time-reversed processes, as evidenced by the precognitive findings outlined above. Bierman (2018) has also suggested that the more coherent the brain the stronger the time restoration effect would be which in turn may lead to a larger precognitive effect. It is not entirely clear at this time precisely what aspect of brain coherence the model refers to but it does at least lend itself to formulating some testable predictions.

Block universe model

Intriguingly, Taylor (2014) has suggested that precognition would be consistent with a block universe account which suggests that information transfer may be influenced by the phase synchrony of brain states at the two times. That is, a resonance may occur between the spatiotemporal neuronal network that encodes the original stimuli and the one that is used to process it again at a later date. The assumption is that this overlap, or match, in neural network patterns leads to a greater coherence which in turn could produce a greater activation of the original network leading to a greater level of recall. The greater level of resonance between the neural network of the present and the future is proposed as the basis for precognition in the here and now. In essence, the information is transferred from the future brain to the present brain of the same person. This idea bears certain similarities to theories suggesting that precognition may rely on non-local quantum self-correlates of the brain at different time points (e.g., Sheehan & Cyrus, 2018; von Lucadou, 2018). Such a proposal is necessarily speculative given our current understanding of the nature of time and consciousness. However, it is interesting to note that recent research examining the neural connectivity of parent-child dyads has shown associations between the level of neural connectivity and complex emotions of both parent and child (Lee, Miernicki, & Telaer, 2017). Furthermore, whilst the proposal that neural phase synchrony over time may mediate precognition is necessarily speculative it does at least offer a potential mechanism that can be tested.

Overview

Precognition generally refers to the notion that an individual obtains information about a future event via a non-normal route. This information could then influence present behaviour, albeit consciously, as a flash of insight, or unconsciously as an autonomic response. The idea that it may be possible to catch a glimpse of the future raises certain paradoxes and challenges our everyday perceptions of the nature of time. However, the fact that the equations of time are symmetrical means that such findings do not represent a fundamental challenge to the current understanding of the underlying physics of time. It may also be that such flashes of insight are glimpses into possible futures as opposed to actual futures and hence free will remains viable as present behaviour may or may not be influenced by such future outcomes. Though some have raised the idea that precognition is the *only* form of psi, the evidence for this is not robust. Nevertheless, experimental research has developed a range of explicit, implicit and dream type paradigms to elicit and assess precognition. At present, it is not clear whether these methods are tapping different types of precognition or simply represent the same underlying processes. Overall, the evidence for explicit type paradigms is less robust than that found for implicit paradigms, which have shown small but reliable effect sizes across a range of implicit tasks. Intriguingly, the evidence is particularly substantial for physiological presentiment effects. So much so that some have begun to examine potential applications for these autonomic responses and this could represent a very useful future avenue of research. Dream precognition, utilising a procedure where dreamers are allowed to sleep in their own homes, also shows some encouraging findings and is logistically less resource intensive than lab-based dream research. The positive precognitive findings from non-human animals are particularly interesting as they provide support for the idea that such effects are generic across all conscious organisms and counter the notion that they are the result of expectation effects. In terms of mediating factors that might help facilitate such precognitive effects it seems that recruiting those with an open mind who have exhibited some prior psi ability and keeping the delay between exposure and test may be helpful. Other factors that have been suggested to benefit performance include the type of target, the possibility of a reward and the necessity of feedback, though the evidence for the influence of these is ambiguous. In terms of theoretical accounts, a primary assumption seems to be that some form of information is transferred from the future to the present. Possible mechanisms for this include changes in entropic energy and a high level of cortical self-correlations at two distinct time points. Overall, there is a substantial amount of evidence to suggest that an individual can obtain some insights or influences from the future. Nevertheless, how such a process occurs remains at present the domain of future research.

Reflective questions

Some questions that may prove helpful when reflecting on the material covered in this chapter.

- Have you ever had a precognitive experience – if so how would you account for it?
- Do you think precognition could be an evolutionary adaptive trait?
- Do you think the different types of precognition represent different aspects of psi?
- Do you think we have a full understanding of the nature of time or consciousness?
- Given the findings for presentiment what other applications of this can you think of?
- What, if any, are the benefits of testing precognition using non-human animals?
- What model or theory do you think would best account for precognition?
- What would you expect a model or theory of precognition to look like?

References

Alvarez, F. (2010). Anticipatory alarm behaviour in Bengalese finches. *Journal of Scientific Exploration*, *24*(4), 599–610.

Alvarez, F. (2016). An experiment on precognition with planarian worms. *Journal of Scientific Exploration*, *30*(2), 217–226.

Andreassi, J. L. (2000). *Psychophysiology: Human behaviour and physiological response* (4 edn). Mahwah, NJ: Lawrence Erlbaum.

Baruss, I., & Rabier, V. (2014). Failure to replicate retrocausal recall. *Psychology of Consciousness: Theory, Research and Practice*, *1*(1), 82–91.

Baumgart, S. L., Franklin, M. S., Jimbo, H. K., Su, S. J., & Schooler, J. (2017). *Prediction of truly random future events using analysis of prestimulus electroencehpalographic data*. Paper presented at the AIP Conference Proceedings.

Bem, D. J. (2011). Feeling the future: Experimental evidence for anomalous retroactive influences on cognition and affect. *Journal of Personality and Social Psychology*, *100*, 407–425.

Bem, D. J., Tressoldi, P., Rabeyron, T., & Duggan, M. (2015). Feeling the future: A meta-analysis of 90 experiments on the anomalous anticipation of random future events. *F1000 Research*, *4*, 1–33. doi: 10.12688/f1000research.7177.2.

Bierman, D. J. (1988). A world with retrocausation. *Systematica*, *6–7*, 45–54.

Bierman, D. J. (2010). Consciousness induced restoration of time symmetry (CIRTS). A psychophysical theoretical perspective. *Journal of Parapsychology*, *24*, 273–300.

Bierman, D. J. (2018). Consciousness-induced restoration of time-symmetry (CIRTS). *Mindfield*, *10*(3), 103–108.

Bierman, D. J., & Bijl, A. (2014). Anomalous retrocausal effects on performance in a go/nogo task. *Journal of Scientific Exploration*, *28*(3), 437–452.

Bierman, D. J., & Radin, D. (1997). Anomalous anticipatory response on randomized future conditions. *Perceptual and Motor Skills*, *84*, 689–690.

Bierman, D. J., & Scholte, H. S. (2002). A fMRI brain imaging study of presentiment. *Journal of International Society of Life Information Science*, *20*(2), 380–388.

Bode, S., He, A. H., Soon, C. S., Trampel, R., Turner, R., & Haynes, J. D. (2011). Tracking the unconscious generation of free decisions using ultra-high field fMRI. *PloS One*, *6*(6), e21612. doi: 10.1371/journal.pone.0021612.

Bornstein, R. F. (1989). Exposure and affect: Overview and meta-analysis of research, 1968–1987. *Psychological Bulletin*, *106*(2), 265.

Briggs, G. A. D., Butterfield, J. N., & Zeilinger, A. (2013). The Oxford questions on the foundations of quantum physics. *Proceedings of the Royal Society A: Mathematical, Physical and Engineering Sciences*, *469*(2157). doi: 10.1098/rspa.2013.0299.

Broughton, R. S. (2004). *Exploring the reliabiltiy of the presentiment effect*. Paper presented at the The Parapsychological Association Convention.

Brown, S. C., & Craik, F. I. M. (2000). Encoding and retrieval of information. In E. Tulving & F. I. M. Craik (Eds.), *The Oxford handbook of memory* (pp. 93–107). New York: Oxford University Press.

Cytowic, R. E. (2002). *Synaesthesia: A union of the senses*. Cambridge: MIT Press.

De Beauregard, O. C. (1998). The paranormal is not excluded from physics. *Journal of Scientific Exploration*, *12*, 315–320.

Duggan, M., & Tressoldi, P. (2018). Predictive physiological anticipation preceding seemingly unpredictable stimuli: An update of Mossbridge et al.'s meta-analysis. *F1000 Research*.

Duma, G. M., Mento, G., Manari, T., Martinelli, M., & Tressoldi, P. (2017). Driving with intuition: A preregistered study about the EEG anticipation of simulated random car accidents. *PloS One*, 1–15. doi: 10.1371/journal.pone.0170370.

Franklin, M. S., Baumgart, S. L., & Schooler, J. W. (2014). Future directions in precognition research: More research can bridge the gap between skeptics and proponents. *Frontiers in Psychology, 5*(907), 1–4. doi: 10.3389/fpsyg.2014.00907.

Franklin, M. S., & Schooler, J. (2011). *Using retrocausal practice effects to predict on-line roulette spins.* Paper presented at the Society for Experimental Social Psychology, Consciousness., Washington, USA.

Galak, J., LeBouf, R. A., Nelson, L. D., & Simmons, J. P. (2012). Correcting the past: Failures to replicate psi. *Journal of Personality and Social Psychology, 103*(6), 933–948. doi: 10. 1037/a0029709.

Greene, B. (2011). *The hidden reality: Parallel universes and the deep laws of the cosmos.* New York, NY: Alfred A. Knopf.

Haraldsson, E. (1970). Subject selection in a machine test precognition test. *Journal of Parapsychology, 34*(3), 182–191.

Haraldsson, E. (1985). Representative national surveys of psychic phenomena: Iceland, Great Britain, Sweden, USA and Gallup's multinational survey. *Journal of the Society for Psychical Research, 53,* 145–158.

Hitchman, G. A., Pfeuffer, C. U., Roe, C. A., & Sherwood, S. J. (2016). The effects of experimenter-participant interaction qualities in a goal-oriented nonintentional precognition task. *Journal of Parapsychology, 80*(1), 45–69.

Hitchman, G. A., Sherwood, S. J., & Roe, C. A. (2015). The relationship between latent inhibition and performance at a non-intentional precognition task. *EXPLORE, 11*(2), 118–126.

Honorton, C., & Ferrari, D. C. (1989). Future telling: A meta-analysis of forced-choice precognition experiments, 1935–1987. *Journal of Parapsychology, 53,* 281–308.

Khoshnoud, F., de Silva, C. W., & Esat, I. I. (2015). Bioinspired psi intelligent control for autonomous dynamic systems. *Control and Intelligent Systems, 43*(4), 205–211.

Kittenis, M. (2018). *Anomalous anticipatory event-related EEG activity in a face recognition memory task.* Paper presented at the 42nd SPR International Conference, Newcastle, UK.

Kolb, B., Whishaw, I. Q., & Teskey, G. C. (2016). *An introduction to brain and behaviour* (Vol. 5). New York: Worth.

Lee, T., Miernicki, M., & Telaer, E. H. (2017). Families that fire together smile together: Resting state connectome similarity and daily emotional synchrony in parent-child dyads. *Neuroimage, 152,* 31–37.

Lobach, E. (2009). Presentiment research: Past, present and future. In C. A. Roe, L. Coly, & W. Kramer (Eds.), *Utrecht II: Charting the future of parapsychology* (pp. 22–45). New York, NY: Parapsychology Foundation.

Luke, D., Delanoy, D., & Sherwood, S. J. (2008). Psi may look like luck: Perceived luckiness and beliefs about luck in relation to precognition. *Journal of the Society for Psychical Research, 72,* 193–207.

Luke, D., & Morin, S. (2014). Exploration of the validity and utility of a reward contingency in a non-intentional forced-choice precognition task. *Journal of the Society for Psychical Research, 78*(917), 207–218.

Luke, D., Roe, C. A., & Davison, J. (2008). Testing for forced-choice precognition using a hidden task: Two replications. *The Journal of Parapsychology, 72,* 133–154.

Mack, J., & Powell, L. (2005). Perceptions of non-local communication: Incidences associated with mdia consumption and individual differences. *Journal of Parapsychology, 7*(2), 279–294.

Maier, M. A., Buchner, V. L., Kuhbandner, C., Pflitsch, M., Fernandez-Capo, M., & Gamiz-Sanfeliu, M. (2014). Feeling the future again: Retroactive avoidance of negative stimuli. *Journal of Consciousness Studies, 21*(9–10), 121–152.

Marwaha, S. B., & May, E. C. (2016). Precognition: The only form of psi? *Journal of Consciousness Studies*, *23*(3–4), 76–100.

May, E. C., Paulinyi, T., & Vassy, Z. (2005). Anomalous anticipatory skin conductance response to acoustic stimlui: Experimental results and speculation about a mechanism. *Journal of Alternative and Complementary Medicine*, *11*(4), 695–702.

McCraty, R., Atkinson, M., & Bradley, R. T. (2004). Electrophysiological evidence of intuition: Part 1. The surprising role of the heart. *The Journal of Complementary Medicine*, *10*(1), 133–143. doi: 10.1089/107555304322849057.

Milton, J. (1997). Meta-analysis of free-response ESP studies without altered states of consciousness. *Journal of Parapsychology*, *61*, 279–319.

Mossbridge, J. A., & Radin, D. (2018). Precognition as a from of prospection: A review of the evidence. *Psychology of Consciousness: Theory, Research and Practice*, *5*(1), 78–93. doi: 10.1037/cns0000121.

Mossbridge, J. A., Tressoldi, P., & Utts, J. (2012). Predictive physiological anticipation preceding seemingly unpredictable stimuli: A meta-analysis. *Frontiers in Psychology*, *3*, 390. doi: 10.3389/fpsyg.2012.00390.

Mossbridge, J. A., Tressoldi, P., Utts, J., Ives, J. A., & Radin, D. (2014). Predicting the unpredictable: critical analysis and practical implications of predictive anticipatory activity. *Frontiers in Human Neuroscience*, *8*(146), 1–10. doi: 10.3389/fnhum.2014.00146.

Parker, A., & Sjoden, B. (2010). Do some of us habituate to future emotional events? *Journal of Parapsychology*, *74*(1), 99–115.

Radin, D. (1997). Unconscious perception of future emotions: An experiment in presentiment. *Journal of Scientific Exploration*, *11*, 163–180.

Radin, D. (2004). Electrodermal presentiments of future emotion. *Journal of Scientific Exploration*, *18*(2), 253–273.

Radin, D. (2017). Unorthodox forms of anticipation. In M. Nadin (Ed.), *Anticipation and Medicine* (pp. 281–292). Switzerland: Springer International.

Radin, D., & Borges, A. (2009). Intuition through time: What does the seer see? *Explore*, *5*(4), 200–211. doi: 10.1016/j.explore.2009.04.002.

Radin, D., & May, E. C. (2001). *Evidence for a retrocausal effect in the human nervous system*. Paper presented at the 43rd Annual Convention of the Parapsychological Association, Columbus, OH.

Radin, D., Vieten, C., Michel, L., & Delorme, A. (2011). Electrocortical activity prior to unpredictable stimuli in meditators and nonmeditators. *EXPLORE*, *7*(5), 286–299.

Ratcliff, R., & McKoon, G. (2000). Memory models. In E. Tulving & F. I. M. Craik (Eds.), *The Oxford handbook of memory* (pp. 571–582). New York: OUP.

Rhine, J. B. (1947). *The reach of the mind*. New York: William Sloane Associates.

Rhine, L. E. (1955). Precognition and intervention. *The Journal of Parapsychology*, *19*(1), 1–34.

Ritchie, S. J., Wiseman, R., & French, C. C. (2012). Failing the future: Three unsuccessful attempts to replicate Bem's retroactive facilitation of recall effect. *PloS One*, *7*(3), e33423.

Roediger, H. L., Buckner, R. L., & McDermott, K. B. (1999). Components of processing. In J. K. Foster & M. Jelicic (Eds.), *Memory: systems, process or function?* (pp. 31–65). Oxford: University Press.

Savva, L., Child, R., & Smith, M. D. (2004). *The precognitie habituation effect: An adaptation using spider stimuli*. Paper presented at the The Parapsychological Association Convention.

Schacter, D. L., & Tulving, E. (1994). *Memory systems*. Cambridge, MA: MIT Press.

Schmidt, H. (1969). Precognition of a quantum process. *Journal of Parapsychology*, *33*, 99–108.

Schönwetter, T., Ambach, W., & Vaitl, D. (2011). Does autonomic nervous system activity correlate with events conventionally considered as unperceivable? Using a guessing task with physiological measurement. *Journal of Parapsychology*, *75*(2), 327.

Schredl, M. (2009). Frequency of precognitive dreams: Association with dream recall and personality variables. *Journal of the Society for Psychical Research*, 73, 83–91.

Schredl, M., Götz, S., & Ehrhardt-Knutsen, S. (2010). Precognitive dreams: A pilot diary study. *Journal of the Society for Psychical Research*, 74(900), 168–175.

Sheehan, D. P. (2006). *Retrocausation and the thermodynamic arrow of time*. Paper presented at the AIP Conference Proceedings.

Sheehan, D. P. (2015). Rememberance of things future: A case for retrocausation and precognition. In E. C. May & S. B. Marwaha (Eds.), *Extrasensory perception: Support, skepticism and science* (pp. 85–109). Santa Barbara, CA: Praeger/ABC-CLIO.

Sheehan, D. P., & Cyrus, P. C. (2018). The thermodynamic retrocausal (TDRC) model of precognition. *Mindfield*, 10(3), 98–102.

Siller, A., Ambach, W., & Vaitl, D. (2015). Investigating expectation effects using multiple physiological measures. *Frontiers in Psychology*, 6(1553), 1–14. doi: 10.3389/fpsyg.2015.01553.

Spottiswoode, J. P., & May, E. C. (2003). Skin conductance prestimulus response: Analysis, artifacts and a pilot study. *Journal of Scientific Exploration*, 17(4), 617–641.

Steinkamp, F., Milton, J., & Morris, R. L. (1998). A meta-analysis of forced-choice experiments comparing clairvoyance and precognition. *Journal of Parapsychology*, 62, 193–218.

Storm, L., Tressoldi, P., & Di Risio, L. (2012). Meta-analysis of ESP studies, 1987–2010: Assessing the success of the forced-choice design in parapsychology. *Journal of Parapsychology*, 76(2), 243–273.

Subbotsky, E. (2013). Sensing the future: Reversed causality or a non-standard observer effect? *The Open Psychology Journal*, 6, 81–93.

Sutherland, R. I. (2017). How retrocausality helps. *American Institute of Physics Conference Proceedings*, 1841(1), 020001.

Taggart, W., & Torrance, E. (1984). *Administrator's manual for the Human Information Processing survey*. Bensenville, IL: Scholastic Testing Service.

Taylor, J. (2014). The nature of precognition. *Journal of Parapsychology*, 78(1), 19–38.

Thalbourne, M. A. (1994). The SPR centenary census: II. The survey of beliefs and experiences. *Journal of the Society for Psychical Research*, 59, 420–431.

Traxler, M. J., Foss, D. J., Podali, R., & Zirnstein, M. (2012). Feeling the past: The absence of experimental evidence for anomalous retroactive influences on text processing. *Memory and Cognition*, 40, 1366–1372. doi: 10.3758/s13421-012-0232-2.

Tressoldi, P. (2011). Extraordinary claims require extraordinary evidence: The case of non-local perception, a classical and Bayesian review of the evidence. *Frontiers in Psychology*, 2(117), 1–5. doi: 10.3389/fpsyg.2011.00117.

Valasek, M., & Watt, C. (2015). Individual differences in prophetic dream belief and experience: Exploring demographic and sleep-related correlates. *Personality and Individual Differences*, 87, 65–69. doi: 10.1016/j.paid.2015.07.028.

Vernon, D. (2015). Exploring precognition using a repetition priming paradigm. *Journal of the Society for Psychical Research*, 79(919), 65–79.

Vernon, D. (2017a). Attempting to elicit a precall effect using emotive images and participants with high levels of belief in psi. *Journal of Consciousness Studies*, 24(11–12), 216–237.

Vernon, D. (2017b). Exploring precall using arousing images and utilising a memory recall practise task on-line. *Journal of the Society for Psychical Research*, 81(2), 65–79.

Vernon, D. (2018). A test of reward contingent precall. *Journal of Parapsychology*, 82(1), 8–23.

Vernon, D., & Ivencevic, L. (2018). *Testing precognition using a novel computer driving game*. Paper presented at the 42nd International SPR Annual Conference, Newcastle Upon Tyne.

von Lucadou, W. (2018). The model of pragmatic information (MPI) and generalized quantum theory. *Mindfield*, 10(3), 109–115.

Wagenmakers, E., Wetzels, R., Borsboom, D., & van der Maas, H. L. (2011). Why psychologists must change the way they analyze their data: The case of psi: Comment on Bem (2011). *Journal of Personality and Social Psychology, 100*(3), 426–432.

Watt, C. (2014). Precognitive dreaming: Investigating anomalous cognition and psychological factors. *Journal of Parapsychology, 78*(1), 115–125.

Watt, C., Valasek, M., & Donald, E. (2015). *Precognitive dreaming: A replication study using an innovative and efficient diary checklist method*. Paper presented at the 39th SPR International Annual Conference, Greenwich, UK.

Watt, C., Vuillaume, L., & Wiseman, R. (2015). Dream precognition and sensory incorporation: A controlled sleep laboratory study. *Journal of Consciousness Studies, 22*(5–6), 172–190.

Zajonc, R. B. (1968). Attitudinal effects of mere exposures. *Journal of Personality and Social Psychology, 9*(2), 1–27.

Zdrenka, M., & Wilson, M. S. (2017). Individual difference correlates of psi performance in forced-choice precognition experiments: A meta-analysis. *Journal of Parapsychology, 81*(1), 9–32.

Chapter 6

Psychokinesis

Many people have probably imagined themselves staring at a distant object, such as their mug of hot coffee, and simply by thought alone willing it to lift and float across to their outstretched hand. Such ideas are prevalent in modern science fiction films where both heroes and villains display astonishing levels of mind control over items large and small. This ability or aspect of psi behaviour is referred to as psychokinesis (PK) and is the focus of this chapter. The chapter begins with a brief definition and outline of psychokinesis and then moves on to explore the three main areas of research. First is the field of macro PK which ranges from the early spirit raps and table levitations to the more recent findings using spinning mobiles. This is followed by an exploration of micro PK research which focuses on human and non-human animal intentions to influence the output of random generators. The chapter then examines an area of PK research that focuses on the direct mental influence on living systems. This includes changes in human physiology, the notion of remote helping as well as attempts made to influence animal behaviour. The chapter ends by briefly exploring some factors thought to influence PK performance and possible mechanisms for such effects.

Psychokinesis

The word 'psychokinesis' stems from the words psyche, relating to 'of the mind' and kinesis referring to 'movement'. Hence, it literally refers to the ability of the mind to influence or move a distant physical object or organism by conscious intention alone. According to Kennedy (1978) it should be viewed as a goal oriented process in the sense that it is thought to emerge to help the individual achieve their goals. The idea of using the mind to control or move an object with thought alone has been around a long time. Early researchers referred to it as *mental suggestion* (Vasiliev, 1963) and since then others have referred to it as *mind over matter* (Rhine & Rhine, 1943), *expressive psi* (Roll, 2003), *telekinesis* (Dullin & Jamet, 2018) and *anomalous perturbation* (Vilenskaya & May, 1994). Some have even suggested that a more cautious label be used such as *mind-matter correlations* which does not postulate any direct causal link between conscious intention and the action but merely suggests that they occur together (Grote, 2015).

Belief in PK is evident but limited. For example, in a survey by Palmer (1979) examining reported psychic experiences, of those that responded, 7% claimed to have seen an object move without any known mechanism. Furthermore, in a 1991 poll conducted in America, of those that responded, 17% of American adults believed in the ability of the mind to move or influence an object using mental energy alone (Gallup & Newport, 1991). However, it is not clear at present whether PK is distinct from general psi abilities, and/or whether the three main areas of PK research each represent a distinct aspect of the phenomenon or whether there is something fundamentally typical underlying the process and/or ability to levitate a table as well as influence the outcome of a random device (Braude, 2015; S. Schmidt, 2015; Varvoglis & Bancel, 2015, 2016). It may be that these differences simply reflect the labels given to the various methodologies used rather than some fundamental difference in the nature of the effect.

Macro PK

Research focusing on macro PK effects generally involves the attempted movement of larger, more clearly visible objects. In a sense this may be one of the least controversial areas of PK research as observers would be expected to agree if an object were to move without any normal physical interaction. Such a result would not rely on or require statistical interpretation which should lead to a clear agreement on the outcome. Indeed, Dullin and Jamet (2018) highlight such points as incentives for conducting research in this area. Macro PK research includes the findings from physical mediums, the early laboratory work of Rhine, the case studies of exceptional individuals and the effect of PK on spinning mobiles.

Spirit manifestations

It has long been documented that physical mediums have been alleged to produce apports, materialisations and movement of distant objects without any physical interaction (Braude, 1986). An apport refers to the paranormal transference of an article from one place to another, or the appearance of an item from an unknown source that is often associated with poltergeist activity or spiritualistic séances. Object movements also include table tipping and levitations (Batcheldor, 1966). According to Alvarado (2006) this form of psychic force, which is assumed to emanate from the body of the physical medium, represents an example of macro PK. The idea is that it is the conscious intention of the medium that produces or elicits such physical phenomena. Over time there have been some intriguing reports based on individuals and groups. Prominent individual cases reporting evidence of macro PK effects include that of D. D. Home, who was alleged to be able to produce musical notes from instruments sealed away in wire cages (Alvarado, 1993, 2017), the more recent Bindelof case, which included table tipping and other physical phenomena (Rosemarie Pilkington, 2006) and the so-called *Gold Leaf Lady*, which referred to a woman in Florida who allegedly manifested quantities of a golden coloured foil under bright, clear and easily observable conditions (see Box 6.1).

One group that proved controversial was identified in the Scole report which described many physical phenomena, from the sudden appearance of lights to the remote influence on sealed camera film (Keen, Ellison, & Fontana, 1999). However, whilst many interesting phenomena have been reported it is often very difficult to prove beyond reasonable doubt precisely how and why such phenomena occurred.

Box 6.1   The Case of the Gold Leaf Lady

I was seated across a table from a woman, no more than three feet away. And while we were talking, a small piece of gold-coloured foil appeared suddenly on her face. I knew that her hands were nowhere near her face when this happened. In fact, I was certain they were in full view on the table the entire time. I knew also that if her husband, seated next to her, had placed the material on her face, I would have clearly seen it. But nobody's hands had been anywhere near her face. So I knew that the material hadn't been placed there; it *appeared* there, evidently without normal assistance.

(Excerpt from Braude, 2007, p. 1, with permission)

According to Braude (2015) many recoil at the suggestion that these phenomena could be genuine, in part because of exposed fraud of some earlier cases which often casts a shadow over the area as a whole. As such, the effects from physical mediums are generally not viewed as providing much in the way of supporting evidence for PK as they often rely on human eyewitness testimony, something which is known to be less than accurate (e.g., Loftus & Palmer, 1996). Others have argued that eye-witness testimony is accepted in many other areas of life and as such it should also trusted it in this context (Murdie, 2015). Indeed, Braude (2015) suggests that it is not in fact the reliability of testimony in general that is of paramount concern but whether the best cases can satisfy conditions for reliability. Importantly, he argues that in the best of cases there is good evidence of accurate eyewitness testimony. Hence, it is not possible to simply side-step the potential PK effects produce by such physical mediums.

Alongside the effects reported from physical mediums there are many reports of alleged movement of distant objects occurring in cases of poltergeist activity. A popular interpretation of poltergeist activity is that the disturbances, when not fraud, are the result of a mischievous or boisterous spirit (Holder, 2012). However, the activity is often elusive and difficult to observe and focused around a particular individual, usually a teenager and often going through puberty or some other emotional turmoil. An interesting alternative explanation for the object movements reported in poltergeist cases is that it is a form of recurrent, spontaneous psychokinetic (RSPK) behaviour, which is a form of macro PK (Roll, 2003). According to Mischo (1968) these phenomena are often linked to or centred around a particular individual and the objects have been suggested to be substitute objects in the sense that they are closely associated with an individual who is the target of the ill feeling of the person at the centre of the RSPK events. Reported movement of distant objects has included ceramics, furniture and tools (see, Roll, 2003), though it is invariably the case that such items move without the need for anyone to focus attention on them. That is, the PK effect seems to occur unconsciously. This may fit with the suggestion by Roll (2003) that it represents a distinct form of PK as the effect is often seen to decline with increasing distance from the source, something that is not mirrored in other findings (Dunne & Jahn, 1992; Tressoldi, Pederzoli, Matteoli, Prati, & Kruth, 2016). There have been suggestions that such PK activity is associated with abnormal cortical activity in the person at the centre of the poltergeist activity (Roll & Persinger, 1998), though there is a lack of physical evidence for abnormal brain activity in people who experience such phenomena (Kruth & Joines, 2016). Nevertheless, it has been suggested that RSPK remains a strong candidate for explaining such phenomena.

Rhine's lab and dice

According to Rhine and Rhine (1943) amateur gamblers often believed that they were able to influence the fall of dice. This struck them as a simple yet effective way of testing potential PK effects by examining precisely whether participants could influence the fall of dice using intention alone. Early procedures involved an individual rolling a pair of dice either by hand or using some form of mechanical thrower. The objective of this early research was to have participants attempt to cause a single dice to land with a particular face up, such as 3 or 6. However, a problem identified when using single dice is that the probability of obtaining a specific number is not equally distributed across all faces of the dice because the side with the six, often identified by six pips cut into the dice, means that this side has the least mass and as such is more likely to land face up. To some extent this could be addressed by using more than one die and asking participants to roll a set number, such as 11, or have the pair of dice come up 'high', that is with both faces totalling above a specific number (Rhine & Rhine, 1943). They would then complete several runs and their success rates could be compared to chance. According to such early work participants were able to produce more high scores than would be expected by chance (Rhine & Rhine, 1943). Rhine (1970) also used this approach to test whether participants could obtain a number higher than 7 and then later repeated the study but had the participants try to score less than 7. Both times, above chance performance was obtained. Such findings led to the tentative conclusion that PK was occurring though the researchers stressed the need and importance of extensive repetitions to corroborate such effects. Later methodological refinements included the use of better-quality dice, that were more precisely balanced, as well as mechanical spinning devices used to provide a more objective manipulation and release of the dice.

Since the beginning of such research a number of studies have been conducted attempting to elicit such macro PK effects. To obtain an overview of the findings researchers have since relied on meta-analyses. However, these have not always produced consistent results. For instance, a meta-analysis of 148 experimental studies that took place between 1935 and 1987, controlling for the potential dice face bias, still showed a significant effect of PK on the fall of the dice, indicating that the dice fell with the face showing that was intended more often than would be expected by chance (Radin & Ferrari, 1991). Radin and Ferrari (1991) argued that the effect cannot be accounted for in terms of experimenter artefact, statistical outliers or methodological quality of the study, which led them to conclude that the evidence suggests a weak but genuine effect is present. This led some to argue that the evidence for macro PK effects is both clearer and more compelling than that found for micro PK effects (Braude, 2015). However, a meta-analysis by others argued that the effects could more easily be accounted for in terms of a publication bias (Bosch, Steinkamp, & Boller, 2006a). Though, as Henry (2005) points out, to cancel out such a positive effect would require approximately

18,000 unreported studies with null findings, which she argues is almost impossible as there are insufficient researchers in the field to conduct such work. Others agree that selective reporting is unlikely to account for such phenomena and argue that there is a genuine PK effect (Radin, Nelson, Dobyns, & Houtkooper, 2006).

Exceptional individuals

The dice studies outlined above often relied upon opportunity sampling, which would suggest that PK, if real, may well exist in the population at large. However, Braude (2016) has suggested that if this is the case then, much like any other skill, there may be those who have an exceptional level of PK. Over time a few of these exceptional individuals have emerged to demonstrate seemingly extraordinary levels of PK skill. They include Nina Kulagina, Felicia Parise, Uri Geller and Ted Serios. It is worth examining such individual cases as they may be able to shed light on the broader issues relating to PK ability in general.

Probably one of the most notable cases of an individual exhibiting exceptional macro PK ability is that of the Russian woman Nina Kulagina. Kulagina was studied for her ability to move small objects and deflect compass needles and researchers at the time suggested that her abilities appeared genuine. Indeed, a series of experiments with Kulagina found her able to move a hydrometer inside a tumbler, influence radiometers placed side by side and deviate a compass needle by up to 70° (Cassirer, 1974; Keil, Herbert, Ullman, & Pratt, 1976; Pratt & Keil, 1973). Kulagina was also reported to be able to alter her heart rate and the concentrated level of energy required to complete such tasks often resulted in her suffering significant weight loss (Henry, 2005). Unfortunately, due to lack of support from the Russian authorities at the time, investigations of Kulagina's alleged abilities often took place in her home or in a hotel room with far from ideal controls. Nevertheless, some have suggested that such behaviours were seen and filmed without any apparent trickery (Irwin & Watt, 2007).

Such findings were reported to have inspired the American Felicia Parise to train herself to move small objects, such as the needle of a compass, under controlled conditions (R. Pilkington, 2015; Watkins & Watkins, 1973). According to Honorton (1993) Parise was able to move small pill bottles and compass needles. In an interview with Pilkington (2015) Parise recounts being able to move a small plastic bottle that she used for keeping her eyelashes in simply by focused intention. According to Pilkington (2015) she did this by relaxing her mind and visualising the bottle moving. Interestingly, Parise also reported that such attempts required a lot of effort.

No chapter on PK would be complete without some mention of the now infamous Uri Geller and his claims to bend spoons and fix watches and clocks. Geller's claims and his demonstrations generated much interest in the idea that the mind could exert power over matter (see, Targ & Puthoff, 1977). Opinion remains mixed in terms of whether the claims made by Geller are genuine or not and the authenticity of his performances is still debated. Some have suggested that Geller prefers the more lucrative television appearances to the more rigorous scientific studies (Irwin & Watt, 2007). Nevertheless, rigorous attempts to monitor the bending of metal strips sealed in glass tubes or observe the changes in electrical resistance as a metal strip is bent have produced some positive evidence. For example, Randall and Davis (1982)

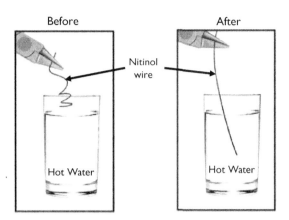

Figure 6.1 Nitinol wire that has been bent out of shape (left), and when heated in hot water regains its original shape (right).

reported that Geller was able to permanently alter a piece of nitinol wire that had been treated to ensure it remained straight simply by stroking it. Nitinol is a type of alloy that once treated is able to retain a unique shape memory such that after any deformation if it is exposed to heat will recover its original shape (see Figure 6.1). Interestingly, attempts to straighten the wire Geller had bent using heat failed. The suggestion was that PK had been used to destroy the shape memory held within the nitinol wire.

A lot of interest was also generated by the American psychic Ted Serios, who demonstrated the apparent ability to project an image on to photographic film using conscious intention alone (e.g., Eisenbud, 1972). The typical procedure would involve a researcher pointing the camera at Serios and then pressing the shutter release button when signalled to do so. The images produced by such an approach included completely black or completely white photographs, fuzzy shadows, silhouettes and pictures of varying clarity (Braude, 2004; Eisenbud, 1972). Serios could often produce images on Polaroid film even when housed away from the camera in a Faraday cage and clothed in a one-piece suit provided by the experimenter (Eisenbud, Pratt, & Stevenson, 1981). Furthermore, sceptics have not succeeded in fully explaining these results, much less duplicating them under conditions similar to those experienced by Serios (Braude, 2015).

As a field, the examination of such exceptional individuals remains controversial and is limited by the low number of such PK superstars. It is interesting to speculate why so few individuals come forward. On the one hand it may simply be that few if any exhibit such skills. On the other hand, they may be reluctant to admit such abilities. For instance, when Parise was asked why she stopped taking part in PK research she responded by saying that she found the accusations of fraud difficult to deal with and simply 'got tired: your integrity is under fire all the time' (Pilkington, 2015, p. 102). Such a response is somewhat disheartening. If PK is real then examination of those that excel at such behaviours is likely to help illuminate and improve understanding of the processes and mechanisms involved.

Spinning PK detectors

Over time there have been a number of attempts to use PK to move or rotate a spinning wheel that may be housed in a glass jar. According to Alvarado (2006) an early French physician by the name of Baraduc created such an instrument called a *biometer,* which consisted of a needle suspended above a circular numbered surface by a thread inside a glass jar. The idea was that any movement of the needle in either direction would be easily identifiable by monitoring precisely where on the wheel the needle pointed. Others, such as Le Comte de Tromelin, also created devices based on similar principles. This usually involved a needle or pointer suspended or finely balanced to allow easy movement or spin and the whole thing contained within a glass bell jar to restrict any physical contact. This led to the development of various types of *psi wheel.* A popular version consists of a folded piece of paper balanced on a pin held in a stable base, which some claimed could be rotated by placing your hands nearby. Unfortunately, this has nothing to do with PK and everything to do with thermodynamics. It is simply heat from the hands creating an upward airflow that causes the paper wheel to spin. However, recent research has used circular plastic mobiles to counter the claims that such movements are the result of thermodynamic effects (see Figure 6.2).

Dullin and Jamet (2018) recruited individuals who showed potential PK ability and created psi wheels using a plastic dome shaped mobile balanced on the top of a pin inserted into a plastic support or cork for stability. Then, they examined the aerodynamic forces influencing the mobile by monitoring the flow of smoke around it which was introduced using a fog machine. They did this under three different

Figure 6.2 The type of plastic mobile device used in the PK experiments by Dullin and Jamet (2018). The clear mobile dome is decorated with ink marks making it easier to identify any movement (courtesy of Eric Dullin).

conditions. First, when the surrounding airflow was blown using a fine jet of air to move the mobile. Second, when a motor was attached to the mobile and finally with a trained PK participant who attempted to move the mobile using only focused conscious intention. The rationale was that if the movement of the mobile was caused by thermodynamic changes in airflow the expectation would be that the surrounding airflow should move at a faster rate than the mobile itself. Specifically, the ratio of air flow movement to mobile movement would be above one. Such movement in the surrounding air would then cause the mobile to move. This was indeed what they found in the first condition when air was blown at the device increasing the surrounding airflow and moving the mobile. However, surrounding air flow was not moving at a rate that was faster than the mobile when using either a small motor or when PK was focused on it (see Figure 6.3).

This led them to conclude that the spinning mobile in the PK conditions was not caused by changes in the surrounding airflow and as such cannot be accounted for in terms of thermodynamics. Instead, they argue that the results provide a clear indication of a macro PK effect from a trained participant. Such a result is encouraging; however, it needs to be replicated in other laboratories ideally by other researchers in order to ascertain whether this effect can generalise. It does of course require participants who have given over sufficient time and effort in order to train themselves to do this.

Micro PK

Within the field of micro PK the effects tend to be small scale and are not usually perceptible; invariably they are only revealed via statistical analysis. An implicit assumption that provides part of the logic of such an approach is that it may be 'easier' to influence such small scale targets requiring less energy. H. Schmidt (1969b) was one of the first researchers to focus on this area using his classic 'lamps' set-up. This was followed by an expanding field focusing on remote PK effects on various random event and random number generators. This is exemplified by the research conducted at the Princeton Engineering Anomalies Research (PEAR) lab and the consortium

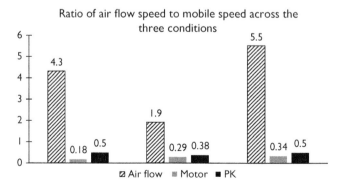

Figure 6.3 Showing the ratio of air flow speed compared to mobile speed (i.e., higher ratio means the air around the mobile is moving faster) when air was blown at the mobile (i.e., Air flow), a motor was used to rotate it (Motor) and PK was used (adapted from Dullin & Jamet, 2018).

replication attempt. There have also been some interesting PK studies based on non-human animals.

Schmidt's lamps

H. Schmidt (1969a, 1969b, 1970b) was one of the first to test for this type of PK using the randomly generated output of information based on a radioactive source. This involved a detector counting the emission rate of particles to determine a random target, which in the early cases was the switching on of a specific sequence of lightbulbs. Given that the emission of a particle from a radioactive source occurs at a random interval the idea was that it would not be possible to predict when the next particle emission will occur. Hence, if a counter or target is selected based on the emission of such a particle it is to all intents and purposes random. In a similar way those based on electronic noise, rather like the intermittent radio static heard between radio stations, rely on the occurrence and/or strength of a signal. Again, the assumption here is that it is not theoretically possible to predict with any degree of certainty when this will occur. Hence, any output reliant on such a signal will be random. A key point is the participants focus their intention or PK on producing non-random output in a desired or pre-specified direction. For example, H. Schmidt's (1969a, 1969b) early work required participants to focus attention on influencing the random output so that the lights on his light box moved in a pre-ordained direction, either clockwise or anti-clockwise. Using this type of set-up produced some very positive effects of micro PK showing that participants could significantly influence the direction of the lights (H. Schmidt, 1969a, 1969b, 1970b, 1974). That is, by conscious thought alone, directly influence the output of a random event generator (REG). Over time he developed his research and argued that such PK effects are goal oriented based primarily on the participant's intentions and mental state. H. Schmidt (1974) also developed an *equivalence principle* which referred to the idea that irrespective of the type of binary random generator used, PK could produce a significant effect (see Figure 6.4).

Given the random binary output the expectation would be that the number of 0's or 1's would be at mean chance, which is 50%. This is what was found in the no PK control trials. However, as can be seen in the PK trials there is a significantly

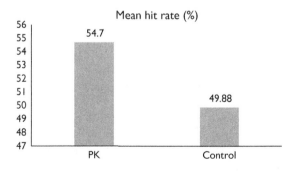

Figure 6.4 Mean percentage hit rate during PK trials (left), based on the output from two different binary random event generators, and no PK control (right) trials (adapted from H. Schmidt, 1974).

higher hit rate suggesting that the output deviates from random. Such findings led H. Schmidt (1976) to argue that PK may even be used retroactively. This would involve participants attempting to influence the output of a random device which had been played and the output pre-recorded without them knowing. Hence, the participant would be attempting to influence the output of a device that had in fact produced its output some time previously. In a series of three experiments conducted to test this idea H. Schmidt (1976) found clear evidence of a PK effect above that expected by chance alone. Indeed, the pattern of PK performance on conventional micro PK tests was similar to that for tests incorporating pre-recorded targets which led him to suggest that the same underlying mechanism may be supporting both types of effect, and that PK could influence data generated at an earlier time.

Overall Schmidt's work represents extremely strong evidence for micro PK. However, some have voiced concerns about the reliability of the random number generator devices (Hyman, 1987) though others have pointed out that there is no evidence to suggest that they were not random or were systematically deviating in some way which could account for the data (Varvoglis & Bancel, 2015). One key point however regarding Schmidt's success was his reliance on selectively recruiting participants that had displayed some success in micro PK work. He argued against opportunity sampling, as any small PK effect would be diluted to the extent that it would be undetectable and that pre-selecting promising participants was a more effective procedure. This included mediums, psychics and people who reported experiencing extraordinary events. However, he did admit that this recruitment process can be both time consuming and frustrating.

Use of RNG and REG devices

With the advent of advanced computer technology, a range of random devices have been developed. Some of these are random number generators (RNG) or random event generators (REG) based on radioactive decay, electronic noise and more recently the use of quantum-based RNG and REG devices, so-called true random generators. According to Varvoglis and Bancel (2015) the use of such devices has now become the standard in micro PK research. In particular the use of quantum-based random event generators has been suggested to provide 'true' random output, providing an optimal source of randomness (Maier, Dechamps, & Pflitsch, 2018). Such devices can be attached to computers and the output displayed as a specific target or visual representation (such as a line) with the participants required to *raise* or *lower* the line (see Figure 6.5). Alternatively, the target may be a picture of snow with a varied rate of fall or a more sophisticated computer game where responses are based on random output. The benefit of these kinds of experiments is that they are largely automatic which makes fraud difficult. They may also be more engaging and help to hold the attention of the participant.

There have been many studies using such a procedure to test the possibility that conscious thought can produce a tangible effect on RNGs and REGs. Possibly one of the most eminent groups was housed at the Princeton Engineering Anomalies Research (PEAR) laboratory founded by Robert Jahn which focused primarily on RNG or REG PK type research. In contrast to Schmidt the PEAR lab used opportunity sampling, or *unselected participants*, to take part in their research based only on willingness and availability. In addition, lab staff were at times also required to act as participants. This opportunity sampling may have helped them obtain large sample sizes but Varvoglis

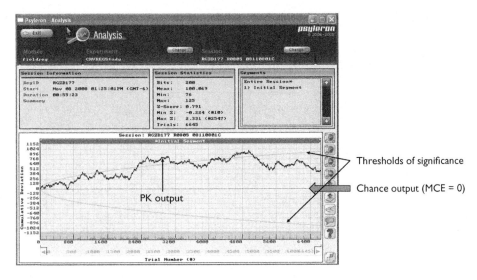

Figure 6.5 The output of one PK session where the aim is to increase the number of 1's which is translated into raising the dark line above a threshold mark. When this dark line crosses the feint parabolic curved line it means that the output is statistically significantly different from what would be expected if the output were purely random.

and Bancel (2016) have suggested that such a recruitment approach may also have watered down any effects found. A strong plus was that the PEAR lab published all its results so there can be no file drawer problem. Furthermore, PEAR utilised a *tripolar protocol* which involved three PK trials of equal length focused on increasing output (high), decreasing it (low) or remaining at baseline (baseline) (Varvoglis & Bancel, 2016). The prediction was that high runs would produce a positive deviation and low runs a negative deviation with no difference for the baseline runs. A good example of this type of protocol is presented by Iqbal (2013) who used an algorithmic or random generator to produce a list of 30 random numbers, between one and ten, and compute the average to one decimal place. He then ran three sets of 30 trials during which two participants either did nothing (i.e., control), or attempted to raise the overall average of the numbers that were output (i.e., high) or lower the overall average (i.e., low). Iqbal (2013) argued that focusing on attempting to increase or decrease the numbers would provide a better indication of any emerging trend in the random numbers. The results were significant in both directions in that he found that the average of the numbers increased when participants were told to produce higher scores and was lower when they focused on reducing scores, compared to a no PK control session (see Figure 6.6).

This led Iqbal (2013) to conclude that human thought had significantly influenced the RNG used in the computer program. Such a positive effect mirrors that reported by the PEAR group. For instance, across a period of 12 years they collected over 2.5 million trials from 91 participants, which overall showed a very significant effect (see, Jahn, Dunne, Nelson, Dobyns, & Bradish, 1997; Varvoglis & Bancel, 2016).

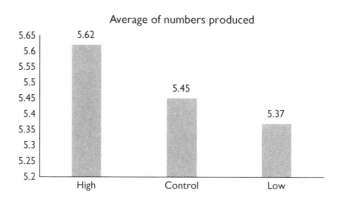

Figure 6.6 The average of the numbers produced by random sequencing when aiming High (left), no aim or Control (centre), and aiming Low (right) (adapted from Iqbal, 2013).

In 1996 PEAR formed a consortium with two German based labs and undertook an extensive replication of the PEAR lab's original findings. The replication used the same tripolar protocol, uniform RNGs, with an equal contribution of trials from each lab. Approximately 750,000 trials per condition were collected from 227 participants over a period of 3 years. However, the results were disappointing and showed no clear evidence of a PK effect (Jahn et al., 2000). Nevertheless, when Varvoglis and Bancel (2016) re-examined the original PEAR data they found that many of the positive findings were the result of two seemingly gifted participants. As such, they suggested that the failure of the consortium to replicate the original PEAR findings could be because it was either underpowered or that it needed to selectively recruit participants rather than rely on opportunity sampling.

More recently Maier and Dechamps (2018) reported conflicting evidence of PK with one experiment showing positive support but a second study failed to replicate the effect. In a follow-up series using an online study they again failed to find any evidence of micro PK effects (Maier et al., 2018). Such failed attempts to replicate the micro PK effect continue to bring its validity into question. However, there are many methodological differences between this study and earlier accounts that report positive PK effects. For example, this latter study was run online, which could reduce motivation or involvement; the participants were also simply told to relax and then presented with either positive or negative images. The assumption was that the participants would implicitly prefer to see positive images and as such the number of positive images should be greater than chance (i.e., 50%). However, there was no conscious intention or effort made on the part of the participants to influence the outcome which seems to be a hallmark of many of the earlier more successful micro PK studies.

To try to obtain an overview of the findings regarding micro PK studies researchers have turned to meta-analyses. For example, one meta-analysis by Radin and Nelson (1989), which included studies conducted up to 1987, reported a strong micro PK effect. More recently when Radin and Nelson (2003) conducted a meta-analysis of all published RNG type PK experiments from 1959 up to 2000, which included over 500 published experiments, they reported that the evidence for a PK type effect persists.

Radin and Nelson (2003) concluded by stating that having completed a meta-analysis on over 500 RNG type experiments conducted by over 90 researchers covering a span of more than 40 years the evidence clearly shows a small magnitude but repeatable and robust PK effect. Such results, they argued, cannot be attributable to either chance or poor methodology. More recently another meta-analysis of over three hundred studies, this time carried out by Bosch et al. (2006a), also reported a small but significant effect of PK. However, given the high level of heterogeneity across the studies they suggested that the findings could more easily be accounted for in terms of a publication bias, particularly in the form of the non-reporting of null effects. This led them to conclude that after nearly four decades of work the field of micro PK has yet to demonstrate a convincing effect. Unsurprisingly, those in the field clearly disagree with this conclusion arguing that the idea that positive PK effects are the result of a publication bias is highly implausible and hence the PK effect is genuine (Radin et al., 2006). They also argue that the heterogeneity in effect size is more likely to be the result of differences in sample size across the various studies. Others have called into question the methodological rigour of the Bosch et al. (2006a) meta-analysis suggesting that it included generic ESP studies which would weaken the findings regarding micro PK (Kugel, 2011). In addition, Kugel (2011) suggested that the Bosch et al. (2006a) meta-analysis included data selection bias, incorrect data coding and a problematic statistical analysis leading to erroneous inter-pretation of the results. Bosch, Steinkamp, and Boller (2006b) responded by suggesting that it would be the province of future studies that underwent rigorous pre-registration to ensure full transparency to help shed light on the issue. However, others have also argued against the idea that the positive effects found for micro PK are the result of a publication bias. For instance, estimates of what is referred to as the *failsafe file drawer* suggests that for each of the published PK studies '90 unpublished studies would be required' to eliminate the effect (Varvoglis & Bancel, 2015, p. 273). Varvoglis and Bancel (2015) argue that this is an unreasonably large number which would suggest that the data supporting PK based effects is more likely to be an accurate indication of what is occurring. Hence, at present there does seem to be clear evidence of a small and robust effect, though it may be that in some instances this is more reliant upon the skilled performance of a few than the general ability of the many.

Animal micro PK

Micro PK studies utilising non-human animals as participants provide additional insights into the potential processes and mechanisms underlying such behaviour. For instance, it may be that such PK effects provide an evolutionary advantage particu-larly if they improve survival rates. Levin (1996) disagrees and suggests that ob-servation of animals in action does not support such an interpretation. Others agree, suggesting that if this were the case then both predator and prey would be simulta-neously attempting to manipulate the context using PK which would lead to an evolutionary arms race between the two species (see e.g., Dawkins & Krebs, 1979). Nevertheless, there have been a variety of studies examining potential micro PK effects across a range of animal species. One early study by H. Schmidt (1970a) placed cockroaches on a 'shocking grid' that was connected to a RNG in order to see if they could influence the device and avoid being shocked. However, it was found that they received more shocks than would be expected.

Braud (1976) reported some initial PK effects with aggressive tropical fish but the effects did not remain stable and declined over time. Since then Chauvin (1986) reported that mice were able to influence a randomly moving object using PK which has been replicated by others (Courtial & Peoc'h, 2016; Peoc'h, 1995). It is unlikely that the animals were aware of the RNG or its influence or control of the device and hence this may be the result of some form of conscious intention on the outcome rather than on the device itself. That is, they may have desired the device to be near or far as opposed to trying to influence the output of the RNG per se. Recently Alvarez (2012) tested whether finches would be able to influence a REG that controlled the presence/absence of the image of a snake, a known predator of finches. The rationale was that finches, as natural prey of snakes, would influence the device such that the image of a snake would appear *less* often. This was exactly what he found when a finch was in the cage and nearby compared to when the cage was empty (see Figure 6.7).

This led Alvarez to conclude that PK was evident and that it could act to benefit the organism in question. However, he does admit that it may not only be the prey that is endowed with such PK skills, as predators may be equally endowed in their attempts to obtain food. Such effects he suggests could make such micro PK effects less visible to outside observers as one species would not exhibit a clear dominance over another.

Direct mental influence on living systems (DMILS)

The third and final area of PK research is one that focuses on the *direct mental influence on living systems*, often referred to as DMILS research (Braud & Schlitz, 2003; Delanoy, 2001; S. Schmidt, 2015). Specifically, such research involves the directed intentional effort of one person, the *influencer*, to change a defined variable of a remote living system, the *recipient*, that is situated at a distance and shielded from all conventional informational and energy influences and cues. Trials where the influencer attempts to alter some aspect of the remote recipient are then compared to

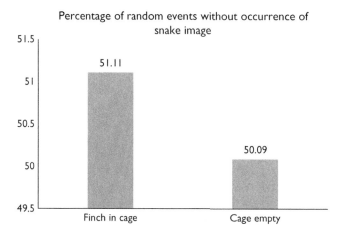

Figure 6.7 The percentage of events occurring *without* the presence of a predatory snake image when a finch was in the cage (left) and when no finch was in the cage (right) (adapted from Alvarez, 2012).

control trials where no attempt is made to elicit any changes and this provides systematic and objective data which can rule out chance, expectancy effects, subtle cues and other possible artefacts. Such measures are also useful as they generally occur outside the conscious volitional control of the target recipient and hence may be less influenced by cognitive filtering and processing. Given the often-positive intention of the influencer there is some similarity here between DMILS and distant healing and spiritual practices. However, it should be noted that intention doesn't have to mean positive intention. Intention can be either positive or negative, depending on the situation, target and context. In addition, in some instances the influencer may be provided with real time feedback of the specific physiological measure from the recipient. This has been suggested to aid in the development of different strategies that may help to elicit positive effects; however it has also been noted that whilst this may help it is not essential to the occurrence of DMILS effects (Braud & Schlitz, 2003). Delanoy (2001) has also pointed out that at present it is not entirely clear if such effects represent a true measure of PK, that is, the distant influence of one individual on or over another. Delanoy (2001) notes that such effects could occur via some form of information transfer, much as might be found in telepathy, between the sender and receiver or possibly between the experimenter and receiver, or indeed a combination of all these effects. In general, the focus of DMILS research has been on producing changes in human physiology, attempts at remote helping and remotely influencing animal behaviour.

Physiological effects

Possibly the most common DMILS paradigm involves attempts to alter the electrodermal activity (EDA) of the recipient, often referred to as EDA DMILS research (Braud & Schlitz, 2003). Such an experiment usually involves an influencer and a recipient, each occupying separate rooms or housed in distinct locations. During a trial the recipient simply remains awake and relaxed. Meanwhile, the influencer focuses their intention on arousing or supressing the EDA of the receiver. Each trail can then be divided into a number of epochs each with a particular focus to either enhance or suppress EDA in the receiver. The specific sequence of epochs should be randomised and balanced to ensure there is no bias. If the specified differences are evident in the receiver's physiology and all other possible reasons can be excluded then the DMILS effect has been successful (see for example Figure 6.8).

Reviews of the evidence have suggested that the effects are significant but small, with clear differences in EDA visible between influence and control periods in the predicted direction (Delanoy, 2001; Schlitz & Braud, 1997). For instance, when Braud and Schlitz (2003) reviewed thirteen studies they had conducted which focused on eliciting EDA changes they found that the overall scores were highly significant in the expected direction. However, despite such positive findings some have criticised the methodology; in particular Fowles et al. (1981) suggested that the EDA measurement procedures did not meet with international standards. This was particularly the case for the electrode locations, use of gels and voltage levels. This led to a follow-up review of such methodological practices by S. Schmidt and Walach (2000) who found that many of the parapsychological studies failed to report their methods completely. In particular, they found that studies used inadequate electrodes and

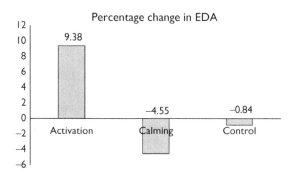

Figure 6.8 The percentage change in electrodermal activity (EDA) as a function of the distant intention to activate (left), remain calm (middle) or leave stable (control: right) (adapted from Braud & Schlitz, 2003).

methods of attachment, gel, that were not suitable to the needs of EDA recording and equipment with inadequate sampling rates. All of which, they argued, reduced the impact of such research.

Indeed, a meta-analyses utilising stringent inclusion/exclusion criteria found that when the analyses were restricted to the higher quality DMILS studies the PK results were no different from chance (S. Schmidt, Schneider, Utts, & Walach, 2004). However, more recently Schmidt (2015) examined all studies completed up to the year 2000 and assessed the quality of the studies in terms of their methodological safeguards, their EDA methodology and their methodological quality. Interestingly there were negative correlations found between study quality and effect size, which would suggest that at least in part such effects may have been due to methodological weaknesses. However, even when these factors were taken into account there remained a small but significant difference in EDA activity suggestive of a PK effect.

Remote helping

The *remote helping* paradigm is sometimes referred to in terms of *attention focused facilitation* and has the influencer attempting to either help or hinder the recipient, sometimes referred to as the *helpee* (S. Schmidt, 2012; S. Schmidt, Han-Gue, Whittman, Ambach, & Kubel, 2018). For instance, the recipient, or helpee, may be required to stare at a candle flame continuously, which requires a level of sustained and focused attention. During this task their mind may wander and they will be required to bring their attention back to the target candle. If this happens they are required to press a button to indicate that they were distracted. As part of the trial the influencer would be required to focus their intention on either helping the receiver focus on the candle or inhibit them. The assumption is that the number of button presses made by the recipient, to indicate the number of distractions from the task, would be lower when the influencer is 'helping' compared to when they are not (Braud, Shafer, McNeill, & Guerra, 1995). Such a paradigm has produced some intriguingly encouraging results with positive behavioural effects shown for focused attention (Edge, Suryani, Tiliopoulous, & Morris, 2004; Watt & Ramakers, 2003). However, attempts to replicate such effects have not always proved possible (e.g., Watt & Baker, 2002). For instance, S. Schmidt et al. (2018) recruited individuals with meditation experience and then had them work in pairs. One of the pair would be required to maintain focused attention on a candle and press a button whenever their mind wandered, whilst the other would be placed remotely and randomly focus either on helping their partner or reading a passage of text.

They found that those receiving the help made slightly more button presses when they were being helped, though the difference was not significant (see Figure 6.9). Such a pattern is contrary to what would be expected. However, they did admit that the study may have lacked sufficient statistical power to elicit the small PK effect that is often reported. Indeed, a meta-analysis which examined eleven studies, all concentrating on supporting the focused attention of a distant recipient, showed a clear and robust difference between those periods in which the recipient was helped compared to those in which they were not in the predicted direction (S. Schmidt, 2012). This led S. Schmidt (2012) to conclude that under certain circumstances one person can intentionally interact with or influence another from a distance, although the effect may be very limited in size and power. More research is needed to ascertain what, if any, are the limits of such influence and what types of behaviour may or may not be helped or impeded. Indeed, it is not just focused attention that has been facilitated by such remote help. For instance Tressoldi, Massaccesi, Martinelli and Cappato (2011) randomly presented non-Chinese speaking participants with a range of real and decoy (i.e., false) Chinese ideograms and asked the participants to classify them as either real or not. At the same time a helper was located at a remote location and was simultaneously presented with the same sequence of ideograms with the aim of helping the participant to correctly classify them by mentally suggesting the correct response. They found that such help did lead to a higher hit rate (i.e., correct classification) compared to when no help was given (see Figure 6.10).

This led Tressoldi et al. (2011) to conclude that the human mind may exhibit non-local properties, though at this stage it is not clear whether such information is transferred from one mind to another or whether the minds of the two individuals are entangled and as such correlate in their outputs. They also suggest that, as in other areas of psi research (e.g., Sheldrake & Beharee, 2009), the strength of the emotional bond between the individuals may influence the effect. The emotional closeness may

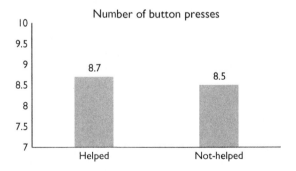

Figure 6.9 Number of button presses (indicating lapse of attention) when remotely helped (left) or not (right) (adapted from Schmidt et al., 2018).

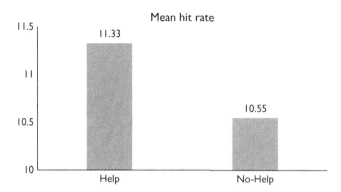

Figure 6.10 Mean hit rate when remote help was given (left) and when no help was provided (right) (adapted from Tressoldi et al., 2011).

make it easier for them to communicate ideas in a non-local way. Furthermore, they argued that such findings suggest practical applications for such DMILS type paradigms. That is, it may be possible to remotely influence the performance of another person. Of course, this could be for the good or ill of the recipient, which in itself raises some interesting moral and ethical issues.

Animal behaviour

In addition to focusing on changes in human behaviour some researchers have attempted to alter non-human animal behaviour by having a remote influencer focus their thoughts on eliciting a particular type of behaviour. In one series of experiments attempts were made to encourage fish to spend more time swimming in a particular orientation relative to the outer walls of their container (Braud & Schlitz, 2003). Out of four experiments examining this, Braud and Schlitz (2003) reported three that showed significantly positive effects. That is, the fish spent more time oriented in the direction encouraged by the influencer compared to no-influence control sessions. Similar positive effects were reported by Braud and Schlitz (2003) when a remote influencer randomly attempted to encourage a gerbil to spend more time on an activity or not (control). Again, three of the four studies showed significant effects in the predicted direction. That is, the gerbils spent more time on the wheel during the randomly interspersed 'movement' trials compared to the no-movement control trials. Such findings led them to suggest that the effect is one that occurs in a goal directed manner. That is, the influencer need not know or be aware of how such changes in behaviour are brought about. It is more that the person's intention remains focused on the goal to bring about the changes. Hence, intentionality appears to be a key aspect of such PK activity. Overall, Braud and Schlitz (2003) reported on thirty-seven experiments that produced effects in the desired directions which led them to conclude that a person is 'able to mentally influence remote biological systems, even when those systems are isolated at distant locations and screened from all conventional information' (p. 103).

Overall the level of evidence for each of the three main PK paradigms seems very similar, something which led Schmidt (2015) to conclude that there is a clear effect of conscious intention influencing distant events and behaviours. However, given the small effect sizes reported Schmidt (2015) pointed out that in many cases such an effect may go unnoticed if the sample size of the study is insufficient. This in turn would lead to a lack of statistical power and result in an erroneous conclusion regarding the possibility of such PK type behaviours.

Mediating factors

Very little is clearly known regarding which factors can potentially influence PK performance. Early research did suggest that priming those taking part by providing them with positive information regarding the effects of PK can induce the illusion of control, and that those with higher levels of belief and an internal locus of control tend to overestimate their performance ability. However, this does not always clearly lead to positive PK effects (Benassi, Sweeney, & Drevno, 1979). Some have suggested that when attempting PK the passive visualisation of the desired outcome may be more helpful than actively thinking about influencing the target in some way (Morris, Nanko, & Phillips, 1982). Others have suggested that performance may be better if the PK task is presented as a type of game and that the participant is relaxed yet highly motivated (Gissurarson, 1991), whilst others have shown that the experimenter-participant interactions seem to be of little or no importance in aiding the emergence of PK (Schneider, Binder, & Walach, 2000). Nevertheless, there is some agreement that PK effects do not seem to be influenced by the distance between the influencer and the recipient (Braud & Schlitz, 2003; Dunne & Jahn, 1992). For instance, H. Schmidt and Braud (1993) and Dunne and Jahn (1992) have both reported positive PK effects when using a random generator located at considerable distance. More recently research has shown that individuals were able to influence a photomultiplier device, which is useful for light detection of very weak signals, placed at a distance of 7300 km (Tressoldi et al., 2016). There is also some suggestion that PK effects may work over time (H. Schmidt, Morris, & Rudolph, 1986). For instance, H. Schmidt et al. (1986) utilised an approach that tested for PK with targets that had been *pre-recorded*, or when the target had been selected *after* the participant had made their choice. Intriguingly both protocols generated positive results consistent with the positive effects found in real-time experiments. In addition, there have been suggestions that the emotiveness of the target used may influence the outcome of a PK study. For instance, it may be that either emotive targets or an emotional link to the target helps to elicit a PK effect. Maier and Dechamps (2018) tested this idea by recruiting participants who identified themselves as either regular smokers or non-smokers and then presented them with a random sequence of images, half of which contained smoking related information. The question was whether the desire for cigarettes by the smokers would influence the RNG output which in turn would alter the number of smoking related images they would see compared to a group of non-smokers. Interestingly they found that when each group was randomly presented with four hundred images the number of smoking related images presented to the smokers was significantly lower than chance (i.e., less than 200), though there was no difference for the non-smokers (see Figure 6.11).

Unfortunately, in a follow-up study they failed to replicate the effect which led them to conclude that there is as yet no robust evidence for micro PK. They speculate that such findings may be accounted for by a decline effect which would be consistent with the notion of pragmatic information preserving the no-signal theorem, as put forward by von Lucadou (1995).

It should be noted that recent suggestions by Varvoglis and Bancel (2016) point to the possibility that PK ability may not be something that is widely and/or normally distributed across the population but rather may represent an exceptional ability or skill. As such, researchers may need to identify gifted individuals and focus their tests on such highly skilled individuals rather than conduct unproductive replications on unselected individuals which are likely to show no clear effects. This view echoes the early research of H. Schmidt (1969a) who was one of the first to suggest that it would be better to test gifted individuals as the poor scores of the majority would dilute any effects that might exist. This idea of testing those who have already shown some prerequisite skill has been echoed by others (e.g., Braude, 2015; Tart, 1983), though Henry (2005) has pointed out that it may be possible to train micro PK type skills using a goal-focused strategy that requires the individual to focus their intention on the outcome but remain calm and relaxed.

Mechanisms of PK

Attempts to try and understand the mechanisms of PK have led to some interesting suggestions. For instance, Braud and Schlitz (2003) have suggested that extremely low frequency electromagnetic radiation may be a conceivable candidate mechanism. However, it is not clear yet how such a signal could be influenced by the thoughts or intentions of the PK adept. The findings from micro PK research have led to suggestions that such effects may be the result of selection or influence. The *selection* approach suggests that participants may use precognition or some generic form of psi to time their action so that they select a data segment that coincides with their intention. That is, rather than directly alter the output of a REG/RNG device they precognitively select when to start their trial so that the output provides a greater match with their desired goal. According to May, Utts and Spottiswoode (1995) the selection model approach

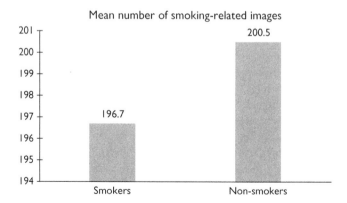

Figure 6.11 Showing Mean number of smoking related images seen by smokers (left) and non-smokers (right) when 200 smoking related images would be the expected chance level (adapted from Maier & Dechamps, 2018).

provides a better statistical fit with the evident data. However, others disagree and suggest that the *influence* approach provides a better account (Bancel, 2011, 2014; Dobyns, 2000). This model puts forward the idea that the conscious intention of the influencer in some way interacts with the target or random device to produce the desired outcome. According to Dobyns (2000) this possibility provides a better fit for the data. Indeed, some have gone so far as to speculate how conscious intention can produce such changes. For example, Pederzoli, Giroldini, Prati and Tressoldi (2017) suggest that the interference could occur directly on electrons in the device by ultraviolet photons produced by the mind of the participant. Such changes would alter the output of the device to become less random and more biased towards producing zeros or ones. They fully recognise that the notion of a human mind generating photons from a distance which interact with a desired target simply as a result of conscious intention is speculative at this point in time. Furthermore, they suggest that to overcome the distances it is necessary to postulate a quantum-like mind-matter entanglement mechanism which implies that consciousness may be able to operate using quantum non-local properties. Nevertheless, even if the influence model is deemed more acceptable, or provides a better fit for the data, it is not entirely clear precisely where this influence is coming from. For instance, in any PK study there is the possible confound of *experimenter PK*, in that any PK effects evident in the experiment, are more likely the result of the intention of the experimenter than the participant (Braude, 2007, 2015). Such a possibility would fit with the idea that the experimenter is probably the most motivated person in the situation. Of course, it should be noted that if experimenter PK is the cause of such effects then this is unlikely to be restricted to psi research alone, but is likely to influence the results of any study where an experimenter is motivated to obtain a particular outcome. This highlights an on-going challenge when dealing with the supposed effects of conscious intention that may be able to operate across space and time (Byrne, 2018). That is, it may not be possible to eliminate the hopes and intentions of the researcher from the research itself, something which could fundamentally challenge the notion of objective research.

Overview

Psychokinesis refers to the idea that it may be possible to influence a distant object or organism by conscious intention alone. Interestingly, belief in such a phenomenon seems reasonably widespread, though this may be influenced by how common such ideas appear in mainstream media. Research on PK has generally taken one of three routes. The first looks at larger, more visible effects and is referred to as macro PK. This field encapsulates the findings from physical mediums as well as attempts to account for poltergeist activity in terms of recurrent spontaneous PK activity. Such findings are not without controversy given their inherent reliance on eye-witness testimony. However, some of the reported effects produced are intriguing and withstand the necessary scrutiny. The findings from lab-based research focusing on the roll of one or more dice have also shown some clear and reliable PK effects, which remained evident when potential methodological issues were more tightly controlled. Furthermore, such effects are unlikely to be accounted for purely in terms of a publication bias. A limited number of exceptional individuals have emerged over time who demonstrated seemingly encouraging macro PK effects. In particular, the findings related to Kulagina, Parise and Serios are certainly noteworthy. Such exceptional abilities suggest that efforts should be made to identify and study modern-day skilled PK practitioners. Furthermore, the recent findings from Dullin and Jamet (2018) using a modern-day psi wheel to measure macro PK effects are both suggestive and worthy of further study. The second area of research which focuses on micro PK effects is more evident in the statistical perturbations of random generators. Over time these studies have amassed quite a substantial amount of positive evidence for such micro PK effects, in particular when selectively recruiting participants who display some skill at the task and when tested on non-human animals. Though some have suggested, again, that such effects may be more parsimoniously explained by a publication bias, the number of non-published studies required to eliminate such a positive effect hardly seems credible. The third and final area of PK research is that focusing on the direct mental influence on a living system. Despite the claims that some of the EDA DMILS research suffers from poor methodological quality the overall effects are suggestive of a small yet robust PK effect. The findings from remote helping are less clear but this may in part be due to the more complex behaviours involved. It is also encouraging to note that non-human animals have also been shown to be susceptible to such remote PK influence, though the precise limits of such influence have yet to be clearly established. Furthermore, it is not yet clear what factors may influence PK performance, though distance to the target has been suggested to have little or no impact. In addition, it may be possible that PK effects can operate outside of time, be influenced by the emotiveness of the target and rely to a great extent on the ability or skill of the individual, though additional confirmation of such issues is clearly needed. Overall, whilst some may argue that it is too soon to reach any firm conclusions regarding the possibility and/or nature of PK, there is certainly sufficient evidence here to indicate that something unusual is occurring.

Review questions

Some questions that may prove helpful when reflecting on the material covered in this chapter.

- Do you think PK is a single unitary construct or do the different paradigms (i.e., micro, macro and DMILS) each measure distinct aspects of psi?
- Do you think it would be easier to use PK to influence a large or small object; why?
- How could you exclude thermodynamics as a reason for a spinning psi wheel?
- What other reasons can you think of for why a psi wheel might spin?
- Do you think it would be easier to alter the random output of an RNG/REG device; why?
- How would you go about testing micro PK effects on animals?
- If conscious intention alone is sufficient to influence a distant object or organism what are some of the implications of this?
- Can you think of any moral or ethical issues that emerge from DMILS research?
- What physiological changes do you think may be amenable to change via PK?
- Do you think remote helping would be more or less effective compared to remotely hindering?
- What practical applications can you think of for DMILS type procedures?
- How would you design an experiment that controlled for experimenter PK?

References

Alvarado, C. S. (1993). Gifted subjects' contributions to psychical research: The case of Eusapia Palladino. *Journal of the Society for Psychical Research, 59,* 269–292.

Alvarado, C. S. (2006). Human radiations: Concepts of force in mesmerism, spiritualism and psychical research. *Journal of the Society for Psychical Research, 70*(884), 138–162.

Alvarado, C. S. (2017). Telepathy, mediumship, and psychology: Psychical research at the international congresses of psychology 1889–1905. *Journal of Scientific Exploration, 31*(2), 255–292.

Alvarez, F. (2012). A PK experiment with zebra finches. *Journal of Scientific Exploration, 26*(2), 261–271.

Bancel, P. A. (2011). Reply to May and Spottiswoode's 'The Global Consciousness Project: Identifying the source of psi'. *Journal of Scientific Exploration, 25*(4), 690–694.

Bancel, P. A. (2014). An analysis of the global consciousness project. In D. Broderick & B. Goertzel (Eds.), *Evidence for psi: Thirteen empirical research reports* (pp. 255–277). Jefferson, NC: McFarland Press.

Batcheldor, K. J. (1966). Report on a case of table levitation and associated phenomena. *Journal of the Society for Psychical Research, 43,* 339–356.

Benassi, V. A., Sweeney, P. D., & Drevno, G. E. (1979). Mind over matter: Perceived success at psychokinesis. *Journal of Personality and Social Psychology, 37*(8), 1377–1386.

Bosch, H., Steinkamp, F., & Boller, E. (2006a). Examining psychokinesis: The interaction of human intention with random number generators – a meta-analysis. *Psychological Bulletin, 132,* 497–523.

Bosch, H., Steinkamp, F., & Boller, E. (2006b). In the eye of the beholder: Reply to Wilson and Shadish (2006) and Radin, Nelso, Dobyns and Houtkeeper (2006). *Psychological Bulletin, 132*(4), 533–537. doi: 10.1037/0033-2909.132.4.533.

Braud, W. (1976). Psychokinesis in aggressive and non-aggresive fish with mirror presentation feedback for hits: Some preliminary experiments. *Journal of Parapsychology, 40*(4), 296–307.

Braud, W., & Schlitz, M. (2003). Mental interactions with remote biological systems. In W. Braud (Ed.), *Distant mental influence: Its contributions to science, healing, and human interactions.* Charlottesville, VA: Hampton Roads Publishing Co.

Braud, W., Shafer, D., McNeill, K., & Guerra, V. (1995). Attention focused facilitation through remote mental interaction. *Journal of the American Society for Psychical Research, 89,* 103–115.

Braude, S. E. (1986). *The limits of influence: Psychokinesis and the philosophy of science.* New York: Law Book Co.

Braude, S. E. (2004). The thoughtography of Ted Serios. In C. Chéroux, A. Fischer, F. Apraxine, D. Canguilhem, & S. Schmit (Eds.), *The perfect medium: Photography and the occult.* New Haven and London: Yale University Press.

Braude, S. E. (2007). *The gold leaf lady: And other parapsychological investigations.* London: University of Chicago Press.

Braude, S. E. (2015). Macro-psychokinesis. In E. Cardena, J. Palmer, & D. Marcusson-Clavertz (Eds.), *Parapsychology: A handbook for the 21st century* (pp. 258–265). Jefferson, NC: McFarland & Company Inc.

Braude, S. E. (2016). *Crimes of reason: On mind, nature, and the paranormal.* Boulder, CO: Rowman & Littlefield.

Byrne, M. E. (2018). A basis for the non-local events of quantum mechanics and psi. *Journal of the Society for Psychical Research, 82*(2), 65–80.

Cassirer, M. (1974). Experiments with Nina Kulagina. *Journal of the Society for Psychical Research*, 47, 315–318.

Chauvin, R. (1986). A PK experiment with mice. *Journal of the Society for Psychical Research*, 53(804), 348–351.

Courtial, J. P., & Peoc'h, R. (2016). Psychokinesis analysed through morphic resonance. *Journal of the Society for Psychical Research*, 80(923), 78–85.

Dawkins, R., & Krebs, J. R. (1979). Arms races between and within species. *Proceedings of the Royal Society of London. Series B. Biological Sciences*, 205(1161), 489–511.

Delanoy, D. (2001). Anomalous psychophysiological responses to remote cognition: The DMILS studies. *Journal of the American Society for Psychical Research*, 16, 30–41.

Dobyns, Y. H. (2000). Overview of several theoretical models on PEAR data. *Journal of Scientific Exploration*, 14(2), 163–194.

Dullin, E., & Jamet, D. (2018). A methodology proposal for conducting a macro-PK test on light spinning objects, in a non-confined environment. *Journal of Scientific Exploration*, 32(3), 514–554. doi: 10.31275/2018.1266.

Dunne, B. J., & Jahn, R. G. (1992). Experiments in remote human/machine interaction. *Journal of Scientific Exploration*, 6(4), 311–332.

Edge, H., Suryani, L. K., Tiliopoulous, N., & Morris, R. L. (2004). Two cogntiive DMILS studies in Bali. *Journal of Parapsychology*, 68, 289–321.

Eisenbud, J. (1972). The Serios 'blackies' and related phenomena. *Journal of the American Society for Psychical Research*, 66(2), 180–192.

Eisenbud, J., Pratt, J. G., & Stevenson, I. (1981). Distortions in the photographs of Ted Serios. *Journal of the American Society for Psychical Research*, 75(2), 143–153.

Fowles, D. C., Christie, M. J., Edelberg, R., Grings, W. W., Lykken, D. T., & Venebles, P. H. (1981). Publication recommendations for electro-dermal measurements. *Psychopyhyiology*, 18, 232–239.

Gallup, G. H., & Newport, F. (1991). Belief in paranormal phenomena among adult Americans. *Skeptical Inquirer*, 15(2), 137–146.

Gissurarson, L. R. (1991). Some PK attitudes as determinants of PK performance. *European Journal of Parapsychology*, 8, 112–122.

Grote, H. (2015). A correlation study between human intention and the output of a binary random event generator. *Journal of Scientific Exploration*, 29(2), 265–290.

Henry, J. (2005). Psychokinesis. In J. Henry (Ed.), *Parapsychology: Research on exceptional experiences* (pp. 125–136). Hove, East Sussex: Routeledge.

Holder, G. (2012). *What is a poltergeist? Understanding poltergeist activity*. New York, NY: F+W Media, Inc.

Honorton, C. (1993). A moving experience. *Journal of the American Society for Psychical Research*, 87, 329–340.

Hyman, R. (1987). Parapsychology: The science of ostensible anomalies. *Behavioral and Brain Sciences*, 10(4), 593–594.

Iqbal, A. (2013). A replication of the slight effect of human thought on a pseudorandom number generator. *NeuroQuantology*, 11(4), 519–526.

Irwin, H. J., & Watt, C. (2007). *An introduction to parapsychology* (5th edn). Jefferson, North Carolina: McFarland & Co.

Jahn, R., Dunne, B., Bradish, G., Dobyns, Y., Lettieri, A., Nelson, R.,... & Walter, B. (2000). Mind/machine interaction consortium: PortREG replication experiments. *Journal of Scientific Exploration*, 14(4), 499–555.

Jahn, R., Dunne, B., Nelson, R., Dobyns, Y., & Bradish, G. J. (1997). Corre lations of random binary sequences with pre-stated operator intention: A review of a 12-year program. *Journal of Scientific Exploration*, 11(3), 345–367.

Keen, M., Ellison, A., & Fontana, D. (1999). The Scole report. *Proceedings for the Society for Psychical Research*, 58(220), 149–152.

Keil, H. H., Herbert, B., Ullman, M., & Pratt, J. G. (1976). Directly observable voluntary PK effects: A survey and tentative interpretation of available findings from Nina Kulagina and known causes of recent date. *Proceedings of the Society for Psychical Research*, 56(210), 197–235.

Kennedy, J. E. (1978). The role of task complexity in PK: A review. *Journal of Parapsychology*, 42, 89–122.

Kruth, J. G., & Joines, W. T. (2016). Taming the ghost within: An approach toward addressing apparent electronic poltergeist activity. *The Journal of Parapsychology*, 80(1), 70–86.

Kugel, W. (2011). A faulty PK meta-analysis. *Journal of Scientific Exploration*, 25(1), 47–62.

Levin, M. (1996). On the lack of evidence for the evolution of psi as an argument against the reality of the paranormal. *Journal of the American Society for Psychical Research*, 90, 221–230.

Loftus, E. F., & Palmer, J. C. (1996). Eyewitness testimony. In P. Banyard & A. Grayson (Eds.), *Introducing psychological research* (pp. 305–309). London: Springer.

Maier, M. A., & Dechamps, M. C. (2018). Observer effects on quantum randomness: Testing micro-psychokinetic effects of smokers on addiction-related stimuli. *Journal of Scientific Exploration*, 32(2), 261–293.

Maier, M. A., Dechamps, M. C., & Pflitsch, M. (2018). Intentional observer effects on quantum randomness: A Bayesian analysis reveals evidence against micro-psychokinesis. *Frontiers in Psychology*, 9(379), 1–11. doi: 10.3389/fpsyg.2018.00379.

May, E. C., Utts, J., & Spottiswoode, S. P. (1995). Decision augmentation theory: Toward a model of anomalous mental phenomena. *Journal of Parapsychology*, 59, 196–220.

Mischo, J. (1968). Personality structure of psychokinetic mediums. *Proceedings of the Parapsychological Association*, 5, 35–37.

Morris, R. L., Nanko, M., & Phillips, D. (1982). A comparison of two popularly advocated visual imagery strategies in a psychokinesis task. *The Journal of Parapsychology*, 46(1), 1–16.

Murdie, A. (2015). *Extraordinary evidence versus similar fact evidence: proving the occurance of psi outside the laboratory*. Paper presented at the 39th SPR International Annual Conference, University of Greenwich.

Palmer, J. (1979). A community mail survey of psychic experiences. *Journal of the American Society for Psychical Research*, 73, 221–251.

Pederzoli, L., Giroldini, W., Prati, E., & Tressoldi, P. (2017). The physics of mind-matter interaction at a distance. *NeuroQuantology*, 15(3), 114–119.

Peoc'h, R. (1995). Psychokinetic action of young chicks on the path of an illuminated source. *Journal of Scientific Exploration*, 9(2), 223–223.

Pilkington, R. (2006). *The spirit of Dr. Bindelof: The enigma of seance phenomena*. Charlottesville, VA: Anomalist Books.

Pilkington, R. (2015). Interview with Felicia Parise, August 6, 2013. *Journal of Scientific Exploration*, 29(1), 75–108.

Pratt, J. G., & Keil, H. H. (1973). Firsthand observations of Nina S. Kulagina suggestive of PK upon static objects. *Journal of the American Society for Psychical Research*, 67, 381–390.

Radin, D., & Ferrari, D. C. (1991). Effects of consciousness on the fall of dice: A meta-analysis. *Journal of Scientific Exploration*, 5(1), 61–83.

Radin, D., & Nelson, L. D. (1989). Evidence for consciousness-related anomalies in random physical systems. *Foundations of Physics*, 19(12), 1499–1514.

Radin, D., & Nelson, L. D. (2003). Meta-analysis of mind-matter interaction experiments: 1959–2000. In W. Jonas & C. Crawford (Eds.), *Healing, intention and energy medicine*. London: Harcourt Health Sciences.

Radin, D., Nelson, L. D., Dobyns, Y., & Houtkooper, J. (2006). Reexamining psychokinesis: Comment on the Bosch, Steinkamp, and Boller (2006) meta-analysis. *Psychological Bulletin*, 132, 529–532.

Randall, J. L., & Davis, C. P. (1982). Paranormal deformation of nitinol wire: A confirmatory experiment. *Journal of the Society for Psychical Research*, 51(792), 368–373.

Rhine, L. E. (1970). *Mind over matter: Psychokinesis*. New York: Collier.

Rhine, L. E., & Rhine, J. B. (1943). The psychokinetic effect: I. The first experiment. *The Journal of Parapsychology*, 7, 20–43.

Roll, W. G. (2003). Poltergeists, electromagnetism and consciousness. *Journal of Scientific Exploration*, 17(1), 75–86.

Roll, W. G., & Persinger, M. (1998). Poltergeist and nonlocality: Energetic aspects of RSPK. *The Journal of Parapsychology*, 62(1), 118–119.

Schlitz, M., & Braud, W. (1997). Distant intentionality and healing: Assessing the evidence. *Alternative Therapies in Health and Medicine*, 3(6), 62–73.

Schmidt, H. (1969a). Clairvoyance tests with a machine. *The Journal of Parapsychology*, 33(4), 300–306.

Schmidt, H. (1969b). Precognition of a quantum process. *Journal of Parapsychology*, 33, 99–108.

Schmidt, H. (1970a). PK experiments with animals as subjects. *Journal of Parapsychology*, 255–261.

Schmidt, H. (1970b). A quantum mechanical random number generator for psi tests. *Journal of Parapsychology*, 34, 219–224.

Schmidt, H. (1974). Comparison of PK action on two different random number generators. *Journal of Parapsychology*, 38, 47–55.

Schmidt, H. (1976). PK effect on pre-recorded targets. *Journal of the American Society for Psychical Research*, 70(3), 267–291.

Schmidt, H., & Braud, W. (1993). New PK tests with an independent observer. *The Journal of Parapsychology*, 57(3), 227–240.

Schmidt, H., Morris, R. L., & Rudolph, L. (1986). Channelling evidence for a PK effect to observers. *Journal of Parapsychology*, 50, 1–16.

Schmidt, S. (2012). Can we help just by good intentions? A meta-analysis of experiments on distant intention effects. *The Journal of Alternative and Complementary Medicine*, 18(6), 529–533. doi: 10.1089/acm.2011.0321.

Schmidt, S. (2015). Experimental research on distant intention phenomena. In E. Cardena, J. Palmer, & D. Marcusson-Clavertz (Eds.), *Parapsychology: A handbook for the 21st century* (pp. 244–257). Jefferson, NC: McFarland & Company Inc.

Schmidt, S., Han-Gue, J., Whittman, M., Ambach, W., & Kubel, S. (2018). Remote meditation support – a multimodal distant intention experiment. *Explore*. doi: 10.1016/j.explore.2018. 12.002.

Schmidt, S., Schneider, R., Utts, J., & Walach, H. (2004). Distant intentionality and the feeling of being stared at: Two meta-analyses. *British Journal of Psychology*, 95(2), 235–247.

Schmidt, S., & Walach, H. (2000). Electrodermal activity (EDA) state-of-the-art measurement and techniques for parapsychological purposes. *Journal of Parapsychology*, 64(2), 139–163.

Schneider, R., Binder, M., & Walach, H. (2000). Examining the role of the neutral versus personal experimenter-participant interaction: An EDA-DMILS experiment. *Journal of Parapsychology*, 64(2), 182–195.

Sheldrake, R., & Beharee, A. (2009). A rapid online telepathy test. *Psychological Reports*, 104(3), 957–970.

Targ, R., & Puthoff, H. (1977). *Mind-Reach: Positive proof that ESP exists*. London: Paladin.

Tart, C. T. (1983). Information acquisition rates in forced-choice ESP experiments: Precognition does not work as well as present-time ESP. *Journal of the American Society for Psychical Research, 77,* 293–311.

Tressoldi, P., Massaccesi, S., Martinelli, M., & Cappato, S. (2011). Mental connection at a distance: Useful for solving difficult tasks? *Psychology, 2*(8), 853–858.

Tressoldi, P., Pederzoli, L., Matteoli, M., Prati, E., & Kruth, J. G. (2016). Can our minds emit light at 7300 km distance? A pre-registered confirmatory experiment of mental entanglement with a photomultiplier. *NeuroQuantology, 14*(3), 447–455. doi: 10.14704/nq.2016.14.3.906.

Varvoglis, M., & Bancel, P. A. (2015). Micro-psychokinesis. In E. Cardena, J. Palmer, & D. Marcusson-Clavertz (Eds.), *Parapsychology: A handbook for the 21st century* (pp. 266–281). Jefferson, NC.: McFarland & Company Inc.

Varvoglis, M., & Bancel, P. A. (2016). Micro-psychokinesis: Exceptional or universal? *Journal of Parapsychology, 80*(1), 37–44.

Vasiliev, L. L. (1963). *Experiments in mental suggestion.* Hampshire, UK: Gally Hill Press.

Vilenskaya, L., & May, E. C. (1994). Anomalous mental phenomena research in Russia and the former Soviet Union: A follow up. *Subtle Energies & Energy Medicine Journal Archives, 4*(3), 231–250.

von Lucadou, W. (1995). The model of pragmatic information (MPI). *European Journal of Parapsychology, 11,* 58–75.

Watkins, G. K., & Watkins, A. M. (1973). Apparent psychokinesis on static objects by a gifted subject: A laboratory demonstration. In W. G. Roll, R. L. Morris, & J. D. Morris (Eds.), *Research in parapsychology* (pp. 132–134). Metuchen, NJ: Scarecros Press.

Watt, C., & Baker, I. S. (2002). Remote facilitation of attention focusing with psi-supportive versus psi-unsupportive experimenter suggestions. *Journal of Parapsychology, 66,* 151–168.

Watt, C., & Ramakers, P. (2003). Experimenter effects with a remote facilitation of attention focusing task: A study with multiple believer and disbeliever experimenters. *The Journal of Parapsychology, 67*(1), 99–116.

Chapter 7

Fields of consciousness

Imagine a field of consciousness surrounding the planet, called a noosphere. And now imagine this field being subtly influenced by situations which involve the concerted action of large groups of individuals, all focused coherently on a particular topic or event. This is the idea behind two interesting areas of research called the *global consciousness project* and the *Maharishi effect*. In examining these effects this chapter will begin by briefly exploring the idea of a noosphere. It then outlines the development of the global consciousness project from field-based research. The chapter then examines attempts to register the effects of global consciousness at large-scale events including acts of terror and tragedy, religion and ritual, concern and compassion as well as celebration. This is followed by an examination of some factors suggested to influence these effects. This includes the distance between the sensor devices and the event, the size and emotional response of the crowd as well as the timing. The chapter then moves on to explore the Maharishi effect and how it developed. This is followed by an exploration of evidence suggesting such an effect can produce reductions in crime, conflict and mortality. The chapter then explores some factors suggested to influence the Maharishi effect, including the timing and duration, the size of the meditating group and their level of experience. This is followed by a brief exploration of some potential confounds before the chapter ends by exploring possible mechanisms which could account for both these effects.

The noosphere

The term noosphere derives from the Greek words 'νοῦς' meaning nous or mind, and 'σφαῖρα' referring to sphaira or sphere in the sense that it envelopes the Earth. In this way it can been seen to be related to the terms geosphere and biosphere which contain all living matter (see e.g., Vernadsky, 1945). Taken literally it refers to a sort of *mind-sphere* surrounding the Earth. It is a concept that was jointly developed by three men: the French philosopher and priest Pierre Teilhard de Chardin, the French philosopher and mathematician Édouard Le Roy and the Russian geochemist Vladimir Vernadsky (Serafin, 1988; Vernadsky, 1945). The noosphere is thought to represent a natural component of the Earth's make-up, much like the biosphere and the atmosphere. Indeed, Vernadsky (1945) suggested that it reflects the increasing level of complex consciousness on the planet, from simple life forms, to human consciousness, to a collective human consciousness. In this way it was conceptualised as representing the changing state of the planet from one that has a biosphere to one that develops a noosphere. Hence, it is assumed to emerge from the interaction of multiple conscious minds. In a way the development of the noosphere reflects the development of humanity. As humanity organises itself into ever more complex and coherent social networks, the noosphere is assumed to grow in awareness. Furthermore, according to Vernadsky (1945), this developing noosphere becomes an increasing force for change. Such arguments indicate that the idea of a form of consciousness surrounding the world is not new. However, findings from both the global consciousness project and the Maharishi effect may be the first subtle indications that it exists.

The global consciousness project (GCP)

According to Nelson (2015) what we think and feel can seem ephemeral and subjective but such thoughts and feelings may have a very real presence in the world, a presence that is both observable and measurable via the output from random devices set to produce two types of output, equivalent to a 0 and a 1, or the head and tail of a coin toss. Such random devices have been used in a variety of psi research with some success (see Psychokinesis: Chapter 6). As technology has developed, these random event generators (REG) and random number generators (RNG) have relied more on quantum level processes for the fundamental source of their output to ensure that the production is evenly split between the 0's and the 1's such that the chance of obtaining one or the other remains at 50% (Radin & Nelson, 1989). Such devices can be used to examine the possibility of human consciousness-machine interactions in the sense that conscious intention may influence the sequence of outputs to the extent that it differs significantly from random. That is, the output is more coherent and less random.

Field REG/RNG studies

The success of lab based micro PK research meant that when developments in technology led to a reduction in the size of such devices, they could be connected to a laptop and taken outside of the lab, allowing researchers to ask whether such devices would be influenced by the shared thoughts and/or emotions of a group of people whose consciousness was focused on a particular event, such as a concert or religious ceremony. In such instances control data could be collected from locations that were not thought to inspire coherent levels of consciousness, such as business meetings and shopping centres (Nelson, Bradish, Dobyns, Dunne, & Jahn, 1996). Since the start of such *field REG* studies there have been many attempts to examine whether the random output of such a device is influenced by a possible *field of consciousness*, the coherence of which would interact with the device in question causing it to act in a non-random manner (e.g., Divya, Nagendra, & Ram, 2016; Hirukawa & Ishikawa, 2004; Kokubo, 2016). For instance, researchers adopting this approach have reported significant deviations in the random output of such devices during large festivals (Divya et al., 2016) as well as at the cinema (Shimizu, Yamamoto, & Ishikawa, 2017). Furthermore, Radin et al. (2017) also found significant decreases in random output from devices placed at and around the Burning Man festival that is held each year in Black Rock Desert, USA and attracts large numbers of people. Such findings inspired Nelson and others to create an internet-based array of continuously recording REG devices, or nodes, situated at distinct locations around the world. Metaphorically, it has been referred to as taking an *electrogaiagram*, akin to taking an EEG from the head of a single person and was called the global consciousness project (GCP; see, Bancel & Nelson, 2008; Nelson, 2001, 2008a, 2008b, 2013, 2015; Nelson, Bradish, Dobyns, Dunne, & Jahn, 1998; Nelson, Radin, Shoup, & Bancel, 2002; Radin, 2002).

GCP

The main idea was that the GCP would create a network extending the single field REG work to a global scale. According to Nelson (2008a) it is first and foremost an empirical exercise. It allows questions to be asked regarding the non-random structure of data from the network that corresponds to global events. The idea is that when global events engage the attention of large groups there will be an in-teraction between 'communal consciousness and the physical world' (Nelson, 2013, p. 16). This interaction is thought to influence the outcome of the network of REGs to the extent that they no longer produce random output. More specifically, that periods of collective emotional or focused attention that spread across large parts of the population would correlate with significant deviations in the random output of one or more devices (Bancel & Nelson, 2008). It is important to note here that it is not simply that the REG devices no longer produce output that is random, but that the output of two or more of the devices becomes synchronised. Hence, there is a loss of randomness or an increase in coherence, *across* the net-work. Interestingly, unlike many other areas of psi research this is one where the effect is not produced by the *goal directed* intention of the individuals in question. That is, the group, crowd or population in question may not even know there are multiple REG devices in place.

Data collection on the GCP began in 1998 and over time many REG devices, or nodes, were placed at various locations around the world from Alaska to New Zealand, with the majority in Europe and North America, continuously generating random output (see Figure 7.1; Bancel & Nelson, 2008; Nelson, 2015). At each of the host sites around the world a REG device is attached to a computer running the relevant software. Throughout the day the various trials are recorded and stored on the host computer and at regular intervals the data is then relayed in packets to a server located in Princeton, USA, which then permanently archives the data file.

According to Nelson (2013) the data is subject to rigorous procedures to ensure it is free from artefacts and defects, such as electrical surges and/or failures, as well as interference from other sources such as mobile phone activity. This data can then be examined to ascertain whether there are any periods of non-random structure that correlate with major events in the world. According to current un-derstanding there should be no relationship between the output of these REGs and world events. This allows the formation of a priori research questions which can then be tested using the data from the archive. If a hypothesis is proposed and registered, the data are extracted and subject to standard statistical analysis with the results posted online at the GCP website (see http://www.global-mind.org). In a way, Nelson (2013) has suggested that this may represent a way to measure the emerging noosphere.

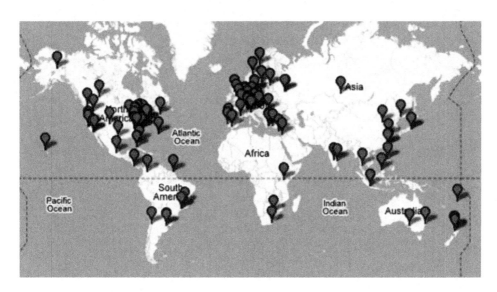

Figure 7.1 Distribution of REG devices (indicated by markers) across the world which go to make up the GCP network (from Bancel & Nelson, 2008, p. 315, with permission).

Evidence for GCP

Since the inception of the GCP project in 1998 the continuous collection of trials from multiple devices has led to the creation of a database containing over 26 billion time stamped trials, as of May 2016 (Bancel, 2017). This allows researchers to look at various historical events that have occurred during this time and ask whether prior, during or after such events there were any noticeable changes in the random output of the devices. According to Nelson (2015) the answer to this is a clear 'yes'. The findings from such research are often grouped under headings relating directly to the events that inspired them and include terror and tragedy, religion and ritual, concern and compassion, and celebrations.

Terror and tragedy

Attempts to register the influence of group consciousness at large events related to terrorist activity has shown significant effects. Perhaps unsurprisingly one of the most widely reported events examined was the terrorist attack on the World Trade Centre in New York, USA on 11 September 2001. When the data from the various REG units was examined it was found to have significantly deviated from random (see Figure 7.2; Nelson et al., 2002; Radin, 2002). The data also showed a substantial increase in structure which correlated with the most intense and widely shared periods of emotional reactions to the event (Nelson, 2002, 2014, 2015).

This was taken as evidence of a coherent global conscious response to the terrorist attack. Radin (2002) agreed, suggesting that this work pointed to some form of entanglement between mind and matter/machine. Furthermore, Nelson (2002) argued that such a pattern cannot be accounted for in terms of an electrical disturbance and/or

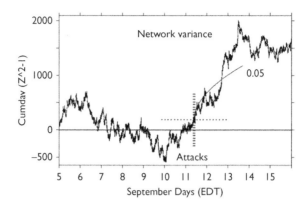

Figure 7.2 Cumulative deviation of GCP network up to 11 September 2001 (marked) and beyond (from Nelson et al., 2002, p. 6, with permission).

increased mobile phone use. However, not all agree with this outcome. For instance, May and Spottiswoode (2011) suggested that if the time window were altered making it either shorter or longer the effects would not have achieved significance. Nelson (2015) takes issue with this claim calling it 'unacceptable post-hoc data selection' (p. 286).

This, however, is not the only tragic event to show up in the GCP network. For instance, the funeral of Princess Diana provided a global event with the focus of many millions of people. Monitoring these events the GCP network again showed significant deviations from random chance (Nelson et al., 1998). Interestingly, a week later during the funeral of Mother Theresa, however, there was no clear deviation from random. It is of course difficult to control for the variety and nature of such naturally occurring events. Some may be more important, or deemed more important than others and as such the emotional response will differ. However, more recently Nelson (2011a) reported on an international event which involved the Israeli navy sending commandoes to stop a flotilla carrying humanitarian aid to Gaza in May 2010. This event caused the reported deaths of at least 10 pro-Palestinian activists and many more were injured in the skirmish. This sparked an international diplomatic crisis causing further strains on relationships between Israel and Turkey and led to condemnations by the United Nations and the European Union. During this crisis, examination of the GCP network showed a significant deviation from random chance (see Figure 7.3).

However, not all such events that have been examined have been shown to elicit significant effects. For instance, during 2009 there was a period of time when global concern peaked regarding a possible pandemic of the very deadly swine flu. When Nelson (2010) examined the data he did find a trend, in that there was a period of time when the data cumulatively showed a shift away from the random baseline, but there was no overall effect (see Figure 7.4).

The lack of an effect here may be because the effect itself was subtle and or the number of those involved may not have been sufficiently high, or the emotiveness not sufficiently engaging. It is certainly the case that the outbreak was not as serious as originally expected and the World Health Organisation officially declared the

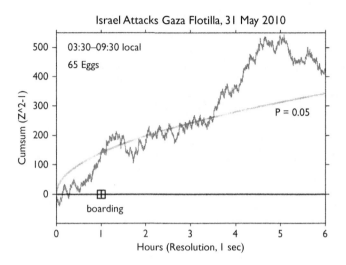

Figure 7.3 Cumulative deviation of GCP network during a 6-hour period representing the Israeli attack on the Gaza flotilla (from Nelson, 2011, with permission).

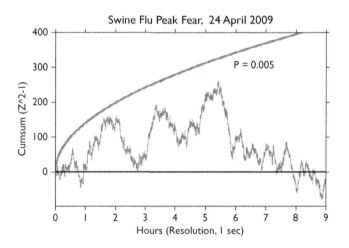

Figure 7.4 Cumulative deviation during possible swine flu pandemic of 2009 (from Nelson, 2010, p. 7, with permission).

pandemic over in 2010. Hence, the nature of the event and the emotive response it evokes may influence the outcome.

Religion and ritual

According to Nelson (1997) a large organised global meditation event called 'Gaiamind' produced positive results. Another more recent religious event that

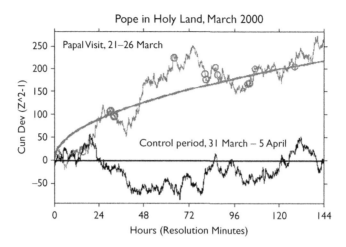

Figure 7.5 Changes in the GCP network during the Papal visit (top jagged line) compared to a control period (bottom jagged line) (from Nelson, 2019, p. 4, with permission).

attracted a lot of media attention was the week-long pilgrimage of Pope John Paul II to various sacred religious sites in the Middle East in March 2000 (Nelson, 2013, 2019). According to Nelson (2019) the data from the GCP network showed a persistent and non-random trend that was not evident when a later 'control' dataset was extracted (see Figure 7.5).

Such a finding is consistent with the data from a field REG approach which used two REG devices in an effort to detect possible changes in random output due to a nearby religious ceremony (Kokubo, 2016).

Concern and compassion

Nelson (2013) has also reported on the peace demonstrations during February 2003, aimed to show worldwide support for a peaceful resolution to the conflict in Iraq and the Middle East. During these demonstrations Nelson (2013) found that data from the GCP network was clearly random until about 11am, when crowds of people gathered in cities such as Rome, London and Berlin. Then the data showed a clear departure from random which continued for the rest of the day.

Celebrations

A good candidate for identifying a priori widespread engagement in a global celebration is New Year's Eve. Everybody knows when it occurs, it happens every year and there is widespread engagement and media coverage. When Nelson (2013) reported on 10 years of GCP data from 1998 to 2008, the prediction was that the random variance of the REGs would *decrease* as midnight approached and then *increase* again after midnight. Averaged over all time zones and across all 10 years the data clearly showed a non-random pattern, which confirmed this prediction. According to Nelson (2013, 2014, 2015) the pattern exhibited across the devices

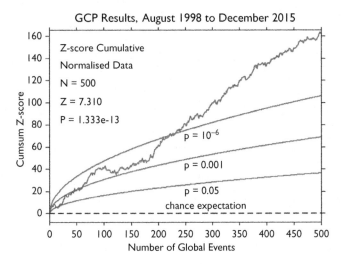

Figure 7.6 Cumulative changes (represented by the jagged line) in the GCP network from 1998 to 2015 along with the probability levels indicating that such changes are distinct from chance (from http://noosphere.princeton.edu with permission).

shows that the effects are real and robust, yet small. Because of the small effect size, it may well be the case that single events do not always produce a clear effect. However, Nelson (2013, 2014, 2015) has argued that a more comprehensive picture can be obtained by examining the cumulative effects of various trials from the GCP network since its inception (see Figure 7.6).

The jagged line in Figure 7.6 shows the cumulative sum of deviations from 500 tests compared to chance expectation with smooth lines to indicate statistically significant levels of 0.05, 0.001 and 10^{-6} (or 0.000001). According to Nelson (2014) the pattern to date shows an overall effect with odds of about one in a million that the correlations are due to random chance fluctuations. Such findings have led Nelson (2015) to argue that that amount of data collected and the pattern it exhibits provides highly significant evidence for something influencing the devices such that the output is no longer random. Indeed, Nelson (2014) reported that over the previous 15-year period positive correlations in the network that match predictions have been found in about two out of three cases. Though the effect for single trials tends to be small the composite results are robustly significant and deviate from chance expectations by seven standard deviations. Furthermore, resampling the output not linked to global events shows the expected random output. Hence, the non-random output is not something inherent in the output of the devices. The general consensus of opinion is that the findings from the GCP provides a clear indication of a correlation among globally distributed systems and human consciousness (Bancel, 2011, 2014; Bancel & Nelson, 2008; Nelson, 2001, 2002, 2010, 2011a, 2013, 2014, 2015; Nelson et al., 1998; Nelson et al., 2002; Radin, 2002). The implications of such correlations suggest that consciousness may create order though it is not clear yet what factors may influence this.

Mediating factors

Trying to understand what factors may influence or mediate the cohesiveness of the GCP network will not only help to shed light on the possible processes involved but also benefit attempts to model or explain such structure. To date researchers have examined the distance between devices and from the device to the event, the size of the event and the emotional response it produces as well as the timing of the event.

Distance

An interesting question is whether the correlations seen in the GCP network depend on the precise location of the various devices. Current understanding informed by the inverse square law would suggest that the intensity of any effect should change as a function of the square of the distance from the source. That is, as the distance between the source of the effect and the REG devices registering it increases the effect itself should decrease or weaken. However, as Nelson (2013) has pointed out, it is not always easy to precisely identify the spatial location of an event. For example, the Asian tsunami on December 26 2004 produced disastrous impact locally; however the response to the news reporting was literally global. Hence, it can be difficult to determine with any degree of precision the locus of an effect. It is not clear if data should only be collected from the location of the physical event or extended to capture the reaction to spreading news reports. Nevertheless, Nelson and Bancel (2011) have reported suggestive evidence of a linear regression effect with regards to distance. That is, the correlation between pairs of devices within the network decreases as the distance between them increases. Indeed, Nelson (2013) reported that the inter-device correlations decreased as the distances increased from 8,000 to 10,000 km, providing strong support for spatial structure in the data. However, Nelson (2015) points out that non-random output can still be found between devices that are separated by large distances during 'global events'. There is also agreement that more work is needed to explore this in order to ascertain whether it applies uniformly or only to certain kinds of events. As such, any model attempting to describe the data would need to incorporate such structure in order to describe the data adequately.

Size of the event

It should be possible to separate events in terms of their size, based on estimates of the number of people attending or involved. In this way it should be possible to compare large global based events to more local ones. An intuitive expectation would be that larger more global events would produce more robust effects in the GCP network. Indeed, Bancel and Nelson (2008) reported that events engaging a very large number of people do produce significantly more deviations in the GCP network than minor events with fewer people. Nelson (2013, 2015) confirmed this, stating that such comparisons show that larger effects are found with global scale events compared to smaller local events. This would suggest that the number of people involved in an event would influence its cohesiveness. Furthermore, that these people would be required to respond in a similar way at a similar time for this coherence to occur and then influence the GCP network.

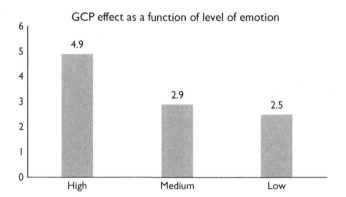

Figure 7.7 The GCP effect as a function of high (left), medium (middle) and low (right) levels of emotion (adapted from Nelson, 2008).

Emotive response

Several emotions are identifiable at various levels in the world events, and subjective ratings can be made with good reliability. While not all events can easily be assigned to a specific class or category, such as 'fear/anxiety', 'positive feeling' and 'compassion/love', all yield adequate samples to assess the presence of a high, medium or low emotional response. Bancel and Nelson (2008) suggested early on that events may require a strong emotional response from a large proportion of the population for an effect to clearly emerge. Indeed, when Nelson (2008a) examined the data he found that high emotional events tended to produce much greater effects than those that elicited either medium or low levels of emotion (see Figure 7.7).

Hence, the stronger or more intense the emotion related to the event the stronger the effect on the GCP network. Interestingly, it is the events that seem to provoke the extremes of these emotional responses, whether positive or negative, that produce the most powerful effects. That is, events with either strong positive or strong negative valence produce significant effects whereas neutral non-emotional events do not (Nelson, 2008a). According to Nelson (2008a, 2008b, 2013) the largest contributions come from events characterised by high levels of fear or compassion and love.

Timing

In terms of timing it is not always clear when to look for an effect or how long an event may last. This may be because, as Nelson and Bancel (2011) point out, an event need not be constrained by the moment of occurrence but also includes the spreading reactions to it. For instance, in response to most events human reactions will initially grow, persist whilst interest is maintained or fed by mainstream media and then possibly spike, and thereafter dissipate as attention moves on to other things. Given that the GCP reflects the level of emotional engagement of the people it is difficult to say precisely at what time a certain number of people will be engaged and as such it may only be possible to approximate the timing of an event. This has important implications as Bancel and Nelson (2008) point out; changing the time window that defines an event may influence the outcome. Nevertheless, Nelson (2013) suggests that data correlations should correspond to the human response to an event, rather than the event itself. As such, any effect may take some time to appear and would likely persist for a short period of time whilst people attend to and focus on the event and then disappear as interest and attention wanes. Indeed, Nelson (2013) reports that correlations between devices grows to significance between 45 minutes to an hour from the start of an event. The correlation has a broad peak of approximately two hours and then begins to diminish. This suggests that the effect may not always be immediate but may take time to build up to a level that is detectable. It may then remain stable for a brief period of time whilst interest in the event is maintained. This pattern is likely to be influenced by the type of event and the level of response.

The Maharishi effect (ME)

The second effect to be explored is based upon group meditation. Meditation is an umbrella term often used to refer to an *approach* adopted to achieve both physical and mental relaxation and focus rather than any specific single technique. For instance, there is Transcendental meditation, Buddhist meditation, yoga mantra meditation and Vipassana meditation, to name but a few. Whilst there may be many different approaches Goleman (1972) pointed out that they often share two core components: *mindfulness* and *concentration*. Mindfulness generally refers to the idea of maintaining a non-judgemental awareness of the current situation where a person is aware of the thoughts and feelings they are having but does not allow themselves to be caught up in them. Concentration invariably involves the state of a single-minded focus of attention on a particular phrase or mantra, or on one's own physiology such as listening to the rhythm of the heart. Hence, meditation is an active process and one that invariably requires time and practice to master. Nevertheless, with continued practice it has been suggested that meditation can lead to a degree of self-regulation of the mind and body (see, Cahn & Polich, 2006). Indeed, there is good evidence that meditation is beneficial both for general health and cognition (see e.g., Anderson, Liu, & Kryscio, 2008; Vernon, 2009).

According to Maharishi Mahesh Yogi, who developed the Transcendental Meditation (TM) technique, if a number of individuals participate together in such meditative practice this will have a wider beneficial effect on the surrounding life and society. The suggestion is that TM encourages the individual to shift their conscious mind from the everyday waking state to a distinct transcendent level of consciousness and this will radiate outwards producing a transition in society towards more orderly and harmonious functioning (Morris, 1992; University, 1977). In honour of the developer this is more generally referred to as the *Maharishi effect* (Borland & Landrith, 1976). The TM technique is broadly described as a simple, effortless technique that can be used to promote full development of human consciousness, and should be practised for 15 to 20 minutes morning and evening with eyes closed (Roth, 1994). The procedure is thought to allow the individual to experience more silent levels of awareness which in turn are thought to lead to the experience of 'pure consciousness' – which is consciousness without the usual mental activity of perception and thought.

According to Maharishi (1978) a society can be characterised by the quality of its collective consciousness which arises from and has a reciprocal influence on the consciousness of all the members of that particular society. Hence, an increase in the coherence and harmony of the collective consciousness brought about as a result of individual members practising TM will in turn have a positive influence on the quality of life of society in general. A key point of the Maharishi effect (ME) is that it does not require any particular external conditions, only that a minimum group size is met in order for the meditative practice to elicit a change in the wider field of consciousness (Orme-Johnson, 2003). It should be made clear that there is no evidence that the various individuals practising TM need to do so together in a single group, and/or specifically focus their intent on reducing crime or violence (see, Orme-Johnson, 2003). It is much more the case that the practice will by its very nature lead to wider changes much like the ripples in a pond reaching out to influence the water surrounding the location of the pebble thrown in. In this sense, the emerging result is seen as a property of TM or a by-product of its practice (Despande & Kowall, 2017).

Evidence for the Maharishi effect

Over time a substantial amount of evidence has been gathered indicating that group practice of TM may be associated with reductions in crime, international conflict and reduced mortality rates.

Reductions in crime

Initial evidence to suggest that groups practising TM may be associated with reduced crime rates was reported by Borland and Landrith (1976). They compared 11 cities from the USA with a population of over 25,000 where almost 1% were practising TM (0.97%) to 11 control cities matched for resident and college population levels and geographic region. The control cities were also identified as having an average 0.29% of their populations practise TM. Crime rates were obtained for each of the cities from the 'Uniform Crime Reports' compiled by the Federal Bureau of Investigations (FBI) and compared from 1967 to 1973 with 1972 representing the year when the TM cities reached their almost 1% threshold level. The researchers found that there were no clear differences in the level of reported crime between the two groups of cities from 1967 to 1972 but in 1973 those cities with around 1% of TM practitioners showed a significant reduction in crime rates compared to the non-TM cities, as can be seen in Figure 7.8.

The idea that crime rate may be reduced when a certain percentage of the population take part in TM has also been reported by Dillbeck, Landrith III and Orme-Johnson (1981). Here the researchers reported a decrease in reported crime rate in 1973 among 24 cities with populations larger than 10,000 where 1% were participating in TM by the end of 1972 compared with 24 cities matched for geographic region and population. Others have also reported similar findings (see e.g., Dillbeck, Banus, Polanzi, & Landrith III, 1988; Dillbeck, Cavanaugh, Glenn, Orme-Johnson, & Mittlefehldt, 1987; Hatchard, Deans, Cavanaugh, & Orme-Johnson, 1996; Orme-Johnson, Dillbeck, Alexander, Chandler, & Cranson, 2003). One review also found that not only had crime reduced but quality of life showed a

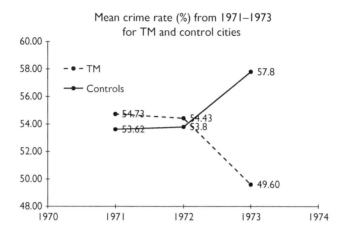

Figure 7.8 Mean percentage crime rate for TM (dotted line) and control (unbroken line) cities across the years 1971–1973 (adapted from Borland & Landrith, 1976).

concurrent increase when 1% of the population took part in such meditative practices (Orme-Johnson, 2003).

Dillbeck et al. (1988) extended these early findings to show a similar decrease in crime rates across 160 cities across the USA and Canada from 1972–1978 when controlling for other variables known to influence crime rates such as education, unemployment, income, percentage of families in poverty, stability of residence, percentage over the age of 65 years, population size and density as well as the ratio of police per population. Even when controlling for such potential confounding variables as age, population, seasonality or possible long-term trends, Dillbeck (1990) found that the practice of TM techniques was associated with a reduction in the number of violent deaths in the American state of Iowa between 1982 and 1985. Dillbeck et al. (1981) also used a cross-lagged panel correlation technique to identify whether the relationship between the 1% of TM practitioners and the reduction in crime was causal or spurious. A cross-lagged panel correlation provides a way of drawing tentative causal conclusions from a study in which none of the variables is manipulated. They reported good 'evidence for a causal influence associated with practice of the TM technique' (p. 25).

Such studies are by their very nature retrospective in that they look back at crime rates and examine the number of individuals participating in TM to see if there is any association between the two. Such an approach is naturally limited in terms of identifying clear causal mechanisms. However, others have taken a more *prospective approach* in an effort to experimentally test such ideas and make the causal links clearer. For example, Orme-Johnson, Alexander, Davies, Chandler and Larimore (1988) reported on a prospective approach to testing the ME in the Middle East. The aim was to utilise TM to reduce stress and improve the overall quality of life in the area. Specifically, they predicted that a group practising TM during August and September 1983 in Jerusalem would be associated with clear reductions in population stress. Stress in this instance was measured using a range of variables including total number of crimes per day in Jerusalem, Israel and Lebanon, as well as automobile accidents, number of fires and war deaths in Lebanon. They found clear reductions in all variables measured as a function of TM practice. More recently, Hagelin et al. (1999) reported on the results of a 'Demonstration Project' which tested the ability of TM to reduce crime in the District of Columbia, USA, between the periods of June and July 1993. A research protocol was devised and agreed upon in advance which predicted that during the time period in question there would be a substantial fall in the level of reported violent crime. During this time a group of approximately 4000 TM practitioners gathered in Washington from 82 different countries. The results showed that during this time there was a highly significant reduction in violent crimes. At its peak there was a reported reduction in crime of 23.3%. Importantly, the statistical analyses took account of external factors also known to influence crime rates, including the weather, daylight hours and changes in police staffing. Furthermore, a time series analysis of the same time period in the preceding five years showed no clear decrease in crime rate. Hence, the drop in crime rates were not due to an annual drop in crime rates during the summer period. Recent attempts to replicate such positive findings have proven fruitful. For instance, Dillbeck and Cavanaugh (2016) found that the percentage of reported violent crimes and homicides across 206 cities in the USA was reduced after the intervention of group TM practice (see Figure 7.9).

They argue that such a pattern cannot easily be accounted for in terms of increased unemployment, incarceration rates, changes in average temperature and possible changes in policing strategies. Furthermore, this pattern replicates prior research showing a positive effect for such group TM practices.

International conflict

Researchers have also suggested that such meditative practices have been associated with reduced terrorism and international conflict at a global level. For example, Orme-Johnson, Dillbeck and Alexander (2003) reported that at three time points en-capsulating three different locations (Iowa, USA; Holland; Washington, USA) between

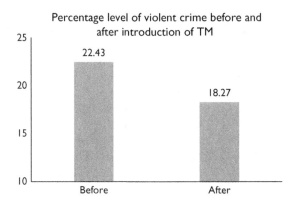

Figure 7.9 Mean percentage levels of violent crime before (left) and after (right) the introduction of group TM practices (adapted from Dillbeck & Cavanaugh, 2016).

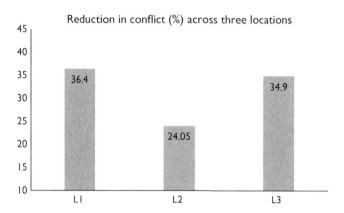

Figure 7.10 Percentage reduction in conflict at location 1 (i.e., L1: Iowa), location 2 (L2: Holland) and location 3 (L3: Washington) as a function of the TM intervention (adapted from Orme-Johnson et al., 2003).

the years 1983–1985 when TM practitioners were assembled in sufficient numbers at each location there was an associated drop in terrorism and international conflict (see Figure 7.10). These assembled practices involved large groups meditating twice a day, once in the morning and then again in the afternoon. Since then others have also reported that group practice of meditation was associated with improved cooperation and reduced conflict in the Lebanon war crises (Davies & Alexander, 2005).

Reduced mortality

A recent study by Dillbeck and Cavanaugh (2017) also examined the effect of a large group of meditating individuals on rates of infant mortality and drug-related deaths in North America. During the time of the intervention they found significant reductions in the trends of both infant mortality and drug-related deaths (see Figure 7.11).

This intervention involved over 1000 individuals gathering each day to meditate. Furthermore, it occurred despite the negative impact of the economic recession that started in 2008. Dillbeck and Cavanaugh (2017) have argued that there is a clear and significant association between such large group meditative practice and the health benefits seen in reduced mortality rates across the wider population. They also argue that such effects cannot be accounted for in terms of seasonality effects, temporal trends, reduced sales of drugs or economic stressors. As such, they claim that there is no clear plausible alternative that would satisfactorily explain the reductions in mortality rates seen as part of the intervention. Alongside these changes researchers have also reported that such meditative practices are associated with improved quality of life (Assimakis & Dillbeck, 1995; Cavanaugh, King, & Ertuna, 1989; Dillbeck et al., 1987) as well as a reduction in motor vehicle fatalities (Cavanaugh & Dillbeck, 2017).

It is not clear if such effects would be elicited with any type of meditative practice or whether they are specific to TM only, as there are many aspects of the meditative practice that are shared by different approaches. Nevertheless, a meta-analysis of the

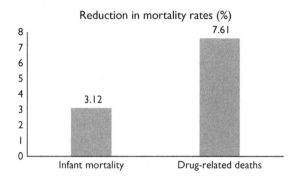

Reduction in mortality rates (%)

Figure 7.11 Percentage reductions in infant mortality rate (left) and drug-related deaths (right) as a function of the TM intervention (adapted from Dillbeck & Cavanaugh, 2017).

effects of TM by Alexander, Rainforth and Gelderloos (1991) has shown that TM can elicit behavioural and relaxation changes not evident in other meditation and relaxation techniques. Such a finding could suggest that TM may represent a distinct type of meditative practice. However, clear and direct comparisons between groups conducting TM type meditation and a coherent alternative need to be conducted to fully explore this idea. In addition to this, Fales and Markovsky (1997) have queried why such an effect, if real, would *only* elicit positive behavioural effects. Orme-Johnson and Oates (2009) suggest this may be due to the innate and naturally adaptive changes in behaviour that move an organism away from noxious events towards more life sustaining/ enhancing events. An important point made by Orme-Johnson (2003) is that the implementation of a TM type programme across the United States could significantly reduce crime and save 'over $600 billion annually' (p. 281). A similar call has been made by Dillbeck and Cavanaugh (2017) in terms of the benefits for reducing public stress-related parameters.

Influencing factors

There are a number of factors that have been examined due to their potential influence on the ME. This includes how much time may be needed for an effect to emerge and the duration of such an effect, as well as the impact of group size and experience.

Time

Trying to understand how much time is needed for an effect to emerge and how long any such effect would last may help to shed light on the underlying processes involved. However, the pattern of effects is not always clear. For example, Orme-Johnson et al. (1988) reported a zero lag cross-correlation between war-related variables and the practice of TM. Such a finding is consistent with the notion of a sudden and system wide change, or phase transition, to a more coherent state. Importantly, this has not been the case for all variables assessed. For instance, Dillbeck (1990) found a decline in reported levels of violent deaths one week after the threshold level of 1% of the population practising TM had been reached, whereas Orme-Johnson, Dillbeck and Alexander (2003) reported evidence for both an *immediate* effect in two locations and a *gradual* effect occurring in a third. This gradual effect was evident two days after the beginning of the meditation assembly. They suggest this may be due to the way in which conflict was assessed and/or the overall severity level of conflict at that time. Hence, the potential time delay between the practice of TM and the emergent effect may depend on the nature of the variable measured as well as other factors, only some of which have been explored. In terms of how long these effects last, once they have emerged, the evidence seems to suggest a reasonably enduring duration. For example, Dillbeck et al. (1981) reported that the decreased crime rate associated with 1% of the population taking part in TM in 1973 continued to show a decrease over the following five years. More recently Hagelin et al. (1999) also found that the decrease in reported crime rates associated with a TM intervention remained 'for several months before returning to predicted levels' (p. 175) after the TM group had departed. This would suggest that the ME elicits an effect that may last for some time after the end of the TM session(s).

Size and experience

It has been suggested that the number of individuals participating in the meditative practice in order to generate an effect is between 1% and the square root of 1% of the societal group under focus. This would suggest a distinct threshold effect rather than a more linear effect where the impact of TM is directly proportional to the size of the group meditating. However, it may be that a certain threshold is initially needed and then a linear trend develops. Indeed, Borland and Landrith (1976) reported a positive effect when the average number of people participating in TM was only 0.97% of the overall population. It is not clear why the threshold of 1% is used and/or whether this has any clear empirical basis beyond the predicted claims of the founder of TM (see Borland & Landrith, 1976). Nevertheless, Borland and Landrith (1976) have suggested that there may be some form of threshold phenomenon whereby the effect emerges more strongly once a certain number of people join the mediation (see Figure 7.12).

However, others have found more linear type effects. For instance, Dillbeck et al. (1988) conducted a time series analysis on weekly crime figures from October 1981 to October 1983 and found increased group participation in TM was followed by reductions in violent crime. Dillbeck (1990) also reported a clear association between increasing TM group size and a corresponding decrease in the number of violent deaths reported. Hence, the pattern may not be as simple as originally assumed. It may also be influenced by the type of TM and the experience of the practitioners (Orme-Johnson et al., 1988). For example, Maharishi (1996) suggested that practice of the more powerful TM-Sidhi technique could produce society-wide benefits even when practised by less than 1% of the population. Indeed, the suggestion was that the square root of 1% of the population, if practising the advanced technique, would be sufficient to elicit wider changes. Such a view is consistent with the suggestion of Hagelin et al. (1999) who argued that stronger, more robust effects may emerge if the individuals are more advanced and practise the TM-Sidhi set of mental techniques.

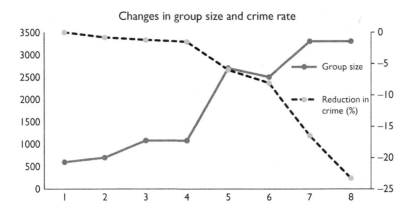

Figure 7.12 Changes in group size (unbroken line measured in 100's using left-hand axis) and reduction in crime rate (dotted line measured in % using right-hand axis) over an 8-week
period (adapted from Hagelin et al., 1999).

Indeed, a review of the ME found that smaller groups could be as effective as larger
ones if they practised the more advanced TM-Sidhi technique (Orme-Johnson, 2003).

Potential confounds

The evidence from the various studies examining the ME seem to suggest that when
groups of a sufficient size gather together to conduct TM positive effects occur in the
nearby environment. However, there are many known variables that are likely to influence rates of crime, conflict and possible mortality. These include the weather, reporting levels, unemployment, population, economic variables, type of crime, age range
of the population, educational level, general trends and time of year to name but a few.
Orme-Johnson, Dillbeck and Alexander (2003) have argued that the researchers are
fully aware of such potential confounds and make attempts, where possible, to control
for them. Nevertheless, Schrodt (1990) has argued that there are a number of methodological weaknesses that limit the interpretation in favour of TM having a discernible effect and that such weaknesses provide a more obvious interpretation of the
results. According to Schrodt (1990) there are problems with the fact that the measurements used to identify the number of active TM practitioners are unclear and incorrect, treatment and controls are often not randomly allocated to conditions, and the
reported effects may have been the result of the statistical tests used. In terms of incorrect measurement of the number of TM practitioners Schrodt (1990) argues that the
population figures used are often defined using *political boundaries* as opposed to
geographical boundaries. According to Schrodt (1990) if 'one uses distance rather than
political boundaries the square root of 1% threshold was never reached' (p. 748). The
second point is that the lack of controls means that it is not possible to eliminate a
possible reverse causality. That is, if participants taking part in the TM technique were
interested in the outcome they would be likely to monitor crime/violence or the focus of
the intervention and as information showed these moving in the desired direction they
would then be more likely to participate. Hence, for example, it is the awareness of the

general reduction in violence that leads to an increase in TM participation and not the TM itself. Finally, Schrodt (1990) has argued that the statistical tests used simply identify probabilities that are not equal to zero, and do not test whether the model is correct or not. As such, it is more likely that spurious significant correlations will occur.

However, researchers have responded to these criticisms by pointing out that the measurement of TM group size was consistent with both theory and prior research. For example, Orme-Johnson, Alexander and Davies (1990) argue that prior successful research utilised a quantification of the number of TM participants based upon political boundaries rather than simple geographical distance. Furthermore, they point out that these represent *community boundaries* and are likely to elicit greater homogeneity and closeness, which would engender a greater spread of the predicted coherent effects of meditation. As such, Orme-Johnson et al. (1990) argue that these community or political boundaries would be more likely to influence the spreading effect of the collective consciousness. In terms of a possible inverse effect whereby a reduction in conflict led potential practitioners to engage in meditative practice, Orme-Johnson et al. (1990) point out that the counterintuitive assumption would also need to be made that if/when conflict increased such individuals would remain at home. They argue that such a view would seem at odds with the assumed motivations of those taking part in such meditative practices. They also point out that the meditations invariably took place in the morning and the afternoon, often before reported crime and conflict took place. Hence, such information would be unlikely to influence engagement in prior meditations. In terms of randomly allocating individuals to conditions Orme-Johnson et al. (1990) argue that such a process is not logistically feasible or practical. With regards to the robustness of the statistical techniques used Orme-Johnson et al. (1990) point out that a re-analysis of their data using different specifications produced the same results. Also, when incorporating randomised pseudo-intervention periods to see if any spurious effects were found they report 'no significant autocorrelation structure in the randomised' (p. 765) control conditions. They argue that these findings strongly support the use of the methods adopted and the original findings reported.

Mechanisms

This chapter has reported on two areas of research that elicit similar effects. That is, the coherent emotive response of many people to a global event produces a synchrony in the feelings and shared consciousness of those involved. This in turn influences the network of the GCP. In a similar way, the ME is the result of an increase in coherence and harmony of the collective consciousness of the meditators. Two models have been put forward to account for the GCP data: the first is a selective model and the second a field-based model. Less research has been carried out on developing models for the ME; however one recent attempt suggests a form of holographic entanglement.

Selection model

The idea here is that the findings from the GCP are largely the result of *experimenter psi* (May & Spottiswoode, 2011). More specifically, that Nelson used psi, either implicitly or explicitly, to select trials from the database to confirm his hypotheses.

Such a proposal fits nicely within *Decision Augmentation Theory* (DAT), which relates to the idea that decisions to select one or more trials over another are augmented by implicit psi to achieve the desired outcome. Psi in this instance could act via precognition based on the feedback obtained in the future that the chosen trials show the expected outcome. May and Spottiswoode (2011) argue that because the devices do not respond in a symmetrical manner to similar events a more parsimonious interpretation is that the experimenters, and in particular Nelson himself as a key researcher in the field of GCP research, are responsible for the effects.

Unsurprisingly, Nelson (2013) disagrees, and argues that attempting to account for the GCP data in terms of experimenter psi is both unconvincing and simplistic. He admits that it is possible that experimenter effects may contribute to the outcome but they are an inadequate explanation for the structure found in the data. Nelson (2011b) has also pointed out that no claims regarding the symmetry of GCP data have been put forward and as such this is a *straw man* argument (i.e., putting forth a weak argument because it will be easy to knock down/refute, etc.). Furthermore, the data and the deviations have an internal structure that makes the 'effect' more compelling and much less likely to be the result of mere selection (Nelson, 2011a, 2011b). Nelson and Bancel (2009) agree that the data do not fit an experimenter model effect. Indeed an analysis of the GCP data by Bancel (2011, 2014) rejected the selection model idea with a high level of confidence (see also, Nelson, 2010, 2011a). They argue that the data, which contains an inherent structure, is more accurately described with reference to field-like models.

However, Bancel (2017) later changed his mind and argued that the GCP data were due to what he called the goal-oriented selection effects of individuals associated with the project, in particular, the notion that those involved in the research have the freedom to select or restrict the parameters of interest – what Bancel (2017) refers to as *self-referential fine tuning*. This is not thought to be the result of a conscious process but rather an anomalous effect based on the experimenter's actions which include the design and implementation of the study. Again Nelson (2017) disagrees with this view and thinks such a suggestion is both preliminary and incomplete. For instance, he points out that many questions examined via GCP were post hoc and as such were not part of the experimenter's initial expectations or intentions. There are other points Nelson (2017) highlights that are also incompatible with a goal-oriented model. For example, the internal structure of the data, including both distance and temporal effects, are more consistent with a field-oriented model.

Field model

In mainstream science many 'at a distance effects' have been accounted for in terms of the existence of underlying fields. Hence, many have argued that both the GCP data and the ME could be accounted for in terms of a field of consciousness extending from the mind of each individual interacting with the extended fields of other minds creating various levels of coherence and interference depending on the intentions and level of shared engagement of the individuals in question (Dillbeck et al., 1987; Hagelin et al., 1999; Nelson, 2010, 2015; Orme-Johnson, 2003; Orme-Johnson & Oates, 2009; Radin et al., 2017). In general, during normal waking life individuals are all busy with a multitude of separate thoughts and feelings and as such any interaction between such fields of consciousness is likely to be random. However, during a shared event or experience the various thoughts, feelings and emotions of those taking part become more coherent and constructively interact, reinforcing each other and producing a higher level of resonance. Hence, the patterns of data seen in the nodes of the GCP and the ME are the result of harmonious and coherently generated fields of consciousness. The notion that consciousness may act and/or operate in a field-like manner is not new. Such a view has a long history within psychology and the social sciences (e.g., Durkheim, 1951; James, 1890). According to Nelson (2010) a non-linear dynamic field model could indicate that individual minds are interactive and that these interactions give rise to an emergent field which is dependent upon individual consciousness but not reducible to it. The suggestion here is that it is the subtle interactions of such a field with the physical world that is evident in the changes produced by the GCP network. In a similar manner Orme-Johnson and Oates (2009) suggest that during meditation the individual provides a harmonious and coherent influence on the surrounding field of consciousness. Such ideas are no doubt provocative but Nelson (2010) argues that it is the most viable of the alternatives currently on offer.

Holographic model

According to Duval (1988) the ideas of a unified field and collective consciousness do not fit within mainstream thinking. Indeed, Fales and Markovsky (1997) criticise the findings related to the ME for suggesting that the effect is based on some form of collective consciousness that is both non-material and omnidirectional. However, Orme-Johnson and Oates (2009) respond by suggesting that the ME operates or connects with the Planck scale quantum field, which defies characterisation in the normal temporal and spatial sense. Nevertheless, a recent attempt was made by Despande and Kowall (2017) to provide a more coherent explanation of the ME with reference to the holographic principle of modern physics. They suggest that the ME represents a form of quantum entanglement with the consciousness of each individual overlapping with that of others, as in the overlapping circles of a Venn diagram. The overlap would be greater between loved ones, or those with close emotional ties, and less so for others, hence the idea that an individual can become more or less psychically connected to anyone. Unfortunately, Despande and Kowall (2017) incorrectly state that during the ME the meditators are focused on reducing crime and hence become connected to criminals. This connection encourages feelings of love in the criminals which in turn makes them less likely to commit crimes. However, as many others have stated, meditation is often self-focused and is invariably not focused on external factors (Orme-Johnson, 2003). As such, the changes seen in the environment may be a by-product of the meditation process.

Overview

This chapter explored the idea that a noosphere, or field of consciousness, surrounding the Earth may be subtly influenced by the coming together of large groups of people in response to an event or as part of a focused meditative practice. The former effect is encapsulated in the global consciousness project and the latter in the Maharishi effect. Data from the GCP shows clear deviations during global terror attacks, as well as suggestive changes during events marked by compassion or celebration. Such findings are likely to be influenced by the nature and type of event as well as the emotional response to it and the possible distance between the event and the recording devices. Nevertheless, the cumulative effects seen in the GCP network are very significant and cannot be accounted for in terms of problematic methodological issues. Such data clearly suggest a link between human consciousness and a distributed system of random output devices. Given this it is interesting to note that the effects are evident despite the absence of any focused intention on the devices themselves. Furthermore, there is no feedback given to the groups in question regarding the level and/or nature of the cohesiveness of their reaction to any event. The implications of this are that it is not important for people experiencing an event to 'know' about the devices or give them any conscious thought. The Maharishi effect also suggests that groups of individuals coming together to react in a coherent and focused way can produce widespread effects on surrounding life and society. Again, this effect is not reliant on the focused intentions of those taking part but rather appears as an emergent property of the group meditation itself. The practice of large group-based TM has been shown to reliably lead to reductions in crime, conflict and mortality rates. Such beneficial effects may take some time to occur and rely to some extent on the size and experience of the meditating group, though such beneficial effects have been shown to persist beyond the end of the meditation practice. In terms of attempts to account for the GCP and ME effects the proposed field type model seems to most closely fit the data. However, whilst the idea that consciousness may act like a field is not new it certainly remains contentious.

Reflective questions

Some questions that may prove helpful when reflecting on the material covered in this chapter.

- Do you think it is possible for a planet to develop a field of conscious awareness?
- How would you measure the noosphere?
- How would you test for global consciousness controlling for experimenter expectations?
- Do you think global consciousness is growing and/or changing over time?
- What events do you think would be associated with non-random outputs in the GCP?
- Do you think governments should sponsor the recording of global consciousness?
- Do you think governments should respond to reactions in global consciousness?
- Given the ME, do you think TM lessons should be freely available?
- Should TM or other types of meditation be compulsory?
- Should TM groups be sent to visit prisons?
- Should TM groups be sent to areas of high crime and violence to help bring such behaviours under control?
- If consciousness is a field how can we measure it?
- What are some of the implications that all conscious beings are linked together?

References

Alexander, C. N., Rainforth, M. V., & Gelderloos, P. (1991). Trancendental meditation, self-actualization, and psychological health: A conceptual overview and statistical meta-analysis. *Journal of Social Behavior and Personality, 6*(5), 189–247.

Anderson, J. W., Liu, C., & Kryscio, R. J. (2008). Blood pressure response to Transcendental Meditation: A meta-analysis. *American Journal of Hypertension, 21*(3), 310–316.

Assimakis, P. D., & Dillbeck, M. C. (1995). Time series analysis of improved quality of life in Canada: Social change, collective consciousness, and the TM-Sidhi program. *Psychological Reports, 76*(3Suppl), 1171–1193.

Bancel, P. A. (2011). Reply to May and Spottiswoode's 'The Global Consciousness Project: Identifying the source of psi'. *Journal of Scientific Exploration, 25*(4), 690–694.

Bancel, P. A. (2014). An analysis of the global consciousness project. In D. Broderick & B. Goertzel (Eds.), *Evidence for Psi: Thirteen empirical research reports* (pp. 255–277). Jefferson, NC: McFarland Press.

Bancel, P. A. (2017). Searching for global consciousness: A 17 year exploration. *Explore, 13*(2), 94–101. doi: 10.1016/j.explore.2016.12.003.

Bancel, P. A., & Nelson, R. D. (2008). The GCP event experiment: Design, analytical methods, results. *Journal of Scientific Exploration, 22*(3), 309–333.

Borland, C., & Landrith, G. S. (1976). Improved quality of city life through the Transcendental Meditation program: Decreased crime rate. In D. W. Orme-Johnson & J. T. Farrow (Eds.), *Scientific research on the Transcendental Meditation program: Collected papers* (Vol. 1, pp. 639–648). Rheinweiler, West Germany: MERU Press.

Cahn, B. R., & Polich, J. (2006). Meditation states and traits: EEG, ERP, and neuroimaging studies. *Psychological Bulletin, 132*(2), 180–211. doi: 10.1037/0033-2909.132.2.180.

Cavanaugh, K. L., & Dillbeck, M. C. (2017). The contribution of proposed field effects of consciousness to the prevention of US accidental fatalities: Theory and empirical tests. *Journal of Consciousness Studies, 24*(1–2), 53–86.

Cavanaugh, K. L., King, K. D., & Ertuna, C. (1989). *A multiple-input transfer function model of Okun's misery index: An empirical test of the Maharishi effect.* Paper presented at the Proceedings of the American Statistical Association, Business and Economics Statistics Section.

Davies, J. L., & Alexander, C. N. (2005). Alleviating political violence through reducing collective tension: Impact assessment analysis of the Lebanon war. *Journal of Social Behaviour and Personality, 17*, 285–338.

Despande, P. B., & Kowall, J. P. (2017). Explanation of the Maharishsi effect by holographic principles. *Journal of Consciousnes Exploration & Research, 8*(10), 797–805.

Dillbeck, M. C. (1990). Test of a field theory of consciousness and social change: Time series analysis of participation in the TM-Sidhi program and reduction of violent death in the US. *Social Indicators Research, 22*, 399–418.

Dillbeck, M. C., Banus, C. B., Polanzi, C., & Landrith III, G. (1988). Test of a field model of consciousness and social change: The Transcendental Meditation and TM-Sidhi program and decreased urban crime. *The Journal of Mind and Behavior Research Methods, 9*(4), 457–486.

Dillbeck, M. C., & Cavanaugh, K. L. (2016). Societal violence and collective consciousness: Reduction of US homicide and urban violent crime rates. *SAGE Open* (April–June), 1–16. doi: 10.1177/2158244016637891.

Dillbeck, M. C., & Cavanaugh, K. L. (2017). Group practice of the Transcendental Meditation (R) and TM-Sidhi(R) program and reductions in infant mortality and drug-related death: A quasi-experimental analysis. *SAGE Open.* doi: 10.1177/2158244017697164.

Dillbeck, M. C., Cavanaugh, K. L., Glenn, T., Orme-Johnson, D. W., & Mittlefehldt, V. (1987). Consciousness as a field: The Transcendental Meditation and TM-Sidhi program and changes in social indicators. *The Journal of Mind and Behavior*, 67–103.

Dillbeck, M. C., Landrith III, G., & Orme-Johnson, D. W. (1981). The Transcendental Meditation program and crime rate change in a sample of forty-eight cities. *Journal of Crime and Justice*, 4(1), 24–45.

Divya, B. R., Nagendra, H. R., & Ram, A. (2016). Effect of consciousness fields on random events at public gatherings: An exploratory study. *International Journal of Preventive and Public Health Sciences*, 1(5), 26–31.

Durkheim, E. (1951). *Suicide: A study in sociology* (JA Spaulding & G. Simpson, trans.). Glencoe, IL: Free Press. (Original work published 1897).

Duval, R. (1988). TM or not TM? *Journal of Conflict Resolution*, 32(4), 813–817.

Fales, E., & Markovsky, B. (1997). Evaluating heterodox theories. *Social Forces*, 76(2), 511–525.

Goleman, D. (1972). The Buddha on meditation and sates of consciousness, part I: A typology of meditation techniques. *Journal of Transpersonal Psychology*, 4(2), 151–210.

Hagelin, J. S., Rainforth, M. V., Orme-Johnson, D. W., Cavanaugh, K. L., Alexander, C. N., Shatkin, S. F., … & Ross, E. (1999). Effects of group practice of the Transcendental Meditation program on preventing violent crime in Washington, DC: Results of the national Demonstration Project, June–July 1993. *Social Indicators Research*, 47(2), 153–201.

Hatchard, G. D., Deans, A. J., Cavanaugh, K. L., & Orme-Johnson, D. W. (1996). The Maharishi effect: A model for social improvement. Time series analysis of a phase transition to reduced crime in Merseyside metropolitan area. *Psychology, Crime and Law*, 2(3), 165–174.

Hirukawa, T., & Ishikawa, M. (2004). *Anomalous fluctuation of RNG data in Nebuta: Summer festival in northeast Japan*. Paper presented at the The Parapsychological Association Convention.

James, W. (1890). *The principles of psychology*, Vol. 2. New York: Henry Holt and Company.

Kokubo, H. (2016). Weak periodic effect in a long-term field REG measurement. *Journal of International Society of Life Information Science*, 34(1), 14–19.

Maharishi, M. Y. (1978). *Enlightenment and invincibility*. Rheinweiler, Germany: Maharishi European Resarch University Press.

Maharishi, M. Y. (1996). *Maharishi's absolute theory of defence*. India: Age of Enlightenment Publications.

May, E. C., & Spottiswoode, J. P. (2011). The Global Consciousness Project: Identifying the source of psi. *Journal of Scientific Exploration*, 25(4), 663–682.

Morris, B. (1992). Maharishi's vedic science and technology: The only means to create world peace. *Modern Science and Vedic Science*, 5(1–2), 199–207.

Nelson, R. D. (1997). Multiple field REG/RNG recordings during a global event. *Electronic Journal Anomalous Phenomenon*. Retrieved from http://noosphere.princeton.edu/ejap/gaiamind/intro_b.html.

Nelson, R. D. (2001). Correlation of global events with REG data: An internet-based, non-local anomalies experiment. *The Journal of Parapsychology*, 65, 241–271.

Nelson, R. D. (2002). Cohernet consciousness and reduced randomness: Correlations on September 11, 2001. *Journal of Scientific Exploration*, 16(4), 549–570.

Nelson, R. D. (2008a). *The emotional nature of global consciousness*. Paper presented at the Behind and Beyond the Brain 7th Symposium of the Bial Foundation, Porto.

Nelson, R. D. (2008b). *Emotions in global consciousness*. Paper presented at the 7th Symposium of the Bial Foundation, Porto, Portugal.

Nelson, R. D. (2010). *Scientific evidence for the existence of a true noosphere: Foundation for a noo-constitution*. Paper presented at the World Forum of Spiritual Culture, 18–20 October, Astana, Kazakhstan.

Nelson, R. D. (2011a). Detecting mass consciousness: Effects of globally shared attention and emotion. *Journal of Cosmology*, 14, 1–15.

Nelson, R. D. (2011b). Reply to May and Spottiswoode on experimenter effect as the explanation for GCP results. *Journal of Scientific Exploration*, 25(4), 683–689.

Nelson, R. D. (2013). The global consciousness project: Meaningful patterns in random data. In S. Krippner, A. J. Rock, J. Beischel, H. L. Friedman, & C. L. Fracasso (Eds.), *Advances in parapsychological research 9* (pp. 15–37). Jefferson, NC: McFarland & Company Inc.

Nelson, R. D. (2014). The global consciousness project. *Journal of International Society of Life Information Science*, 32(2), 185–188.

Nelson, R. D. (2015). Implicit physical psi: The global consciousness project. In E. Cardena, J. Palmer, & D. Marcusson-Clavertz (Eds.), *Parapsychology: A handbook for the 21st century* (pp. 282–292). Jefferson, NC: McFarland & Company Inc.

Nelson, R. D. (2017). Weighting the parameters, a response to Bancel's 'Searching for global consciousness: A seventeen year exploration'. *EXPLORE*, 13(2), 102–105.

Nelson, R. D. (2019). *The global consciousness project: Is there a noosphere?* Retrieved November 27, 2019, from http://teilhard.global-mind.org/papers/GCPnoosphere.pdf.

Nelson, R. D., & Bancel, P. A. (2009). Response to Schmidt's commentary on the Global Consciousness Project, letter to the editor. *Journal of Scientific Exploration*, 23, 510–516.

Nelson, R. D., & Bancel, P. A. (2011). Effects of mass consciousness: Changes in random data during globa events. *Explore*, 7(6), 373–383. doi: 10.1016/j.explore.2011.08.003.

Nelson, R. D., Bradish, G. J., Dobyns, Y., Dunne, B. J., & Jahn, R. G. (1996). FieldREG anomalies in group situations. *Journal of Scientific Exploration*, 10, 111–141.

Nelson, R. D., Bradish, G. J., Dobyns, Y., Dunne, B. J., & Jahn, R. G. (1998). FieldREG II: Consciousness field effects. Replications and explorations. *Journal of Scientific Exploration*, 14, 425–454.

Nelson, R. D., Radin, D., Shoup, R., & Bancel, P. A. (2002). Correlations of continuous random data with major world events. *Foundation of Physics Letters*, 15, 537–550.

Orme-Johnson, D. W. (2003). Preventing crime through the Maharishi effect. *Journal of Offender Rehabilitation*, 36(1–4), 257–281. doi: 10.1300/J076v36n01_12.

Orme-Johnson, D. W., Alexander, C. N., & Davies, J. L. (1990). The effects of the Maharishi Technology of the Unified Field: Reply to a methodologial critique. *Journal of Conflict Resolution*, 34(4), 756–768.

Orme-Johnson, D. W., Alexander, C. N., Davies, J. L., Chandler, H. M., & Larimore, W. E. (1988). International peace projectr in the Middle East. *Journal of Conflict Resolution*, 32(4), 776–812.

Orme-Johnson, D. W., Dillbeck, M. C., & Alexander, C. N. (2003). Preventing terrorism and international conflict. *Journal of Offender Rehabilitation*, 36(1–4), 283–302. doi: 10.1300/J076v36n01.

Orme-Johnson, D. W., Dillbeck, M. C., Alexander, C. N., Chandler, H. M., & Cranson, R. W. (2003). Effects of large assemblies of participants in the Transcendental Meditation and TM-Sidhi program on reducing international conflict and terrorism. *Journal of Offender Rehabilitation*, 36(1–4), 283–302.

Orme-Johnson, D. W., & Oates, R. M. (2009). A field-theoretic view of consciousness: Reply to critics. *Journal of Scientific Exploration*, 23(2), 139–166.

Radin, D. (2002). Exploring relationships between random physical events and mass human attention: Asking for whom the bell tolls. *Journal of Scientific Exploration*, 16(4), 533–547.

Radin, D., Bailey, S., Bjune, E., Burnett, J., Carpenter, L., Delorme, A., ... & Welss, C. (2017). *A disturbance in the force: Exploring collective consciousness at Burning Man: A report on five years of exploratory experiments.* San Francisco, CA: Institute of Noetic Sciences.

Radin, D., & Nelson, L. D. (1989). Evidence for consciousness-related anomalies in random physical systems. *Foundations of Physics*, 19(12), 1499–1514.

Roth, R. (1994). *Maharishi Mahesh Yogi's Transcendental Meditation.* New York: Primus.

Schrodt, P. A. (1990). A methodological critque of a test of the effects of the Maharishi Technology of the Unified Field. *Journal of Conflict Resolution, 34*(4), 745–755.

Serafin, R. (1988). Noosphere, Gaia, and the science of the biosphere. *Environmental Ethics, 10*(2), 121–137. doi: 10.5840/enviroethics19881023.

Shimizu, T., Yamamoto, K., & Ishikawa, M. (2017). A field RNG experiment: Use of digital RNG at movie theatres. *NeuroQuantology, 15*(1), 60–66. doi: 10.14704/nq.2017.15.1.964.

University, M. I. (1977). *Creating an ideal society*. New York: MIU Press.

Vernadsky, W. I. (1945). The biosphere and the noosphere. *American Scientist, 33*(1), 1–12.

Vernon, D. (2009). *Human potential: Exploring techniques used to enhance human performance*. London: Routledge.

Chapter 8

Energy healing

Imagine a situation whereby the thoughts and intentions of one person can help to heal the physical and/or psychological problems of another, even at a distance. The idea of some form of subtle energy healing is not new and is one scientists have grappled with for decades. Given this, it is no surprise that there is a wealth of literature on the topic and a comprehensive review exploring all the various types of healing and their effects is beyond the scope of a single chapter. Nevertheless, the aim of this chapter is to explore some aspects of energy healing practices to provide insights into what may occur and why. The chapter begins by exploring the notion of energy healing and what it refers to. A brief outline of some of the key approaches used is then provided and this is followed by data on those who access such treatments, the prevalence of use and their satisfaction with such interventions. The chapter then examines evidence of healing from three domains. The first examines the effects on humans, both physical and psychological. The second explores studies conducted on non-human animals and the final domain examines in-vitro research. Each of these areas provides some unique insights into the potential beneficial effects of energy healing. The chapter then briefly examines some effects which have been shown to mediate or influence the outcome of such healing sessions. This includes the number of sessions and the skill or experience of the healer. The chapter ends with a brief exploration of proposed mechanisms that may account for such healing effects. However, before venturing into the field of subtle energy healing it should be stressed that the evidence presented here in no way should be taken to suggest that modern healthcare and/or biomedicine is in any way inadequate. Subtle energy healing simply provides a complementary approach.

Subtle energy healing

The idea that energy, in some form or other, could aid the healing process is one that is found throughout the world in most cultures and across religions (Levin, 2011; S. A. Schwartz, 2017). For instance, the ancient Greeks and Egyptians used magnetite to stimulate damaged tissue, and before that shocks from electric eels were used to help the healing process (DiNucci, 2005). The term *energy healing* itself broadly encapsulates a range of various types of healing practices. For example, the National Centre for Complementary and Integrative Health (NCCIH) has defined energy healing as involving the channelling of healing energy through the hands of a practitioner into a client's body to restore a normal energy balance and, therefore, health.

Such approaches are often grouped under the broad general heading of complementary and alternative medicine, or CAM (Tindle, Davis, Phillips, & Eisenberg, 2005). For instance, in the UK the House of Lords Science and Technology Committee (Lords, 2000) has acknowledged that healing should be recognised as a form of complementary medicine. Hence the idea is that the focused intention of one person, the healer or practitioner, can influence another, the patient or recipient, possibly at a distance and in a non-invasive way that is assumed to pose little or no risk and without utilising known physical means of intervention (Astin, Harkness, & Ernst, 2000; Benor, 2005; Jonas & Crawford, 2003). This healing is based around the manipulation and/or direction of some form of energy. It should be noted that whilst the term 'energy' is used this does not refer to any known source of energy. Therefore, some refer to this as *subtle energy healing* to indicate that the form of energy is a subtle and as yet unknown one (Jonas & Crawford, 2003), though Schwartz (2017) has speculated that such healing effects may be due to the transfer of information from practitioner to recipient rather than energy per se. Nevertheless, the fact that the underlying mechanism(s) of healing are not clearly understood and/or known represents a key challenge to the field.

Types of energy healing

Subtle energy healing represents a wide range of techniques and approaches rather than a single unique system. Here the focus will be on energy healing techniques that allegedly heal via the exchange and/or focused channelling of some form of supra-physical energy, such as Johrei, Reiki, Therapeutic Touch (TT) and prayer. One way to conceptualise such techniques is as a lens used to help focus energy onto or into the recipient (see Figure 8.1).

Whilst these techniques may be more common, there are many other forms of energy healing approaches such as *healing touch*, or *IRECA, Qigong, quantum touch* and *biofield therapy* to name but a few (DiNucci, 2005; Jain & Mills, 2010; Levin, 2011; Rubik, Muehsam, Hammerschlag, & Jain, 2015; Vitale, 2007). This plethora of techniques or approaches represents another challenge for the field as it is not always clear precisely what approach or technique has been used in a particular research study. In fact, some do not distinguish between the various techniques and

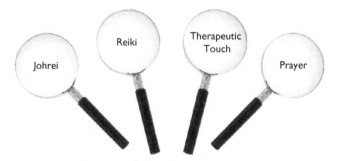

Figure 8.1 Each of the energy healing techniques as a distinct lens which can be used to focus the necessary energy onto/into the recipient.

default to the generic term of energy healing (Bunnell, 1999). However, this is problematic as it may well be that there are slight differences between the various techniques and that one may be better than another at treating a specific problem. As such, more work is needed to delineate the specific effects of the various techniques and identify their unique benefit.

Johrei

Johrei represents a philosophy and healing approach developed in Japan by Mokichi Okada in the 1930s (see, Buzzetti et al., 2013; Naito et al., 2003). According to Okada, Johrei is essentially a method of spiritual purification. Adherents claim that it is a method for channelling energy, or divine light, through the hands of the healer and into the recipient by means of focused conscious intention. For instance, Johrei healing may involve the practitioner sitting opposite and facing the recipient and raising their hand to focus the energy into/onto the recipient (see Figure 8.2).

Hence the trained Johrei practitioner provides energy healing through their open raised hand. As such, the practitioner can focus the healing energy onto the recipient without needing to touch them. Johrei can be learnt and practised by anyone and is seen as a two-way process that benefits both the healer and the person healed (Reece, Schwartz, Brooks, & Nangle, 2005).

Figure 8.2 A Johrei practitioner on the left with raised a hand focusing energy onto/into the recipient on the right (picture taken by author).

Reiki

Reiki is another popular Japanese energy healing technique. It began, or was created, by Dr Mikao Usui who personally experienced a healing energy which he subsequently used to help his family and others (Thrane & Cohen, 2014). Reiki is described as a vibrational or subtle energy therapy most commonly facilitated by light touch on or above the body. Key features of Reiki are hand positions on the front and back of the body and the use of symbols to aid the healing process. Reiki is seen as a way for the practitioner to guide the healing energy to the recipient to facilitate the healing process (see Box 8.1). The practitioners themselves do not generate the energy nor do they cause the healing. They are instead seen as providing a channel. Generally, a session of Reiki can last from between 30 to 90 minutes and consists of a clothed recipient laying down whilst the practitioner places their hands on or above the body in a set sequence. The aim of Reiki is to recharge, rebalance and/or realign the human energy fields, creating optimal conditions for the body's natural healing to emerge (van der Vaart, Gijsen, de Wildt, & Koren, 2009; Vitale, 2007). In this way it encourages a compassionate connection between the practitioner and the recipient with the intent to heal. According to Reiki spiritual masters, Reiki attunement opens and expands the energy holding capacity of the practitioner (Lubeck, Petter, & Rand, 2001). Such attunement is an advanced spiritual practice, which involves the transmission of energy from the teacher to the student (Trepper, Strozier, Carpenter, & Hecker, 2013). Those that have received such attunements describe powerful experiences of love and peace.

Box 8.1   The Reiki healing process

When asked how the Reiki healing process unfolds a Reiki master responded:

> when I initiate the Reiki process, I usually begin by connecting to the energy with my hands raised and channelling the energy towards my sacral chakra (the Tanden). I allow the energy to build and when I feel it has accumulated I would then treat the client. This is usually done from head to toe and laying on of hands in appropriate areas if the client is happy for the physical touch, otherwise, the hands will remain in the area above the body and I would just allow the energy to flow. The thought process for me is to let go of all expectation and let the energy go to where it needs to. I see myself purely as a bridge to the energy that is required.

> A full Reiki treatment usually lasts for between 40 minutes to an hour, although shorter treatments are also used for events such as fairs or where someone just wishes for a short blast so to speak.
> (from Reiki Master Practitioner Gary Hewitt, with permission)

Reiki training involves several levels. According to van der Vaart et al. (2009) the focus of Level I training is to encourage the body to recover its natural healing ability and is generally used for self-help or for helping others through a light touch. Level II teaches a deeper understanding of the energetic flow and may introduce symbols to aid in treatment efficiency. It can also include the notion of healing at a distance where the practitioner can *send* energy to a recipient located at a distance. Level III, or master level, focuses on the inner spiritual development of the practitioner, in particular the development of a spiritual consciousness (van der Vaart et al., 2009). It also involves extensive practice and may include training others (Thrane & Cohen, 2014). Being classified as a Reiki master implies a level of expertise and experience and is usually only given after a practitioner has been practising Level II Reiki for at least one year.

Therapeutic touch

According to Peters (1999) the idea of Therapeutic Touch (TT) was derived originally from the notion of healing by the laying on of hands. As a method of healing it is based on the work of Krieger (1995) and, in a similar way to Johrei and Reiki, it assumes an energy or life force surrounding the body that can be influenced, or controlled by TT. During the process the practitioner directs healing energy to the recipient and assists them in modulating their energy field to correct any imbalances (Krieger, 1995). Hence, the idea is that the energy field of the recipient can be manipulated or influenced by the TT practitioner and over time this has shifted from using direct physical touch to relying more on focused conscious intention. As such, despite the name, direct physical contact is not necessary. According to Krieger (1995) TT involves several stages. First, the practitioner prepares for the healing session by focusing on centring themself via meditative practice. Second, the practitioner will evaluate the recipient's energy field assessing any possible imbalances or disturbances around the body. Third, there is a re-balancing or re-synchronisation of the recipient's energy field which is achieved by the practitioner sending healing energy to areas that may require attention. Finally, the practitioner will reassess the energy field to ensure it is correctly balanced. However, it should be noted that attempts to assess whether TT practitioners are able to detect such energy fields have not been successful. For instance, Rosa, Rosa, Sarner and Barrett (1998) tested 21 experienced practitioners of TT under blinded conditions and found they were unable to identify which of their hands was in or near the energy field of one of the experimenters. Rosa et al. (1998) concluded that suggestions TT practitioners could detect and/or manipulate such energy fields is both groundless and unjustified. Nevertheless, others have pointed out that even if the mechanism of TT is unknown this does not invalidate it as a potential therapeutic intervention if it can produce clinically measurable effects (O'Mathuna, Pryjmachuk, Spencer, Stanwick, & Matthiesen, 2002).

Prayer

According to Simao, Caldeira and Campos de Carvalho (2016) prayer has been used since ancient times to promote both self-healing and the healing of others. It has been suggested to be the best known and most widely practised form of such healing (McCullough, 1995). Indeed, a survey of American adults by the US Centres for

Disease Control and Prevention, National Centre for Health Statistics found that of the top five most popular complementary approaches, three involved prayer. The most popular complementary and alternative healing practice was prayer for oneself and the second most popular was prayer for another (Barnes, Powell-Griner, McFann, & Nahin, 2004). This highlights that there are several variants of prayer. For instance, *personal prayer* involves an individual praying for themself (Hodge, 2007). This is thought to provide hope to the individual by providing a connection with a sacred self-transcending dimension (Simao et al., 2016). Such prayers can take the form of a *supplication*, which represents a request for a specific type of outcome, or *non-directed* prayers, which are a more passive and generic form of prayer whereby the individual praying does not request any specific outcome (Astin et al., 2000). There is also *intercessory prayer* which is characterised by petitions on behalf of others for their health and well-being. It is advocated in many religions and philosophies and involves an effort on behalf of someone with a special need, aiming to alleviate ill-health and promote well-being. However, it need not be religious and can refer to any means of concentrated mental effort to influence reality in a particular way, by appealing to a force. Sometimes this is carried out far from the target recipient and then it is generally called distant intercessory prayer.

Conscious intention

A key point worth noting is that whilst the above healing techniques may have some subtle differences in the way they approach the process of healing there are also many similarities. All methods include both proximal and distal healing, though without the need for direct physical contact. Indeed, some have argued that there are relatively few meaningful differences between the distinct healing approaches (Rahtz, Child, Knight, Warber, & Dieppe, 2019). For instance, a central commonality in such approaches is the underlying core of a shared compassionate conscious intention to put self aside and focus on healing the recipient. This intentional mental effort has been suggested to be an essential part of the process (Schlitz et al., 2003). In fact, some have found that the precise healing approach may be less important than the focused intention to heal. For example, researchers have shown changes in cellular growth using mental imagery without recourse to any particular healing approach (Rider & Achterberg, 1989) and that such imagery alone can influence tumour growth or remission (Achterberg & Lawlis, 1984). However, this should not be taken to indicate that the particular healing technique is irrelevant, rather that it is unclear as yet what the potential differential effects of the various healing techniques may be. There has been very little research directly comparing different healing techniques. Most research to date has been focused on comparing an active healing intervention to a placebo or non-active control group to assess what, if any, beneficial effects emerge. However, many researchers have argued that more needs to be done to fully describe and categorise the various techniques and their effects in order to provide a more comprehensive understanding of the field (Jonas & Crawford, 2003; Rahtz et al., 2019; Schlitz et al., 2003). It is also worth pointing out that it is not clear yet whether healing represents more of an innate ability or a learnt skill. Some have suggested it can be taught to anyone (Benor, 1992). For instance, Nash (1982) found that individuals with no prior skill or healing ability could be trained to significantly influence the growth of bacteria in-vitro. Others have suggested that there is insufficient evidence and the question remains empirically unresolved (Bengston & Murphy, 2008).

Prevalence and demographics

It is worth just taking a moment to question how many people access this type of healing, who are they, why they do this, what the outcomes are and what the implications of this are for the field in general. Despite the seeming over-reliance on mainstream medicine access to and use of CAM approaches is reasonably widespread. According to various surveys examining how many people access healing as a form of treatment, the figures provided show around 35% to 40% of the adult population have accessed at least one form of healing or another and approximately 12% of children (Astin et al., 2000; Jain & Mills, 2010; Jonas & Crawford, 2003; Tindle et al., 2005; van der Vaart et al., 2009). There is also suggestive evidence that the number seeking such alternatives is on the increase. According to DiNucci (2005) visits to CAM practitioners has increased by 47.3% since 1990. Umberger (2019) pointed out that in the USA alone this equates to over 75 million adults seeking some form of complementary approach. Interestingly, the number of practitioners offering distant healing also increased over the years (Astin et al., 2000).

In terms of who accesses such healing interventions it is very likely to be influenced by cultural norms. For instance, it may be more common for certain cultural or ethnic groups to seek spiritual healing in the form of prayer (Schlitz et al., 2003). Nevertheless, surveys show that of those visiting healers the majority tends to be female (>76%) and of a more mature age (>48 years) group, with around 45% educated up to university level (Kristoffersen, Stub, Knudsen-Baas, Udal, & Musial, 2019; Rahtz et al., 2019; Tindle et al., 2005). It should be noted that the difference in gender represents a general trend that is also evident in mainstream biomedicine (Wang, Hunt, Nazareth, Freemantle, & Petersen, 2013). Furthermore, healthcare workers themselves have also been known to visit healers, in part because they are interested in therapies that are non-invasive and not dependent on expensive technologies (Vitale, 2007).

In terms of why people use such approaches, research suggests that users are more likely to have positive attitudes and beliefs about the practitioner's competence and abilities (Kristoffersen et al., 2019) and some even use this as a *treat* rather than a *treatment* (Bishop, Yardley, & Lewith, 2008). Some also use it as a coping mechanism for helping them deal with illness (Söllner et al., 2000); others like the fact that they are able to actively opt for such treatments (Vincent & Furnham, 1996), offering a new and integrative approach and greater choice to patients, emphasising a multi-perspective view of healthcare which incorporates multiple therapeutic approaches (Rubik et al., 2015). According to Rahtz et al. (2019) approximately one-third are attempting to find treatment for a single problem whereas up to two-thirds had two or more problems they wanted addressing (see also, Kristoffersen et al., 2019). The most common problem cited was mental health (47%) followed by pain (29%). Finally, others have also found that use of CAM may also be influenced by the cost, the view that such alternative approaches are safer and carry fewer negative side effects, as well as the notion that it may be more natural and holistic (Jordan & Croft, 2018).

In general, the outcomes from such visits tend to be positive and those receiving healing seem to be satisfied. According to one survey conducted in the USA 92% of those who had accessed an energy healing intervention indicated a high level of satisfaction (DiNucci, 2005). Of course, this may simply be a dissonance effect (i.e., attempting to avoid internal conflict that may arise when belief and behaviour do not align) resulting from the high possibility that such interventions need to be paid for. Nevertheless, given that most healthcare in the USA requires some form of payment and that payment for healthcare in the USA is more common, this is unlikely to completely account for such high levels of satisfaction. Furthermore, such positive outcomes have been reported by others. For instance, a survey of those receiving TT showed that 90% found it to be very helpful (Newshan & Schuller-Civitella, 2003). Similarly, a recent survey of those accessing healers in the UK showed that, of those that responded, 93% reported some benefit and 68% made a further appointment (Rahtz et al., 2019). Also, nearly a third of those receiving energy healing reported a sensory experience such as seeing lights, or feeling heat or tingling sensations. However, it is worth noting that a small minority have reported some adverse effects from visiting healing practitioners, such as tiredness, back pain and headache, albeit in only a very few cases (see, Kristoffersen et al., 2019). As such, the overall pattern would suggest that those receiving energy healing are highly satisfied with the outcome.

There are several implications that emerge from this. First is the necessity to provide solid empirical support for such interventions. Given the increasing use and/or access to such energy therapies van der Vaart et al. (2009), among many others, have argued that it is essential that good quality trials are conducted to ascertain the potential effectiveness of such healing interventions (Astin et al., 2000; Jonas & Crawford, 2003; Rao, Hickman, Sibbritt, Newton, & Phillips, 2016; Schlitz & Braud, 1997; Schouten, 1993). The increasing widespread use may make it easier for mainstream medical health professionals to refer patients to healers. For example, a survey of medical professionals in the California region of the USA showed that 13% reported using or recommending complementary healing approaches (Schlitz et al., 2003). However, it may not always be easy for healthcare professionals to advocate a healing approach. Initially, such a proposal could be seen as suggesting an alternative approach to the standard model of care on offer. Furthermore, such professionals may feel that they are exposing themselves to ridicule and worse, particularly in terms of career progression, if they advocate something their employers do not see as acceptable.

Evidence

It is worth noting that while the focus here is on the beneficial effects of healing on the recipient there are many studies showing that learning to use and practise these techniques can have significant beneficial effects on improving relaxation and reducing stress of the practitioner (e.g., Cuneo et al., 2011; Quinn & Strelkauskas, 1993). Hence, there seems to be a positive impact on those that practise such techniques (Kemper, 2016). Nevertheless, according to van der Vaart et al. (2009) subtle energy healing techniques remain controversial for two key reasons. First, because there is a lack of clear and robust empirical data supporting the claims of healing practitioners which leads to scepticism. Second, because the alleged *energy* that is assumed to form the basis of such healing cannot, or at least has not, been measured in any objective manner. The latter point may be difficult to address and require developments in both theory and technology to move forward. However, the former can be addressed using current standards and methods applied in biomedicine.

The generally accepted *gold standard* method for clinical intervention studies is the randomised double blind placebo controlled approach (Misra, 2012). This has been suggested to provide the best evidence for identifying cause-effect relationships. However, Verhoef et al. (2005) have argued that such studies often rely only on quantitative measures and fail to take note of the qualitative impact of the intervention. They point out that energy healing approaches often take a more holistic approach to dealing with and treating the person and as such the research should incorporate both quantitative and qualitative evidence. These differences may, to some extent, account for the inconsistencies in the data. For instance, a number of reviews of energy healing have shown it to produce small but significantly positive effects (e.g., Astin et al., 2000; DiNucci, 2005; Hodge, 2007; Jahnke, Larkey, Rogers, Etnier, & Lin, 2010; Jonas & Crawford, 2003; Rao et al., 2016; Schouten, 1993), whilst others have found no clear evidence of any benefit (Joyce & Herbison, 2015; Roberts, Ahmed, & Davison, 2009; Robinson, Biley, & Dolk, 2007; Taft et al., 2003). Such contradictory outcomes are very likely to be the result of the many differences in methodology between the studies, which includes variability in illnesses, and the grouping together of multiple healing techniques under the rubric of energy healing, to name but a few (Abbott, 2000; Astin et al., 2000; Rao et al., 2016; Schouten, 1993).

Such findings highlight the challenges faced when attempting to ascertain what, if any, evidence there is to support energy healing. Asking is there any evidence to support energy healing is akin to asking 'does therapy work?' – an interesting and no doubt useful question but one that needs further qualification. For instance, what type of therapy, delivered by whom, for how long and in what way? And perhaps more importantly, treating what specific illness? Such questions should give an indication of the broad range of questions that can be asked and to provide comprehensive answers would require many chapters if not a book (see e.g., Edwards, 2016). Hence, the aim here is not to provide comprehensive reviews of all types of healing across every instance of illness but rather provide a brief overview of some key findings examining the benefits of Reiki, Johrei, TT and prayer from three main areas: first, looking at evidence of energy healing for human physical and psychological problems; second, looking at evidence from non-human animal research; and finally in-vitro studies.

Human physical

Physical pain is a common symptom and can often lead to other more complicated issues. Such pain may be associated with injury, disease, treatment or surgery (Dogan, 2018). Many researchers have found that Reiki healing can lead to significant reductions in pain perception, or reports of pain by patients (Jain & Mills, 2010; Vitale & O'Connor, 2006). For instance, Midilli and Eser (2015) reported on a randomly controlled study that showed significant reductions in post-caesarean delivery pain

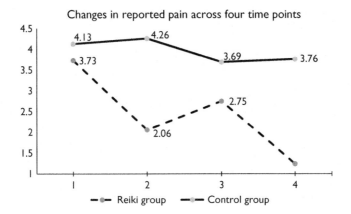

Figure 8.3 Changes in reported levels of pain for Reiki group (lower dotted line) and rest-only control group (upper solid line) across the four time points (adapted from Midilli & Eser, 2015).

for a group receiving Reiki compared to a resting control group, across four time points (see Figure 8.3).

Such findings have led researchers to argue that the pain reducing effects of Reiki are beyond what might be expected from non-specific placebo effects (Jain & Mills, 2010; McManus, 2017). Some have even suggested that Reiki given at a distance can be helpful in reducing the perceived pain of hospitalised patients (Demir, Can, Kelam, & Aydiner, 2015). Indeed, a meta-analysis of the potential benefits of Reiki for pain management, looking only at randomised controlled trials, showed that Reiki interventions led to a significant reduction in reported pain levels compared to non-Reiki control groups (Dogan, 2018).

Similar pain reducing benefits have been reported from those receiving Johrei treatments (e.g., Navarro-Rodriguez et al., 2008). Johrei has also been found to be effective in patients with functional chest pain (Gasiorowska et al., 2009). Here, Johrei treatment resulted in significant reductions in symptom intensity compared to a no treatment control group. However, it is important to note that the perceived level of physical problems, such as pain, are often reliant on subjective reports by the patient via a standardised scale or questionnaire (e.g., Visual Analogue Scale for Pain: McCormack, Horne, & Sheather, 1988). As such, it is possible that the score obtained on such scales may not always be truly representative of how much pain the individual is experiencing. For instance, researchers have shown that visiting a healer when undergoing radiotherapy for cancer can lead to subjective reports of improved tolerance to the radiotherapy. However, objective measures based on radiation toxicities and related fatigue and pain showed no clear indication of any enhanced tolerance (Guy et al., 2017). Hence, patient perceptions had changed but the objective measures did not reflect this. Nevertheless, attempts have been made to identify more objective changes resulting from energy healing. For instance, Naito et al. (2003) examined the immune function of three groups by taking blood samples before and after an intervention. The first were given Johrei healing, the second were a non-healing control group and the third were given mock neurofeedback. The researchers used the blood samples to examine NK cell activity which acted as an objective marker for immune system functioning. Using this approach Naito et al. (2003) found that only the Johrei group showed an increase in NK cell activity compared to both control groups. Hence, it may well be the case that the reported changes seen in the scales are representative of changes in the underlying physiology of the recipient, though more needs to be done here to identify and monitor such changes over time.

Therapeutic Touch (TT) has also been shown to be an effective intervention for pain relief (Aghabati, Mohammadi, & Pour Esmaiel, 2008; Gordon, Merenstein, D'Amico, & Hudgens, 1998; Tabatabaee et al., 2016a, 2016b; Wardell, Rintala, & Tan, 2008). For example, chronic back pain is a common complaint and as such has become a costly treatment option. In a pre-post randomly controlled trial researchers showed that TT alongside the standard medication treatment option led to significant reductions in reports of chronic back pain compared to those receiving only the medication (see Figure 8.4; Mueller, Palli, & Schumacher, 2019). Importantly, there was no difference in reported levels of pain between the two groups prior to the intervention. This, they argue, provides a non-pharmacological approach for the management of pain.

However, not all agree with the view that TT can elicit beneficial health effects. For example, O'Mathuna et al. (2002) have argued that there is insufficient evidence for TT and as such it is unethical to promote its use on anyone not clearly informed of the speculative and unproven nature of the intervention. They also highlight the fact that TT has an unknown mechanism of action which brings it into question. Nevertheless, many others examining the effects of TT for reducing pain have suggested that there are sufficient positive findings to recommend it, particularly as there are no clearly identified negative risks (e.g., Anderson & Taylor, 2012; Bulette Coakley & Duffy, 2010; Dorri & Bahrami, 2014). Some have even suggested that TT could be used to help reduce pain in newborn babies, who are more sensitive to such pain (see e.g., Mir, Behnam Vashani, Sadeghi, Boskabadi, & Khorshahi, 2018). Alongside pain reduction TT has been shown to provide benefits to those living with dementia (Woods, Craven, & Whitney, 2005); improving the physical health of patients suffering from cancer (Tabatabaee et al., 2016b); helping those living with heart failure (Shields, 2008); and providing benefits prior to medical interventions (Madrid, Barrett, & Winstead-Fry, 2010).

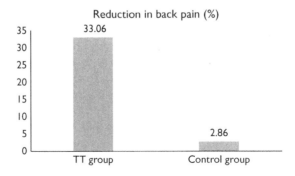

Figure 8.4 Percentage reduction in back pain for Therapeutic Touch group (left) and Control group (right) after four days of treatment (adapted from Mueller et al., 2019).

In terms of prayer the physical health benefits are more generic. For instance, an early study by Byrd (1988) reported on the distant healing effect of prayer on patients with cardiac problems. This involved healing prayers *sent* to one group of patients whilst another group acted as the controls. Neither patients themselves nor their physicians knew which condition an individual patient had been allocated to. However, those receiving the prayers showed significant benefits in terms of lower incidences of intubation/ventilation, use of antibiotics, cardiopulmonary arrest, congestive heart failure, pneumonia and the use of diuretics. Such positive general health benefits resulting from prayer have also been reported by others (e.g., Cha, Wirth, & Lobo, 2001; Harris et al., 1999; Hodge, 2007; Simao et al., 2016). However, Hodge (2007) has noted that various methodological difficulties and the heterogeneity across studies limits the applicability of the findings. For instance, it is not clear what the minimal amount of prayer is that is needed, or for how long praying should continue, or whether praying should be carried out individually or in groups, and what specific type of prayer should be used as well as the experience of the individual or group conducting the praying. Nevertheless, those receiving positive prayers have shown fewer physical complications when undergoing medical procedures (Krucoff et al., 2005); improved health for those suffering from AIDS (Sicher, Targ, Moore, & Smith, 1998); and improved fertility rates when undergoing IVF (Cha et al., 2001). There have even been suggestions that prayer could have retroactive effects. That is, prayer may help patients *after* they have been diagnosed and treated (Leibovici, 2001). Though, unsurprisingly, others suggest that such findings may be more parsimoniously accounted for in terms of problematic methodological issues (Olshansky & Dossey, 2003). However, a review by Roberts et al. (2009) published in the Cochrane database comes to a different conclusion. They argue that the findings are equivocal and, although some of the results of individual studies suggest a positive effect of intercessory prayer, the majority do not and the evidence does not support a recommendation either in favour or against the use of intercessory prayer. However, a more recent randomised blinded study of patients with cancer who received intercessory prayer showed a small but significant improvement in well-being (Olver & Dutney, 2012).

Human psychological

A review by Vitale (2007) showed only limited benefits for using Reiki to reduce stress and improve depression, though others have reported clear improvements in anxiety and depression following Reiki treatment (e.g., Hulse, Stuart-Shor, & Russo, 2010; Richeson, Spross, Lutz, & Peng, 2010). However, a follow-up review of the evidence for Reiki found that many of the studies were of low methodological quality which severely limited the findings (van der Vaart et al., 2009). Indeed, a systematic review published in the Cochrane database examining the possible benefits of Reiki for treating anxiety and depression concluded that very few people with anxiety or depression, or both, had been included in randomised trials and as such there was insufficient data to reach a firm conclusion regarding the usefulness of Reiki for the treatment of anxiety and depression (Herbison, 2015). Others have pointed to the lack of statistical power due to small sample sizes and the difficulties inherent in recruiting individuals, and monitoring them for long periods of time when attempting to study the possible benefits of Reiki (Thrane & Cohen, 2014).

There has been only limited research examining the psychological benefits of Johrei. For example, one study measuring the stress levels of students around exam time showed that those who learnt Johrei exhibited a boost in their immune function compared to a relaxation control group which helped them to moderate their levels of stress (Naito et al., 2003). In a follow-up study stressed participants exposed to Johrei showed improved mood and reduced anxiety compared to a resting control group (Laidlaw et al., 2006), though, as noted above, these participants were students and not clinically anxious and/or depressed individuals. Hence, the severity of the psychological distress experienced by the individual is very likely to influence the outcome. Nevertheless, others have shown that incorporating Johrei into a programme dealing with individuals receiving treatment for substance abuse helped to decrease stress/depression and physical pain and increased positive emotional/spiritual state, energy and overall well-being (Brooks, Schwartz, Reece, & Nangle, 2006).

Therapeutic Touch (TT) has also garnered support for its role in alleviating stress and anxiety as well as improving mood. For instance, Lafreniere et al. (1999) examined the effect of TT on physiological measures including changes in cortisol, dopamine, nitric oxide in urine, as well as mood disturbance and anxiety. After three consecutive monthly sessions, significant positive post-treatment changes were found in the experimental group in nitric oxide, mood disturbance and stress levels when compared to a control group. A meta-analysis by Peters (1999) also suggested that there was reasonable evidence to support the idea that TT leads to positive outcomes. However, she also noted that insufficient information and methodological weaknesses in the early research meant a clear conclusion could not be reached. Since then many others have conducted research to examine the potential benefits of TT and found improved positive mood (Quinn & Strelkauskas, 1993); improved well-being for patients with terminal cancer (Giasson & Bouchard, 1998); the alleviation of stress related illnesses (Newshan & Schuller-Civitella, 2003); and improved mood and anxiety of those suffering from dementia (Woods, Beck, & Sinha, 2009; Woods & Dimond, 2002). Such findings have led researchers to argue that TT is both a safe and tolerable complementary therapy and can be of particular benefit for those suffering from dementia (Senderovich et al., 2016; Woods et al., 2005). However, whilst some have found that TT may ameliorate symptoms such as pain, sleep disturbances, depression, stress and anxiety in patients suffering from both malignant and non-malignant terminal illnesses (e.g., Gregory & Verdouw, 2005; Hawranik, Johnston, & Deatrich, 2008; Montalto, Bhargava, & Hong, 2006) a Cochrane review by Robinson et al. (2007) was unable to reach any clear conclusions due to the lack of randomised or quasi-randomised controlled trials examining the effects of TT for anxiety disorders. However, since then a number of randomised controlled and quasi-experimental studies have been conducted. Most recently Zolfaghari, Eybpoosh and Hazrati (2012) conducted a quasi-experimental study exploring the impact of TT on anxiety. They found that patients undergoing cardiac catheterisation who received TT exhibited significant decreases in state anxiety compared to an equal contact placebo control group (see Figure 8.5).

Such findings suggest that TT can be effective in managing state anxiety in such patients. It also adds weight to the suggestion by Robinson et al. (2007) highlighting the need for more robust clinical trials.

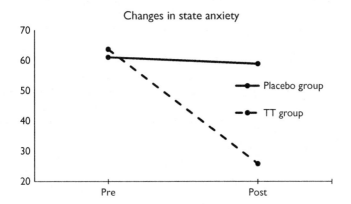

Figure 8.5 Changes in state anxiety levels, from pre- to post-intervention, for the Placebo Control group (solid top line) and the Therapeutic Touch group (dotted bottom line) (adapted from Zolfaghari et al., 2012).

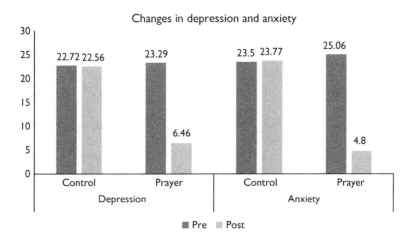

Figure 8.6 Changes in levels of Depression (left panel) and Anxiety (right panel) before (left columns) and after (right columns) Prayer intervention compared to Controls (adapted from Boelens et al., 2009).

Prayer has also been shown to produce positive psychological benefits (e.g., Tloczynski & Fritzsch, 2002), though not always (see Astin et al., 2000). For instance, Boelens, Reeves, Replogle, and Koenig (2009) found that six 1-hour direct person-to-person prayer sessions led to significant reductions in both depression and anxiety compared to a control group (see Figure 8.6).

Interestingly when Boelens, Reeves, Replogle and Koenig (2012) conducted a follow-up after one year they found that the reduced levels of depression and anxiety were maintained. Such findings are consistent with others who have reported that prayer, whether intercessory or petition, used in clinical practice led to reductions in depression and anxiety (e.g., Johnson, 2018; Olver & Dutney, 2012; Sadeghimoghaddam, Alavi,

Mehrabi, & Bankpoor-Fard, 2016; Simao et al., 2016). Whilst these results are certainly suggestive, more research needs to be done to examine the various potential mediating factors: for instance, the religious or spiritual beliefs of those praying and of the individual being prayed for, as well as the heterogeneous nature of the illness and/or problems of those being prayed for, and the specific instructions regarding the nature of intention and prayer, frequency and length of each prayer and duration of the praying intervention. Also, it is not clear why a supposedly compassionate God or higher power would only respond to the needs of those who pray or are prayed for.

Non-human animal studies

Non-human animal models are often used as a way to explore and refine particular clinical interventions (e.g., de Souza, Rosa, Blanco, Passaglia, & Stabile, 2017). For instance, animal experiments have contributed much to our understanding of the mechanisms of disease, though many have argued that their value is limited and human clinical trials would always be essential to be sufficiently certain of the effectiveness of any intervention (see e.g., Jucker, 2010). Nevertheless, they provide an additional branch of research exploring the potential benefits of energy healing and are invariably assessed using *wound reduction* effects or behaviour following the *injection of toxic cells*. For example, early work that inflicted similar sized wounds on mice and then randomly allocated them to either a healing condition or a no-intervention control condition found that those mice given healing showed significantly accelerated healing levels (Grad, 1965). Such positive findings have been replicated by others adopting a randomised double-blind approach and using prayer to encourage wound healing in primates (Lesniak, 2006). More recently de Souza et al. (2017) reported a significant reduction in the size of the wound area of rats treated with TT compared to an equal contact control group (see Figure 8.7).

De Souza et al. (2017) argued that TT benefited skin healing by accelerating skin tissue repair and increasing the number of biological cells that help structure tissue (i.e., fibroblasts), though they admit that it is not entirely clear yet precisely how TT produces such an effect. Nevertheless, given it is a low-cost intervention and is both relatively easy to use and has no clearly reported negative side effects, it would be a useful adjunct for treating tissue repair. However, they are cautious and point out the

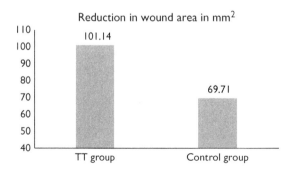

Figure 8.7 Reduction in wound size (in mm^2) for Therapeutic Touch group (left) and Control group (right) after intervention (adapted from de Souza et al., 2017).

need for more research, ideally on human tissue samples, to explore potential mediating factors to gain a better understanding of the healing effects of TT.

The injection of toxic cells into animals usually takes the form of cancer cells. Following such injections, the researchers then examine the effects of energy healing compared to a no-healing condition on the remission and/or growth rate of the cancerous tumours. Early work showed reduced tumour growth in mice that were treated with healing compared to an untreated control group (Onetto & Elguin, 1966), a finding which has since been replicated by many others. For instance, Bengston and Krinsley (2000) found that following a brief training period it was possible for an individual to utilise energy healing to dramatically raise the remittance rate of mice infected with an incurable cancer (see Figure 8.8). Interestingly, the level of 'belief' exhibited by the healer did not seem to influence the outcome.

A follow-up study again showed that an energy healer was able to heal mice injected with mammary cancer cells (Bengston & Moga, 2007). Others have found similar benefits using TT which has been shown to significantly reduce the growth of cancerous tumours in mice compared to mock-treated controls (Gronowicz, Secor, Flynn, Jellison, & Kuhn, 2015). A meta-analysis of 11 animal based healing studies by Roe, Sonnex and Roxburgh (2015) showed a significant effect of healing intention. Hence, those animals allocated to the active energy treatment conditions achieved better outcomes than those allocated to control conditions. Such findings have led to suggestions that future research should focus on attempting to shed light on the underlying mechanisms by which such healing occurs (Bengston & Krinsley, 2000).

In-vitro studies

One way to try and address the methodological limitations of relying on human and/ or non-human animal participants is to focus on more controlled studies using bacteria that can be monitored and precisely controlled. In-vitro studies can be performed in tightly controlled environments that minimise various confounding variables, such as expectancy and belief. Another benefit is that in-vitro studies can focus on specific cell lines such as cancer cells, bone cells, skin cells, etc. to see which, if any, respond to such treatments. Furthermore, those conducting the statistical

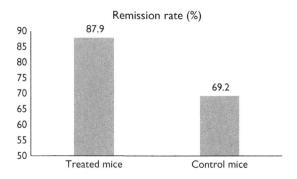

Figure 8.8 Percentage remission rates for mice given healing (left) compared to no-healing controls (right) (adapted from Bengston & Krinsley, 2000).

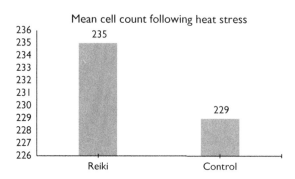

Figure 8.9 Mean bacteria cell count for culture treated with Reiki healing (left) and untreated controls (right) (adapted from Rubik et al., 2006).

analyses of such interventions can be easily blinded to the conditions. A wide range of research examining the in-vitro effects of energy healing has shown positive benefits. For instance, an early report by Nash (1982) showed that it was possible to retard the growth of bacterial and fungal infections. Rubik, Brooks and Schwartz (2006) have also reported some positive results from randomised controlled research comparing the effect of Reiki healing on cell cultures. They found that, after stressing cell cultures using a standard heat shock technique, a greater number of cells survived when given Reiki healing compared to no-healing controls (see Figure 8.9).

This led Rubik et al. (2006) to suggest that Reiki healing has growth-promoting potential for cell cultures. Others have also found that energy healing can influence the growth or survival of stressed cells (Mager et al., 2007) as well as influence the growth of *Excherichia coli* (E. coli) bacteria (Trivedi, Pati, Shettigar, Gangwar, & Jana, 2015).

Given the large number of people that die from the various forms of cancer each year it is unsurprising that many in-vitro studies have examined energy healing effects on cancer cells. For instance, early work by Shah et al. (1999) examined the effect of energy healing on in-vitro tumour cell growth. They compared the effects of a healer to that of a medical student mimicking the healer along with another control sample left at an ambient temperature to control for non-specific effects. They found that the healer was significantly more able to inhibit tumour cell growth compared to the medical student. Since then many others have replicated such effects showing that energy healing can inhibit or influence cultured human cancer cells in experiments comparing treated cells with untreated control cells (Monzillo & Gronowicz, 2011; Ohnishi, Ohnishi, Nishino, Tsurusaki, & Yamaguchi, 2005; Trivedi et al., 2015; Yount et al., 2012). For example, researchers found significant reductions in the density of human gastric cancer cells after four days of Johrei treatment compared to a no intervention control group (see Figure 8.10; Abe, Ichinomiya, Kanai, & Yamamoto, 2012).

Abe et al. (2012) noted that the loss of cancer cells in the Johrei condition was due mainly to cell death and a decreased proliferation. Furthermore, they found that certain types of cancer cells were more influenced by Johrei than others. This, they suggested, shows that whilst Johrei can induce a loss of cancer cells, the specific rate

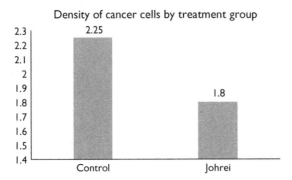

Density of cancer cells by treatment group

Figure 8.10 The density of human gastric cancer cells in the Control condition (left) and the Johrei condition (right) after four days of treatment (adapted from Abe et al., 2012).

of responsiveness may be influenced by the type of cancer cell. Such healing effects have even been suggested to occur when the healer focuses their energy on sterilised cotton rolls which are then placed by cancer cell cultures (Beseme, Bengston, Radin, Turner, & McMichael, 2018).

Interestingly, the in-vitro energy healing research has not only shown that negative cell growth can be inhibited but also that positive healthy cell growth can be encouraged. For instance, Radin, Taft, and Yount (2004) reported that energy healing was associated with the growth of healthy human brain cells. Others have also shown that TT can increase healthy cell proliferation (Gronowicz, Jhaveri, Clarke, Aronow, & Smith, 2008) and significantly increase human bone cell synthesis, differentiation and mineralisation compared with both a placebo control and an untreated control sample (Jhaveri, Walsh, Wang, McCarthy, & Gronowicz, 2008).

However not all have not found evidence of such beneficial effects. For instance, Taft et al. (2003) examined the effect of Johrei on cultured brain tumour cells and found no difference in cell death or proliferation in cultures treated by Johrei practitioners and controls. Similar negative effects have been found in cells exposed to ionising radiation (Hall, Luu, Moore, & Yount, 2006). Again, Johrei treatment did not reduce cell death compared to a no treatment control group. The difference in results is likely due to the differences in methodology. This can include the type of healing, the specific cancer cell, the climate and treatment settings and the duration and number of sessions. It may even be that combining multiple healing approaches is more effective. However, at present, whilst the results are extremely encouraging more work is needed to identify the specific role of each type of healing on the various types of cell culture. Nevertheless, a recent meta-analysis of 22 in-vitro studies by Roe et al. (2015) showed them to be heterogenous but significant. That is, energy healing elicited significantly positive effects across in-vitro cell cultures and tissue samples.

Mediating factors

Radin, Schlitz and Baur (2015) are among those who have pointed out that there are many and varied factors that could introduce unknown sources of variance, which could either enhance or inhibit the outcome of energy healing interventions. Unfortunately, despite a wealth of research exploring the potential benefits of energy healing there have been few studies examining the various factors likely to mediate such effects. Nevertheless, there are some indications that repeated sessions can elicit more robust effects and that the skill or experience of the healer may play a part.

Repetition of sessions

In mainstream biomedicine there is often a clear relationship between the dose of the medicine and the response to it, encapsulated within the *dose-response curve* (e.g., Kolb, Whishaw, & Teskey, 2016). The more medicine given the greater the initial response until a point of saturation is reached where increased medication may then lead to negative side effects. In a similar way researchers have shown that there is a relationship between the number of healing sessions attended and the reported positive effects (Jain & Mills, 2010). For example, Radin et al. (2004) examined the effect of multiple Johrei healing sessions on growth cultures of human brain cells. Initially, they found that healing did not influence cell growth on the first two days compared to controls. However, on the third day there was a clear increase in cell growth for those cells given healing compared to controls (see Figure 8.11).

This led them to suggest that the effects of such healing may be weak, but cumulative. That is, a single healing session may be insufficient to elicit a measurable effect whereas multiple repeated sessions may build the effect up over time producing more robust outcomes. Others have also reported such dose related relationships when examining the potential benefits of energy healing. For instance, Jhaveri et al. (2008) reported that using an intervention of TT was only able to elicit positive effects on cell cultures after repeated treatments over a two-week period. Such findings clearly indicate that it may take some time for the beneficial effects of energy healing to emerge and that multiple treatment sessions may be optimal. However, it is not clear yet precisely how many sessions would be needed and whether it would be the same for each of the various healing approaches. A related point is the duration of the sessions. It may be that longer sessions provide a more optimal intervention than

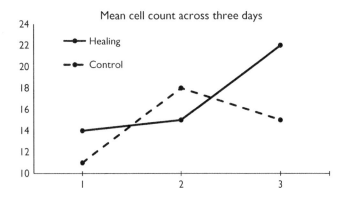

Figure 8.11 Mean cell count for cell cultures treated with Healing (top solid line) and Control cultures (bottom dotted line) across three days (adapted from Radin et al., 2004).

shorter sessions; however, there is no research directly addressing this question. Hence, the findings regarding repeated sessions are useful but much more needs to be done to clarify the precise role the length and number of sessions has on outcome.

Skill/experience of healer

It would seem logical that recruiting experienced healers with a certain level of practice and skill may lead to a more efficacious outcome, irrespective of their approach. Indeed, Astin et al. (2000) have suggested that healers should have at least three years of practice before they are considered to be optimally effective. Such suggestions are consistent with the findings reported by Kemper (2016) who found that many healers report that their intuitions and perceptions improve over time with practice. The idea that the skill or experience of the healer leads to more positive outcomes has some support from the literature. For example, a review by van der Vaart et al. (2009) reported that of the nine studies they examined that showed positive effects eight of them used a Reiki master, whereas no significant effects were found when using Reiki practitioners with less than three years of experience. Others have also reported beneficial effects when recruiting practitioners with five, or more, years of experience (Sicher et al., 1998). On a related note some have suggested that it is not just the experience of the practitioner that needs to be taken into account but also their mood and well-being (Rubik et al., 2006). For instance, Rubik et al. (2006) reported that the well-being of the practitioners can have an impact on the outcome of the healing sessions. That is, those with greater levels of well-being produced more positive effects than those with low well-being scores. However, as with repeated sessions, it is not clear yet whether level of skill and practitioner mood and well-being have a similar impact on the outcome for the different healing techniques. As such, whilst the findings certainly suggest that skill and well-being may be essential components in eliciting clear healing effects more needs to be done to clarify the role of such factors within each of the different healing approaches.

Indeed, there are many other factors that are likely to influence the outcome of an energy healing intervention which have received either only limited or no attention. For instance, some have suggested that the distance between the healer and the recipient does not appear to influence the effectiveness of the healing intervention (e.g., Benor, 2005; Radin et al., 2015), though more empirical work is needed to clearly examine this across healing approaches and for the various interventions. Others have suggested that the context in which the healing is conducted may also influence the outcome. For instance, Rubik et al. (2006) suggest that a positive supportive context is important and that research that fails to take this into account may not be providing an optimal setting in which to assess energy healing effects.

Mechanisms

The evidence outlined above provides a glimpse of some of the key findings in energy healing research. If such evidence is accepted the next obvious question is how can this be happening? Unfortunately, as yet there is no clearly established mechanism by which energy healing can occur which may be a potential barrier to the acceptance of such techniques as most scientists and clinicians are cautious about accepting ideas and approaches that cannot be clearly explained using current scientific thinking and mechanisms. Many sceptics are also keen to point out the problems associated with the idea of action at a distance effects, despite the many experiments in quantum field theory which clearly show that the very essence of the cosmos may be non-local (Schlitz et al., 2003). Though there is no agreed upon mechanism of action for energy healing, several potential alternatives have been proposed. They include placebo effects, biological mechanisms, psychological effects and the notion of subtle energy fields (e.g., Benor, 1992, 2005; Krieger, 1995).

Placebo

In the absence of a clear and fully understood mechanism it is not surprising that many sceptics adopt a view that is more in line with the suggestion that any perceived benefits are simply the result of a placebo effect. Placebo effects are often considered to be the result of an inert substance, such as a sugar pill, that has no active ingredients, but this characterisation has been suggested to be somewhat limited. For instance, Wager and Atlas (2015) argue that placebo effects are the beneficial effects attributable to the brain–mind responses of the individual to the context in which a treatment is delivered rather than to the specific actions of any biomedicine. In a broad sense, placebo effects are improvements in patients' symptoms that are attributable to their participation in the therapeutic encounter, with its rituals, symbols and interactions. Indeed, research has shown that the effects of a placebo are both powerful and effective and that administering a placebo can significantly benefit a range of health-related issues (Flik et al., 2017). Furthermore, research has also shown that increasing the dosage of the placebo is associated with improved healing (de Craen et al., 1999), and that more complex and detailed placebo interventions (e.g., sham surgery) are associated with better responses compared to placebo medication alone (Meissner, Fassler, & Rucker, 2013). Interestingly, the placebo effect continues to work even when people know they are being given a sham treatment (Kam-Hansen et al., 2014).

Given the high levels of reported belief in energy healing techniques and the perceived notion that they provide a more holistic and natural approach (e.g., Wallis & McDowell, 1996) it is easy to see how such beliefs can translate into high expectations and a possible placebo effect (French & Stone, 2014). However, whilst such beliefs and expectations *may* influence the outcome of energy healing research, as they no doubt do in all clinical interventions (e.g., Razza et al., 2018; Yeung, Sharpe, Glozier, Hackett, & Colagiuri, 2018), they cannot fully account for the data for a number of reasons. First, it has been argued that placebo treatments remain consistent across studies from different laboratories (Wager & Atlas, 2015). This is not the case for energy healing research (see e.g., Roe et al., 2015). Benor (2005) has also argued that attempting to account for energy healing effects in terms of placebo or spontaneous remission fails to account for data when double-blind trials are used. Jain and Mills (2010) agree, arguing that the effects of energy healing go beyond any non-specific effects that may be mediated by placebo effects. Finally, and perhaps most damning of all, placebo, beliefs and expectations cannot in any way account for the data from non-human animal studies and the very tightly controlled in-vitro research.

Biological mechanisms

Several potential biological mechanisms have been proposed to account for the beneficial effects seen in energy healing. One speculative possibility is based on the fact that the human body is approximately 55 65% water (e.g., Watson, Watson, & Batt, 1980). The idea here is that healing may work via changes in hydrogen bonding (S. Schwartz, De Mattei, Brame, & Spottiswoode, 2015). An alternative is that healing may work via the enhanced action of enzymes in the body, which act to catalyse the various reactions throughout the body (Smith, 1972). Other possibilities include the enhanced activation of hormones (Benor, 2005), as well as increased production of antibodies (Bengston & Krinsley, 2000). Some have also suggested that changes in brain activity of the recipient alone (Achterberg et al., 2005; P. R. Baldwin, Velasquez, Koenig, Salas, & Boelens, 2016; Giroldini & Pederzoli, 2018; Pike, Vernon, & Hald, 2014) or synchronous changes in both practitioner and healer (Ventura, Saroka, & Persinger, 2014) may underpin such healing effects. It may be that any one, or more, of these biological processes underpins the effects of energy healing. However, what remains unclear is how such biological changes can be brought about. That is, what is it that causes the potential changes in hydrogen bonding, enzyme, antibody or brain activity? Hence, these suggested biological processes simply shift the field of enquiry from asking how can healing produce a beneficial effect to how can healing influence biology.

Psychological mechanisms

Given that some healers claim that illness may be the product of psychological dis-harmony it should not come as much of a surprise that one possible way healing may influence healthy outcomes is via the various psychological routes (DiNucci, 2005; Jain & Mills, 2010). One obvious possibility is that improved healing could be the result of reductions in anxiety (see, O'Laoire, 1997). Simply having someone to talk with, share the problem and receive both emotional and psychological support would be expected to positively influence the health of the recipient. It may also be that taking the conscious decision to seek out and access such complementary health care interventions leads to an enhanced sense of self control and/or self-efficacy which could positively influence the outcome (Targ, 1997). However, whilst such psychological mechanisms may have some influence they are unlikely to be able to provide a full account given the various blinded and placebo-controlled methods used. Reduced anxiety and/or enhanced self-control are also unlikely to account for the findings from non-human animal studies and the in-vitro data.

Subtle energy

Energy healing practitioners often suggest that illness may be the result of disruptions to the individual's energy field (DiNucci, 2005). Healing may then occur by the practitioner modifying and/or directing this subtle energy in a particular way to aid the healing process. For instance, the reported sensations of heat felt during the healing process are often taken to suggest that an exchange of *energy* has occurred (Benor, 2005). This energy is often assumed to be representative of some form of universal energy, or the energy of God or another spiritual source. This energy is referred to by different names in separate cultures, such as chi in China, ki in Japan, prana in India and light energy in Christian-based cultures. Alternatively, it has been suggested that this energy emerges from the zero-point field that is theorised to pervade all aspects of the universe (DiNucci, 2005). It is this subtle energy that is channelled by the conscious focused intention of the practitioner onto areas of interest in the recipient (Bengston & Moga, 2007). Recourse to such an idea may seem to provide an explanation for the beneficial effects of energy healing. However, it should be noted that, to date, no one has been able to identify or measure the alleged interaction between a human and such proposed subtle energy fields (O'Mathuna et al., 2002). Indeed, the findings whilst suggestive are at best equivocal. For instance, Zimmerman (1990) reported that when a healer focused on healing a patient the surrounding energy field of the healer increased in size as measured by a Superconducting Quantum Interference Device (SQUID). This led to suggestions that such a field provides the basis for either the emission or transmission of subtle energy from practitioner to recipient. However, an early study examining whether those trained in TT could *feel* whether another person's hand was held above their own showed they were unable to do this (Rosa et al., 1998). This was taken as a failure on the part of the therapists to identify the alleged subtle energy field of another person with any degree of accuracy. Others have also found that Reiki does not produce any evidence of high-intensity electromagnetic fields from either the heart or hands (A. L. Baldwin, Rand, & Schwartz, 2013). Hence, as yet, there is no clear evidence of any such subtle energy field existing nor any robust support for the notion that energy healing practitioners can identify it. Nevertheless, it is important to realise that this does not mean that such potential subtle energies do not exist. Simply, for now, we have been unable to clearly identify and measure them. The snapshot of evidence reviewed above clearly indicates that something positive can occur when an individual receives energy healing. Hence, many have argued that more research is needed to provide a greater understanding of the mechanisms of such effects (e.g., Astin et al., 2000; DiNucci, 2005; Hodge, 2007; Jain & Mills, 2010; Jonas & Crawford, 2003; Levin, 2011; Rao et al., 2016; Schlitz et al., 2003; Schwartz, 2017; Thrane & Cohen, 2014; van der Vaart et al., 2009).

Overview

Healing refers to the notion that a practitioner can channel or manipulate a form of subtle energy that is focused on, or into, the recipient, possibly at a distance, to restore normal energy balance and health. Over time many techniques have been developed that can help the practitioner learn to focus such energy in a healing context. Such techniques may act as metaphorical lenses helping to focus both the conscious intention of the practitioner and the subtle energy assumed to underpin such healing. However, give the large number of potential approaches it is not clear yet precisely what, if any, differential effects such techniques can elicit. Hence, more work is needed to delineate the unique healing effect of each approach. To provide a flavour of some of the various techniques the chapter examined Johrei, Reiki, Therapeutic Touch (TT) and prayer. Whilst there are subtle differences between these approaches there are also some similarities. For instance, all rely on the focused conscious intention of the practitioner to direct positive healing energy and/or thoughts towards the recipient, though it is not clear yet to what extent the ability to heal is something that is innate or a skill that can be learnt. In addition, access to and use of such complementary healing approaches are both widespread and increasing. The reasons given for this vary widely from attempting to deal with multiple problems to viewing such interventions as a treat, though such options are likely influenced by social norms as well as the financial costs. Nevertheless, the majority of those accessing such healing interventions are satisfied with the outcomes. A key implication of this is the need for clear robust empirical support for such interventions. Many reviews of the evidence have suggested that the effects of energy healing tend to be small but are significantly positive. For instance, there is good evidence showing the pain reducing benefits of Reiki, Johrei and TT. Prayer has also been shown to benefit general health, particularly for those in hospital. The potential benefits for psychological problems are more ambiguous, with the effects of Reiki limited by poor methodology and lack of statistical power. In contrast, Johrei has been shown to improve mood and reduce anxiety, with similar effects reported for TT and prayer. Alongside this the non-human animal studies have shown good evidence of wound reduction and improved remission rates following energy healing interventions. The evidence for energy healing is also bolstered by the findings from in-vitro research. Here researchers have shown that healing can protect stressed cell cultures and inhibit the growth of cancerous tumours. Interestingly some have also reported positive effects with healthy cells showing improved growth and proliferation. In terms of the potential mediating factors there is a lack of good research examining such possibilities. Nevertheless, there is some evidence to suggest that the small positive effects of energy healing can be enhanced by incorporating multiple treatment sessions and relying on skilled practitioners, though clearly more needs to be done in this area to identify what other factors may enhance or inhibit the outcome of such interventions. Finally, it is not clear yet what mechanism(s) underpin such healing interventions. As with all clinical treatments some aspect will be reliant on placebo effects but this cannot provide a full account of the data. Suggestions for biological and psychological mechanisms are also appealing but again do not fully account for the data. The idea that such healing is reliant on some form of subtle energy is both compelling and provocative. However, the current level of evidence to support this is both vague and ambiguous. Hence, more work is needed that focuses on identifying the potential mechanism(s) of action, because when such mechanism(s) are identified the potential implications and benefits for humanity will be significant.

Reflective questions

Some questions that may prove helpful when reflecting on the material covered in this chapter.

- How would you design a study to test for energy healing effects controlling for non-relevant intentions?
- Are there any ethical/moral concerns regarding energy healing?
- Should energy healing be made available on the NHS?
- Should energy healing be offered for all terminal cases?

- Should doctors and nurses be trained in energy healing techniques?
- Should energy healers be accredited to indicate a sufficient level of skill/expertise?
- Would you like to have the option of energy healing?
- Given the findings from energy healing research how would you account for the data?

References

Abbott, N. C. (2000). Healing as a therapy for human disease: a systematic review. *Journal of Alternative and Complementary Medicine, 6*(2), 159–169.

Abe, K., Ichinomiya, R., Kanai, T., & Yamamoto, K. (2012). Effect of Japanese energy healing method known as Johrei on viability and proliferation of cultured cancer cells in vitro. *The Journal of Alternative and Complementary Medicine, 18*(3), 221–228.

Achterberg, J., Cooke, K., Richards, T., Standish, L. J., Kozak, L., & Lake, J. (2005). Evidence for correlations between distant intentionality and brain function in recipients: A functional magnetic resonance imaging analysis. *Journal of Alternative and Complementary Medicine, 11*(6), 965–971. doi: 10.1089/acm.2005.11.965.

Achterberg, J., & Lawlis, G. (1984). *Imagery and disease.* Champaign, IL: Institute for Personality and Ability Testing.

Aghabati, N., Mohammadi, E., & Pour Esmaiel, Z. (2008). The effect of therapeutic touch on pain and fatigue of cancer patients undergoing chemotherapy. *Evidence-Based Complementary and Alternative Medicine, 7,* 375–381. doi: 10.1093/ecam/nen006.

Anderson, J. G., & Taylor, A. G. (2012). Use of complementary therapies for cancer symptom management: Results of the 2007 National Health Interview Survey. *The Journal of Alternative and Complementary Medicine, 18*(3), 235–241.

Astin, J. A., Harkness, E., & Ernst, E. (2000). The efficacy of 'Distant Healing': A systematic review of randomized trials. *Annals of Internal Medicine, 132*(11), 903–910.

Baldwin, A. L., Rand, W. L., & Schwartz, G. E. (2013). Practicing Reiki does not appear to routinely produce high-intensity electromagnetic fields from the heart or hands of Reiki practitioners. *Journal of Alternative and Complementary Medicine, 19*(6), 518–526.

Baldwin, P. R., Velasquez, K., Koenig, H. G., Salas, R., & Boelens, P. A. (2016). Neural correlates of healing prayers, depression and traumatic memories: A preliminary study. *Complementary Therapies in Medicine, 27,* 123–129. doi: 10.1016/j.ctim.2016.07.002.

Barnes, P. M., Powell-Griner, E., McFann, K., & Nahin, R. L. (2004). *Complementary and alternative medicine use among adults: United States, 2002. (National Center for Health Statistics No. 343).* Hyattsville, MD: Centers for Disease Control.

Bengston, W., & Krinsley, D. (2000). The effect of the 'laying on of hands' on transplanted breast cancer in mice. *Journal of Scientific Exploration, 14*(3), 353–364.

Bengston, W., & Moga, M. (2007). Resonance, placebo effects and type II errors: Some implications from healing research for experimental methods. *Journal of Alternative and Complementary Medicine, 13*(3), 317–327. doi: 10.1089/acm.2007.6300.

Bengston, W., & Murphy, D. G. (2008). Can healing be taught? *Explore, 4*(3), 197–200. doi: 10.1016/j.explore.2008.02.004.

Benor, D. (1992). Lessons from spiritual healing research & practice. *Subtle Energies & Energy Medicine Journal Archives, 3*(1), 73–88.

Benor, D. (2005). Healing. In J. Henry (Ed.), *Parapsychology: Research on exceptional experiences* (pp. 137–148). Hove, East Sussex: Routledge.

Beseme, S., Bengston, W., Radin, D., Turner, M., & McMichael, J. (2018). Transcriptional changes in cancer cells induced by exposure to healing method. *Dose Response, 16*(3), 1–8. doi: 10.1177/1559325818782843.

Bishop, F. L., Yardley, L., & Lewith, G. T. (2008). Treat or treatment: A qualitative study analyzing patients' use of complementary and alternative medicine. *American Journal of Public Health*, 98(9), 1700–1705.

Boelens, P. A., Reeves, R. R., Replogle, W. H., & Koenig, H. G. (2009). A randomized trial of the effect of prayer on depression and anxiety. *International Journal of Psychiatry in Medicine*, 39(4), 377–392. doi: 10.2190/PM.39.4.c.

Boelens, P. A., Reeves, R. R., Replogle, W. H., & Koenig, H. G. (2012). The effect of prayer on depression and anxiety: Maintenance of positive influence one year after prayer intervention. *The International Journal of Psychiatry in Medicine*, 43(1), 85–98. doi: 10.2190/PM.43.1.f.

Brooks, A. J., Schwartz, G. E., Reece, K., & Nangle, G. (2006). The effect of Johrei healing on substance abuse recovery: A pilot study. *Journal of Alternative and Complementary Medicine*, 12(7), 625–631.

Bulette Coakley, A., & Duffy, M. E. (2010). The effect of therapeutic touch on postoperative patients. *Journal of Holistic Nursing*, 28(3), 193–200.

Bunnell, T. (1999). The effect of 'healing with intent' on pepsin enzyme activity. *Journal of Scientific Exploration*, 13(2), 139–148.

Buzzetti, R. A., Hinojosa-Kurtzberg, M., Shea, T. J., Ibuki, Y., Sirakis, G., & Parthasarathy, S. (2013). Effect of Johrei therapy on sleep in a murine model. *Explore*, 9(2), 100–105. doi: 10.1016/j.explore.2012.12.004.

Byrd, R. (1988). Positive therapuetic effects of intercessary prayer in a coronary care population. *Southern Medical Journal*, 81, 826–829.

Cha, K. Y., Wirth, D. P., & Lobo, R. A. (2001). Does prayer influence the success of in vitro fertilization-embryo transfer?: Report of a masked, randomized trial. *Journal of Reproductive Medicine*, 46(9), 781–787.

Cuneo, C. L., Curtis Cooper, M. R., Drew, C. S., Naoum-Heffernan, C., Sherman, T., Walz, K., & Weinberg, J. (2011). The effect of Reiki on work-related stress of the registered nurse. *Journal of Holistic Nursing*, 29(1), 33–43.

de Craen, A. J. M., Moerman, D. E., Heisterkamp, S. H., Tytgat, G. N. J., Tijssen, J. G. P., & Kleijnen, J. (1999). Placebo effect in the treatment of duodenal ulcer. *British Journal of Clinical Pharmacology*, 48(6), 853–860. doi: 10.1046/j.1365-2125.1999.00094.x.

de Souza, A. L. T., Rosa, D. P. C., Blanco, B. A., Passaglia, P., & Stabile, A. M. (2017). Effects of therapeutic touch on healing of the skin in rats. *Explore*, 13(5), 333–338. doi: 10.1016/j.explore.2017.06.006.

Demir, M., Can, G., Kelam, A., & Aydiner, A. (2015). Effects of distant reiki on pain, anxiety and fatigue in oncology patients in Turkey: A pilot study. *Asian Pacific Journal of Cancer Prevention*, 16(12), 4859–4862.

DiNucci, E. M. (2005). Energy healing: A complementary treatment for orthopaedic and other conditions. *Orthopaedic Nursing*, 24(4), 259–269.

Dogan, M. D. (2018). The effect of reiki on pain: A meta-analysis. *Complementary Therapies in Clinical Practice*, 31, 384–387. doi: 10.1016/j.ctcp.2018.02.020.

Dorri, S., & Bahrami, M. (2014). The effect of Therapeutic Touch on pain relief in patients with cancer. *The Journal of Urmia Nursing and Midwifery Faculty*, 12(8), 767–776.

Edwards, S. (2016). *Healing in a hospital: Scientific evidence that spiritual healing improves health*. Amazon: Sandy Edwards.

Flik, C. E., Bakker, L., Laan, W., van Rood, Y. R., Smout, A. J. P., & de Wit, N. J. (2017). Systematic review: The placebo effect of psychological interventions in the treatment of irritable bowel syndrome. *World Journal of Gastroenterology*, 23(12), 2223–2233. doi: 10.3748/wjg.v23.i12.2223.

French, C. C., & Stone, A. (2014). *Anomalistic psychology: Exploring paranormal belief and experience*. Hampshire, UK: Palgrave Macmillan.

Gasiorowska, A., Navarro-Rodriguez, T., Dickman, R., Wendel, C., Moty, B., Powers, J., ... & Thai, H. (2009). Clinical trial: The effect of Johrei on symptoms of patients with functional chest pain. *Alimentary Pharmacology & Therapeutics*, 29(1), 126–134.

Giasson, M., & Bouchard, L. (1998). Effect of therapeutic touch on the well-being of persons with terminal cancer. *Journal of Holistic Nursing*, 16(3), 383–398.

Giroldini, W., & Pederzoli, L. (2018). Brain-to-brain interaction at a distance based on EEG analysis. *Journal of Consciousnes Exploration & Research*, 9(6), 501–513.

Gordon, A., Merenstein, J. H., D'Amico, F., & Hudgens, D. (1998). The effects of therapeutic touch on patients with osteoarthritis of the knee. *Journal of Family Practice*, 47(4), 271–278.

Grad, B. (1965). Some biological effects of the 'laying on of hands': A review of experiments with animals and plants. *Journal of the American Society for Psychical Research*, 59(2), 95–129.

Gregory, S., & Verdouw, J. (2005). Therapeutic touch: Its application for residents in aged care. *Australian Nursing Journal*, 12(7), 23–25.

Gronowicz, G. A., Jhaveri, A., Clarke, L. W., Aronow, M. S., & Smith, T. H. (2008). Therapeutic touch stimulates the proliferation of human cells in culture. *Journal of Alternative and Complementary Medicine*, 14(3), 233–239. doi: 10.1089/acm.2007.7163.

Gronowicz, G. A., Secor, E. R., Flynn, J. R., Jellison, E. R., & Kuhn, L. T. (2015). Therapeutic touch has significant effects on mouse breast cancer metastasis and immune response but not primary tumor size. *Evidence Based Complementary and Alternative Medicine*, 2015, Article ID 926565. doi: 10.1155/2015/926565.

Guy, J. B., Bard-Reboul, S., Trone, J. C., Vallard, A., Espenel, S., Langrand-Escure, J., ... & Rancoule, C. (2017). Healing touch in radiation therapy: is the benefit tangible? *Oncotarget*, 8(46), 81485–81491. doi: 10.18632/oncotarget.20594.

Hall, Z., Luu, T., Moore, D., & Yount, G. (2006). Radiation response of cultured human cells is unafected by Johrei. *Evidence Based Complementary and Alternative Medicine*, 4(2), 191–194. doi: 10.1093/ecam/ne1078.

Harris, W. S., Gowda, M., Kolb, J. W., Strychacz, C. P., Vacek, J. L., Jones, P. G., ... & McCallister, B. D. (1999). A randomised controlled trial of the effects of remote intercessory prayer on outcomes in patients admitted to the coronary care unit. *Archives of Internal Medicine*, 159(19), 2273–2278.

Hawranik, P., Johnston, P., & Deatrich, J. (2008). Therapeutic touch and agitation in individuals with Alzheimer's disease. *Western Journal of Nursing Research*, 30(4), 417–434.

Herbison, J. J. (2015). Reiki for depression and anxiety. *Cochrane Database of Systematic Reviews* (4). doi: 10.1002/14651858.CD006833.pub2.

Hodge, D. R. (2007). A systematic review of the empirical literature on intercessory prayer. *Research on Social Work Practice*, 17(2), 174–187.

Hulse, R. S., Stuart-Shor, E. M., & Russo, J. (2010). Endoscopic procedure with a modified Reiki intervention: a pilot study. *Gastroenterology Nursing*, 33(1), 20–26.

Jahnke, R., Larkey, L., Rogers, C., Etnier, J., & Lin, F. (2010). A comprehensive review of health benefits of qigong and tai chi. *American Journal of Health Promotion*, 24(6), 1–25.

Jain, S., & Mills, P. J. (2010). Biofield therapies: helpful or full of hype? A best evidence synthesis. *International Journal of Behavioral Medicine*, 17, 1–16.

Jhaveri, A., Walsh, S., Wang, Y., McCarthy, M., & Gronowicz, G. A. (2008). Therapeutic touch effects DNA synthesis and mineralization of human osteoblasts in culture. *Journal of Orthopaedic Research*, 26(1), 1541–1546.

Johnson, K. A. (2018). Prayer: A helpful aid in recovery from depression. *Journal of Religion and Health*, 57(6), 2290–2300. doi: 10.1007/s10943-018-0564-8.

Jonas, W. B., & Crawford, C. C. (2003). Science and spritual healing: A critical review of spiritual healing, 'energy' medicine, and intentionality. *Alternative Therapies in Health and Medicine*, 9(2), 56–61.

Jordan, J. L., & Croft, P. R. (2018). Justifications for using complementary and alternative medicine reported by persons with musculoskeletal conditions: A narrative literature synthesis. *PloS One, 13*(7), e0200879.

Joyce, J., & Herbison, G. P. (2015). Reiki for depression and anxiety. *Cochrane Database of Systematic Reviews* (4).

Jucker, M. (2010). The benefits and limitations of animal models for translational research in neurodegenerative diseases. *Nature Medicine, 16*(11), 1210.

Kam-Hansen, S., Jakubowski, M., Kelley, J. M., Kirsch, I., Hoaglin, D. C., & Kaptchu, T. J. (2014). Altered placebo and drug labeling changes the outcome of episodic migraine attacks. *Science Translational Medicine, 6*(218), 218ra215. doi: 10.1126/scitranslmed.3006175.

Kemper, K. J. (2016). Authentic healing: Effects on recipients and healers. *Alternative and Complimentary Therapies, 22*(3), 105–110. doi: 10.1089/act.2016.29057.kjk.

Kolb, B., Whishaw, I. Q., & Teskey, G. C. (2016). *An introduction to brain and behaviour.* (Vol. 5). New York: Worth.

Krieger, D. (1995). *Therapeutic touch: Modern version of the ancient technique of laying on of hands.* Sao Palo: Cultrix.

Kristoffersen, A. E., Stub, T., Knudsen-Baas, O., Udal, A. H., & Musial, F. (2019). Self-reported effects of energy healing: A prospective observational study with pre-post design. *Explore, 15*(2), 115–125. doi: 10.1016/j.explore.2018.06.009.

Krucoff, M. W., Crater, S. W., Gallup, D., Blankenship, J. C., Cuffe, M., Guarneri, M., ... & Oz, M. (2005). Music, imagery, touch, and prayer as adjuncts to interventional cardiac care: The Monitoring and Actualisation of Noetic Trainings (MANTRA) II randomised study. *The Lancet, 366*(9481), 211–217.

Lafreniere, K. D., Mutus, B., Camerson, S., Tannous, M., Gianotti, M., Abu-Zahra, H., & Laukkanen, E. (1999). Effects of Therapeutic Touch on biochemical and mood indicators of women. *The Journal of Alternative and Complementary Medicine, 5*(4), 367–370. doi: 10. 1089/acm.1999.5.367.

Laidlaw, T. M., Naito, A., Dwivedi, P., Hansi, N. K., Henderson, D. C., & Gruzelier, J. H. (2006). The influence of 10 min of the Johrei healing method on laboratory stress. *Complementary Therapies in Medicine, 14*(2), 127–132.

Leibovici, L. (2001). Effects of remote, retroactive intercessory prayer on outcomes in patients with bloodstream infection: Randomised controlled trial. *British Medical Journal, 323*(22–29), 1450–1451.

Lesniak, K. T. (2006). The effect of intercessory prayer on wound healing in nonhuman primates. *Alternative Therapies in Health & Medicine, 12*(6), 42–48.

Levin, J. (2011). Energy healers: Who are they and what do they do. *Explore, 7*(1), 13–26.

Lords, House of (2000). Complementary and alternative medicine. Retrieved November, 2019, from https://publications.parliament.uk/pa/ld199900/ldselect/ldsctech/123/12302.htm.

Lubeck, W., Petter, F. A., & Rand, W. L. (2001). *The spirit of Reiki: From tradition to the present fundamental lines of transmission, original writings, mastery, symbols treatments, Reiki as a spiritual path and much more.* Twin Lakes, WI: Lotus Press.

Madrid, M. M., Barrett, E. A., & Winstead-Fry, P. (2010). A study of the feasibility of introducing therapeutic touch into the operative environment with patients undergoing cerebral angiography. *Journal of Holistic Nursing, 28*(3), 168–174.

Mager, J., Moore, D., Bendl, D., Wong, B., Rachlin, K., & Yount, G. (2007). Evaluating biofield treatments in a cell culture model of oxidative stress. *Explore, 3*(4), 386–390. doi: 10.1016/j.explore.2007.04.010.

McCormack, H. M., Horne, D. J., & Sheather, S. (1988). Clinical applications of visual analogue scales: a critical review. *Psychological Medicine, 18*(4), 1007–1019.

McCullough, M. E. (1995). Prayer and health: conceptual issues, research review, and research agenda. *Journal of Psychology and Theology, 23*(1), 15–29. doi: 10.1177/009164719502300102.

McManus, D. E. (2017). Reiki is better than placebo and has broad potential as a complementary health therapy. *Journal of Evidence-Based Complementary & Alternative Medicine, 22*(4), 1051–1057. doi: 10.1177/2156587217728644.

Meissner, K., Fassler, M., & Rucker, G. (2013). Differential effectiveness of placebo treatments. *JAMA Internal Medicine, 173*(21), 1941–1951. doi: 10.1001/jamainternmed.2013.10391.

Midilli, T. S., & Eser, I. (2015). Effects of reiki on post-cesarean delivery pain, anxiety, and hemodynamic parameters: A randomised controlled clinical trial. *Pain Management Nursing, 16*(3), 388–399. doi: 10.1016/j.pmn.2014.09.005.

Mir, M., Behnam Vashani, H., Sadeghi, T., Boskabadi, H., & Khorshahi, A. (2018). Effects of Yakson therapeutic touch and heel warming on pain caused by heel stick procedure, vital signs, and cry duration in full-term neonates. *Evidence Based Care, 8*(2), 49–57.

Misra, S. (2012). Randomized double blind placebo controlled studies, the 'Gold Standard' in intervention based studies. *Indian Journal of Sexually Transmitted Diseases and AIDS, 33*(2), 131–134. doi: 10.4103/2589-0557.102130.

Montalto, C. P., Bhargava, V., & Hong, G. S. (2006). Use of complementary and alternative medicine by older adults: An exploratory study. *Complementary Health Practice Review, 11*(1), 27–46.

Monzillo, E., & Gronowicz, G. A. (2011). New insights on therapeutic touch: A discussion of experimental methodology and design that resulted in significant effects on normal human cells and osteosarcoma. *Explore, 7*(1), 44–51. doi: 10.1016/j.explore.2010.10.001.

Mueller, G., Palli, C., & Schumacher, P. (2019). The effect of therapeutic touch on back pain in adults on a neurological unit: An experimental pilot study. *Pain Management Nursing, 20*, 75–81. doi: 10.1016/j.pmn.2018.09.002.

Naito, A., Laidlaw, T. M., Henderson, D. C., Farahani, L., Dwivedi, P., & Gruzelier, J. H. (2003). The impact of self-hypnosis and Johrei on lymphocyte subpopulations at exam time: A controlled study. *Brain Research Bulletin, 62*(3), 241–253.

Nash, C. (1982). Psychokinetic control of bacterial growth. *Journal of the Society for Psychical Research, 51*, 217–221.

Navarro-Rodriguez, T., Gasiorowska, A., Ibuki, Y., Dickman, R., Moty, B., Powers, J., ... & Fass, R. (2008). W1814 The effect of Johrei (Energy healing) versus wait-list on symptoms of patients with functional chest pain (Fcp) of presumed esophageal origin – a randomized trial. *Gastroenterology, 134*(4), A-721.

Newshan, G., & Schuller-Civitella, D. (2003). Large clinical study shows value of therapeutic touch program. *Holistic Nursing Practice, 17*(4), 189–192.

O'Laoire, S. (1997). An experimental study of the effects of distant, intercessory prayer on self-esteem, anxiety and depression. *Alternative Therapies in Health and Medicine, 3*(6), 38–53.

O'Mathuna, D. P., Pryjmachuk, S., Spencer, W., Stanwick, M., & Matthiesen, S. (2002). A critical evaluation of the theory and practice of therapeutic touch. *Nursing Philosophy, 3*, 163–176.

Ohnishi, T., Ohnishi, T., Nishino, K., Tsurusaki, Y., & Yamaguchi, M. (2005). Growth inhibition of cultured human liver carcinoma cells by Ki-energy (life-energy): Scientific evidence for Ki-effects on cancer cells. *Evidence-Based Complementary and Alternative Medicine, 2*(3), 387–393.

Olshansky, B., & Dossey, L. (2003). Retroactive prayer: A preposterous hypothesis? *British Medical Journal, 327*(7429), 1465–1468.

Olver, I. N., & Dutney, A. (2012). A randomized, blinded study of the impact of intercessory prayer on spiritual well-being in patients with cancer. *Alternative Therapies in Health and Medicine, 18*(5), 18–27.

Onetto, B. H., & Elguin, G. H. (1966). Psychokineses in experimental tumourgenesis. *Journal of Parapsychology, 30,* 220.

Peters, R. M. (1999). The effectiveness of Therapeutic Touch: A meta-analytic review. *Nursing Science Quarterly, 12*(1), 52–61.

Pike, C., Vernon, D., & Hald, L. (2014). Asymmetric activation of the anterior cerebral cortex in recipients of IRECA: Preliminary evidence for the energetic effects of an intention-based biofield treatment modality on human neurophysiology. *Journal of Alternative and Complementary Medicine, 20*(10), 780–786. doi: 10.1089/acm.2014.0074.

Quinn, J. F., & Strelkauskas, A. (1993). Psychoimmunologic effects of therapeutic touch on practitioners and recently bereaved recipients: A pilot study. *Advances in Nursing Science, 15*(4), 13–26.

Radin, D., Schlitz, M., & Baur, C. (2015). Distant healing intention therapies: An overview of the scientific evidence. *Global Advances in Health Medicine, 4,* 67–71. doi: 10.7453/gahmj.2015.012.

Radin, D., Taft, R., & Yount, G. (2004). Effects of healing intention on cultured cells and truly random events. *The Journal of Alternative and Complementary Medicine, 10*(1), 103–112.

Rahtz, E., Child, S., Knight, S., Warber, S. L., & Dieppe, P. (2019). Clients of UK healers: A mixed methods survey of their demography, health problems, and experiences of healing. *Complementary Therapies in Clinical Practice, 35,* 72–77. doi: 10.1016/j.ctcp.2019.01.012.

Rao, A., Hickman, L. D., Sibbritt, D., Newton, P. J., & Phillips, J. L. (2016). Is energy healing an effective non-pharmacological therapy for improving symptom management of chronic illness? A systematic review. *Complementary Therapies in Clinical Practice, 25,* 26–41. doi: 10.1016/j.ctcp.2016.07.003.

Razza, L. B., Moffa, A. H., Moreno, M. L., Carvalho, A. F., Padberg, F., Fregni, F., & Brunoni, A. R. (2018). A systematic review and meta-analysis on placebo response to repetitive transcranial magnetic stimulation for depression trials. *Progress in Neuro-Psychopharmacology and Biological Psychiatry, 81*(2), 105–113. doi: 10.1016/j.pnpbp.2017.10.016.

Reece, K., Schwartz, G. E., Brooks, A. J., & Nangle, G. (2005). Positive well-being changes associated with giving and receiving Johrei healing. *Journal of Alternative and Complementary Medicine, 11*(3), 455–457.

Richeson, N. E., Spross, J. A., Lutz, K., & Peng, C. (2010). Effects of Reiki on anxiety, depression, pain, and physiological factors in community-dwelling older adults. *Research in Gerontological Nursing, 3*(3), 187–199.

Rider, M. S., & Achterberg, J. (1989). Effect of music-assisted imagery on neutrophils and lymphocytes. *Biofeedback and Self-Regulation, 14*(3), 247–257.

Roberts, L., Ahmed, I., & Davison, A. (2009). Intercessory prayer for the alleviation of ill health. *Cochrane Database of Systematic Reviews.* Retrieved from http://www.cochrane.org/cochrane/revabstr/ab000368.htm.

Robinson, J., Biley, F. C., & Dolk, H. (2007). Therapeutic touch for anxiety disorders. *Cochrane Database of Systematic Reviews* (3). doi: 10.1002/14651858.CD006240.pub2.

Roe, C. A., Sonnex, C., & Roxburgh, E. C. (2015). Two meta-analyses of noncontact healing studies. *Explore, 11*(1), 11–23. doi: 10.1016/j.explore.2014.10.001.

Rosa, L., Rosa, E., Sarner, L., & Barrett, S. (1998). A close look at therapeutic touch. *JAMA Internal Medicine, 279*(13), 1005–1010.

Rubik, B., Brooks, A. J., & Schwartz, G. E. (2006). In vitro effect of Reiki treatment on bacterial cultures: Role of experimental context and practitioner well-being. *The Journal of Alternative and Complementary Medicine, 12*(1), 7–13. doi: 10.1089/acm.2006.12.7.

Rubik, B., Muehsam, D., Hammerschlag, R., & Jain, S. (2015). Biofield science and healing: History, terminology and concepts. *Global Advances in Health Medicine, 4,* 8–14. doi: 10.7453/gahmj.2015.038.suppl.

Sadeghimoghaddam, S., Alavi, M., Mehrabi, T., & Bankpoor-Fard, A. (2016). The effect of two methods of relaxation and prayer therapy on anxiety and hope in patients with coronary artery disease: A quasi-experimental study. *Iranian Journal of Nursing and Midwifery Research*, 24(2), 102–107.

Schlitz, M., & Braud, W. (1997). Distant intentionality and healing: Assessing the evidence. *Alternative Therapies in Health and Medicine*, 3(6), 62–73.

Schlitz, M., Radin, D., Malle, B., Schmidt, S., Utts, J., & Yount, G. L. (2003). Distant healing intention: Definitions and evolving guidelines for laboratory studies. *Alternative Therapies in Health and Medicine*, 9, 31–43.

Schouten, S. (1993). Applied parapsychology studies of psychics and healers. *Journal of Scientific Exploration*, 7, 375–401.

Schwartz, S., De Mattei, R. J., Brame, E. G., & Spottiswoode, J. P. (2015). Infrared spectra alterations in water proximate to the psalms of therapeutic practitioners. *Explore: The Journal of Science and Healing*, 11(2), 143–155. doi: 10.1016/j.explore.2014.12.008.

Schwartz, S. A. (2017). Therapeutic intervention: into the next generation. *Explore*, 13(3), 1–6.

Senderovich, H., Ip, M. L., Berall, A., Karuza, J., Gordon, M., Binns, M., … & Dunal, L. (2016). Therapeutic touch in a geriatric palliative care unit – a retrospective review. *Complementary Therapies in Clinical Practice*, 24, 134–138.

Shah, S., Ogden, A. T., Pettker, C. M., Raffo, A., Itescu, S., & Oz, M. C. (1999). A study of the effect of energy healing on in vitro tumor cell proliferation. *The Journal of Alternative and Complementary Medicine*, 5(4), 359–365.

Shields, D. (2008). Healing as a lifeway: A path to inner peace. The lived experience of receiving Therapeutic Touch. *International Journal of Human Caring*, 12(3), 98–98.

Sicher, F., Targ, R., Moore, D., & Smith, H. S. (1998). A randomised double-blind study of the effects of distant healing in a population with advanced AIDS. *Western Journal of Medicine*, 169, 356–363.

Simao, T. P., Caldeira, S., & Campos de Carvalho, E. (2016). The effect of prayer on patients' health: systematic literature review. *Religions*, 7(11), 1–11. doi: 10.3390/rel7010011.

Smith, J. (1972). *The influence on enzyme growth by the 'laying on of hands.' The dimensions of healing*: A symposium. Los Altos, CA: The Academy of Parapsychology and Medicine.

Söllner, W., Maislinger, S., DeVries, A., Steixner, E., Rumpold, G., & Lukas, P. (2000). Use of complementary and alternative medicine by cancer patients is not associated with perceived distress or poor compliance with standard treatment but with active coping behavior: A survey. *Cancer: Interdisciplinary International Journal of the American Cancer Society*, 89(4), 873–880.

Tabatabaee, A., Tafreshi, M. Z., Rassouli, M., Aledavood, S. A., AlaviMajd, H., & Farahmand, S. K. (2016a). Effect of Therapeutic Touch in patients with cancer: A literature review. *Medical Archives*, 70(2), 142–147. doi: 10.5455/medarh.2016.70.142–147.

Tabatabaee, A., Tafreshi, M. Z., Rassouli, M., Aledavood, S. A., AlaviMajd, H., & Farahmand, S. K. (2016b). Effect of therapeutic touch on pain related parameters in patients with cancer: A randomized clinical trial. *Materia Socio-Medica*, 28(3), 220–223. doi: 10.5455/msm.2016.28.220-223.

Taft, R., Nieto, L., Luu, T., Pennucci, A., Moore, D., & Yount, G. (2003). Cultured human brain tumor cells do not responds to Johrei treatment. *Subtle Energies & Energy Medicine*, 14(3), 253–265.

Targ, E. (1997). Evaluating distant healing: A research review. *Alternative Therapies in Health & Medicine*, 3(6), 74–78.

Thrane, S., & Cohen, S. M. (2014). Effect of Reiki therapy on pain and anxiety in adults: An in-depth literature review of randomized trials with effect size calculations. *Pain Management Nursing*, 15(4), 897–908.

Tindle, H. A., Davis, R. B., Phillips, R. S., & Eisenberg, D. M. (2005). Trends in use of complementary and alternative medicine by US adults: 1997–2002. *Alternative Therapies in Health and Medicine, 11*(1), 42–49.

Tloczynski, J., & Fritzsch, S. (2002). Intercessory prayer in psychological well-being: Using a multiple baseline, across-subjects design. *Psychological Reports, 91*(3), 731–741. doi: 10. 2466/pr0.2002.91.3.731.

Trepper, T. S., Strozier, A., Carpenter, J. E., & Hecker, L. L. (2013). *Introduction to alternative and complementary therapies*. New York: Routledge.

Trivedi, M. K., Pati, l. S., Shettigar, H., Gangwar, M., & Jana, S. (2015). In vitro evaluation of biofield treatment on cancer biomarkers involved in endometrial and prostate cancer cell lines. *Cancer, Science and Therapy, 7*(8), 253–257. doi: 10.4172/1948-5956.1000358.

Umberger, W. (2019). Complementary and integrative approaches to pain and patient preference. *Pain Management Nursing, 20*, 1–2. doi: 10.1016/j.pmn.2018.11.059.

van der Vaart, S., Gijsen, V. M. G. J., de Wildt, S. N., & Koren, G. (2009). A systematic review of the therapeutic effects of Reiki. *The Journal of Alternative and Complementary Medicine, 15*(11), 1157–1169. doi: 10.1089/acm.2009.0036.

Ventura, A. C., Saroka, K. S., & Persinger, M. A. (2014). Non-locality changes in intercerebral theta band coherence between practitioners and subjects during distant Reiki procedures. *Journal of Nonlocality, 3*(1), 1–25.

Verhoef, M. J., Lewith, G., Ritenbaugh, C., Boon, H., Fleishman, S., & Leis, A. (2005). Complementary and alternative medicine whole systems research: Beyond identification of inadequacies of RCT. *Complementary Therapies in Medicine, 13*, 206–212. doi: 10.1016/j. ctim.2005.05.001.

Vincent, C., & Furnham, A. (1996). Why do patients turn to complementary medicine? An empirical study. *British Journal of Clinical Psychology, 35*(1), 37–48.

Vitale, A. (2007). An integrative review of Reiki touch therapy research. *Holistic Nursing Practice, 21*(4), 167–179. doi: 10.1097/01.HNP.0000280927.83506.f6.

Vitale, A., & O'Connor, P. C. (2006). The effect of Reiki on pain and anxiety in women with abdominal hysterectomies: A quasi-experimental pilot study. *Holistic Nursing Practice, 20*(6), 263–272.

Wager, T. D., & Atlas, L. Y. (2015). The neuroscience of placebo effects: Connecting context, learning and health. *Nature Reviews Neuroscience, 16*, 403. doi: 10.1038/nrn3976.

Wallis, C., & McDowell, J. (1996). Faith & healing. *Time, 147*(26), 58–63.

Wang, Y., Hunt, K., Nazareth, I., Freemantle, N., & Petersen, I. (2013). Do men consult less than women? An analysis of routinely collected UK general practice data. *BMJ Open, 3*(8), e003320.

Wardell, D. W., Rintala, D., & Tan, G. (2008). Study descriptions of healing touch with veterans experiencing chronic neuropathic pain from spinal cord injury. *EXPLORE, 4*(3), 187–195.

Watson, P. E., Watson, I. D., & Batt, R. D. (1980). Total body water volumes for adult males and females estimated from simple anthropometric measurements. *The American Journal of Clinical Nutrition, 33*(1), 27–39.

Woods, D. L., Beck, C., & Sinha, K. (2009). The effect of therapeutic touch on behavioral symptoms and cortisol in persons with dementia. *Complementary Medicine Research, 16*(3), 181–189.

Woods, D. L., Craven, R. F., & Whitney, J. (2005). The effect of Therapeutic Touch on behavioural symptoms of persons with dementia. *Alternative Therapies in Health and Medicine, 11*(1), 66–74.

Woods, D. L., & Dimond, M. (2002). The effect of Therapeutic Touch on agitated behavior and cortisol in persons with Alzheimer's disease. *Biological Research for Nursing, 4*(2), 104–114.

Yeung, V., Sharpe, L., Glozier, N., Hackett, M. L., & Colagiuri, B. (2018). A systematic review and meta-analysis of placebo versus no treatment for insomnia symptoms. *Sleep Medicine Reviews*, *38*, 17–27. doi: 10.1016/j.smrv.2017.03.006.

Yount, G. L., Patil, S., Dave, U., Alves-dos-Santos, L., Gon, K., Arauz, R., & Rachlin, K. (2012). Evaluation of biofield treatment dose and distance in a model of cancer cell death. *Journal of Alternative and Complementary Medicine*, *19*(2), 124–127.

Zimmerman, J. (1990). Laying-on-of-hands healing and therapeutic touch: A testable theory. *Journal of the Bioelectromagnetics Institute*, *24*, 8–17.

Zolfaghari, M., Eybpoosh, S., & Hazrati, M. (2012). Effects of Therapeutic Touch on anxiety, vital signs, and cardiac dysrhythmia in a sample of Iranian women undergoing cardiac catheterization. *Journal of Holistic Nursing*, *30*(4), 225–234. doi: 10.1177/0898010112453325.

Chapter 9

Out of body experiences

Imagine the feeling of falling asleep, or undergoing a relaxing meditative experience, only to suddenly feel yourself floating and upon opening your eyes looking down to see yourself below. For some this might be an intriguing experience with profound implications, whilst others may find it bewildering and disorienting. Such an event is encapsulated within the fascinating concept of an *out of body experience* (OBE), which is the focus of this chapter. The chapter begins by attempting to define an OBE, identifying some of the core components which make up the experience. This is followed by an exploration of the main characteristics of the OBE. It then examines how common such experiences are, under what conditions they occur and to whom. The chapter then examines four main approaches in the field of OBE research. This includes attempts to detect the subtle second body, obtain veridical information from such excursions, identify possible psychophysiological changes and more recently the work on inducing such experiences. The chapter then examines the three main types of explanation. These are encapsulated within the broad headings of psychological, neurological and projection theories. Finally, the chapter briefly considers some of the implications that arise from the OBE.

What is an OBE?

Initially it may seem a straight forward concept to define. The out of body experience is precisely that: the subjective experience of being, or existing, outside of the physical body whilst remaining consciously aware of the disconnection from the physical (e.g., Blackmore, 2005; Neppe, 2011; Tart, 1998; Twemlow, Gabbard, & Jones, 1982). Other terms are also used, including *astral projection, spirit travel* and *travelling clairvoyance* (e.g., Braude, 2001; J. C. Smith, 2010; Steiger, 1982). However, there are many features of the OBE that suggest it is a far more complex and less unitary experience than originally thought. For instance, all would agree that the element of conscious awareness needs to be spatially distinct from the physical body. In addition, some would argue that the OBE also needs to include the idea that the experient observes the world from an elevated viewpoint that remains distant from the physical body (Anzellotti et al., 2011; Bunning & Blanke, 2005; Holt, Simmonds-Moore, Luke, & French, 2012). A slightly more contentious point is the suggestion that during the OBE the individual needs to have the experience of seeing their own body (e.g., Anzellotti et al., 2011; Blanke & Arzy, 2005; Blanke & Mohr, 2005; Bunning & Blanke, 2005; Tart, 1998). This is problematic because others have reported that many OBE experients do not report seeing their own physical body (e.g., Irwin, 1985; Jones, Gabbard, & Twemlow, 1984). For instance, Braithwaite, Broglia, Bagshaw and Wilkins (2013) found that only 53% of those who experienced an OBE reported seeing their own body. Furthermore, not all those who report an OBE feel that they are *in* a body in the sense of being encapsulated within a particular form. Some feel as though they are simply a disembodied point of conscious awareness, like a bubble or spot of light (Blackmore, 2005). Others have reported multiple bodies including a physical body, a distinct *psychic body* and an intermediate called the *subtle body* (Tressoldi et al., 2015). Furthermore, others have found that up to 20% report the existence of a *silvery cord* linking their conscious awareness to their spatially distant physical body (e.g., Alvarado, 2012; Alvarado & Zingrone, 1998; Alvarado, Zingrone, & Dalton, 1999; Hurd, 2016) and others have argued that the OBE includes obtaining information which is later validated as correct (e.g., Osis & McCormick, 1980; Palmer & Lieberman, 1975; Tressoldi et al., 2014). The examples from Green (1968) in Box 9.1 nicely illustrate some of these elements.

Box 9.1   Elements of the out of body experience

Dislocation

> I was sitting at the rear of the bus looking out through the window. When without warning I found myself looking at myself from the stairs of the bus. All my senses, sight and feelings and so on seemed to be on the stairs only my actual body remained at the seat. (p. 20)

Elevated perspective

> I was resting on the bed in the afternoon, when suddenly I saw myself on the bed. I was so surprised, I couldn't believe it … There was no doubt at all that I was outside of my body looking down on myself. (p. 62)

Travel

> I cannot ever remember having to consciously think about opening doors etc., there seemed to be no physical barrier as to where I go … the mind seems just to roam anywhere. (p. 127)

Veridical perceptions

> I looked down at my body then kind of floated out of the room into a street and stopped before a house and I entered and went to a bedroom facing the stairs. The man lying in bed was a very old friend whom I had not seen for a year or two … When I [later] told him he lived in an upstairs flat and how the furniture was placed in the bedroom, he wanted to know how I knew. (p. 126)
>
> (Green, 1968)

What the findings outlined above show is that there is no clear consensus on what precisely an OBE represents. This has led to suggestions that the OBE is not a single unitary experience at all, but more accurately represents a diverse range of potential experiences across a spectrum (see Figure 9.1) that range from imagination to a full-blown OBE with veridical reports of distant target information (see e.g., Braithwaite & Dent, 2011a; Neppe, 2011; Tart, 1998; Twemlow et al., 1982). This has important implications because the various types of OBE may be supported by and/or influenced by distinct underlying psychological or neurological mechanisms. As Neppe (2011) has pointed out, to classify all OBEs under a single heading may be both erroneous and misleading. For instance, there may be distinct stages within the OBE realm of experiences as well as distinct sub-types of OBE. Some have suggested that the OBE contains specific multiple components, but as yet there is no agreement on precisely what those components should be (e.g., Anzellotti et al., 2011; Bunning & Blanke, 2005; Neppe, 2011; Tart, 1998). Hence, the differences in the way the experience may be defined are likely to account for the mixed findings in the literature. In addition, this lack of a clear definition represents a challenge for those exploring potential concomitants of the OBE. For instance, when examining personality features that may be associated with the OBE researchers often ask participants 'have you ever felt your consciousness to be separate from your physical body', and if the answer is affirmative the individual is classified as having had an OBE (e.g., Alvarado et al., 1999; Gow, Lang, & Chant, 2004; Murray & Fox, 2005; Parra, 2010). This is problematic for several reasons. First, it is not clear whether the participant's understanding of what constitutes a separate consciousness is the same as that for the researchers. Second, there is often no verification that the experience referred to was an OBE and if so what type. For instance, when given the above question a participant could legitimately answer yes when thinking about a lucid dream.

It is important to point out that whilst these issues are limitations, which may hinder the research conducted in the field, it does not mean that the OBE does not exist, simply that, as Neppe (2011) has argued, a more detailed level of screening and

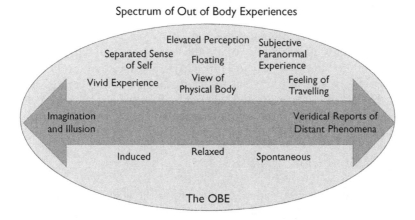

Figure 9.1 The various elements reported during and OBE and the possible range of experiences from imagination and illusion at one end (i.e., the left) to the veridical perception of distant target information at the other (i.e., the right).

classification of such experiences is required to ensure that similar experiences are grouped together, and that relying on a single question to examine OBEs is inadequate.

Characteristics of the OBE

According to Hurd (2016) the OBE may represent a unique experience for the individual in question; however, there are certain aspects that appear across multiple reports which may help to provide some insights into the nature of such an experience. These include physical sensations, sensory experiences, the vividness of the experience, the level of control over the experience, the number of OBEs that an individual experiences and the duration of the experience.

Physical experiences

During an OBE many report the physical sensation of floating which can include movement to distant locations (Alvarado, 1992; Sellers, 2017, 2018), though Twemlow et al. (1982) found that 58% of their sample who reported OBEs remained in the same physical environment as their body. Some also report feeling physical vibrations move throughout their body, particularly at the beginning and end of the experience (Blackmore, 2005; Hurd, 2016; Twemlow et al., 1982) as well as hearing noises (Irwin, 1985). Interestingly, whilst Twemlow et al. (1982) found that 68% of their sample reported that their OBE form was similar to that of their physical body, others have reported feeling as though they were a disembodied form of consciousness, a ball of light or a silvery-white cloud (e.g., Alvarado, 2000; Blackmore, 2005; Tressoldi et al., 2015). Nevertheless, most report that during the OBE it is not possible for them to interact with physical objects and/or people in the world. Such attempts often result in the hand of the experient passing unnoticed through the object or person.

Sensory experience

Given that vision is the dominant sense in humans (e.g., Kolb, Whishaw, & Teskey, 2016) it is perhaps unsurprising that OBEs are predominantly visual in nature (Blackmore, 2005; Holt et al., 2012; Hurd, 2016; Sellers, 2018), although the precise nature of such visual sensations can differ in that experients report being able to see through solid objects, or around them as well as being able to see clearly in the dark. The involvement of the other sense seems to mirror that in normal perceptual experiences.

Vividness

A point raised by many who experience an OBE is the vivid and intense nature of the experience. For example, Twemlow et al. (1982) found that 93% of their sample reported that their OBE was more real than a dream. Others have also found that individuals report highly vivid and extremely clear experiences often associated with heightened sensory processing abilities that are more acute, bright and richly coloured than in the normal waking state (Blackmore, 2005; Hurd, 2016; Sellers, 2017). Such findings are consistent with the notion that the experience often produces a profound effect in the individual.

Control

The ability to control the OBE is one that has been reported by the more adept individuals (e.g., Monroe, 1971; Muldoon & Carrington, 1929; Steiger, 1982), though for others it is often much less. For instance Alvarado and Zingrone (1998) reported that 30% of their OBE sample reported having some level of control, with 38% responding that they had no control at all. In addition, Irwin (1985) found that females reported greater control compared to males. The ability to exert control over the OBE is predominantly used to define the location or individual focus of the experience. Such movement and focus have been reported to be regulated by intention rather than relying on or being influenced by physical ability. For example, attempts by Tressoldi et al. (2014) to induce an OBE showed that control of the process, which in this instance was the acquisition of visual information, was purely regulated by the participant's focused conscious intention. They reported that the act of perceiving a distant object was achieved by zooming in on it using conscious intention and the ability to focus.

Number of OBEs

There is limited data on the precise number of OBEs any one individual has experienced. This is further complicated by many researchers attempting to classify such experiences in a dichotomous manner, labelling them as either *one* or *more than one* (e.g., Twemlow et al., 1982). This latter category offers a very wide range of possibilities but provides little precise detail. Hence, future researchers should clearly identify the precise number of OBEs any one individual has experienced. That said, the limited reports do suggest that the majority of those that have reported such experiences often had more than one OBE (e.g., Palmer, 1979; Parra, 2010; Sellers, 2017). This would fit with the findings suggesting that the majority find such an experience to be pleasant and beneficial. Indeed, Twemlow et al. (1982) noted that 84% of their sample that had experienced an OBE indicated they would try it again. As such, it may be that those who have already experienced an OBE are more likely to experience another, possibly in part due to their positive initial reaction.

Duration

Again it is not always clear how long such an experience may last. Sellers (2017) reported on a single case study of OBEs that could last from minutes to hours. However, such self-reports need to be interpreted with caution given the findings suggesting that those who experience an OBE may lose their sense of time when involved in an OBE (Alvarado et al., 1999; Twemlow et al., 1982). For instance, a phenomenological comparison among OBEs experienced both spontaneously and induced via hypnosis showed that perception of time changed during the experience (De Foe, Al Khafaji, Pederzoli, Prati, & Tressoldi, 2017). Reports indicated that the perception of time was counterintuitive to normal perception and that it was not perceived the same way, becoming faster or slower.

Demographics

In exploring the nature of the OBE, it is useful to know how common such an experience is, what the conditions are that may lead to it and whether there is anything specific about the individuals who undergo such an experience. Such information may provide useful insights into the nature of the experience which in turn may help to classify the OBE as one of a particular type.

Prevalence

Over time several surveys have been conducted to ascertain how many people have had such an experience. For the general population the reported rates range from 10% to 27% (Alvarado, 2000; Blackmore, 2005; Palmer & Dennis, 1975; Twemlow et al., 1982), which rises from 20% up to 48% for student populations (Blackmore, 2005; Green, 1967; Irwin, 1985; Murray & Fox, 2005; Twemlow et al., 1982). That student numbers tend to be higher overall may simply reflect a greater willingness to report such incidences. In addition, the lack of precision in the figures may reflect the somewhat vague structure utilised to define an OBE. Nevertheless, there is some overall agreement that the OBE is a widespread phenomenon that occurs across populations and cultures (Metzinger, 2005). Indeed, a recent estimate by Abreu, Madurell and Perego (2013) suggests that across multiple countries more than 70 million people worldwide have reported some type of lucid projection of their conscious selves. Such findings have led to the argument that the universality of the OBE has been clearly and fully established (Hurd, 2016).

Conditions

Given the wide range of possible OBE type experiences it should come as no surprise that an OBE may occur as a result of a wide variety of conditions. However, by far the most common conditions are those in which the individual is feeling physically and mentally calm and relaxed, which may include meditative states and dreaming (Sellers, 2017; Twemlow et al., 1982). Though some have suggested that OBEs may occur when taking drugs (J. C. Smith, 2010) or during a life threatening situation (Myers, Austrin, Grisso, & Nickeson, 1983), others have found this relates to only a small minority of the reported conditions (Twemlow et al., 1982). Indeed, OBEs have been suggested to occur due to some neurological abnormality (e.g., Bunning & Blanke, 2005) and even during childbirth (Bateman, Jones, & Jomeen, 2017). Alongside this there are suggestions that the illusion of an OBE may be obtained using virtual reality (Ehrsson, 2007), or induced using some form of neural stimulation or hypnosis (e.g., Daltrozzo, Kotchoubey, Gueler, & Karim, 2016; Tressoldi et al., 2014). However, it is not always clear to what extent these various attempts to elicit or induce an OBE manage to produce specific and relevant OBE type experiences. Hence, whilst the majority of reported OBEs occur during periods of deep mental and physical relaxation (e.g., Gow et al., 2004) there is no single unique event that leads to such an experience.

Individuals

Many researchers have examined the individuals reporting such experiences to ascertain whether there is anything distinct or unique about them; however, the findings tend to be mixed. For instance, there is general agreement that factors such as age, gender, marital status, education and religious belief are not related to reports of OBE experiences (e.g., Blackmore, 2015; Irwin, 1985; Myers et al., 1983; Twemlow et al., 1982). However, other factors such as belief in psi, fantasy proneness, absorption and personality have produced more inconsistent results. For example, some have reported that experients of an OBE often report higher levels of belief in psi phenomena (Tobacyk & Mitchell, 1987). However, more recently researchers have shown that there was no difference in the level of belief in psi between those identified as believers who had experienced an OBE and those that had not (Gow et al., 2004). This would suggest, somewhat counterintuitively, that the OBE does not increase the belief in psi score but it may indicate that those with higher levels of belief in psi may be more open to the possibility of such an experience. Similar inconsistencies have been reported in terms of *fantasy proneness* and measures of *absorption*.

Fantasy proneness refers to people who tend to have a rich inner life to the extent that as children they may have played with imaginary friends, have a rich imagination, enjoy reading and/or being read to as a child (Stanford, 1987). Like most things in life if taken to its extreme it may result in some confusion between imagined fantasy events and real events which can lead to fantasy prone adults living in isolation in a make-believe world (Wilson & Barber, 1983). Some have suggested that those reporting OBEs are more fantasy prone than those who do not report such experiences (e.g., Alvarado, 2000; Parra, 2010). However, others have shown that whilst those with high levels of belief in psi may be more fantasy prone than those with low levels of belief, there was no difference in fantasy proneness between believers in psi who had experienced an OBE and those who had not (Gow et al., 2004). This would suggest that fantasy proneness may be more generically associated with belief in unusual phenomena than an OBE per se. Imaginative absorption refers to the idea that individuals can become fully engrossed in their own thoughts, activities and feelings, such as reading a book or watching a film (Tellegen & Atkinson, 1974). The idea of absorption is that the individual in question focuses all resources on the current object or target whilst excluding all other information. Some have suggested that experients of OBEs tend to report a greater capacity for absorption (e.g., Alvarado, 2000; Irwin, 1980, 2000). However, Gow et al. (2004) showed that whilst those with high levels of generic belief in psi did exhibit a higher capacity for absorption compared to low-belief controls, those who had experienced an OBE showed no difference in absorption compared to those who had not.

Hence, there does not seem to be anything unique or special about those who report an OBE. Such a finding could be taken to suggest that the experience is potentially open to anyone willing to attempt it. However, the inconsistencies in the data are also likely to be a result of the different questions used to identify the OBE itself and/or the specific nature of the experience. As such, future research could more clearly examine such factors by more precisely defining the OBE.

Experimental research

Much of the evidence for OBEs comes from anecdotal reports, testimonials and individual case studies, which are often written up after the event and as such contain all the advantages and disadvantages of such approaches. However, just because OBEs are invariably subjective experiences does not mean that they should be ignored, any more than other subjective phenomena, such as dreams (see, Tart, 1998). Hence, experimental research has invariably focused on four questions. First, whether it is possible to detect the subtle second body that is assumed to house consciousness during the OBE. Second, if veridical information can be obtained during the OBE. Third, if during the OBE the experient exhibits a particular or specific psychophysiological profile, and finally, whether it is possible to induce an OBE.

Detecting the OBE subtle body

If a double, or subtle, body exists and is able to travel beyond the bounds of the physical body then it may be detectable at its new location by a device or other people (see, Alvarado, 1982, 1989). Such approaches have included attempts to photograph the projected body or consciousness of the individual, weigh it or take some other measure such as looking for possible changes in the magnetic field and temperature as well as using ultra violet and infra-red detectors (Blackmore, 1982, 2005, 2015). For instance Osis and McCormick (1980) worked with Alex Tanous, an adept at self-induced OBEs, and asked him to go out of his body and localise himself in a distant shielded chamber containing a sensitive strain gauge. The chamber itself was only 18 inches in diameter and suspended from the ceiling of the laboratory to reduce any environmental vibrations and contained two metal sensor plates connected via a highly sensitive strain gauge device that would be able to measure very small movements or vibrations. On arrival at the lab Tanous was required to lie down in a sound-attenuated darkened room and attempt to send his consciousness out of his body to the distant shielded chamber. This would represent a single trial and would be repeated many times across multiple sessions. Osis and McCormick (1980) found

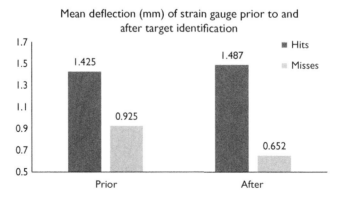

Figure 9.2 Mean deflection (in mm) of a strain gauge when Tanous correctly identified a distant target (hit) compared to when he did not (miss) prior to his OBE (left) and directly after it (right: adapted from Osis & McCormick, 1980).

that the mean strain gauge activation was significantly higher when Tanous correctly reported on targets located beside the shielded chamber and that such differences occurred just prior to and following the OBE (see Figure 9.2).

This led them to argue that the results suggested that some form of kinetic effect was picked up when Tanous underwent an OBE, travelled to the location and correctly identified the target. Interestingly, they point out that no mention was made to Tanous regarding the strain gauge prior to or during the experiment, and that all attention was focused on obtaining accurate reports of the target. This led them to tentatively suggest that the deflections were caused by the OBE visit of Tanous to the location of the shielded chamber.

A further study tested whether an individual alleged to be able to self-induce OBEs could visit distant locations and interact with the physical environment such that their presence would be detected (Morris, Harary, Janis, Hartwell, & Roll, 1978). There was some indication that human detectors showed a tendency to respond to such visits. In addition, a pet kitten was significantly less active during the initial visits but during later visits showed no tendency to orient towards the location of the participant's OBE location. Overall, this led the researchers to conclude that the range of detectors were unable to consistently identify and respond in a way that could provide clear evidence of the detection of an extended self. Overall, the level of success at identifying a possible distinct subtle body during an OBE is limited at best. Nevertheless, the data from Osis and McCormick (1980) is intriguing and warrants further examination, though it also requires replication.

Veridical reports from an OBE

Given the claims that during an OBE consciousness leaves the body the idea here is to test whether the experient can obtain information from their sojourn into the wider world, information which they would not be able to obtain using any normal route of sensation or perception. This could involve placing target letters or objects at specific distant locations and then asking the individual to induce an OBE and visit the location to view the target (see, Alvarado, 1982, 2000). Unfortunately, attempts to obtain veridical information from someone who has allegedly had an OBE are both sparse and inconsistent. One early attempt involved the creation of a device that was assumed to be able to differentiate between results occurring via generic psi (i.e., clairvoyance or telepathy) and those relying on what was referred to as exteriorised sight (Osis, 1975), that is, the requirement to look through a viewing window to correctly ascertain the target. Osis (1975) claimed that a few specially trained participants were able to obtain statistically significant results. In addition, Palmer and Lieberman (1975) found that those reportedly undergoing an OBE were able to identify remote targets at a statistically significant level of accuracy. Other attempts to assess whether those experiencing an OBE can obtain information during the experience have met with only limited success. For instance, Tart (1998) reported on six case studies, only one of which was able to identify a five digit number when exteriorised from their physical body. Whilst not overly impressive Tart points out that the odds of correctly guessing the five digit number are 100,000 to 1, making it a 'remarkable event' (p. 81). However, it should be noted that when Tart (1998) conducted a follow-up study with the adept OBEr

Robert Monroe he failed to find any evidence that Monroe was correctly identifying distant targets. Others have also attempted to induce OBEs in participants and have them travel to distant locations and identify a target. However, the participant's ability to describe such remote targets was at chance (Morris et al., 1978; Palmer & Lieberman, 1975). Overall, such findings are suggestive; however, it has been argued that the results could more easily have been obtained via another psychic route, such as clairvoyance or remote viewing and as such there is no need to propose the notion of an OBE (see, Braude, 2001).

Given the proposal that a key component of an OBE is the idea that the conscious awareness of the individual travels beyond the physical body it would seem essential to document this with reports of such journeys which could then be assessed for their veracity. The ability to report accurate information from a journey outside of the body would provide strong support for the notion that some form of consciousness may indeed be capable of travelling to distant locations. However, despite the many claims made by individuals who experience an OBE suggesting that they can see and experience their surroundings from a distinct viewpoint there is little empirical research supporting this. As such, future research would do well to focus on this area as without any clear evidence that consciousness travels beyond the physical body there is little need to postulate the existence of OBEs.

Psychophysiological profile

In a sense there are two questions that are pursued within this line of research. The first is whether there is a specific or unique electroencephalographic (EEG) profile exhibited in the brain of someone undergoing an OBE. The second would take this one step further and use such a profile to train others via neurofeedback to ascertain whether it would be possible to induce an OBE (see e.g., Vernon, 2009). Unfortunately, the research showing clear changes in the EEG during an OBE is limited and inconsistent. For example, early work by Osis and Mitchell (1977) showed a reduction in overall EEG amplitude, predominantly in the right occipital region, as well as reduced alpha wave activity in the left hemisphere during an alleged OBE. Others have also reported slowed alpha activity during an OBE (Tart, 1968) along with activity similar to that seen in ordinary Stage I sleep (Tart, 1998). Such limited findings led Blackmore (2005) to argue that the OBE does not seem to be associated with any unique or distinct physiological state, beyond that of simply being relaxed and/or on the edge of sleep. It may be that the OBE, as mentioned above, represents more of a range of possible behaviours and as such it is not likely that these potentially distinct states are underpinned by a single EEG profile. However, there is also the challenge of attempting to identify precisely when an OBE begins and ends in someone who is deeply relaxed with their eyes closed. It may be that such a challenge could be informed by research on lucid dreaming. For instance, in order to identify when someone was having a lucid dream researchers required the dreamer to perform a pre-determined physical response using specific eye movement signals (LaBerge, Levitan, & Dement, 1986). Future researchers interested in identifying possible EEG profiles associated with an OBE need to develop a way for the relaxed participant to signal the experimenter.

Induced OBE

The aims of inducing an OBE are twofold. First, there is the straightforward goal of attempting to elicit an OBE which should ideally be verified to ensure the authenticity of the reported experience. Second, if an OBE occurs then researchers can explore the potential range of factors that may be associated with an OBE as well as the phenomenological experience of the individual themselves. To some degree this field of research emerged from an early case study of a patient reporting an OBE type experience during an awake craniotomy (Penfield & Erickson, 1941). During the procedure the right temporal gyrus of the brain was electrically stimulated and the patient described feeling as if they were floating away from themself. Since then others have also been able to induce mild floating sensations using weak magnetic pulses (e.g., Persinger, Saroka, Mulligan, & Murphy, 2010) and more recently subcortical stimulation of the left temporoparietal junction during an awake craniotomy led to induced feelings of OBE type experiences which included the patient reporting they were floating just below the ceiling and saw their own body lying on the operating table below (Bos, Spoor, Smits, Schouten, & Vincent, 2016). Stimulation of the brain is only one way to attempt to induce an OBE, other methods include using virtual reality, drugs and hypnosis (e.g., Bunning & Blanke, 2005; Ehrsson, 2007; Tressoldi et al., 2015; Tressoldi et al., 2014). For instance, Tressoldi et al. (2014) had a small group of five people complete an hypnotic induction to induce an OBE and then attempt to identify remote target images. They found that the target hit rate was significantly greater than would be expected by chance alone (see Figure 9.3).

The researchers cautiously claimed that this provides supporting evidence for the notion that the participants involved had an OBE and visited the distant target. However, they point out that independent replications are needed to confirm the findings. They also suggest that future research should focus on attempting to capture some form of physical interaction between the individual having the OBE and the distant physical environment. They argue that this would provide more convincing support for the idea that some form of disembodied consciousness travels beyond the physical body and may address the concerns of those who suggest such findings are simply the result of generic psi behaviours (see e.g., Braude, 2001).

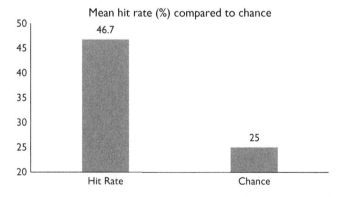

Figure 9.3 Mean percentage hit rate (left) compared to chance (right) during an hypnotically induced OBE (adapted from Tressoldi et al., 2014).

Others have examined possible changes in mood, consciousness and physiology when an OBE is induced via hypnosis compared to simply imagining having such an experience (Facco et al., 2019). Here the researchers found that those who underwent the hypnotic induction reported higher scores on self-reported measures of altered states, positive affect, altered experience and attention. These phenomenological experiences were also associated with reductions in beta and gamma band EEG activity in the right temporoparietal region, leading to the claim that an induced OBE can produce distinct phenomenological states, possibly with distinct changes in brainwave activity.

However, when examining the data from studies attempting to induce an OBE it is important to keep two essential points in mind. First, not all researchers have been successful in attempting to induce OBE type behaviours (e.g., Nash, Lynn, & Stanley, 1984; Tart, 1998; Tressoldi & Del Prete, 2007). Hence, there is no guarantee that attempting to induce an OBE, whether by cortical stimulation or hypnosis, will produce the desired effect. Second, it is very likely that the OBE type experiences produced by such induction methods are distinct in many ways from the more natural and spontaneous OBEs (Neppe, 2011; Pederzoli et al., 2016). Hence, whilst the approach may be able to provide some useful insights into the nature and processes involved in an OBE, as well as model some of the experiences of those reporting an OBE, it is unlikely to be able to provide a full picture. This is clear from the cortical stimulation research inducing feelings of floating. Whilst the feeling of floating certainly represents a component of the OBE, possibly even a core component, the OBE is also much more than this alone.

Explanations

Whilst it is not clear, yet, precisely what occurs during an OBE several ideas have been put forward to account for the pattern of reported behaviours. It would not be accurate to call them 'theories' in the strict sense that a theory allows for the development of clear predictions which in turn can be tested. Nevertheless, the ideas proposed can be grouped under the three broad headings of psychological, neurological and projection accounts.

Psychological

Psychological accounts have attempted to explain the OBE in terms of reduced sensory input, a form of lucid dreaming, reliance upon an altered model of reality and the combination of dissociation and absorption.

Reduced proprioceptive input

Proprioception refers to the perception and movement of body parts, based on sensory information from those body parts. Proprioception is what allows you to know where your arms and legs are without having to look. As such, the idea here is that there is some change in proprioceptive feedback from the body which leads to a subtle change in body concept. This change in the perceived body concept was suggested to represent a threat to the individual's sense of identity and as a result of this unconscious processes were assumed to be activated in an attempt to re-establish the individual's sense of a coherent identity (Palmer, 1978). This approach appeals to Freudian descriptors relating to psychodynamics, possibly including fantasies and/or hallucinatory experiences, which may lead to a sense of self existing outside of the body which is what produces the OBE. Once the normal body concept has been re-established the OBE comes to an end. There is only limited support for this idea based on the changes in body concept that occur during an OBE (e.g., Neppe & Palmer, 2005).

Lucid dreaming

During a lucid dream the dreamer becomes consciously aware of the fact that they are dreaming and this conscious awareness provides them with a level of control over the content and nature of the dream itself. In addition, as with most dreams, sleep paralysis ensures that the physical body does not move and this can help to create the feeling of dissociation from the physical body. Indeed, LaBerge (1985) has suggested that OBEs may be similar to the lucid dreams that occur during the hypnogogic phase of sleep onset. The hypnogogic phase refers to the transitional state that takes a person from full conscious wakefulness to sleep. During this state individuals may experience sleep paralysis, lucid dreaming and subjective para-normal experiences (Holt et al., 2012). The idea that OBEs are lucid dreams gains some support from two areas. First, is the idea that OBEs often rely on lucid dreaming, or dream control, to elicit an OBE (Rogo, 1983), and second are the reported associations between those who experience an OBE and those who have lucid dreams (Irwin, 1985; Palmer, 1979). For instance, Palmer (1979) reported a positive correlation between the reported incidence of OBEs and lucid dreams. Poynton (1975) also found a clear increase in the number of reported OBEs as participants moved from simply being relaxed (16%), through dozing (20%) to sleeping (27%). Such changes were argued to be the result of a clear relationship between sleep, dreaming and the OBE state.

However, Rogo (1984) has argued that lucid dreams are simply a sub-type of normal dreaming and that they exhibit distinct psychophysiological profiles from those seen when an individual is undergoing an OBE. Others have also reported that whilst changes in the EEG can occur during the OBE they are not characteristic of normal sleep and dreaming stages (Blackmore, 2005; Twemlow et al., 1982). The possible relationship between lucid dreams and OBEs has also been questioned by Alvarado et al. (1999) who found no evidence of a link between OBEs and reports of lucid dreams. In addition, others have argued that in an OBE there is no clouding of consciousness as is commonly reported in dreams (Twemlow et al., 1982). Furthermore, OBEs are often reported as being more real than a dream in the sense that the individual feels more awake and aware and their experiences seem more vivid and real than those occurring whilst dreaming (see e.g., Alvarado, 2000; Blackmore, 1982). One suggestion put forward by Hurd (2016) is that the OBE may co-occur with certain sleep related phenomena such as lucid dreaming, sleep paralysis and hypnogogic hallucinations. Hence, there may be a common factor that underpins all these behaviours but at present the findings are not consistent with the idea that OBEs simply represent a form of lucid dreaming.

Altered model of reality

This idea is based on the assumption that the cognitive system works by creating multiple models of the world and at any time only one of these models is taken to serve or indicate the external reality of the world (Blackmore, 1984, 2005). In particular, one model is thought to relate to the body image of the individual and relies on the input of somatosensory, visual and other sensory input along with memory. If sensory input is either interrupted or inhibited, as may be the case in meditation or deep relaxation for example, then other pre-constructed models may come to the fore and take over. According to Blackmore (1984) this may rely on the cognitive system building a model that provides a best guess regarding what external reality is. Such a model will be influenced by memory and imagination and many memories are often built from a 'bird's eye view' perspective and it may be this change in perspective that results in the feeling of being distinct from the physical body as well as providing the elevated viewpoint often reported in OBEs. Hence, the suggestion is that if the model based on sensory input is inhibited or breaks down in some way then a model based on memory and imagination takes over. It is the reliance on a model based upon a constructed imaginary world that leads the individual to incorrectly feel as though they are somehow distant and/or distinct from their physical body. Thus, according to this view, for an OBE to occur there needs to be an inhibition and/or failure of sensory input resulting in a switch to a model based on memory and imagination.

This view is to some extent similar to that put forward by Palmer (1978) in that both propose OBEs occur in part due to alterations in the body concept. Moreover, it may be able to account for the various inaccuracies of the world perceived during an OBE as it is constructed from memory and likely to contains errors. Nevertheless, the evidence to support such a view is both limited and tenuous. For instance, Blackmore (1987) has found that OBE reports are more likely from people who are better able to perceive the world from an external observer or bird's-eye-view. Cook and Irwin (1983) also reported that those reporting OBEs were better able to imagine a scene from another perspective. Such findings confirm the intuitive notion that individuals who experience an OBE should be better at external perspective taking and imagery manipulation. However, others have found that those reporting OBEs are poorer at shifting perspective (e.g., Braithwaite & Dent, 2011b; Easton, Blanke, & Mohr, 2009) which led to the suggestion that the processes underlying such perspective taking are not the same as those involved in experiencing an OBE. Furthermore, it is not clear how a change in visual perspective would or should be linked to a change in the *feeling* that one's self has shifted. Indeed, Neppe (2011) argues that such a view denies the subjective experience of the OBE.

Dissociation and absorption

Irwin (2000) put forward a dissociation model to account for the OBE. The idea here is that sensory dissociation and cognitive absorption leads to a perception that the 'self' is no longer located within the physical body and the individual becomes highly absorbed in this idea. There may be a variety of factors that underlie such a dissociation but it should not be assumed to be indicative of any pathological symptoms. Nevertheless, according to Irwin (1985, 2000) the OBE is due to a dissociation between somatic inputs, in which cross modal synaesthetic type experiences take place, resulting in a feeling that the sense of self as located within the physical body is undermined and in turn leads to a disembodied consciousness represented as the self, floating free from the physical body. The individual then becomes highly absorbed in such a dissociated self which explains the high levels of absorption reported by those who have experienced an OBE (e.g., Irwin, 1985, 2000). Indeed, Irwin (2000) argues that high levels of absorption are responsible for the experienced realism of the OBE. In a similar way Murray and Fox (2005) argue that experients of an OBE have a weak sense of physical embodiment which is characterised by a general dissociation between their self and their physical body. However, as noted above, the association between reports of OBEs and absorption is not consistent. There are those who have experienced an OBE but do not exhibit greater levels of absorption (e.g., Gow et al., 2004). In addition, it is important to keep in mind that this view primarily addresses the notion of dissociation which is only one aspect of the OBE range of experiences. Hence, it may be able to account for some of the data but not all of it.

Neurological

Neurological attempts to explain the OBE have perhaps unsurprisingly taken a pathological approach, viewing the behaviour as the result of abnormal brain activity, particularly around the temporoparietal junction (TPJ).

Abnormal TPJ

The idea here is that the healthy normal brain maintains a continuous representation of the sense of self and that a disruption of the sensory information, possibly from damaged and/or disrupted neural pathways, in or around the temporoparietal junction (TPJ), means that this sense of self becomes distorted. Hence, the assumption is that during an OBE there is a failure to integrate sensory information and because of this the normal sense of 'self' that is resident in the physical body is disrupted and becomes located outside the physical body. This gives the 'illusion' of being separate, though it is only an illusion brought about by disrupted sensory information leading to an altered sense of self. Thus, a central assumption of this view is that an OBE is caused by a disintegration of visual, vestibular, proprioceptive and tactile information at the TPJ in the brain which may inhibit the creation of a coherent representation of the sense of self (e.g., Blanke & Arzy, 2005; Blanke, Landis, Spinelli, & Seeck, 2004; Blanke & Mohr, 2005; Bunning & Blanke, 2005). Such cortical disruption leads the individual to mistakenly feel as though their visual perspective has shifted outside the physical body. There are various lines of evidence that have been put forward to support this view. For instance, Easton et al. (2009) showed that when people who had reported having an OBE were asked to imagine that a figure was their own or a mirror image (i.e., reflected) they were poorer at switching between the imagined positions. This poor performance was taken to suggest some potential 'deficit' in the integration of information at the TPJ, hence highlighting a possible link between an OBE and impaired TPJ function. Further support for the TPJ view comes from a study in which healthy volunteers had to imagine themselves experiencing an elevated visual perspective similar to that reported during an OBE. During this task EEG recordings showed the TPJ was significantly more active and that performance on the task was disrupted when transcranial magnetic stimulation was used to disrupt the TPJ (Blanke & Arzy, 2005). Others have also found support for this view when using sensitive equipment to stimulate the brain. For instance, when a weak current was passed through the right angular gyrus of an epileptic patient they reported feeling their body was moving and being able to view their lower body from above (Blanke, Ortigue, Landis, & Seeck, 2002). Such findings are also consistent with reports that those who experience an OBE have a relatively high level of activation of their right hemisphere (e.g., McCreery & Claridge, 1996; Munro & Persinger, 1992), and relatively high levels of temporal lobe abnormalities (Braithwaite et al., 2013). Some have even suggested that OBEs reliant on TPJ disfunction may be caused by epilepsy or migraine (Bunning & Blanke, 2005).

These cases of neural stimulation suggest that it is clearly possible to disrupt the sense of self by stimulating the TPJ which many have argued clearly implicates this region of the brain in mediating OBE-like experiences. However, whilst many report a sense of dislocation, or separateness, they do not report a disruption of the sense of self. Indeed, the sense of self remains intact and coherent; it is simply the location in space-time that is at odds with expected reality. Furthermore, Murray and Fox (2005) point out that it is not clear at all why interference in activity at the TPJ would occur in relaxed and meditative states, nor why, or how a dissociated visual representation of the body is constructed. Neppe (2011) has also raised some concerns regarding the consistency of such cortical stimulation studies noting that stimulation of different regions of the brain have produced similar experiences. For instance, when A. Smith and Messier (2014) examined the cortical activity of a healthy participant who was able to imagine themselves outside of their physical body they found increased levels of activation in the left supplementary motor area. More recently Daltrozzo et al. (2016) found that stimulation of the right TPJ had no impact on abnormal body perceptions. Hence, they argue that the right TPJ may not play a specific role in this process. Others agree and suggest that a more cautious approach needs to be adopted when attempting to interpret OBE-*like* experiences which are induced and assumed to provide insights into real OBE experiences (Neppe, 2011; Neppe & Palmer, 2005; Sellers, 2018). Overall, they suggest that such procedures may be useful in attempting to understand and/or shed light on specific features of the OBE, such as the notion of a distinct perceptual experience, or the feelings of floating and dislocation. In addition, Sellers (2018) has argued that there may be many differences between the induced experience of some altered state via cortical stimulation and a full-blown OBE. Hence, whilst there may be similarities there are also likely to be many differences and the former should not be confused as fully representing the latter.

Projection

The idea that each person has a spiritual body that may mirror their physical one is not new and has been reported across many cultures such as Greek and Egyptian as well as having a rich history in folklore (Alvarado, 2000). The projection model is intuitively appealing as it suggests quite simply that an aspect of conscious awareness, capable of sustaining perceptual and volitional control, leaves the physical body and travels to distant locations. Hence, the core sense of self leaves the body. Such an idea fits with the assumption that an objective aspect of mind is capable of separating from the physical body and can exist independently (e.g., Alvarado, 1989; Crookall, 1970; Crookall & Shepard, 1972). Such an idea is intuitively plausible, particularly to those who undergo an OBE, as there is a distinct feeling of leaving the physical body. Conceptually, it is also parsimonious in the sense that all reported findings are easily and fully accounted for by some form of self-consciousness leaving the physical body (Crookall, 1973). However, robust empirical support for this view is currently lacking. On the one hand the idea that something leaves the physical body during an OBE has some support from anecdotal accounts (Alvarado, 1989, 2000). Unfortunately, whilst such accounts remain interesting and potentially informative, they also carry with them a range of inherent limitations. More objective attempts to detect the 'double' of a person undergoing an OBE have met with limited success (see, Alvarado, 1989; Blackmore, 2005). For instance, whilst some have reported unusual recordings from technical equipment (e.g., Osis & McCormick, 1980) overall the results do not clearly support the notion that anything 'detectable' leaves the physical body. In addition, Irwin and Watt (2007) rightly point out how such an approach attempts to hedge its bets in terms of attempting to account for both accurate and inaccurate information. For instance, if during an OBE an individual reports back something accurate that could not have been obtained via ordinary means this is taken as evidence that the individual's consciousness left the physical body and travelled to the target location. However, if during an OBE the individual reports back information that is not consistent with the reality of the physical world then this is accounted for in terms of the individual's consciousness leaving the physical body and travelling to a related *astral* world which may be similar but not identical to the physical world (see e.g., Monroe, 1971; Steiger, 1982). Hence, whilst such an approach is superficially appealing there is no clear evidence to support it. Furthermore, it is not helpful in that it does not make any clear predictions in terms of the individuals who are more or less likely to have an OBE, or the situations and circumstances in which such events occur.

Need for a multi-etiological approach

Neppe (2011) argues that many of the prior accounts of the OBE offer a unitary approach to understanding the process and experience, that is, the assumption that there is a single broad cause and explanation. The problem with such proposals is that they attempt to account for the OBE as a unitary experience with one single cause when in fact there may be many different types of OBE and hence a multi-perspective may provide a better account. Others agree, pointing out that there is no one single culture less type of OBE (Hurd, 2016; Sellers, 2018). Each OBE may be uniquely bound to the individual, their background, culture, experience and expectations. Given this, it is very likely that there is more than one reason why such experiences occur.

Implications

There are three main implications that emerge from the research into the field of OBEs. First, the experience is predominantly perceived as remarkably positive. After an OBE the individual in question is often inspired to become more interested in psychic phenomena, and lead a more spiritual, fulfilled and less materialistic lifestyle (Sellers, 2019; Twemlow et al., 1982). Second is the implication often made, either implicitly or explicitly, that an OBE would suggest that consciousness may not be solely reliant on the brain (Metzinger, 2005), w hich leads to suggestions that consciousness, or mind, may exist independent of the body. And finally, given this, those who experience an OBE show a clear reduction in their fear of death and dying (e.g., Almeder, 1992; Bourdin, Barberia, Oliva, & Slater, 2017; Paterson, 1995), though some have suggested that non-survivalist explanations that rely more on basic psi phenomena such as clairvoyance and psychokinesis provide a more compelling account (e.g., Braude, 2001). Nevertheless, as Hurd (2016) points out, it may not matter whether OBEs are real or not in the sense that they provide some view of the ontological reality of the cosmos. What may matter more is the effect such an experience can have on the beliefs, behaviours and lifestyle of those that have them.

Overview

Despite the superficial clarity of the term 'out of body experience' there is no clear agreement regarding precisely what aspects of behaviour this refers to. However, it is clear when recording the experiences of those reporting an OBE that it contains a wide range of experiences. As such, the OBE is more likely to be a polymodal experience in the sense that there is no *one* single type of OBE but may be multiple subtypes, each exhibiting distinct behaviours and reliant on different processes. This represents a challenge to the field because researchers need to be clear that when they are referring to an OBE they are in fact talking about the same or similar types of experience. In addition, classifying someone as having experienced an OBE based on an affirmative response to a single ambiguous question is also very problematic. Given the core premise of an OBE it would seem essential, at the very least, that evidence be obtained indicating that some aspect of conscious awareness was distinct from the physical body before classifying the individual in question as having had an OBE. Hence, adopting a more rigorous approach to defining more precisely what an OBE is may help to produce more consistent findings which in turn will move the field forwards. In terms of the key, or core, characteristics of the OBE these include the physical sensations of floating and may include feeling vibrations, with the perceptions of a subtle body that is similar to the physical. The sensory characteristics of the OBE are predominantly visual and tend to be very vivid and intense. Some also report the ability to control the OBE which may be achieved by focused conscious intention. Furthermore, many of those reporting an OBE seem to have had more than one and the majority indicate that they would be happy to try it again. The demographic information shows that OBEs are widely reported across populations and cultures. They can also occur as a result of a wide variety of conditions, though the most common are those in which the individual is deeply relaxed and mentally calm. Interestingly, examination of individual factors such as age, gender, belief, education and personality show there is nothing unique or special about those who report an OBE. This would suggest that such an experience may be available to everyone which in turn may account for the widespread reporting of such a phenomenon. Regarding evidence for the OBE it would be fair to state that at this moment in time the majority of claims are based on anecdotal reports and testimonials. Experimental research attempting to detect the subtle body that is assumed to travel beyond the physical has shown some intriguing though limited support, whilst attempts to test the veridical nature of information obtained during an OBE have so far met with little success. Examination of the psychophysiological profile of those undergoing an OBE has also produced inconsistent results. In part this may be due to the varied nature and/or sub-types of the OBE. It may also be due to methodological difficulties inherent in a paradigm attempting to ascertain precisely when such an experience begins and ends. Nevertheless, attempts to induce an OBE via hypnosis have produced some positive and thought-provoking results. It is not clear precisely how, if at all, such an induced OBE may differ from the more spontaneous naturally occurring experience. Several ideas have been put forward in an attempt to account for the OBE. These include psychological, neurological and projection accounts. However, most are limited by the fact that they tend to focus on only one aspect of what is a rich and varied experience. Hence, at present there is no clear unified theory that can account for the OBE. Overall, the OBE represents an intriguing and challenging phenomenon with rewards that could have wide ranging and potentially paradigm shifting implications.

Reflective questions

Some questions that may prove helpful when reflecting on the material covered in this chapter.

- How would you define an OBE?
- What criteria would you use to classify different types of OBE?
- What evidence should be used to classify someone as having experienced an OBE?
- How would you distinguish an OBE from clairvoyance or remote viewing?
- What type of evidence do you think would best support claims of an OBE?
- Do you think an induced OBE would be the same as a spontaneous one – why?
- Is it ethical to try and induce an OBE?
- What are some of the implications that arise from OBEs?
- How do you think you would feel if you had an OBE?

References

Abreu, N., Madurell, A., & Perego, L. (2013). The Consciential Paradigm: A consciousness-centered framework for expanding the study of reality through bioenergy, OBE, and allied phenomena. *Syntropy*, 2(2), 127–144.

Almeder, R. (1992). *Death and personal survival: The evidence for life after death*. Lanham, MD: Rowman & Littlefield Publishers.

Alvarado, C. S. (1982). ESP during out-of-body experiences: A review of experimental studies. *Journal of Parapsychology*, 46, 209–230.

Alvarado, C. S. (1989). Trends in the study of out-of-body experiences: An overview of developments since the nineteenth century. *Journal of Scientific Exploration*, 3(1), 27–42.

Alvarado, C. S. (1992). The psychological approach to out-of-body experiences: A review of early and modern developments. *Journal of Parapsychology*, 126(3), 237–250.

Alvarado, C. S. (2000). Out-of-body experiences. In E. Carde, S. J. Lynn, & S. Krippner (Eds.), *Varieties of anomalous experience: Examining the scientific evidence* (pp. 183–218). Washington, DC: American Psychological Association.

Alvarado, C. S. (2012). Explorations of the features of out-of-body experiences: An overview and critique of the work of Robert Crookall. *Journal of the Society for Psychical Research*, 76(907), 65–82.

Alvarado, C. S., & Zingrone, N. L. (1998). A study of the features of out-of-body experiences in relation to Sylvan Muldoon's claims. *European Journal of Parapsychology*, 14, 89–99.

Alvarado, C. S., Zingrone, N. L., & Dalton, K. S. (1999). Out-of-body experiences: Alterations of consciousness and the Five-Factor Model of personality. *Imagination, Cognition and Personality*, 18(4), 297–317. doi: 10.2190/293K-3KW9-KYN8-TWKC.

Anzellotti, F., Onofrj, V., Maruotti, V., Ricciardi, L., Franciotti, R., Bonanni, L., ... & Onofrj, M. (2011). Autoscopic phenomena: Case report and review of literature. *Behavioral and Brain Functions*, 7(2), 1–11. doi: 10.1186/1744-9081-7-2.

Bateman, L., Jones, C., & Jomeen, J. (2017). A narrative synthesis of women's out-of-body experiences during childbirth. *Journal of Midwifery and Women's Health*, 62(4), 442–451. doi: 10.1111/jmwh.12655.

Blackmore, S. (1982). Out-of-body experiences, lucid dreams, and imagery: Two surveys. *Journal of the American Society for Psychical Research*, 76(4), 301–317.

Blackmore, S. (1984). A psychological theory of the out-of-body experience. *Journal of Parapsychology*, 48, 201–218.

Blackmore, S. (1987). Where am I? Perspectives in imagery and the out-of-body experience. *Journal of Mental Imagery*, 11(2), 53–66.

Blackmore, S. (2005). Out of body experiences. In J. Henry (Ed.), *Parapsychology: Research on exceptional experiences* (pp. 188–195). Hove, East Sussex: Routledge.

Blackmore, S. (2015). Out-of-body experiences are not evidence for survival. In M. Martin & K. Augustine (Eds.), *The myth of the afterlife* (pp. 393–403). New York: Rowman & Littlefield.

Blanke, O., & Arzy, S. (2005). The out of body experience: Disturbed self-processing at the temporo-parietal junction. *The Neuroscientist*, 11(1), 16–24.

Blanke, O., Landis, T., Spinelli, L., & Seeck, M. (2004). Out-of-body experience and autoscopy of neurological origin. *Brain*, 127, 243–258.

Blanke, O., & Mohr, C. (2005). Out-of-body experience, heutoscopy, and autoscopic hallucination of neurological origin: Implications for neurocognitive mechanisms of corporeal awareness and self consciousness. *Brain Research Reviews*, 50, 184–199.

Blanke, O., Ortigue, S., Landis, T., & Seeck, M. (2002). Neuropsychology: Stimulating illusory own-body perceptions. *Nature*, 419(6904), 269. doi: 10.1038/419269a.

Bos, E. M., Spoor, J. K., Smits, M., Schouten, J. W., & Vincent, A. J. (2016). Out-of-body experience during awake craniotomy. *World Neurosurgery*, 92, 586.e589–586.e513.

Bourdin, P., Barberia, I., Oliva, R., & Slater, M. (2017). A virtual out-of-body experience reduces fear of death. *PloS One*, 12(1), e0169343. doi: 10/1371/journalpone.0169343.

Braithwaite, J. J., Broglia, E., Bagshaw, A. P., & Wilkins, A. J. (2013). Evidence for elevated cortical hyperexcitability and its association with out-of-body experiences in the non-clinical populations. *Cortex*, 49, 793–805.

Braithwaite, J. J., & Dent, K. (2011a). New perspectives on perspective-taking mechanisms and out of body experience. *Cortex*, 47, 628–632.

Braithwaite, J. J., & Dent, K. (2011b). New perspectives on perspective-taking mechanisms and the out-of-body experience. *Cortex*, 47, 628–632. doi: 10.1016/j.cortex.2010.11.008.

Braude, S. E. (2001). Out-of-body experiences and survival after death. *International Journal of Parapsychology*, 12(1), 83–129.

Bunning, S., & Blanke, O. (2005). The out of body experience: Precipitating factors and neural correlates. *Progress in Brain Research*, *150*, 331–350. doi: 10.1016/S0079-6123(05)50024-4.

Cook, A. M., & Irwin, H. J. (1983). Visuospatial skills and the out-of-body experience. *The Journal of Parapsychology*, *47*(1), 23–35.

Crookall, R. (1970). *Out-of-the-body experiences: A fourth analysis*. New York, NY: University Books, Incorporated.

Crookall, R. (1973). *The study and practice of astral projection*. New York, NY: University Books.

Crookall, R., & Shepard, L. (1972). *Case-book of astral projection, 545–746*. Secaucus, NJ: University Books.

Daltrozzo, J., Kotchoubey, B., Gueler, F., & Karim, A. A. (2016). Effects of transcranial magnetic stimulation on body perception: No evidence for specificity of the right temporo-parietal junction. *Brain Topography*, *29*(5), 704–715.

De Foe, A., Al Khafaji, B. E., Pederzoli, L., Prati, E., & Tressoldi, P. E. (2017). Out-of-body-experiences: A phenomenological comparison of different causes. Available at SSRN: https://ssrn.com/abstract=2903827. doi:10.2139/ssrn.2903827.

Easton, S., Blanke, O., & Mohr, C. (2009). A putative implication for fronto-parietal connectivity in out-of-body experiences. *Cortex*, *45*(2), 216–227. doi: 10.1016/j.cortex.2007.07.012.

Ehrsson, H. H. (2007). The experimental induction of out-of-body experiences. *Science*, *317*, 1048. doi: 10.1126/science.1142175.

Facco, E., Casiglia, E., Al Khafaji, B. E., Finatti, F., Duma, G. M., Mento, G., ... & Tressoldi, P. (2019). The neurophenomenology of out-of-body experiences induced by hypnotic suggestions. *International Journal of Clinical and Experimental Hypnosis*, *67*(1), 39–68. doi: 10.1080/00207144.2019.1553762.

Gow, K., Lang, T., & Chant, D. (2004). Fantasy proneness, paranormal beliefs and personality features in out-of-body experiences. *Contemporary Hypnosis*, *21*(3), 107–125.

Green, C. (1967). Ecsomatic experiences and related phenomena. *Journal of the Society for Psychical Research*, *44*, 111–131.

Green, C. (1968). *Out-of-the-body experiences*. Oxford: Institue of Psychophysical Research.

Holt, N. J., Simmonds-Moore, C., Luke, D., & French, C. C. (2012). *Anomalistic psychology*. New York, NY: Palgrave Macmillian.

Hurd, R. (2016). Towards an evolutionary psychology of out-of-body experiences. In A. De Foe (Ed.), *Consciousness beyond the body: Evidence and reflections* (pp. 56–69). Melbourne: Melbourne Centre for Exceptional Human Potential.

Irwin, H. J. (1980). Out-of-body down under: Some cognitive characteristics of Australian students reporting OOBEs. *Journal of the Society for Psychical Research*, *50*, 448–459.

Irwin, H. J. (1985). *Flight of mind: A psychological study of the out-of-body experience*. Metuchen, NJ: Scarecrow Press.

Irwin, H. J. (2000). The disembodied self: An empirical study of dissociation and the out-of-body experience. *Journal of Parapsychology*, *64*, 261–277.

Irwin, H. J., & Watt, C. (2007). *An introduction to parapsychology* (5th edn). Jefferson, NC: McFarland & Co.

Jones, F., Gabbard, G., & Twemlow, S. (1984). Psychological and demographic characteristics of persons reporting out-of-body experiences. *The Hillside Journal of Clinical Psychiatry*, *6*(1),105–115.

Kolb, B., Whishaw, I. Q., & Teskey, G. C. (2016). *An introduction to brain and behaviour* (Vol. 5). New York: Worth.

LaBerge, S. (1985). *Lucid dreaming*. Los Angeles: Tarcher.

LaBerge, S., Levitan, L., & Dement, W. C. (1986). Lucid dreaming: Physiological correlates of consciousness during REM sleep. *The Journal of Mind and Behavior, 7*(2/3), 251–258.

McCreery, C., & Claridge, G. (1996). A study of hallucination in normal subjects – I. Self-report data. *Personality and Individual Differences, 21*(5), 739–747.

Metzinger, T. (2005). Out-of-body experiences as the origin of the concept of a 'soul'. *Mind & Matter, 3*(1), 57–84.

Monroe, R. A. (1971). *Journeys out of the body.* Garden City, NY: Doubleday.

Morris, R. L., Harary, S. B., Janis, J., Hartwell, J., & Roll, W. G. (1978). Studies of communication during out-of-body experiences. *Journal of the American Society for Psychical Research, 72*(1), 1–21.

Muldoon, S. J., & Carrington, H. (1929). *The projection of the astral body.* New York: Rider & Co.

Munro, C., & Persinger, M. A. (1992). Relative right temporal-lobe theta activity correlates with Vingiano's hemispheric quotient and the 'sensed presence'. *Perceptual and Motor Skills, 75*(3), 899–903.

Murray, C. D., & Fox, J. (2005). Dissociational body experiences: Differences between respondents with and without prior out-of-body experience. *The British Journal of Psychology, 96*, 441–456. doi: 10.1348/000712605X49169.

Myers, S. A., Austrin, H. R., Grisso, J. T., & Nickeson, R. C. (1983). Personality characteristics as related to the out-of-body experience. *Journal of Parapsychology, 47*(2), 131–144.

Nash, M. R., Lynn, S. J., & Stanley, S. M. (1984). The direct hypnotic suggestion of altered mind/body perception. *American Journal of Clinical Hypnosis, 27*(2), 95–102.

Neppe, V. M. (2011). Models of the out-of-body experience: A new multi-etiological phenomenological approach. *NeuroQuantology, 9*(1), 72–83.

Neppe, V. M., & Palmer, J. (2005). Subjective anomalous events: Perspectives for the future, voices from the past. In M. A. Thalbourne & L. Storm (Eds.), *Parapsychology in the twenty-first century: Essays on the future of psychical research* (pp. 242–274). Jefferson, NC: McFarland & Co.

Osis, K. (1975). Perceptual experiments on out-of-body experiences. In J. D. Morris, W. G. Roll, & R. L. Morris (Eds.), *Research in parapsychology 1974* (pp. 53–55). Metuchen, NJ: Scarecrow Press.

Osis, K., & McCormick, D. (1980). Kinetic effects at the ostensible location of an out-of-body projection during perceptual testing. *Journal of the American Society for Psychical Research, 74*(3), 319–329.

Osis, K., & Mitchell, J. L. (1977). Physiological correlates of reported out-of-body experiences. *Journal of the Society for Psychical Research, 49*(772), 525–536.

Palmer, J. (1978). The out-of-body experience: A psychological theory. *Parapsychology Review, 9*(5), 19–22.

Palmer, J. (1979). A community mail survey of psychic experiences. *Journal of the American Society for Psychical Research, 73*, 221–251.

Palmer, J., & Dennis, M. (1975). *A community mail. Survey of psychic experiences in research in parapsychology.* Metuchen, NJ: Scarecrow Press.

Palmer, J., & Lieberman, R. (1975). The influence of psychological set on ESP and out-of-body experiences. *Journal of the American Society for Psychical Research, 69*(3), 193–213.

Parra, A. (2010). Out-of-body experiences and hallucinatory experiences: A psychological appraoch. *Imagination, Cognition and Personality, 29*(3), 211–223. doi: 10.2190/IC.29.3.d

Paterson, R. (1995). *Philosophy and the belief in a life after death.* London: Macmillan Press Ltd.

Pederzoli, L., Giroldini, W., Duma, G. M., Mento, G., Prati, E., & Tressoldi, P. E. (2016). Out-of-body experience induced by hypnotic suggestions: An exploratory neurophenomenological study. Available at SSRN 2820689. doi: 10.2139/ssrn.2820689.

Penfield, W., & Erickson, T. C. (1941). *Epilepsy and cerebral localization*. Oxford, England: Charles C. Thomas.

Persinger, M. A., Saroka, K., Mulligan, B. P., & Murphy, T. R. (2010). Experimental elicitation of an out of body experience and concomitant cross-hemispheric electroencephalographic coherence. *NeuroQuantology, 8*(4), 466–477. doi: 10.14704/nq.2010.8.4.302.

Poynton, J. C. (1975). Results of an out-of-the-body survey. In J. C. Poynton (Ed.), *Parapsychology in South Africa* (pp. 109–123). Johannesburg: South African Society for Psychical Research.

Rogo, D. S. (1983). *Leaving the body*. Englewood Cliffs, NJ: Prentice Hall.

Rogo, D. S. (1984). Researching the out-of-body experience: The state of the art. *Anabiosis, 4*, 21–49.

Sellers, J. (2017). Out-of-body experience: Review and a case study. *Journal of Consciousness Exploration & Research, 8*(9), 686–708.

Sellers, J. (2018). A brief review of studies of out-of-body experiences in both the healthy and pathological populations. *Journal of Cognitive Science, 19*(4), 471–491.

Sellers, J. (2019). Transpersonal and transformative potential of out-of-body experiences. *Journal of Exceptional Experiences and Psychology, 6*(2), 7–27.

Smith, A., & Messier, C. (2014). Voluntary out-of-body experience: An fMRI study. *Frontiers in Human Neuroscience, 8*(70), 1–9. doi: 10.3389/fnhum.2014.00070.

Smith, J. C. (2010). *Pseudoscience and extraordinary claims of the paranormal*. West Sussex: Wiley & Sons Ltd.

Stanford, R. G. (1987). The out-of-body experience as an imaginal journey: The developmental perspective. *The Journal of Parapsychology, 51*(2), 137–155.

Steiger, B. (1982). *Astral projection*. Atlan, PA: Whitford Press.

Tart, C. T. (1968). A psychophysiological study of out-of-the-body experiences in a selected subject. *Journal of the American Society for Psychical Research, 62*, 3–27.

Tart, C. T. (1998). Six studies of out-of-body experiences. *Journal of Near-Death Studies., 17*(2), 73–99.

Tellegen, A., & Atkinson, G. (1974). Openness to absorbing and self-altering experiences ('absorption'), a trait related to hypnotic susceptibility. *Journal of Abnormal Psychology, 83*(3), 268–277.

Tobacyk, J. J., & Mitchell, T. P. (1987). The out-of-body experience and personality adjustment. *Journal of Nervous and Mental Disease, 175*(6), 367–370. doi: 10.1097/00005053-198706000-00008.

Tressoldi, P., & Del Prete, G. (2007). ESP under hypnosis: The role of induction instructions and personality characteristics. *Journal of Parapsychology, 71*(1), 125–137.

Tressoldi, P., Pederzoli, L., Caini, P., Ferrini, A., Melloni, S., Prati, E., ... & Trabucco, A. (2015). Hypnotically induced out-of-body experience: How many bodies are there? Unexpected discoveries about the subtle body and psychic body. *SAGE Open, 5*(4), 2158244015615919.

Tressoldi, P., Pederzoli, L., Caini, P., Ferrini, A., Melloni, S., Richeldi, D., & Trabucco, A. (2014). Out of body experience induced by hypnotic suggestion. Part 1: Phenomenology and perceptual characteristics. *SSRN Electronic Journal*. doi: 10.2139/ssrn.2443719.

Twemlow, S. W., Gabbard, G. O., & Jones, F. C. (1982). The out-of-body-experience: A phenomenological typology based on questionnaire responses. *American Journal of Psychiatry, 139*(4), 450–455.

Vernon, D. (2009). *Human potential: Exploring techniques used to enhance human performance*. London: Routledge.

Wilson, S. C., & Barber, T. X. (1983). The fantasy prone personality: Implications for understanding imagery, hypnosis, and parapsychological phenomena. In A. A. Sheikh (Ed.), *Imager, current theory, research and application* (pp. 340–387). New York: Wiley.

Chapter 10

Near-death experiences

Irrespective of age, creed, nationality, gender or wealth everyone will eventually die. It is the one fundamental aspect of life shared by all on the planet. However, precisely what happens when we die is a mystery that is as old as mankind. Nevertheless, some intriguing insights can be obtained from the reported experiences of those that have died and been resuscitated. The fact that an increasing number of people have died and been resuscitated is not the interesting point, though it does acknowledge the advances of modern medicine. The interesting point is that during the time they are clinically dead these individuals report a range of vivid and emotional experiences that have a dramatic impact on their lives. Unsurprisingly, such reports have far reaching implications, not only for the notion of death and dying, but also for understanding the nature of human consciousness. It has also been suggested that the knowledge and insights gained from listening to and trying to understand these reported experiences can help clinicians deal with the anxieties of patients facing death (Parnia & Fenwick, 2002). This chapter explores these reported experiences by initially defining what a near-death experience (NDE) is, highlighting the fact that death is more of a process than a single event. This is followed by an outline of the phenomenology of the near-death experience, how such experiences are classified and their prevalence. The chapter then examines the evidence supporting the veracity of such claims. This is followed by an examination of some of the prevailing explanations put forward to account for such experiences. The chapter ends by exploring some of the implications of an NDE.

A near-death experience (NDE)

The term *near-death experience* (NDE) was coined, or at least popularised, by Dr Raymond Moody in his book *Life After Life* (Moody, 1975). It was based on the collected anecdotal accounts of individuals who had survived cardiac arrest and reported a range of unusual experiences during the time they were thought to have been dead. Moody (1975) labelled this complex cluster of subjective events the near-death experience. Since then, many books have been written describing the varied and interesting cases of those reporting such experiences (e.g., Fenwick & Fenwick, 2008; Parnia & Young, 2013; Rivas, Dirven, & Smit, 2016).

In general, the NDE refers to someone who has died and is brought back to life, with death often defined as an event typified by cardiac arrest, no respiration, fixed or dilated pupils, and may also include flatlined electroencephalogram (EEG) recordings

(Agrillo, 2011; Greyson, 1985, 1998; Roberts & Owen, 1988). The range of measures serves to indicate that death is a process rather than a single event and it is difficult to define with any precision exactly when an individual crosses the border from life to death and back. Such issues are particularly challenging for research into NDEs as it makes it difficult to identify precisely when such experiences occur. For example, they may occur as the person slips into death, during a period of death or when they are returning to life (Rivas et al., 2016). Agrillo (2011) has suggested that the 'near' aspect does not necessarily mean 'almost' dead, but may refer to the experiences of the individual during the early stages of the dying process. Parnia and Young (2013) take a different view suggesting that the experiences should be labelled as 'actual death' experiences rather than 'near death'. Others disagree, pointing out that if death is defined as an irreversible loss of organ function leading to a one-way permanent state, then no one reporting an NDE has died and therefore all such reports relate to the experiences of people who are still alive (Roberts & Owen, 1988). Hence, a precise definition of what an NDE represents remains contentious. Nevertheless, the field of interest surrounding NDEs has grown substantially to include scientific associations that specifically focus on studying and reporting on NDEs (e.g., International Association for Near-Death Studies: IANDS) and includes academic journals specifically targeted at disseminating findings from NDE research (e.g., *Journal of Near-Death Studies*). Hence, it would seem that the study of NDEs, whether to ascertain the veracity of the experience, or attempt to understand why an individual may have such an experience, is widespread and becoming more mainstream (Bailey & Yates, 1996).

Phenomenology of the NDE

Ever since Moody (1975) first coined the term NDE the description of such an experience has been thought to include some or all of the following key elements (see e.g., Corazza, 2008; Lorimer, 2017; Parnia, 2008; Rogo, 1986; van Lommel, 2010):

- Hearing oneself pronounced dead
- Impression of being located beyond the physical body
- Overwhelming feeling of peace
- Floating/drifting, often through a dark tunnel
- Awareness of a golden light
- Encountering beings of light/other 'spirits' and communicating
- Rapid and/or panoramic life review
- Sensing or becoming aware of a border or limit
- Coming back into the body.

Examples of some of these key features are given in Figure 10.1. Ring (1980) classified these as *stages* that an individual may go through, whereas Lundahl (1993) saw them more as a *sequence* of events. However, it is important to note that not all NDEs feature all of these elements and even if they do the order in which they occur differs from one individual to another (see e.g., Bailey & Yates, 1996; Blackmore, 2005; Grey, 1985; Greyson, 2003, 2006; Martial et al., 2017; Ring, 1980; Sabom, 1998). For example, a survey by Ring (1980) of 101 randomly selected survivors of

Impression of being located beyond the physical body

... Then I soared up and was looking down on myself. I was a feet and-a-half to six feet hovering over my body.

(Rogo, 1986, p. 62)

Overwhelming feeling of peace

And the pain, especially the pressure on my lungs, was gone. The atmosphere made me feel totally relaxed. I'd never felt this happy before.

(van Lommel, 2010, p. 18)

Floating/drifting, often through a dark tunnel

I became less and less able to see and feel. Presently, I was going down a long black tunnel with a tremendous alive sort of light bursting in at the end.

(Drab, 1981, p. 126)

Awareness of a golden light, and encountering beings of light/other 'spirits' and communicating

Reaching the light, I was met by other beings of light and very gently encouraged to move forwards ...

(Parnia, 2008, p. 75)

Rapid and/or panoramic life review

I saw my whole past take place in many images, as though on a stage at some distance from me. I saw myself as the chief character in the performance.

(Lorimer, 2017, p. 3)

Reaching a border and returning

My father came to greet me. We walked together for a little while and then he left me and crossed a 'rainbow bridge'. I was about to follow him but he told me not to do so. He said to me 'Go home, go home'. Then I woke up.

(Corazza, 2008, p. 61)

Figure 10.1 Some of the core elements of an NDE.

NDE confirmed that 37% reported out of body experiences, although others have found rates as high as 75% (Greyson & Stevenson, 1980). Typically, people find themselves in a room detached from and suspended above their physical body. The environment may seem normal but senses tend to be heightened and there is a feeling that the self is no longer occupying the physical body. An interesting point however is that the individuals in question do not recall any sensation associated with *leaving* the physical body. This seems to happen 'all at once' as it were.

Given the shift in perspective based on the impression of leaving the physical body it may be unsurprising that many report a sense of emotional detachment or absence of fear and pain. This is also sometimes referred to as a state of happiness and/or joy (Noyes Jr & Slymen, 1979). Depending on the survey, reports range from 56% (van Lommel et al., 2001), to 60% (Ring, 1980) and up to 88% (Fenwick & Fenwick, 1995) of individuals reporting feelings of peace and tranquillity, making it one of the most common features of the NDE. Sometimes the NDE may continue with the experient seeing or travelling along a dark tunnel with a light at the end. This may represent some form of transition phase from the current situation to a distinct realm. Reports of seeing such a tunnel vary from around 25% (see Ring, 1980; Sabom & Kreutiziger, 1982; van Lommel et al., 2001) up to 51% (Fenwick & Fenwick, 1995). Furthermore, the tunnel may represent a social construction specific to the culture of the individual as Westerners may see a tunnel whilst others, such as Melanesians, may see subterranean caves (see, Corazza, 2008). This transition leads the individual to a transcendental realm of supernatural beauty and light. Interestingly, the light is often reported to be highly intense and yet simultaneously reassuring and comforting. This realm is usually perceived as a place of dazzling spiritual beauty, with lush trees and flowers, rich in colour. Having made the transition to a new realm nearly half (~40%) report the presence of a cosmic spirit guide and/or religious figure (Ring, 1980). Communication with this being generally revolves around the issue of whether the individual in question will die or not. Furthermore, some report meeting deceased relatives in this realm (Fenwick & Fenwick, 1995). These meetings may provide a comforting 'marker' for the individual in the sense that this is someone with whom they are familiar. Such meetings may be followed by a life review, or panoramic vision of the experient's physical life, though not always (see e.g., Corazza, 2008). Some have suggested that such life reviews resemble a post-mortem encounter or judgement of one's deeds (Lorimer, 2017). The reported cases of this range from as low as 3% (Fenwick & Fenwick, 1995) up to 25% (Ring, 1980; van Lommel et al., 2001). The review itself may involve vivid representations of the individual's life and can be either the whole life or selected highlights. For example, an examination of the life review experience (LRE) from seven participants who underwent this as part of their NDE revealed several key characteristics in terms of the order of events, their continuity, the period of time they covered, as well as the valence, emotions and perspective taken (Katz, Saadon-Grosman, & Arzy, 2017). This shows the LRE to be a diverse range of sub-components, only some of which any one individual undergoing an NDE may experience. Furthermore, it is worth noting that the life review is not instigated by the individual; rather they are passive observers of the sequence of events. Following the life review the individual may be offered a choice to return or not, or approach a boundary or border which if crossed would mean that they cannot return (see, Corazza, 2008; van Lommel, 2010). The form of this border is many and varied, including for example a river, a wall of thick fog, a valley or a bridge (van Lommel, 2010). Once a decision to return is made the return to the physical body is usually abrupt. Some report a force or wind sucking them back through the tunnel instantly returning them to the physical body. It should be noted that not all make their own choice. In some instances, the individuals seem happy to continue onwards and do not feel the need to return to their physical body, particularly if it is suffering injury and pain. Nevertheless, relatives or key spiritual figures may indicate to them that their time is not yet up and that they have something further to accomplish in life which requires them to return (see, Corazza, 2008).

Overall, for most the NDE represents a positive experience. However, in a few cases individuals may report frightening experiences where they are isolated in dark places or are afraid for various reasons. For instance, Osis and Haraldsson (1977) found that some patients reacted negatively to what they perceived as hallucinatory guides who wished to take them away. These harrowing experiences are sometimes reported as involving similar common elements such as extreme fear, isolation, non-being, confusion and possible torment and guilt. According to van Lommel (2010) such experiences are often known as a 'hell experience' and can be both frightening and stir profound feelings of guilt. Furthermore, it is difficult to know precisely how many people have such a negative NDE as they may keep quiet about their experience out of shame and guilt. According to Greyson and Bush (1992) there are at least three different types of negative NDE. The first involves phenomenology that is similar to a peaceful NDE but that is simply interpreted as unpleasant. The second may include the unpleasant experience of non-existence and the final type may include visions of hellish landscapes and entities. Ring (1994) has also suggested three separate types of negative NDE. The first is characterised by an aversive tone. In the second the experient is thrust into a meaningless environment and may be taunted by voices. The third may include fear that they are about to die. Furthermore, it has also been suggested that there is often an element of judgement about such experiences, whereby the experient feels they are being judged for past behaviour and/or deeds (Irwin & Bramwell, 1988). It is not clear at this stage whether the two types of NDE (i.e., positive and negative) have similar or distinct underlying causes. However, Atwater (1992) has suggested that those experiencing a negative NDE feel somewhat ignored by mainstream research and at the same time they may be reluctant to talk about their experiences due to the stigma attached.

Classification of the NDE

Given the range of experiences that constitute an NDE there is some debate in the literature as to whether it represents a unitary construct or whether there are a variety of sub-types of NDE, each with its own distinct set of causes (Roberts & Owen, 1988). For instance, Ring (1980) has suggested an invariant unitary approach where the NDE is generally the same across demographic, psychological and situational variables. Others disagree and suggest that there may be several classes of NDE each with its own set of unique experiences (Greyson, 1993; Twemlow, Gabbard, & Coyne, 1982). This has important implications, particularly for those conducting research in the field as it is important that any comparisons made are across alike experiences to try to ascertain any unique underlying features. Hence, how an NDE is classified and documented is likely to influence perceptions of the experience.

One early attempt by Ring (1980) to classify NDEs led to the production of a Weighted Core Experience Index (WCEI) based on the presence of 10 weighted items that emerged over time from phenomenological studies. However, while exhibiting some face validity it lacked empirical evidence suggesting it was either internally coherent or reliable. This led Greyson (1983) to develop a Near-Death Experience Scale (NDES) based on the empirical analysis of questionnaire responses identifying the frequency of a wide range of experiences. This scale is based on 16 separate items under four broad headings (see Table 10.1) and is used widely in the field.

Table 10.1 Showing the four main clusters, each with four items, used to classify NDE (adapted from Greyson, 1983)

Cognitive	Affective	Paranormal	Transcendental
Altered time perception	Peace/ pleasantness	Heightened senses	Unearthly environment
Speeded thoughts	Feelings of joy	ESP	Encountering mystical being/presence
Life review	Harmony/unity	Precognitive visions	Encountering deceased/ religious spirits
Understanding everything	Bright light	Separation from the body	Border, point of no return

Each of the 16 items within the four main components can be scored from 0 to a maximum of 2. Hence, each of the four clusters would have a score that ranged from 0 to 8, with the overall maximum being 32. According to Greyson (1983) an overall score of 7 or more would indicate the presence of an NDE, though he notes that dismissing an individual's claim to an NDE based on a single criterion score may be counterproductive. Nevertheless, it highlights the challenge faced by researchers when using a single score to indicate such a range of possible experiences. It may be that when future researchers examine these components in more depth it will lead to a refinement of the sub-scales showing, for example, that each of the core components of an NDE may be made up of multiple sub-components and that with continued research more sensitive questionnaires can be developed to tease these apart (see e.g., Katz et al., 2017).

Prevalence of NDEs

When examining reported NDEs it is interesting to ask how often they occur, to whom and is there anything unusual or special about the people who experience them? Furthermore, are such experiences reported across cultures and situations? In terms of their commonality such events have been reported across time. For instance, one of the earliest accounts of a possible NDE appeared in the 10th book of Plato's Republic, written around 420 BC, in which he describes a solider named Er, who regained consciousness while on his funeral pyre 12 days after he was thought to have been killed in battle (see e.g., Roberts & Owen, 1988; Schwartz, 2015). Once revived, Er described being taken to a mysterious realm where he was confronted with two openings, side by side. Judges sat between these entrances: those judged as righteous were sent to the right and upwards to heaven, with tokens of their deeds attached to them. Those considered unjust were sent on the downward road to the left. From above, happy souls reported visions of beauty; from below came the sounds of wailing, as souls bemoaned thousands of years of dreadful sufferings. Prior to returning to life, each soul drank from the River of Forgetfulness, causing these events to fade from memory. However, Er was not permitted to drink or forget, and so returned to life to tell the tale.

Contemporary estimates of the precise number of people who have had an NDE varies. For instance, reported rates are as low as 6% to 7% (Parnia, Waller, Yeates, & Fenwick, 2001), with larger samples showing averages of 10% (Greyson, 2003; Kondziella & Olsen, 2019; van Lommel, van Wees, Meyers, & Elfferich, 2001) and some suggesting around 22% (Locke & Shontz, 1983), with others going as high as 48% (Ring, 1980). Van Lommel et al. (2001) found that the frequency of the reported experience relied on how the NDE was defined. Though unsurprising, it would account for the varying rates seen in the literature as there is no single agreed upon criterion definition. They also found that the reported levels of NDEs were higher in those patients aged below 60 years. This may to some extent be related to or influenced by the higher rates of survival following cardiac arrest of those below the age of 60. Younger patients have a better chance of surviving such an illness and thus can describe their experiences. Some have suggested that given that a large proportion of those reporting NDEs are self-selected and that they may have both some understanding of the topic and an interest in the experience such rates may be overestimating the precise figures (Roberts & Owen, 1988). Others disagree and point out that the actual occurrence of NDEs may be much higher but people may simply not *remember* the event (Greyson, 2003). The amnesia that often accompanies cardiac arrest may make such recall difficult or impossible. Others have also argued that individuals may be reluctant to come forward and report their experiences for fear of ridicule (see, Fenwick & Fenwick, 2008). Nevertheless, these figures, whilst not precise, would seem to indicate that a large proportion of the population has experienced an NDE at some stage during their life.

Demographics

Researchers have shown that those reporting such experiences do not differ from non-reporting controls in terms of age, race, religion or mental health, place of residence, employment status, personality, IQ or death anxiety (Greyson, 1983, 1998; Kondziella & Olsen, 2019; Locke & Shontz, 1983; Osis & Haraldsson, 1977). Indeed, NDEs reported by children are similar to those reported by adults, though they often lack the life review component as would be expected given their lifespan (see Greyson, 1998). This led Ring (1980) to suggest that however the NDE is brought about the experience itself is much the same across those of different backgrounds. There have been suggestions that women have, and report, deeper experiences compared to men (van Lommel et al., 2001), although, this may represent a reluctance on the part of the males to provide such rich reports of their experiences. Indeed, Moody (1975) found no differences in gender but reported that males were simply less likely to disclose such an experience as they feared ridicule (see also, Greyson, 1983).

Cultural influence

There is evidence of NDE reports coming from a wide variety of cultures (see, Roberts & Owen, 1988). For instance, Kondziella and Olsen (2019) reported cases of NDEs from across 35 different countries worldwide. However, there is some suggestive evidence that NDEs may vary across cultures. For instance, Pasricha and Stevenson (1986) found differences in the reported content of NDEs from American versus Indian experients. The NDEs of native American Indians, for example, included imagery of moccasins, snakes, eagles and bows and arrows, whereas Asian Indians reported encountering Yamraj, the Hindu king of the dead, and Yamdoots, his messengers (see also, Schorer, 1986). Others have reported that apparitions of females were significantly higher in the American population compared to the Indian, though reports of religious figures were fewer for the Americans compared to the Indians, 24% compared to 76%. Also, no Hindu reported seeing Jesus and no Christian a Hindu deity (Osis & Haraldsson, 1977). Such findings clearly suggest that cultural environments can influence and contribute to the content of the NDE (Belanti, Perera, & Jagadheesan, 2008). For instance, Belanti et al. (2008) found notable similarities in the experiences of Mapuche and Hawaiian people, with both including dominant landmarks and no evidence of a life review, as well as between Thai and Indian people who did not report any 'tunnel' type experience or meeting deceased acquaintances. Hence, there are some aspects of the NDE that may be more strongly influenced by culture than others. As such, cultural influences need to be considered when attempting to interpret any NDE.

Situations

NDEs have been reported in a wide variety of situations including childbirth (Greyson & Stevenson, 1980), terminal illness, accidents (Roberts & Owen, 1988) and suicide (Ring & Franklin, 1982). Indeed, an early review by Roberts and Owen (1988) noted that the physical circumstances of the NDE did not appear to have a major impact on its phenomenological consistency, though some have found that the likelihood of reporting an NDE is reduced by brain damage with only a low correlation between illness and experience showing for those on sedative drugs (Gabbard & Twemlow, 1991; Osis & Haraldsson, 1977). Interestingly, one review did find that patients admitted with cardiac arrest reported significantly more NDEs than patients admitted with other cardiac problems (Greyson, 2003). This was suggested to support an association between how near death the individual patient was and the experiences they had, with those suffering cardiac arrest being closer to death and experiencing more of the NDE components. Others have also found that patients judged to have been closer to death during an illness were more likely to report enhanced perception of light and enhanced cognitive powers compared to a group who were ill but not in danger of dying (Owens, Cook, & Stevenson, 1990). However, a more recent survey of reported NDE type experiences across 35 countries found that NDEs occurred equally likely in truly life-threatening situations *and* situations that only felt life-threatening (Kondziella & Olsen, 2019). Hence, the relationship between the NDE and how close to death the individual really is may be more complex than originally thought.

Evidence of an NDE

Throughout the literature there are many case studies detailing the personal experiences of those that have undergone an NDE (e.g., Corazza, 2008; Fenwick & Fenwick, 2008; Lorimer, 2017; Parnia, 2008; Parnia & Young, 2013; van Lommel, 2010). However, it should be noted that some point out that this does not mean that the experiences are real, in the sense that they represent a potential reality (Blackmore, 2005; Fischer & Mitchell-Yellin, 2016). Even if there is life after death, which is by no means certain and remains a contentious point, Blackmore (2005) argues that such experiences cannot constitute proof of such things. For instance, it is always possible to argue that the person did not die and therefore the experience is a part of life and not death (Blackmore, 1996; Roberts & Owen, 1988). Furthermore, given that it is difficult to predict the occurrence of an NDE some have suggested that obtaining direct evidence for the experience may not even be possible (Greyson, 1998, 2015). Indeed, despite the fact that NDEs have been reported and reviewed for over 40 years there is still a lack of empirical data which would allow any firm conclusions to be drawn (Sleutjes, Moreira-Almeida, & Greyson, 2014). Hence, whilst the potential implications of the NDE may be far reaching there is no doubt that it represents a distinct methodological challenge to mainstream science. For example, the gold standard methodology for scientific research often includes a double-blind, randomly controlled, placebo comparison approach. However, it should be obvious that such a method cannot be used here. It is not possible to randomly allocate people to different conditions with the expectation that some *may* have an NDE at some unspecified date in the future. It is also unclear at this stage precisely what a placebo NDE would be. Hence, at present, there is a reliance on case study reports from the following areas of research. The first details cases of reported NDEs from children. The second deals with veridical reports obtained during the NDE. The third relates to perceptions during an NDE that are not possible during waking consciousness, and finally there are cases of meeting individuals during the NDE.

The NDEs of children

An important point relating to NDEs occurring in children is that they are argued to be less likely the result of prior knowledge, or religious expectations (van Lommel, 2010). Interestingly, the rate of children who experience an NDE due to a life-threatening illness is higher than that seen in the adult population (van Lommel et al., 2001), though this may be influenced by their ability to survive a critical illness. Furthermore, the NDE reports made by children are similar to those reported by adults, though they are often more simplistic (Morse, 1994; van Lommel, 2010). For example, surveys of children aged from 3 to 16 years of age who had survived a critical illness and reported NDE type experiences included core components such as the out of body experience, seeing their physical body from above, travelling in a tunnel and a return to the body (Morse, Castillo, Venecia, Milstein, & Tyler, 1986). However, others have suggested that children's reports can be fragmentary and that the sample is too small to enable any firm conclusions to be drawn (Blackmore, 1996).

An illustrative case reported by Morse (1983) describes the NDE of a 7-year-old child who nearly drowned. The child in question, a young girl, was in excellent health prior to experiencing a near-drowning in a community swimming pool. The trauma resulted in her losing consciousness and being hospitalised. After two weeks she showed a full recovery with only mild short-term memory impairment. During an examination she was asked what, if anything, she remembered of her experience. She recalled talking to the 'heavenly Father and then became embarrassed and would not discuss it further' (Morse, 1983, p. 960). At a follow-up interview one week later, the child revealed that during the experience she thought she was dead, then experienced a tunnel which became bright and a woman appeared and together they walked towards heaven (see Box 10.1).

Morse (1983) noted that the child was from a deeply religious background which may to some extent account for the religious content of her experience. Nevertheless, he also points out that the reported events were consistent with the core experiences of a typical NDE, including the tunnel and being of light as well as meeting dead relatives and being offered the choice to return. Such points, he argues, would not necessarily emerge due to her religious background. There are other cases of children reporting such experiences during a critical illness, some as young as nine months (e.g., Corazza, 2008; Ring & Valarino, 2000).

Veridical perceptions during an NDE

Veridical NDEs are where people reportedly have an NDE and observe events or gather information that is later verified by an additional source. Given that the

---

Box 10.1   The case of the child NDE

The following case was reported by a child who nearly drowned. When asked what she remembered of the experience the girl said:

> 'I was dead, then I was in a tunnel and it was dark. A bright light appeared and a tall woman and we walked towards heaven … Heaven was fun, bright with lots of flowers'.

The girl reported meeting many people including her grandparents.

She then reported meeting the heavenly Father and Jesus who asked her if she would like to return. She said no.

However, when asked if she would like to see her mother again she answered yes and immediately woke up in the hospital.

(adapted from Morse, 1983, p. 960)

---

individual in question is either clinically dead, or at the very least unconscious, such perceptions are thought to be physically impossible and not explicable by conventional means. However, verifying the accuracy of such reported cases is often difficult as the focus of medical staff at the time is on the resuscitation of the patient and documenting such experiences often occurs much later in time.

Possibly one of the most well-known cases is that of *Maria*, who while visiting friends in the USA suffered a severe heart attack and was rushed to hospital (Clark, 1984). Whilst in hospital she suffered a cardiac arrest during which she had an unusual out of body experience where she found herself outside the hospital on a ledge of the third floor where she saw a single tennis shoe. Once resuscitated Maria provided details of the shoe to her critical care worker who went to the described location and found the shoe. Clark (1984, p. 243) concluded 'the only way she could have had such a perspective was if she had been floating outside at very close range to the tennis shoe'. Another illustrative case of possible veridical perception during an NDE was reported by van Lommel et al. (2001) and related to a case of a clinically dead person whose dentures were removed from his mouth (see Box 10.2). According to van Lommel et al. (2001) the patient was correct about the location of his dentures and was also able to correctly describe the room he was in during the resuscitation process as well as some of those present. Others have suggested that the patient may have in fact been conscious during the process and as such would have naturally felt his dentures being removed and placed in a typical metal cabinet which is standard hospital furniture (Woerlee, 2004). However, Smit (2008) argues that this does not concur with the reported facts of the case. Others have also shown that Woerlee's (2004) attempted interpretation does not fit the data and is patently wrong (Smit & Rivas, 2010).

Some have also reported on cases of individuals having an NDE reporting *improbable objects* in unlikely locations which were later confirmed by at least one

Box 10.2 The case of the missing dentures

The patient in question arrived at the hospital in a comatose condition and was taken to the resuscitation unit. During the resuscitation process the patient's dentures were removed by a nurse and lost in the chaos of the process. The patient was successfully revived and one week later on seeing the nurse he cried out:

> oh, that nurse knows where my dentures are

The nurse was surprised by this, but the patient continued:

> yes you were there when I was brought into the hospital and you took my dentures out of my mouth and put them onto that cart, it had all these bottles on it and there was this sliding drawer underneath and there you put my teeth.

The nurse was amazed because when this happened the patient was in a deep coma and undergoing CPR.

(from van Lommel et al., 2001, p. 2041)

witness (Ring & Lawrence, 1993). For instance, in one case, a nurse talking to a resuscitated patient told of how the patient reported floating up through the hospital and found herself above the roof looking at the skyline. During this experience the patient saw a red object which turned out to be a shoe but was then whisked off to experience other components of the NDE. However, the nurse on relaying this incident to a colleague reported that the colleague then got a janitor to allow him to access the roof where he found a red shoe. Interestingly, when interviewing the nurse the researchers found she was unaware of the case of Maria's tennis shoe. In a second case they report on a nurse working in an intensive care unit who was wearing a new set of plaid shoelaces when she was involved in resuscitating a patient who later identified her as 'the one with the plaid shoelaces' (Ring & Lawrence, 1993, p. 227). A third case involved a nurse who part way through resuscitating a patient with a flat electrocardiogram had to leave and was replaced by someone else. A few days later when the nurse encountered the resuscitated patient he commented 'you looked so much better in your yellow top' (Ring & Lawrence, 1993, p. 228), which shocked the nurse as she had been wearing a yellow top during the attempted resuscitation.

Some have reported on cases of an NDE experient able to provide an extremely accurate account of the events occurring during the resuscitation process whilst the patient was deeply unconscious with eyes closed (Sartori, Badham, & Fenwick, 2006). The events were verified by the attending nurse and physiotherapist as well as documented in his medical notes. However, Blackmore (1993b) has pointed out that it is possible that the recalled experience was based more on knowledge of resuscitation procedures in general than on the precise occurrence in that instance. Given the nature of the topic and its current reliance on such case reports it is perhaps unsurprising that such reports will invariably be open to criticism. Nevertheless, attempts to assess the overall veracity of such claims have produced some suggestive results. For instance, Holden (2009) examined 107 anecdotal case reports of NDEs and found that 38% contained elements that could be considered to represent accurate perceptions. Unfortunately, close inspection of these claims has led to suggestions that many cases did not involve cardiac arrest and as such may have been based on normal brain function, also that the interviews were often carried much later giving rise to bias and false memories, and that there was little external corroboration (see, Craffert, 2015). In general researchers are aware of these issues and are rightly cautious of their interpretation noting that such cases do not constitute proof of the authenticity of the NDE but simply add to the extant literature on possible veridical perceptions during such experiences (e.g., Corazza, 2008; Fenwick & Fenwick, 2008; Lorimer, 2017; Ring & Valarino, 2000; Rivas et al., 2016).

To date, most of the research examining veridical perceptions during an NDE have been retrospective. That is, they are conducted after the individual in question has reported their experience and what follows is a series of interviews to gather evidence from witnesses who were around at the time. This raises several challenges for the NDE researcher. For instance, there may be a long delay between the event and it being reported. This can make it difficult to obtain witness statements and where such statements are obtained they may be based on old, vague memories which research has shown are all too malleable (e.g., Loftus & Palmer, 1996). Hence, some have proposed a more *prospective* approach to assessing aspects of the NDE (Parnia et al., 2014; Sartori et al., 2006). This approach incorporates the use of hidden targets in locations where hospital patients are resuscitated, such as the intensive therapy units (ITU) or intensive care units (ICU), and adopts a procedure of interviewing all patients who experience cardiac arrest during their stay at a hospital thereby reducing the possible influence of memory distortions due to time delays. For instance, in one prospective study shelves were installed in areas where cardiac arrest resuscitation was likely to occur and images placed on these shelves that could only be seen when viewed from above (Parnia et al., 2014). The idea was that these images represented targets which if a patient reported any visual awareness during cardiac arrest they might be able to identify and then report. Unfortunately, the research team had insufficient numbers to offer any clear insights as very few of the patients (~9%) reported an NDE and none reported seeing the target images on the shelves, though to some extent this was due to 78% of cardiac arrests taking place in areas without the shelves and target images. However, such prospective studies should be applauded and encouraged as they may be able to provide more accurate data on the perceptions of those who undergo an NDE.

Perceptions not possible during consciousness

Given the range of visual experiences often recounted as part of the NDE one question researchers have asked is whether those who are blind report such experiences. Such data, if available, would certainly support the idea that some forms of perception are possible during an NDE and would also raise questions regarding the role of the brain in vision. However, surprisingly very little research has been conducted in this area. The one published report by Ring and Cooper (1997) examined the NDEs of blind respondents to answer three main questions. First, if blind people have NDEs that are similar to those of sighted individuals. Second, whether they report any visual experiences during the NDE and finally whether such claims can be independently corroborated. To test this they interviewed 21 blind individuals, 14 who were blind from birth, who had survived or experienced an NDE. They found that blind people, including those blind from birth, recounted experiences that are consistent with the components of the NDE reported by those with sight. In fact, they found that the narratives of blind participants were indistinguishable from those who were sighted in terms of the elements that help to define an NDE. For example, one participant who suffered optic nerve damage following a premature birth reported visual perceptions during an NDE (see Box 10.3).

According to Ring and Cooper (1997) the individual experienced many of the core components of a typical NDE, including seeing a beautiful scene with trees, flowers and tremendous light, meeting individuals who had already died and having a discussion with a religious figure about returning to her body prior to being shown a life review. They report on other cases that also show that blind individuals experience a clear visual representation of objects and the environment during an NDE. In all, they found that just over 70% of blind respondents claimed to have had some kind of sighted experience during their NDE. This led them to conclude that most blind people who experience an NDE do indeed report visual stimuli during the experience. However, they admit that it proved difficult to identify corroborative reports from reliable independent witnesses that the individuals in question were perceiving something as opposed to simply experiencing a complex hallucination. In many cases the reported NDE occurred a long time ago and identifying witnesses who may have been around at the time was often impossible. Hence, for most reported cases the

---

Box 10.3   The case of a blind person's NDE

This individual had never had any visual experience and reportedly did not understand the nature of light due to her blindness. As a result of an automobile accident she had an NDE and recounted the following experience of seeing herself

> I knew it was me … I was pretty thin then. And I recognised at first that it was a body, but I didn't even know it was mine initially. Then I perceived that I was up on the ceiling, and I thought, 'well, that's kind of weird. What am I doing up here?' I thought, 'well this must me be. Am I dead?'

Later she reported about her visual experienced during the NDE

> I had a hard time relating to it [i.e., the visual experience] because I've never experienced it. And it was something very foreign to me. It was like hearing words and not being able to understand them, but knowing they were words.

(adapted from Ring & Cooper, 1997)

veracity of the claims relies on the truthfulness and accuracy of the individual making the report. Ring and Cooper (1997) acknowledge that as a rule they have no cause to question the sincerity of the respondents but as they accurately point out 'sincerity is not evidence' (p. 120).

If someone who is blind can accurately identify information and/or individuals from their NDE environment this would help deal with issues of contamination via expectation and would also address concerns that someone who may be partially conscious could perceive some aspects of their environment. In fact, there is no need to limit this research to those that are blind. Exploring the NDEs of those who are deaf to ascertain whether they *hear* any of the conversations that occur during their resuscitation could also prove interesting. For now, however, such intriguing questions remain the domain of future research.

NDE meetings

The literature contains many case reports of individuals undergoing an NDE and experiencing the presence of a deceased person (e.g., Bailey & Yates, 1996; Rivas et al., 2016; van Lommel, 2010). This phenomenon is thought to occur widely across different cultures. There are two main types of NDE meetings, the first is with known deceased persons, usually friends or family members that the individual may recognise and feel a strong emotional connection with. The second, and potentially more interesting, is with those the individual does not recognise at the time but is able to later identify (see Box 10.4).

Meeting with deceased relatives or familiar friends is more frequently reported and to some extent may simply represent a level of wish fulfilment. The more intriguing cases are those where the experiencer at the time of the NDE does not know the person and only later finds out who they are. For instance, Rivas et al. (2016) outline five case reports of individuals meeting deceased strangers who following the NDE

Box 10.4   Examples of NDE communication

With deceased friends or family members

> suddenly I recognised all these relatives … my parents were there too.
>
> (van Lommel, 2010, p. 33)

With strangers

> during my NDE following a cardiac arrest … I saw a man who looked at me lovingly but whom I didn't know. Over ten years later my mother confided on her deathbed that I'd been born from an extramarital affair; my biological father was a Jewish man who'd been deported and killed in WWII. My mother showed me a photograph … it was the unfamiliar man I'd seen during my NDE.
>
> (adapted from van Lommel, 2010, p. 33)

are identified as friends or family members. One example is the case of 'Colton Burpo' who during his reported NDE was alleged to have met 'Pop', one of his father's grandfathers, whom he later recognised from a family photograph. Such meetings are at least suggestive of the individual possibly obtaining information in an unusual way.

Explanations

The idea that an individual's consciousness could leave or exist beyond the physical body and that during a period of time when the physical body was classified as 'dead' the individual consciously experiences a range of phenomena has led some to claim that this provides suggestive evidence of the continuation of consciousness beyond death (e.g., Corazza, 2008; Fenwick, 1997; Fenwick & Fenwick, 1995; Rivas et al., 2016; van Lommel, 2010). Nevertheless, many remain unconvinced and suggest that such experiences may be the result of a neurological abnormality, or an hallucination, or simply a misrecalled experience that is influenced by expectations (e.g., Blackmore, 2005; Fischer & Mitchell-Yellin, 2016; French, 2005). In general attempts to explain the NDE can be grouped under the headings of neurological, psychological and survival.

Neurological

Neurological approaches have focused on a range on issues including anoxia, temporal lobe dysfunction, neurochemical reactions and cortical disinhibition.

Cerebral anoxia

A lack of oxygen in the brain, or cerebral anoxia, has been suggested to be a causal factor in the NDE. The idea here is that anoxia may produce a disinhibition of neural firing resulting in a rapid activation of the cortex which in turn is responsible for the unusual experiences associated with an NDE. Rodin (1980) was one of the first to point out the similarities between an NDE and the experiences of an individual suffering from cerebral anoxia. This included characteristic changes in perception and attitude, with a sense of well-being, the loss of critical judgements, and hallucinations and delusions. This led him to conclude that the NDE is a product of an anoxic brain. In addition, Blackmore and Troscianko (1989) have suggested that the organisation of the visual cortex which has a greater number of cells devoted to the centre of the visual field could, if rapidly activated, produce effects of a brighter light at the centre which fades to the periphery, an effect which may account for the 'tunnel like' experiences of an NDE (see also, Blackmore, 1996, 2005). However, Sabom (1998) has argued that anoxia often leads to confused thinking not the clear and lucid thoughts reported by those having an NDE. Others have also shown that the physiological factors resulting from cerebral anoxia are not related to the occurrence of an NDE (van Lommel et al., 2001). Furthermore, a recent study by Parnia et al. (2001) reported that cardiac patients that had experienced an NDE had significantly *higher* levels of oxygen in their brain at the time of the NDE compared to non-experients. Such findings would suggest that anoxia is not a causative factor in NDEs and may in fact mitigate against them.

Temporal lobe activation/dysfunction

Researchers noting the similarities between experiences reported during an NDE and those occurring as a result of temporal lobe epilepsy or dysfunction have led to the formulation of ideas proposing that an NDE may be the result of a temporal lobe dysfunction (e.g., Britton & Bootzin, 2004; Carr, 1982). According to Carr (1982) the extreme stress of being near death induces hyperactivity in the limbic lobe, which may result in the NDE. Indeed, there is some evidence to suggest that increased activity in the temporal lobe may play a role in the NDE. For instance, Persinger (1999) has argued that electrical stimulation of the temporal lobe junction can produce feelings of bodily distortions such that the individual may 'feel' as though they are outside of their physical body (see also, Persinger, Saroka, Mulligan, & Murphy, 2010). Others have also reported greater neural activity in the temporal lobe during sleep of those that experienced an NDE compared to those that had not (Britton & Bootzin, 2004).

Hence, the central idea here is that an NDE, or at the very least that aspect associated with out of body experiences, may be the result of abnormal firing or activation at the temporal-parietal junction. However, it should be noted that the EEG recordings reported by Britton and Bootzin (2004) were taken some time after the NDE experiences and as such it is difficult to disentangle cause and effect. Furthermore, whilst there may be some similarities between distortion of temporal/parietal activity and a sub-component of the NDE there are also distinct differences. For instance, a seizure is often accompanied by feelings of fear, loneliness and distorted perception. This is at odds with many of the reported elements of an NDE (e.g., van Lommel, 2010). There are many other elements of the NDE that do not conform to the pattern evident during a seizure, including the reports of meeting deceased relatives. In addition, epileptics characteristically experience unpleasant burning or rotting olfactory experiences. In contrast, those who experience an NDE often report very positive perfumed, flowery smells (Neppe, 1989). Indeed, such points have led researchers to point out that any brain dysfunction is likely to produce clouded thinking, irritability, fear, idiosyncratic visions quite unlike the clear thinking, peaceful, calm content of the typical NDE (e.g., Greyson, 1998; van Lommel, 2010). Furthermore, claims linking the NDE to abnormalities in temporal/parietal lobe functioning would lead to the proposal that NDEs should be more prominent in this patient group. However, there is no clear evidence of this in the literature. Finally, given the wide range of experiences that make up an NDE Neppe (1989) has pointed out that it would be unlikely for such a range of experiences to derive from, or be associated with, a single anatomical locus. It may well be that the various aspects of the NDE rely on distinct neurological structures and processes.

Neurochemical reactions

When stressed, the brain of an individual may release endorphins, a natural morphine-like substance, which helps the individual cope with such stresses and pains. Such findings led Carr (1982) to suggest that endorphin release may account for the NDE as it can induce feelings of well-being and pleasure, which may be responsible for the positive emotions experienced by those reporting an NDE. However, Jansen (1997) argued that endorphins are not potent enough to elicit the long-lasting effects of an NDE. Nevertheless, many researchers have noted the similarities recorded by those taking various hallucinogenic drugs and the experiences reported by those who have undergone an NDE (see e.g., Martial et al., 2019). For instance, one suggestion is that the experiences of an NDE are similar to the hallucinations brought on by using lysergic acid (Morse, Venecia, & Milstein, 1989). Here, Morse et al. (1989) argue that the NDE may be the result of activation of serotonergic neuronal pathways in the temporal lobes, the activation of which may be the result of severe psychological and/or physiological stress or via the use of certain psychoactive drugs. Indeed, when they applied a scale of NDE type experiences retrospectively to five case histories of patients treated with LSD, three of them scored as having moderate NDEs. They go on to suggest that this may represent a defence mechanism of the brain to severe or stressful situations. Rogo (1984) was one of the first to put forward the idea that many of the NDE elements have been reported by those using the dissociative anaesthetic ketamine. Since then others have noted similarities in the experiences of those taking ketamine to the experiences reported from an NDE (Martial et al., 2019). According to Jansen (1997) the use of ketamine may reproduce an NDE type experience by blocking glutamate receptors in the brain and inducing experiences of tunnels, lights and sensations of telepathic communication with what appear to be mystical entities. Others highlight the similarities between reported experiences induced by *N,N-Dimethyltryptamine (DMT)* and some of the reported components of the NDE (Timmermann et al., 2018).

There is no doubt that it is possible to modify ordinary waking consciousness by ingesting certain chemical substances and that this can provide some interesting insights into states of consciousness. However, the suggestion that such alterations in neurochemical functioning may account for an NDE is questionable as it represents an argument from association which is inherently weak and can be problematic if taken too far (see Box 10.5).

Hence, at best, these various drugs can elicit behaviours and/or experiences that may *mimic* some aspects of the NDE but they do not induce an NDE. It is clear that no one has died during this research and experienced a full NDE. Furthermore, the effects of these drugs are often wide ranging and varied, whereas the reported NDEs tend to be more consistent. In addition, Strassman (1997) has argued that the influence of such psychoactive drugs depends more on the individual in question, what their expectations are and what those who administer the drug also expect. Hence, any model attempting to account for NDEs that included or relied on such drugs would also need to look at the interaction of the substance with the psychology and biology of the individual as well as the social environment. Moreover, unlike the experiences reported during an NDE many ketamine experiences are frequently fearful and rarely regarded as real or pleasant by the experiencer (Fenwick, 1997; Strassman, 1997). In addition, whilst some have reported no clear relationship between medication and the frequency of a reported NDE (e.g., van Lommel et al., 2001), others have found that patients administered anaesthetics or pain killers tend

---

Box 10.5   The limitations of arguing from association

Imagine a situation with three groups of adults, A, B and C. Group A are a healthy control group and take part in a suite of attentional tasks and their performance provides a useful baseline. Group B on the other hand consists of adults diagnosed with attention deficit disorder (ADD). When they take the same suite of attentional tasks their performance is unsurprisingly poorer than the controls. Now, group C consists of a group of otherwise healthy adults who have consumed large quantities of alcohol and as such are intoxicated. When they take the suite of attentional tasks their performance is also worse than the controls. However, it is interesting to note that the pattern of their performance across the various attentional tasks bears a strong similarity to those who suffer from ADD.

Question: Would you infer that ADD is caused by alcohol consumption?

Hopefully not. This, somewhat tongue in cheek example, highlights the problems associated with arguments that attempt to infer causality based only on associations in behaviour and/or performance.

---

to have *less* elaborate and detailed NDEs (see e.g., Blackmore, 1996, Greyson, 1998). Fenwick (1997) has also pointed out that NDEs can occur without any obvious trauma to the brain and/or stress which would mean there was no release of any such chemicals. Hence, a purely neurochemical approach cannot account for the data.

Massive cortical disinhibition

According to Siegel (1980) an NDE is the result of a massive cortical disinhibition, a view echoed by Blackmore (1993a). Here the key point is that normal waking consciousness is reliant upon controlled neural activity and that this is severely disrupted during an NDE which in turn leads to an altered state of consciousness. A key aspect of this disorientation, according to Siegel (1980), is the loss of a clear sense of self. Another is for internally generated visual activity to be misinterpreted as a perceptual-like experience. Hence, the visual experiences that occur during an NDE may be more representative of visual memories re-activated as a function of disordered cortical activity. However, once again this view may account for *some* of the limited experiences that occur during an NDE but it fails to fully account for the data. A key limitation is the point that massive cortical disinhibition would lead to severely disrupted neural behaviour and yet somehow leave the brain sufficiently intact to enable the production of clear and vivid memories. It also fails to explain why such disrupted neural activity would generate specific memories of deceased relatives and produce such positive transformative insights (Greyson, 1998, 2006, 2015).

Psychological

Similarly, a range of psychological explanations have been put forward to account for the NDE, the most prominent being simple expectation effects, depersonalisation, mistimed perceptions and motivated fantasies.

Expectation

According to Blackmore (2005) expectation may play a big part in the NDE as individuals do not need to be physically *near* death in order to have such experiences (see also, Blackmore, 1996). For instance, the feeling of being 'out of the body' has been reported in many other instances that do not involve being near death. Furthermore, some of the experiences reported to occur during an NDE, particularly in terms of encountering a religious presence, often reflect cultural norms or values. Nevertheless, Blackmore (2005) does admit that expectation effects alone cannot provide a comprehensive account of the NDE. Indeed, van Lommel (2010) points out that for many people the content of their NDE does not match their expectations of death. People who believe that death is the end of everything have very similar experiences to those who hold strong beliefs about a possible afterlife. In addition, if the NDE were based largely on expectations these would be expected to change as more information about the various experiences are reported in the popular media. However, Lester (2003) has shown that the reported features of NDE accounts show little variation over time, suggesting that they represent consistent aspects of the experience.

Depersonalisation

Depersonalisation refers to the idea that an individual may experience a psychological detachment from their own body. This depersonalisation may come about as a psychological response to physical trauma, in the form of a defence mechanism (Noyes, 1979; Noyes & Kletti, 1977). According to Noyes (1972) the perception of imminent death is a key prerequisite for the NDE, encouraging a split or depersonalisation of the individual into an observing self and participating self. In a sense the idea is that the person facing death attempts to remove themselves from the situation by becoming a disinterested observer. This dissociation from the awareness of impending death was also thought to characterise the review phase of the NDE process and when the person surrenders to the inevitability of death feelings of fear and anxiety decrease, and more positive feelings of peace and tranquillity are assumed to develop. Indeed, Noyes and Kletti (1977) reported that survivors of life-threatening danger report feelings of depersonalisation, or a feeling of detachment from the environment, as well as distortions in time perception and lack of emotion. However, the concept of depersonalisation also includes a sense of confusion relating to identity of the self, something which is clearly not evident in an NDE. There are also cases of NDE experients not knowing that their life was at stake at the time of the NDE, something which would be difficult to account for if one were to assume it was merely a defence mechanism to trauma. Others have also pointed out that NDEs may differ from depersonalisation on several parameters including the notion that depersonalisation does not usually include feelings of being out of the body; it is also typically unpleasant, unlike most NDEs, is often characterised by feelings of anxiety and panic and rarely occurs in those older than 40 years of age (see Greyson, 1998).

Timing of the NDE

The idea here is that it is not always clear precisely when an NDE occurs. It may be that the brain of the unconscious individual as they move into and out of full unconsciousness is still capable of registering meaningful sounds and events which helps to form memories that later resurface into an imagined reconstruction of what occurred during the period of complete unconsciousness (Fischer & Mitchell-Yellin, 2016). Such cortical processing may be underpinned by a burst of intense cortical hyperconnectivity. This idea has received some support from animal studies showing that dying rat brains exhibit a period of intense coordinated brainwave activity near death (Borjigin et al., 2013). Furthermore, the distortion of the timing of the experience could be similar to that found in dreams. For instance, during the night an individual may have one or more dreams and these dreams can be both lucid and temporally distinct in the sense that in the dream much may occur but in reality very little time may have passed. Hence, the intense brain activity that may occur as an individual nears death underpins the NDE and makes it feel as though the experience continued for longer than it did. Thus, the experiences do not occur when the individual is fully unconscious or noted as clinically dead but as they enter into and emerge from such states. Hence, despite the claims by some that an NDE may have occurred during a period of brain inactivity, which could be taken as evidence to support the notion of such events (see, van Lommel et al., 2001), it is possible, and perhaps more *probable*, that the experience of the individual did not occur when their brain was 'off line', but just before or afterwards, when brain function returned (see e.g., French, 2001). Though an intriguing proposal, others disagree and argue that such changes in cortical functioning would be presumed to limit and/or restrict the possible NDE type experiences, which is not the case (Parnia et al., 2001). Furthermore, changes in cortical activity as an individual transitions into unconsciousness, as measured by EEG in cases of cardiac arrest, are quick and as such it has been suggested that this would not allow sufficient time for such experiences to play out (Parnia et al., 2001). Furthermore, others have argued that experiences occurring during the recovery period are often confused and lack the clarity of an NDE (Parnia & Fenwick, 2002; Parnia et al., 2014). Indeed, Parnia and Fenwick (2002) argue that any injury or illness that leads to a period of unconsciousness is likely to produce both anterograde and retrograde amnesia. Therefore, events occurring prior to or just after a loss of consciousness would not be expected to be recalled. Furthermore, the recovery in such situations is not straightforward and is often slow and disjointed. Hence, whilst it may be possible that such a confused revival may be responsible for the spontaneous occurrence of simple stimuli such as a light or perceived tunnel it is not possible to explain away the detailed and specific visual/motor and emotional memories that result from such experiences.

Motivated fantasy

The idea here is that the individual is motivated by denial of death into producing a fantasy based on popular social images and events of what constitutes an NDE (Walker, 1989). Hence the NDE is the product of imagination, constructed from personal and cultural expectations, to protect the individual from facing the threat and fear of death. Such an idea is superficially simplistic, though there is some support for the notion that those who report NDEs may be more fantasy prone (Council & Greyson, 1985). However, as van Lommel (2010) points out, it is not clear how this would explain why children have very similar NDEs or why people would fantasise about travelling in a dark tunnel. As mentioned above there are also those who report an NDE that may conflict with their religious or spiritual expectations. In addition, familiarity with the phenomenon does not seem to influence the details of the experience (see Greyson, 1998). Furthermore, a comparison of NDE type memories relating to real and imagined events has shown that the real memories are distinctly different from those relating to imagined events (Moore & Greyson, 2017). Memories from a real NDE were rated as containing a greater level of visual detail, spatial and temporal information, clarity and emotional intensity. This they suggest would fit the claims of those who have them as being 'more real' than real events. Hence, the idea that an NDE is the result of a motivated fantasy is not supported by the data.

Survival of consciousness

It is possible that the only agreement between researchers is that of the many attempts that have been put forward to account for the NDE most are, at best, able to account for one or two aspects of the experience whilst none can offer a full account (Bókkon, Mallick, & Tuszynski, 2013). Hence, a plausible alternative is that something beyond the brain is responsible for the experience. That human consciousness can exist independently of the body. According to Greyson (1998) this is the explanation most endorsed by those who have experienced an NDE. That is, that during the experience some aspect of themselves separated from their physical body and experienced a glimpse of something different that may reflect what happens when we naturally and eventually die. Of course, direct and independent evidence to support this view is difficult if not impossible to obtain. In addition, it is important to note that as Roberts and Owen (1988) point out, the individuals reporting such experiences can at best only be considered as having entered the early and reversible phases of the dying process. Others have suggested that our technology may at present be insufficient to accurately identify whether any brain activity is still occurring and that the NDE is in fact evidence for the notion that there is undetected brain activity mediating such experiences (Blackmore, 2005). However, van Lommel et al. (2001) point out that the NDE is pushing at the scientific limits of what is known about brain functioning and consciousness. They also highlight that the current consensus which takes the view that consciousness and memories reside *only* in the brain is an unproven assumption. Indeed, there is evidence from mainstream science showing that memories may be transmitted across generations which would suggest that storage of such events may not rely solely in the brain (e.g., Dias & Ressler, 2013). Hence, many in the field argue that it is important to consider the notion that the NDE is the result of an altered state of consciousness, in which a conscious entity may be capable of functioning independent of an unconscious physical body (e.g., Corazza, 2008; Fenwick & Fenwick, 1995; Parnia, 2008; Parnia & Young, 2013; Rivas et al., 2016; Sabom, 1998; van Lommel, 2010).

Implications

Regardless of the cause of the NDE there is a clear consensus that it dramatically and permanently alters the individual's attitudes, beliefs, values and behaviour. Following the NDE an experient typically undergoes life changes of a kind not usually reported by people who survive a near-death event without experiencing an NDE (Greyson, 2006; Parnia & Fenwick, 2002; Parnia, Spearpoint, & Fenwick, 2007; van Lommel et al., 2001). Indeed, some have suggested that this may be the most important aspect of the NDE (Greyson, 1998). These changes can include some or all of the following:

- An absence or reduced fear of death
- Loss of interest in money and material possessions
- Increased love and compassion for others
- A renewed appreciation for family and friends and for nature
- Feeling part of something larger, more profound and eternal
- Career and relationship upheavals.

Perhaps unsurprisingly, many show an increased level of belief in religious ideas whilst also showing greater tolerance of religious differences (Gabbard & Twemlow, 1991). For instance, Sabom and Kreutziger (1982) found that 69% of their sample who had experienced an NDE showed an increased level of belief in life after death. In general, there is also a shift away from materialistic goals towards finding greater meaning, purpose and fulfilment in life. Interestingly Berman (1974) found that such positive changes were not evident in people who had experienced a close brush with death but not undergone an NDE. However, Greyson and Stevenson (1980) have suggested that the closer the individual may feel to death the more extensive and intense their experience may be. Indeed, Pope (1994) has suggested that it is the brush with death that produces these changes in attitudes and behaviour and not the NDE per se. However, others have shown that those who do experience an NDE report the event as more life changing than those who do not (Bonenfant, 2004). Furthermore, the transformational effects that occur as a result of the NDE may take several years to consolidate (van Lommel et al., 2001).

Overall it would seem that the NDE elicits a positive change in the attitudes and behaviour of the experient. However, the aftereffects of such an experience are not universally positive. For instance, some may exhibit emotional problems including anger and depression at having been resuscitated and 'unwillingly' returned to their life (Greyson, 1998; van Lommel, 2010). They may also have problems adjusting their world view following the experience and the changes in behaviour and values brought about by the experience can also require a period of adjustment, both for the individual in question and for close family and friends. Such adjustments are not always easy and can in some instances have a disruptive effect on family relationships, with those who had the NDE showing not only greater compassion but also an increased fascination with what other family members may perceive as mystical and psychic concepts (e.g., Greyson, 1998, 2006, 2015; Insinger, 1991). This fractionation may be exacerbated by the difficulties reported by experients when they try and fail to communicate what they feel is the ineffable quality of the experience (West, 1998). Some have suggested that counselling may be required to help the individual adjust back into their 'normal life' (Holden, 2009). Unfortunately, the disruptive changes and adjustments that occur following an NDE often lead to divorce between spouses. For instance, up to 75% of the marriages of those who experience an NDE end in divorce, compared to the 40–50% in the general population (Bush, 1991; Christian, 2005). Hence, there is no doubt that those who experience an NDE are transformed by their experience. However, such changes can be challenging both for them and for those around them.

Overview

Death is a thread that connects us all. No one knows with any certainty what happens when we die. However, there are an increasing number of people who have been resuscitated from death, or near death, and report a range of experiences during the time they were assumed to be dead. These near-death experiences can include a variety of components including hearing oneself pronounced dead, feeling separated from and seeing the physical body, strong feelings of peace and tranquillity, bright lights, encounters with spiritual beings and/or deceased relatives and friends, a life review and reaching a border where the decision to go on or return may be made. However, not all NDEs contain all these components and the order may vary from one person to the next. The demographic information shows that there is nothing unique about those that report having an NDE and that such experiences are universally present across different cultures and can occur as a result of various situations. Given the nature of the NDE the veracity of the claims of those who experience such an event are often based primarily on their case reports. Case reports of NDEs from children would at least suggest that such experiences are not based solely on prior knowledge and/or expectations. The data from cases examining veridical perceptions during an NDE are suggestive but not conclusive. It may be that prospective studies, if continued, will be able to shed more light on this area and the examination of NDEs from those who are blind or deaf could potentially be a fruitful area of future research. As such, the overall level of evidence supporting the claims made during NDEs is somewhat limited. However, researchers should continue to study NDEs for a number of reasons. First, such experiences, whether real or not, occur in patients near death and they deserve to be treated with dignity and respect. It is also possible that open discussion of such events may help others to face death. Second, they often lead to profound changes in the behaviour of those that survive. Furthermore, they raise very interesting questions regarding the interaction between mind and brain. Attempts to explain NDEs has led to a number of ideas having been put forward from both neurological and psychological perspectives. Such theories are often able to shed light on one aspect of the NDE; however, at present, there is no clear emerging theory that provides a plausible interpretation of all aspects of what is clearly a multidimensional process. Despite the difficulties in attempting to account for the NDE there is a clear consensus in the literature that undergoing such an experience can often have profound and positive life-changing effects on the experient's attitudes and behaviour. This can be challenging to deal with, both for the individual in question and for those around them. Given the challenges involved in studying NDEs it may be that definitive evidence supporting or refuting the notion that some aspect of human consciousness is able to exist beyond the physical body is simply not possible. Perhaps the reports of these experiences leading to a more open discussion of the nature of death and dying represents the field's primary contribution. It may be that only when we learn to acknowledge the certainty of death that we embrace the transient joy of life.

Useful online resources

* http://www.nderf.org
* https://iands.org/

Reflective questions

Some questions that may prove helpful when reflecting on the material covered in this chapter.

* How would you classify an NDE?
* What are the implications of multiple types/sub-types of NDE?
* Why do you think only some people who die and are resuscitated experience an NDE?
* How would you design a study to examine the veracity of NDE claims?
* What evidence do you find most compelling and why?
* What do you think is the best theoretical account of an NDE?
* What are some of the implications of the NDE?
* If the evidence supporting NDEs was irrefutable how would it change the way you lived?
* What do you think happens to you when you die?

References

Agrillo, C. (2011). Near-death experience: Out-of-body and out-of-brain? *Review of General Psychology, 15*(1), 1–10. doi: 10.1037/a0021992.

Atwater, P. M. (1992). Is there a hell? Surprising observations about the near-death experience. *Journal of Near-Death Studies, 10*(3), 149–160.

Bailey, L. W., & Yates, J. (Eds.). (1996). *The near death experience: A reader.* New York: Routledge.

Belanti, J., Perera, M., & Jagadheesan, K. (2008). Phenomenology of near-death experiences: A cross-cultural perspective. *Transcultural Psychiatry, 45*(1), 121–133.

Berman, A. L. (1974). Belief in afterlife, religion, religiosity and life-threatening experiences. *OMEGA – Journal of Death and Dying, 5*(2), 127–135.

Blackmore, S. (1993a). *Dying to live: Science and the near death experience.* London: Grafton.

Blackmore, S. (1993b). Near-death experiences in India: They have tunnels too. *Journal of Near-Death Studies, 11*(4), 205–217.

Blackmore, S. (1996). Near-death experiences. *Journal of the Royal Society of Medicine, 89*, 73–76.

Blackmore, S. (2005). Near-death experiences. In J. Henry (Ed.), *Parapsychology: Research on exceptional experiences* (pp. 196–203). Hove, East Sussex: Routledge.

Blackmore, S., & Troscianko, T. S. (1989). The physiology of the tunnel. *Journal of Near-Death Studies*, 8(1), 15–28.

Bókkon, I., Mallick, B. N., & Tuszynski, J. A. (2013). Near death experiences: A multi-disciplinary hypothesis. *Frontiers in Human Neuroscience*, 7, 533–544. doi: 10.3389/fnhum.2013.00533.

Bonenfant, R. J. (2004). A comparative study of near-death experience and non-near-death experience outcomes in 56 survivors of clinical death. *Journal of Near-Death Studies*, 22(3), 155–178.

Borjigin, J., Lee, U., Liu, T., Pal, D., Huff, S., Klarr, D., … & Mashour, G. A. (2013). Surge of neurophysiological coherence and connectivity in the dying brain. *Proceedings of the National Academy of Sciences*, 110(35), 14432–14437.

Britton, W. B., & Bootzin, R. R. (2004). Near-death experiences and the temporal lobe. *Psychological Science*, 15(4), 254–258.

Bush, N. E. (1991). Is ten years a life review? *Journal of Near-Death Studies*, 10(1), 5–9.

Carr, D. (1982). Pathophysiology of stress-induced limbic lobe dysfunction: A hypothesis for NDEs. *Anabiosis*, 2, 75–89.

Christian, S. R. (2005). *Marital satisfaction and stability following a near-death experience of one of the marital partners*. University of North Texas, Denton, Texas (unpublished doctoral dissertation).

Clark, K. (1984). Clinical interventions with near-death experiencers. In B. Greyson & C. P. Flynn (Eds.), *The near-death experience: Problems, prospects, perspectives* (pp. 242–255). Springfield, IL: Charles C. Thomas.

Corazza, O. (2008). *Near-death experiences: Exploring the mind-body connection*. London: Routledge.

Council, J. R., & Greyson, B. (1985). *Near-death experiences and the 'FantasyProne' personality: Preliminary findings*. Paper presented at the 93rd Annual American Psychological Association, Los Angeles.

Craffert, P. F. (2015). Do out-of-body and near-death experiences point towards the reality of nonlocal consciousness? A critical evaluation. *The Journal for Transdiciplinary Research in Southern Africa*, 11(1), 1–20.

Dias, B. G., & Ressler, K. J. (2013). Parental olfactory experience influences behaviour and neural structure in subsequent generations. *Nature Neuroscience*, 17, 89–96.

Drab, K. J. (1981). The tunnel experience: Reality or hallucination? *Anabiosis: The Journal of Near-Death Studies*, 1, 126–152.

Fenwick, P. (1997). Is the near-death experience only N-methyl-D-aspartate blocking? *Journal of Near-Death Studies*, 16(1), 43–53.

Fenwick, P., & Fenwick, E. (1995). *The truth in the light: An investigation of over 300 near-death experiences*. New York: Berkley Books.

Fenwick, P., & Fenwick, E. (2008). *The art of dying: A journey to elsewhere*. London: Bloomsbury.

Fischer, J. M., & Mitchell-Yellin, B. (2016). *Near-death experiences: Understanding visions of the afterlife*. New York: Oxford University Press.

French, C. C. (2001). Dying to know the truth: visions of a dying brain, or false memories? *The Lancet*, 358(9298), 2010–2011. doi: 10.1016/S0140-6736(01)07133-1.

French, C. C. (2005). Near-death experiences in cardiac arrest survivors. *Progress in Brain Research*, 150, 351–367.

Gabbard, G. O., & Twemlow, S. W. (1991). Do 'near-death experiences' occur only near death? – revisited. *Journal of Near-Death Studies*, 10(1), 41–47.

Grey, M. (1985). *Return from death: An exploration of the near-death experience*. London: Arcana.

Greyson, B. (1983). The near-death experience scale construction, reliability and validity. *Journal of Nervous and Mental Disease, 171*(6), 369–375.

Greyson, B. (1985). A typology of near-death experiences. *American Journal of Psychiatry, 142*(8), 967–969.

Greyson, B. (1993). Varieties of near-death experience. *Psychiatry, 56*, 390–399.

Greyson, B. (1998). Biological aspects of near-death experiences. *Perspectives in Biology and Medicine, 42*(1), 14–32.

Greyson, B. (2003). Incidence and correlates of near-death experiences in a cardiac care unit. *General Hospital Psychiatry, 25*, 269–276.

Greyson, B. (2006). Near-death experiences and spirituality. *Zygon, 41*(2), 393–414.

Greyson, B. (2015). Western scientific approaches to near-death experiences. *Humanities, 4*, 775–796. doi: 10.3390/h4040775.

Greyson, B., & Bush, N. E. (1992). Distressing near-death experiences. *Psychiatry, 55*, 95–110.

Greyson, B., & Stevenson, I. (1980). The phenomenology of near-death experiences. *The American Journal of Psychiatry, 137*(10), 1193–1196. doi: 10.1176/ajp.137.10.1193.

Holden, J. M. (2009). Veridical perception in near-death experiences. In J. M. Holden, B. Greyson, & D. James (Eds.), *The handbook of near-death experiences: Thirty years of investigation* (pp. 185–211). Santa Barbara, CA: Praeger.

Insinger, M. (1991). The impact of a near-death experience on family relationships. *Journal of Near-Death Studies, 9*(3), 141–181.

Irwin, H. J., & Bramwell, B. A. (1988). The devil in heaven: A near-death experience with both positive and negative facets. *Journal of Near-Death Studies, 7*(1), 38–43.

Jansen, K. L. R. (1997). The ketamine model of the near-death experience: A central role for the n-methyl-d-aspartate receptor. *Journal of Near-Death Studies, 16*(1), 5–26.

Katz, J., Saadon-Grosman, N., & Arzy, S. (2017). The life review experience: Qualitative and quantitative characteristics. *Consciousness and Cognition, 48*, 76–86. doi: 10.1016/j.concog.2016.10.011.

Kondziella, D., & Olsen, M. H. (2019). Prevalence of near-death experiences and REM sleep intrusion in 1034 adults from 35 countries. *bioRxiv.* doi: 10.1101/532341.

Lester, D. (2003). Depth of near-death experiences and confounding factors. *Perceptual and Motor Skills, 96*(1), 18–18.

Locke, T. P., & Shontz, F. C. (1983). Personality correlates of the near-death experience: A preliminary study. *Journal of the American Society for Psychical Research, 77*(4), 311–318.

Loftus, E. F., Palmer, J. C. (1996). Eyewitness testimony. In P. Banyard & A. Grayson (Eds.), *Introducing psychological research* (pp. 305–309). London: Springer.

Lorimer, D. (2017). *Resonant mind: Life review in the near-death experience*. Hove, UK: White Crow Books.

Lundahl, C. R. (1993). The near-death experience: A theoretical summarization. *Journal of Near-Death Studies, 12*(2), 105–118.

Martial, C., Cassol, H., Antonopoulos, G., Charlier, T., Heros, J., Donneau, A.-F., ... & Laureys, S. (2017). Temporality of features in near-death experience narratives. *Frontiers in Human Neuroscience, 11*, 311. doi: 10.3389/fnhum.2017.00311.

Martial, C., Cassol, H., Charland-Verville, V., Pallavicini, C., Sanz, C., Zamberlan, F., ... & Greyson, B. (2019). Neurochemical models of near-death experiences: A large-scale study based on the semantic similarity of written reports. *Consciousness and Cognition, 69*, 52–69.

Moody, R. A. (1975). *Life after life*. San Francisco: Harper.

Moore, L. E., & Greyson, B. (2017). Characteristics of memories for near-death experiences. *Consciousness and Cognition, 51*, 116–124. doi: 10.1016/j.concog.2017.03.003.

Morse, M. (1983). A near-death experience in a 7-year-old child. *American Journal of Diseases of Children, 137,* 959–961.

Morse, M. (1994). Near death experiences and death-related visions in children: Implications for the clinician. *Current Problems in Pediatrics, 24*(2), 55–83. doi: 10.1016/S0045-9380(07)80003-X.

Morse, M., Castillo, P., Venecia, D., Milstein, J., & Tyler, D. C. (1986). Childhood near-death experiences. *American Journal of Diseases of Children, 140*(11), 1110–1114.

Morse, M., Venecia, D., & Milstein, J. (1989). Near-death experiences: A neurophysiologic explanatory model. *Journal of Near-Death Studies, 8*(1), 45–53.

Neppe, V. M. (1989). Near-death experiences: A new challenge in temporal lobe phenomenology? Comments on 'A neurobiological model for near-death experiences'. *Journal of Near-Death Studies, 7*(4), 243–248.

Noyes Jr, R., & Slymen, D. J. (1979). The subjective response to life-threatening danger. *OMEGA – Journal of Death and Dying, 9*(4), 313–321.

Noyes, R. (1979). Near-death experiences: Their interpretation and significance. In R. Kastenbaum (Ed.), *Between life and death* (pp. 73–88). New York: Springer.

Noyes, R., & Kletti, R. (1977). Depersonalization in response to life-threatening danger. *Comprehensive Psychiatry, 18*(4), 375–384.

Osis, K., & Haraldsson, E. (1977). Deathbed observations by physicians and nurses: A cross-cultural survey. *Journal of the American Society for Psychical Research, 71*(3), 237–259.

Owens, J. E., Cook, E. W., & Stevenson, I. (1990). Features of 'near-death experience' in relation to whether or not patients were near death. *The Lancet, 336,* 1175–1177.

Parnia, S. (2008). *What happens when we die: A ground-breaking study into the nature of life and death.* London: Hay House.

Parnia, S., & Fenwick, P. (2002). Near death experiences in cardiac arrest: Visions of a dying brain or visions of a new science of consciousness? *Resuscitation, 52,* 5–11.

Parnia, S., Spearpoint, K., de Vos, G., Fenwick, P., Goldberg, D., Yang, J., ... & Schoenfeld, E. R. (2014). AWARE – AWAreness during REsuscitation – a prospective study. *Resuscitation, 85,* 1799–1805.

Parnia, S., Spearpoint, K., & Fenwick, P. (2007). Near death experiences, cognitive function and psychological outcomes of surviving cardiac arrest. *Resuscitation, 74,* 215–221. doi: 10.1016/j.resuscitation.2007.01.020.

Parnia, S., Waller, D. G., Yeates, R., & Fenwick, P. (2001). A qualitative and quantitative study of the incidence, features and aetiology of near death experiences in cardiac arrest survivors. *Resuscitation, 48*(2), 149–156.

Parnia, S., & Young, J. (2013). *The Lazarus effect: The science that is erasing the boundaries between life and death.* Croydon, UK: Random House.

Pasricha, S., & Stevenson, I. (1986). Near-death experiences in India: A preliminary report. *The Journal of Nervous and Mental Disease, 174*(3), 165–170.

Persinger, M. A. (1999). Near-death experiences and ecstasy: A product of the organization of the human brain. In S. D. Sala (Ed.), *Mind myths: Exploring popular assumptions about the mind and brain* (pp. 85–99). New York, NY: John Wiley & Sons Ltd.

Persinger, M. A., Saroka, K., Mulligan, B. P., & Murphy, T. R. (2010). Experimental elicitation of an out of body experience and concomitant cross-hemispheric electroencephalographic coherence. *NeuroQuantology, 8*(4), 466–477. doi: 10.14704/nq.2010.8.4.302.

Pope, J. E. (1994). Near-death experiences and attitudes towards life, death and suicide. *Australian Parapsychological Review, 19,* 23–26.

Ring, K. (1980). *Life at death: A scientific investigation of the near-death experience.* New York, NY: Coward McCann.

Ring, K. (1994). Frightening near-death experiences revisited: A commentary on responses to my paper by Christopher Bache and Nancy Evans Bush. *Journal of Near-Death Studies, 13*(1), 55–64.

Ring, K., & Cooper, S. (1997). Near-death and out-of-body experiences in the blind: A study of apparent eyeless vision. *Journal of Near-Death Studies, 16*(2), 101–147.

Ring, K., & Franklin, S. (1982). Do suicide survivors report near-death experiences? *OMEGA – Journal of Death and Dying, 12*(3), 191–208.

Ring, K., & Lawrence, M. (1993). Further evidence for veridical perception during near-death experiences. *Journal of Near-Death Studies, 11*(4), 223–229.

Ring, K., & Valarino, E. (2000). *Lessons from the light: What can we learn from the near-death experience?* Cambridge, MA: Moment Point Press.

Rivas, T., Dirven, A., & Smit, R. H. (2016). *The self does not die: Verified paranormal phenomena from near-death experiences.* Durham, NC: IANDS.

Roberts, G., & Owen, J. (1988). The near-death experience. *British Journal of Psychiatry, 153,* 607–617.

Rodin, E. A. (1980). The reality of death experiences: A personal perspective. *Journal of Nervous and Mental Disease, 168*(5), 259–263. doi: 10.1097/00005053-198005000-00001.

Rogo, D. S. (1984). Researching the out-of-body experience: The state of the art. *Anabiosis, 4,* 21–49.

Rogo, D. S. (1986). *Life after death: The case for survival of bodily death.* London: Thorsons Publishing Group.

Sabom, M. B. (1998). *Light and death: One doctor's fascinating account of near-death experiences.* Michigen: Zondervan.

Sabom, M. B., & Kreutziger, S. (1982). Physicians evaluate the near-death experience. In C. R. Lundahl (Ed.), *A collection of near-death research readings.* Chicago: Nelson Hall.

Sartori, P., Badham, P., & Fenwick, P. (2006). A prospectively studied near-death experience with corroborated out-of-body perceptions and unexplained healing. *Journal of Near-Death Studies, 25*(2), 69–84.

Schorer, C. (1986). Two Native American near-death experiences. *OMEGA – Journal of Death and Dying, 16*(2), 111–113.

Schwartz, S. A. (2015). Six protocols, neuroscience, and near death: An emerging paradigm incorporating nonlocal consciousness. *Explore, 11*(4), 252–260.

Siegel, R. (1980). The psychology of life after death. *American Psychologist, 35,* 911–931.

Sleutjes, A., Moreira-Almeida, A., & Greyson, B. (2014). Almost 40 years investigating near-death experinces: An overview of mainstream science journals. *The Journal of Nervous and Mental Disease, 202*(11), 833–836.

Smit, R. H. (2008). Corroboration of the dentures anecdote involving veridical perception in a near-death experience. *Journal of Near-Death Studies, 27*(1), 47–61.

Smit, R. H., & Rivas, T. (2010). Rejoinder to 'Response to corroboration of the dentures anecdote involving veridical perception in a near-death experience'. *Journal of Near-Death Studies, 28*(4), 193–205.

Strassman, R. J. (1997). Endogenous ketamine-line compounds and the NDE: If so, so what? *Journal of Near-Death Studies, 16*(1), 27–41.

Timmermann, C., Roseman, L., Williams, L., Erritzoe, D., Martial, C., Cassol, H., ... & Carhart-Harris, R. (2018). DMT models the near-death experience. *Frontiers in Psychology, 9,* 1424. doi: 10.3389/fpsyg.2018.01424.

Twemlow, S. W., Gabbard, G. O., & Coyne, L. (1982). A multivariate method for the classification of preexisting near-death conditions. *Anabiosis: The Journal of Near-Death Studies, 2*(2), 132–139.

van Lommel, P. (2010). *Consciousness beyond life: The science of the near-death experience.* New York: Harper Collins.

van Lommel, P., van Wees, R., Meyers, V., & Elfferich, I. (2001). Near-death experience in survivors of cardiac arrest: A prospective study in the Netherlands. *The Lancet, 358,* 2039–2045.

Walker, F. O. (1989). A nowhere near-death experience: Heavenly choirs interrupt myelo-graphy. *Journal of the American Medical Association, 261*(22), 3245–3246.

West, T. (1998). On the encounter with a divine presence during a near-death experience. In R. Valle (Ed.), *Phenomenological inquiry in psychology* (pp. 387–405). Boston, MA: Springer.

Woerlee, G. M. (2004). Cardiac arrest and near-death experiences. *Journal of Near-Death Studies, 22,* 235–249.

Chapter 11

Post death phenomena

Many people report experiences or phenomena that relate to someone who has died. In part this may be due to the fact that surveys of the general population often show a large majority (e.g., around 80%) of those who respond state a belief in the survival of something, usually identified as a soul, after death (Bastos Jr, Bastos, Gonçalves, Osório, & Lucchetti, 2015). Indeed, Palmer (1979) noted early on that communication with the dead was one of the most commonly reported paranormal experiences. These post death phenomena may occur in a variety of different ways and circumstances. However, irrespective of the approach used to examine them they all have implications for what is commonly referred to as the *survival hypothesis*. This refers to the idea that some aspect of human consciousness and/or personality survives beyond physical death and that communication with such a discarnate entity may be possible. If so it would have significant implications for our understanding of consciousness and its relationship to the brain, as well as possible implications for assisting the bereaved in dealing with their loss. As such, this chapter explores three lines of enquiry, each of which provides a unique view of some form of post death phenomena. The first relates to spontaneous after death communications. The chapter begins by examining the various types of after death communication along with the reported demographics and prevalence rates. It then examines whether there is any evidence for this and the impact it has on those who experience it before looking at some ideas that have been put forward to account for such experiences. The second line of enquiry examines the assisted mediumistic approach. Here the chapter provides a brief outline of the background and history of mediumship identifying the main types. It then explores the profile of the medium examining research conducted to ascertain whether a medium can obtain accurate information from/or about a deceased individual. The final line of enquiry explores the idea that direct requests for contact with discarnate entities can be made via electronic equipment. This field of research, whilst known about for some time, is still in its infancy and is generally referred to as electronic voice phenomena. Here the chapter briefly explores the background and history of such phenomena and examines whether there is any evidence to support such claims and what explanations have been put forward to account for them.

After death communications

According to LaGrand (2005) encounters with the deceased seem to be common occurrences in the general population and is something that has a long history of reportedly occurring (e.g., Gurney, Myers, & Podmore, 1886; Sidgwick, Sidgwick, & Johnson, 1894). The idea of contact with the dead can take several forms. Here, *after death communication* (ADC) refers to a *spontaneous* event during which a living individual may see, feel or sense the presence of a deceased person (Beischel, 2019; Guggenheim & Guggenheim, 1995; LaGrand, 2005; Sanger, 2009). Other terms have also been used, such as post death contact (Klugman, 2006). According to Beischel (2019) these spontaneous events are likely the most common type of post death phenomenon. Parallel data collected on ADC by researchers in different countries during different eras suggests that the phenomenon itself is real. This has led to suggestions that ADC may demonstrate spirit survival and that surviving discarnates may be able to communicate with the living in a limited way (Wright, 1999, 2006).

Categories of ADC

There is no clear agreement on the precise number and classification of types of ADC. According to Daggett (2005) there are four main categories of ADC. These are visions and dreams, lost-things found, symbolic messages and sightings. However, others also include having a conversation with the deceased (Klugman, 2006), as well as coincidences or synchronicities, communication through electronic devices and other unusual incidents (Beischel, 2014, 2019).

Research suggests that the feeling of a *sensed presence* is one of the most commonly reported ADC experiences (Rees, 1971; Wright, 1999). For example, Barbato, Blunden, Reid, Irwin and Rodriquez (1999) reported that 50% of their respondents experienced the feeling of a sensed presence, making it the most common type of experience. This may range from a vague feeling of the sense of being watched to a stronger sensory experience (G. Bennett & Bennett, 2000). In addition, it is something that may persist, especially if the widow or widower gains comfort from the experience. For instance, G. Bennett and Bennett (2000) found that widows continued to recount such experiences for up to 20 years after a bereavement. Hence, they are not restricted to the early periods of bereavement, though may occur more frequently following such a loss. Other sensory experiences include visual, auditory, tactile and in some cases olfactory sensations (Barbato et al., 1999; G. Bennett & Bennett, 2000; Keen, Murray, & Payne, 2013). In their report Barbato et al. (1999) found that 33% reported auditory, another 33% olfactory, with only 11% tactile and 5% visual, though others have suggested that visual experiences are the most commonly reported sensory type of ADC (Harroldson, 1988). For instance, Wright (1999, p. 261) reported the following account from a 42-year-old female:

> I was lying in bed and saw my Aunt Ruby and she said to me 'Don't worry child everything will be alright', and I felt a brush near my shoulder. When I ran down the hall to tell my mother and father that I'd just seen my Aunt Ruby, someone called and said she had died. The phone call came as I was running down the hallway.

In addition some have suggested ADCs can also occur in dreams (Houck, 2005; Wright, 1999). There is some discussion in the literature regarding precisely how frequently such experiences occur, with some suggesting that they are very common (e.g., Houck, 2005; Wright, 1999), whilst others have found only about 5% of their respondents report such experiences (Barbato et al., 1999). Such varying rates may be due to the biased nature of the samples. For instance, it is often that specific individuals are sought out, such as those recently bereaved, or those who report contact with the dead and are willing to talk about it. Hence, these rates may not be applicable to wider samples. It is also important to note that many individuals have reported ADCs that involve multiple sensory modalities at the same time (Keen et al., 2013).

Demographics and prevalence

By asking about those who have experienced an ADC it may be possible to identify whether there is anything unique about such individuals. Also, examining how often they occur and when may provide insights into the nature of the experience.

Experients of an ADC

Those individuals who have some knowledge or experience from observation or participation are generally referred to as *experients*. Hence, there are two questions that can be posed. First, is there anything unique, or unusual about the experient of an ADC? Second, what is the relationship between the experient and the deceased?

Those who report such experiences come from all socioeconomic and religious/ spiritual groups and across all geographic regions, and include all types of death (Holden, Lankford, & Holmes, 2019; Houck, 2005; Klugman, 2006). They also include both adults and children (Normand, Silverman, & Nickman, 1996; Sanger, 2009), though perhaps unsurprisingly they are more likely to be reported by widows and widowers. Interestingly, some have found that those able to deal more effectively with the bereavement process tended to talk more to their dead spouse (K. M. Bennett, Hughes, & Smith, 2005). Furthermore, many have found that more women report experiencing an ADC than men (Barbato et al., 1999; Wright, 1999). However, it has been noted that this may be because women are more likely to discuss such events with others and men may be reluctant to report such experiences for fear of ridicule or being labelled as mentally unstable (Daggett, 2005). There have also been suggestions that the level of marital harmony may influence whether a widow or widower experiences an ADC with their deceased spouse (Grimby, 1998), though this is not consistently clear in the literature. For instance, some have argued that those with longer happier marriages would be more likely to experience an ADC compared to those with shorter unhappy marriages (G. Bennett & Bennett, 2000). However, Daggett (2005) found no difference in the nature or quality of the relationships between spouses reporting an ADC and those that do not. Hence, across all ages and backgrounds there is nothing out of the ordinary about those that report such events (Sanger, 2009). Such findings have been suggested to imply the universality of such experiences.

With regards to the relationship between the experient and the deceased the ADC usually occurs with someone the living person had a relationship with when alive, such as a close friend or family member. For instance, Barbato et al. (1999) reported that of those reporting an ADC 78% referred to a deceased next of kin with 21% relating to a loved one. Others have found that sensing the presence or reporting contact with a deceased parent is the most common type of experience followed by grandparents, then spouses (G. Bennett & Bennett, 2000; Klugman, 2006). This may be the result of a long relationship and strong bond between child and parent, though it should also be noted that such reports have also been made by those who work in emergency services dealing with the fatal injuries of relative strangers (R. E. Kelly, 2002). Hence, it is not essential for the experient to know the deceased to have an ADC, though a strong bond may make the experience much richer.

Frequency of an ADC

Precise estimates of the number of reported incidents of an ADC are difficult to obtain. At present there is no single standardised ADC questionnaire that has been developed and adopted by the field. Hence, this is something future researchers could usefully focus on. For example, when assessing such experiences some specifically ask whether the experient in question has been contacted by someone who had died (Guggenheim & Guggenheim, 1995), whilst others ask a more generic question regarding a sensed presence (Houck, 2005). Hence, some assume that an ADC means the individual has experienced direct contact with a deceased individual whereas others may see it simply as relating to the feeling of a presence (Holden et al., 2019). Given this variety in definitions it is unsurprising that the incidence rates of ADC experiences range quite broadly from a reasonably conservative estimate of about 20% of Americans (Guggenheim & Guggenheim, 1995), through to 30% to 40% of the general population (e.g., Barbato et al., 1999; Greeley, 1987; Kalish & Reynolds, 1973; LaGrand, 2005), reaching as high as 90% in some instances (Yamamoto, Okonogi, Iwasaki, & Yoshimura, 1969). Yamamoto et al. (1969) noted that openness to maintaining a connection with the deceased in Japan may have contributed to the high prevalence rate reported in their study, which suggests that culture may influence the incidence of these. However, it is also important to keep in mind that many experients may be reluctant to disclose their ADC experience thinking that others may find such experiences difficult to deal with and/or think them mentally ill (Beischel, 2019; Rees, 1971). Those experiencing an ADC during the bereavement period are often unsure about the nature or origin of the experience and whilst many find them comforting, there is an element of fearing a negative reaction which can make revealing such experiences difficult. Fear of ridicule and the negative stigma attached to reporting such experiences are commonly reported issues. Indeed, reports have noted that it is often the case that 'few relatives or friends were willing to believe their stories' (Guggenheim & Guggenheim, 1995, p. 20), which leads experients to feel both rejected and confused in terms of how they are supposed to deal with the experience. Hence, it is difficult to obtain accurate and precise estimates of the frequency of ADC experiences, though they are reasonably common occurrences.

Occurrence of ADC

Barbato et al. (1999) noted that the more recent the loss the more common were ADC reports and that a decline occurs after the first year. This is consistent with others who have found that ADC reports are more common during the first year of bereavement (Beischel, 2019). Others have also found that the incidence rate decreases over time following the bereavement, which may indicate the increasing ability of the bereaved person to cope with the loss (Grimby, 1998; Lindström, 1995). However, more recently Bennett and Bennett (2000) found that the feeling of a sensed presence relating to a deceased spouse can continue for much longer than was originally thought. This in part may be due to the impact such continued communication has on the life of the living partner.

Impact of ADC

Many of those reporting an ADC say it has a strong emotional impact and can lead to lasting changes in their views of death and dying. This impact can be both positive and negative.

From a positive perspective a number of researchers have reported that experiencing an ADC can have widespread beneficial effects on those who have been bereaved (Barbato et al., 1999; Daggett, 2005; Parker, 2005). This includes a sense of comfort and reassurance, feelings of consolation, reduced death anxiety, as well as encouraging personal and/or spiritual growth and interest (Bara & Cooper, 2017; Beischel, Mosher, & Boccuzzi, 2015; Botkin, 2000; LaGrand, 2005). Alongside these positive experiences others suggest it can provide an opportunity to say goodbye and in doing so provides an adaptive outcome to the grief experienced by such loss (Parker, 2005). Others agree, pointing out that such experiences commonly facilitate the healing process and provide an overwhelming benefit to the bereaved (Holden et al., 2019). In contrast, in a very few instances an ADC can be a negative experience that fulfils no apparent bereavement need, provides no comfort and does not facilitate the grieving process or lead to an adaptive outcome (Parker, 2005). For instance, it may be that the ADC acts as a reminder of the loss a bereaved person has suffered and as such it may be perceived as negative (Bara & Cooper, 2017). It may also be that the type of impact the experience has is influenced by the nature of the relationship between the bereaved and the deceased. A potential negative outcome may also be exacerbated if the experient has difficulty talking about their experience. However, if and when they are able to discuss the experience it often has a beneficial effect (Smith & Dunn, 1977). Indeed, Drewry (2003) has suggested that even when such experiences are initially frightening they can ultimately be beneficial. Hence, overall whilst the specific experience can vary in intensity and impact they are generally seen as a normal part of the grieving process and are usually beneficial and comforting (Beischel, 2019).

Evidence for ADC

Given the spontaneous nature of the ADC they are invariably limited to case reports from the bereaved. Such reports are often viewed as the weakest form of evidence as they can be easily influenced by biases and the whims of memory (Howitt, 2013). In addition, they are invariably based on a small biased sample, that is those who choose to come forward and recount their ADC experience. Furthermore, there is often a delay in time between the ADC and any subsequent interview and reporting. For instance, Daggett (2005) reported on the ADC experiences of a group of bereaved individuals with elapsed time since the death to the interview ranging from 8 months to 20 years. However, Vandenbroucke (1999) has argued that the use of case reports is an essential component in bringing potentially new areas of research to the attention of the scientific community. Indeed, others have argued that they are often the first and sometimes major source for detecting rare and unusual events (Albrecht, Werth, & Bigby, 2009). Hence, whilst the limitations of case reports are well known and should be kept in mind when reading them there are many thousands of such reports outlining a wide variety of ADC experiences (see e.g., Barbato et al., 1999; G. Bennett & Bennett, 2000; Daggett, 2005; Devers, 1997; Guggenheim & Guggenheim, 1995; Klugman, 2006; LaGrand, 2005; Sanger, 2009; Wright, 1999). It is beyond the scope of a single chapter to provide a comprehensive outline of all these various reports. However, the following examples provide some illustrations of the main types of reported ADC (see Box 11.1).

This type of report is interesting in part because the experient at the time of the reported ADC was not aware of the fact that her friend had died three days earlier. The following is another case of a death coincidence which refers to an apparent instance of contact with a person who is either dead or dying that takes place from about 12 hours prior to death up to 12 hours after (Wright, 2006). This is an

---

Box 11.1   Maria Angela's experience

I was working in my jewellery store repairing a necklace that my friend Giovanna had dropped in some weeks earlier. Now … I've known Giovanna for most of my life … we were in the girl scouts together when we were teenagers and I had heard that she was ill with cancer.

So … I was working on a bench with the main window in front of me that looked out onto the street. As I was working I looked up and I saw Giovanna looking in through the window. I remember it clearly as I saw she was wearing a head scarf. Then I went to stand up, just to go and talk to her, but in that moment something happened … I felt a light pressure gently pushing me back down. And so, I sat back down and as I did I felt this energy, or cold shiver run down my spine. But I didn't pay any attention to it and just went back to working on the necklace.

Later that day, after leaving my store and walking back to my house on my way back I saw a notice on the wall of the town announcing that Giovanna had died three days ago. I couldn't understand it because it was today I saw her.

I don't know what to think. The experience was real. Absolutely real, and I did not know about her death.

I believe in what I saw, but I know if someone else was telling me this I'm not sure I would believe them.

(from Maria Angela Lippi with permission)

adapted case report by Wright (1999, p. 261) relating to a visual ADC of a 57-year-old retired nurse:

> I had a friend in Hawaii who was dying of AIDS who I had mentored for a couple of years. I was down at the beach on a Sunday morning. I'm sitting there talking to some people and I look over and I say, 'My God, I thought Laurie was in the hospital'. Now here he is sitting with two other people that I had never seen before. They were surrounded by the most incredible white glimmering kind of light. It didn't look a sunlight thing. It was like a halogen light looks. I looked at my watch and the next day I found out that was exactly the time he died.

The following is an example of an auditory ADC adapted from Devers (1997, pp. 47–48) in which a male (Randy) recalls an ADC with his recently deceased father:

> Randy sat in his father's ocean condominium stunned and numb. He felt a profound sense of loss surrounded by all the familiar reminders of the man he loved ... Listening to bird song from an old record he heard his father's voice ... it was clear and happy and it said 'The birds sound better here. No scratches.' Randy felt this message was relayed from his father and it had a beneficial healing effect on him. He later noted ... When people ask me whether I think it really happened, I say, of course it really happened.

Many such case reports serve to support the extant literature on ADC experiences. However, whilst assessing the veracity of such cases is often very difficult, if not impossible, it has been suggested that by validating the claimed experience of the bereaved individual it may help them deal with their loss and grief (Hastings, 1983).

Explanations for ADCs

In general, three main proposals have been put forward to account for ADC experiences. The first centres around the idea that such experiences are the result of some form of neurological abnormality, the second, that they are a form of grief driven hallucination and the final option is that such experiences are what they seem to be, communication with discarnate entities. Interestingly, Bennett and Bennett (2000) note that the explanatory framework adopted is often based on the specific assumptions the researchers involved.

Neurological abnormality

The idea that an ADC may represent a cortical abnormality is based on the work of Persinger (1983, 1993) who suggests that such experiences may be evoked by transient microseizures within the temporal lobe. Such microseizures may occur as a result of a variety of factors including life crises, isolation, changes associated with illness, and medication. Persinger (1983) goes so far as to suggest that personal life crises and dying provide the optimal conditions for such microseizures. Others agree that trauma to the brain, particularly if caused early on in life, may predispose individuals to experience such events (Ross & Joshi, 1992). Persinger (1993) suggests that the pattern of experiences seen across the various ADCs are similar because of the similarities in temporal lobe function, though these may be influenced to some extent by cultural and religious background. However, Houran and Lange (1997) argue that such microseizures alone are not sufficient to fully account for the ADC experience. In addition, feelings of a sensed presence of a recently deceased individual have also been reported by emergency workers who had no symptoms of mental illness and despite the possible stress of the emergency situations were not grieving for those lost in the usual sense (R. E. Kelly, 2002). According to R. E. Kelly (2002) these emergency workers were familiar with death and well grounded in the physical world and aware of how unusual such feelings were, though they were equally adamant that such feelings were real and not imagined.

Hallucinations

Here the idea is that these experiences are descriptively similar to psychiatric hallucinations in that each person perceives the experience as coming from outside of themselves rather than as a self-generated image (Keen et al., 2013). According to this explanatory framework an ADC would be viewed as 'pathological' only in the sense that the individuals make false judgements about the experience believing it to be real. These grief driven hallucinations are an adaptive part of coping with the loss as they can provide some comfort to those who wish to maintain a connection to the deceased. Hence, in the short term such hallucinatory experiences may be a helpful and adaptive coping mechanism designed to comfort the bereaved. However, if they continue and particularly if they become a source of distress then they may be seen as pathological (Keen et al., 2013). Such hallucinatory experiences have been considered as a natural and normal extension of the successful grief resolution during bereavement (Barbato et al., 1999). For instance, in the *Continuing Bonds* model put forward by Klass (1993) a bereaved person does not get over or learn to forget about the deceased. Rather a personal connection is maintained by internally representing the dead person using imagery and imagination. Hence, an ADC may be parsimoniously interpreted as a constructed dialogue with that internally generated representation. In this way the experience may be seen as an adaptive way of coping with the bereavement in which the bereaved can continue their relationship with the deceased (Keen et al., 2013; Root & Exline, 2014). This approach may fit with the findings from Simon-Buller, Christopherson and Jones (1989) who reported that ADC experiences were more likely to emerge in those who had difficulty adjusting to the bereavement, though not all agree with this view (see, Epstein, Kalus, & Berger, 2006). In addition, others have argued that such an experience is in no way a symptom of any mental disorder (Beischel, 2019). In fact, many who report experiencing an ADC are often unaware of such a phenomenon and as such it has been argued that grief driven expectations are unlikely to be able to account for all effects (Daggett, 2005).

Extraordinary experiences

The inability to find conventional explanations for ADC has led some to view them as suggestive of a continued existence beyond physical death (Bara & Cooper, 2017). Here the idea is that they are what they seem to be: sensations and perceptions, albeit anomalous and extraordinary, with deceased entities (e.g., LaGrand, 2005; Parker,

2005). Such an approach avoids pathologising the event in terms of a neurological abnormality and attempting to explain it in terms of an hallucination. However, at this moment in time there is insufficient evidence to clearly identify a dominant candidate to account for ADC experiences.

Mediumship

In contrast to the spontaneous ADC experiences outlined above mediumship refers to an 'active' or 'facilitated' ADC (Beischel, 2014, 2019). For instance, many people who have been bereaved seek out the comfort of a message from a medium relating to their loss. A *medium* is someone who regularly experiences contact with the deceased and is often able to do this 'on demand' and relay obtained information back to the bereaved (Bastos Jr et al., 2015; Beischel, 2014, 2019). They are sometimes referred to as psychic mediums or spirit mediums (Beischel, 2019; O'Keeffe & Wiseman, 2005) and it is a phenomenon that is well known in many cultures around the world (Pierini, 2016).

The idea of mediumship has an important historical role to play as it was primarily for this reason that the Society for Psychical Research (see https://spr.ac.uk) began its activities in terms of collecting and examining the various case reports. For instance, initial tests of mediums carried out in the 1880s allowed investigators attending séances to note down the comments made by mediums, allegedly received from the deceased, and then assess the accuracy of this information. Some of the resulting reports argued in favour of the existence of genuine mediumistic ability, and contained lengthy transcripts of mediumistic messages along with detailed descriptions of the evidence supporting these statements (e.g., Hodgson, 1898). From this work emerged several seemingly remarkable individuals who demonstrated an ability to contact the deceased and/or obtain accurate information. For example, both the American medium Leonora Piper and the British medium Gladys Leonard were particularly acclaimed for their successes (Gauld, 1977; Salter, 1950). However, it should be noted that some have argued that such work often failed to assess whether the seemingly accurate readings could have been the result of various psychological stratagems, such as the mediums engaging in shrewd guesswork or producing very general statements that would be endorsed by the majority of people (see e.g., Gardner, 1992; O'Keeffe & Wiseman, 2005).

Profile of a medium

A number of researchers have examined the personality profiles of mediums to assess whether there is anything unique or distinct about them compared to non-mediums. There is some agreement in the literature that mediums tend to be well-adjusted, healthy, happy, occupationally active individuals (Aurelio et al., 2015). For instance, one study found that mediums scored higher in wellbeing and lower in psychological stress compared to a non-mediumistic control group (Roxburgh & Roe, 2011). Another reported a clear association between mediumship and good mental health and social adaptation (Bastos Jr et al., 2015). Though some have suggested a link between mediumship and the pathological process of dissociation (Negro Jr, Palladino-Negro, & Louzã, 2002), a recent study by Wahbeh and Radin (2017) found that individuals claiming mediumistic experience do tend to score higher than non-claimants on a dissociation scale but not to the extent that their responses would be deemed pathological.

Types of mediumship

There are a variety of methods or approaches that have been developed and adapted for the study of mediumship and often a distinction is made between physical, trance and mental mediumship (Beischel, 2007; Beischel, Mosher, et al., 2015; Beischel & Zingrone, 2015). Physical mediumship usually refers to the generation of physical phenomena such as table tipping and materialisation; it may also include the levitation of objects, and taps on walls or furniture. Trance mediumship may occur in a sleep-like state and involve some aspect of amnesia on the part of the medium whereby they become the instrument of the discarnate entity. Mental mediumship generally refers to a situation where the medium enters into an altered state of consciousness, though remains conscious and awake, and acts as an active intermediary between the living *sitter* and the deceased *discarnate* by gathering and relaying information during a 'reading' (Beischel, Mosher, & Boccuzzi, 2015; Beischel & Zingrone, 2015). The set-up of a reading is outlined in Figure 11.1 and indicates the flow of communication via the directionality of the arrows. For instance, the sitter may ask questions of the medium and receive responses, though questions posed to the discarnate entity by the sitter will be relayed back through the medium.

According to Beischel (2014) a reading involves a complex dynamic between the *sitter*, the *medium* and the invited deceased person, each component of which may influence the outcome. Mental mediums can relay information back to the sitter in a wide variety of formats including drawings, paintings, music and in some cases artistic performances (see, Harris & Alvarado, 2014). However, the main types of mental mediumship are proxy sittings, discarnate directed, drop-in communications, xenoglossy and cross-correspondences.

Proxy sittings

Here the *sitter* may ask the medium for information known only to some third party not present at the meeting. For example, in experimental research the *proxy sitter* may be the experimenter who sits with the medium and poses questions that have been pre-specified by the sitter (see e.g., Beischel, 2007). Using a proxy sitter to pose questions blinds the medium to cues from the original sitter and can also

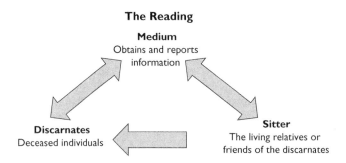

Figure 11.1 The set-up of a reading involving a medium, who obtains and relays information from a discarnate entity to a sitter, who in turn may be a living relative or friend of the deceased.

blind the sitter to the reading until it is later scored. An extension of this is for the proxy sitter to contact the medium via phone or email. In this way the blinded proxy sitter acts for an absent sitter and the medium can conduct the reading in a comfortable location of their choice. Such blinding techniques have been proposed to exclude any possible use of psi by the medium. However, as Irwin and Watt (2007) accurately point out, the precise limits of psi are as yet unknown, if indeed there are any, and as such it is not possible to be completely certain that such an approach excludes all psi-based sources.

Discarnate directed

In this instance the medium may be given the first name of a specific discarnate the sitter wishes to communicate with and sometimes their relationship to the sitter. It has been suggested that by giving the medium such information it may be possible for them to produce generalisations that could give the impression of accuracy (French & Stone, 2014). However, Beischel (2007) has argued that the specific information required from the medium regarding the physical life of a discarnate is not likely to be obtained solely from a first name. Furthermore, Beischel (2007) points out that if a name does provide some culturally specific information, as it would with the clearly Japanese name of Akira, then it should be possible to either provide two names from the same cultural background, only one of which would relate to a discarnate, or provide two names from the same cultural background both referring to discarnates and require the medium to focus on details that would distinguish between the two.

Drop-in communicators

According to Irwin and Watt (2007) this is where an apparently discarnate personality 'drops in' to provide information to the sitters in a séance. In this instance, information obtained from such a discarnate would be unknown to the medium, sitter or experimenter (Beischel, 2007).

Xenoglossy

In some rare cases during a séance the medium may exhibit a skill and/or personality characteristic that was possessed by the discarnate whilst living but that the medium does not have. A classic example is the paranormal ability of the medium to speak and/or write in a language they have not naturally acquired. Although there have been reported cases of such xenoglossy (see, Gauld, 1982, 2005) their methodological rigour leaves many questions unanswered.

Cross-correspondences

Here the idea is that different mediums may receive communications from the same deceased individual. This in turn would lead to a correspondence between the scripts of their meetings or readings which would suggest that the information came from the same source. This would be assuming that the mediums in question never meet. An adaptation of this is where distinct parts of a single message are communicated through different mediums which would only make sense when all the parts are brought together as a whole (Gauld, 2005). This has led to suggestions that such cross-correspondences in communication, if accurate, would indicate that they belong or stem from a single source (Beischel & Zingrone, 2015).

Laboratory based investigations into mediums

Two of the main lab-based approaches used to examine mediumship have been to explore changes in psychophysiological activity to see if there is something distinct about the state of the medium and to examine the veracity of any communication whilst attempting to control for the various normal routes of communication. According to Beischel (2007) all lab-based research examining mediums needs to use detailed reading protocols, clear experimental blinding of those involved, the pre-screening of all those involved in the research and a transparent scoring system to identify the accuracy of the readings. Unfortunately, not all abide by these helpful and rigorous guidelines.

Psychophysiological research

A central idea with this type of research is to examine the cerebral activity of the medium before, during and after the reading to ascertain what, if any, differences in cortical activity are seen in the medium compared to either non-mediums or mediums in a non-reading control condition. For instance, one study utilising Single Positron Emission Tomography (SPECT) showed a reduction of cerebral blood flow (CBF) in a wide range of cortical regions associated with memory, language and planning during mediumistic communication as compared to a control task for more experienced mediums (Peres, Moreira-Almeida, Caixeta, Leao, & Newberg, 2012). There was also a negative correlation between the CBF in these areas and the linguistic complexity of the written text produced. The pattern of data was more complex than would be expected simply by having the individual relax. As such, it was suggested that it indicated the activation of fewer neuronal populations during the reading. In addition, researchers have examined changes in the electrocortical activity of the medium's brain using the electroencephalogram (EEG). For example, work by Krippner (2008) reported increased activity in the EEG frequencies of theta, alpha and beta during mediumistic communication compared to a baseline. In a two-part study Delorme et al. (2013) measured the EEG from mediums during masked readings as well as other mental tasks. This showed some differences in theta brain activity during periods of low accuracy compared to periods of high accuracy. In the follow-up experiment they required mediums to think about a living person, to passively listen to a biography, to think about an imaginary person and finally to mentally communicate with a deceased individual. They found clear differences in gamma band activity between each of these four conditions which was taken to suggest that mediumistic communication represents a distinct mental state from ordinary thinking or imagination and that brain activity during these phases may also be distinct. Others have also compared the EEG of mediums to non-mediums before, during and immediately following a reading. They found greater activity in the theta and beta EEG frequency ranges for the mediums compared to the non-mediums (Bastos Jr et al., 2016). Such increases in theta and beta are usually indicative of greater cognitive demands.

However, there are many methodological issues with this area of research which indicate that its findings need to be interpreted with caution. First, it has been noted that it is a challenge in such psychophysiological research to precisely define when any mediumistic communication begins and ends (Bastos Jr et al., 2015). This makes it difficult to precisely synchronise any potential changes in brain activity to the distinct stages of the reading process. In addition, the various studies utilise mediums with a diverse level of experience. For instance, the study by Peres et al. (2012) examining changes in the brain during mediumistic readings included mediums with between 15 and 47 years of experience. There are also inconsistencies in the offered interpretations across the various imaging studies. For instance, the SPECT study by Peres et al. (2012) suggested a reduction in activation of some key left hemisphere regions whereas the EEG work of Bastos et al. (2016) is indicative of greater cognitive activity. Such contradictory findings are difficult to reconcile. In part, no doubt, this is likely to be due to the complexity of the brain and the task at hand. However, even when clear cortical differences are identified it needs to be made clear that they are not simply a result of other non-specific differences such as the age of the medium, their experience, the number of readings they have conducted, the duration of the reading, as well as the context and setting (see e.g., Beischel, 2007). This will no doubt be a growing area of research as technology develops; nevertheless, more needs to be done in terms of developing clear a-priori ideas as to why a medium would be expected to exhibit a particular cortical profile.

Lab-based sittings/readings

This line of research examines the veracity of information obtained during a mediumistic reading. According to Beischel (2007) the information obtained by the medium is more often received than retrieved and as such is referred to as *anomalous information reception* (AIR). Beischel (2014, 2019) also suggests that the three main types of information obtained by mediums relating to deceased individuals includes information identifying the deceased, information regarding events in the life of the bereaved person including those since the death, and direct messages relayed from the deceased. Such identifying information can include physical appearance, background information including occupation, and personality characteristics. This is thought to help the sitter identify the source as the specific individual they wish to communicate with. Information relating to events in the sitter's life since the death are thought to provide evidence that the deceased individual is still taking an interest in their life. Finally, the relayed messages may simply be messages of love or may specifically refer to things only the sitter would know. However, mediumistic readings have often been criticised for allowing potential artefacts, such as non-verbal cues, clever guesswork and generic statements to be used (French & Stone, 2014; Holt, Simmonds-Moore, Luke, & French, 2012), specifically, the use of Barnum statements and the cold reading approach. The former relies on producing generic truths that encourage the listener to form a specific impression (e.g., O'Keeffe & Wiseman, 2005; Roe, 1996), whereas the latter refers to a set of techniques in which visual and auditory cues from the sitter may be used consciously or unconsciously to fabricate readings (French & Stone, 2014).

Contemporary research

Researchers are fully aware of the use and potential influence of Barnum statements and cold reading and as a consequence contemporary methods have evolved beyond the historical approaches to include a range of rigorous checks and measures. Although there is no single universally accepted methodological gold standard Beischel (2007) has identified a set of procedures that robustly deals with issues of contamination and possible fraud. This includes the use of detailed reading protocols, clear experimental blinding, the pre-screening of all those involved in the research and a transparent scoring system used to identify the accuracy of the readings. A key element of all this is the reliance on using well trained and skilled mediums. For instance, the reading may include protocols that become more specific at each step, requiring more detailed information as the session progresses. Or it may involve asking for a specific discarnate, which would allow for similar discarnate readings to be made across a study. In addition, when rating a given reading the sitter should ideally be given two readings, one that was intended for them and one intended for another sitter. These readings should be matched for discarnates of the same gender to avoid any obvious gender-based cues and the sitter would be required to identify which reading was intended for her. The level of blinding can also become progressively more stringent. For instance, a single-blind condition refers to situations where only the medium is blinded to information regarding the sitter and discarnate. Double-blind conditions are where the medium is blind to all information and the individual rating the reading is also blinded to the origin. Triple-blind procedures include the addition of blinding the experimenter involved in the research (see Beischel, 2007). Nevertheless, whilst these procedures represent a gold standard in terms of methodological rigour there are still many methodological differences in the studies reported in the literature which may to some extent account for the different results.

For example, one study required five professional mediums to each provide a reading to five sitters. The mediums had no contact with the sitters and were provided no information about them. Each sitter was then asked to rate the accuracy of their own readings along with a range of decoy readings. The results failed to show any clear pattern with only one occasion whereby a sitter gave a higher accuracy rating to a reading meant for them (O'Keeffe & Wiseman, 2005). This would suggest that the accuracy of information obtained during a reading is very poor. However, this study was later criticised for containing both descriptive and methodological flaws which included requiring the mediums to produce multiple readings 'on demand', and editing transcripts in such a way as to reduce applicability ratings (Beischel & Zingrone, 2015). That said, others have also attempted to study the veracity of the readings given by mediums when produced under controlled conditions and found no clear evidence of paranormal communication (Jensen & Cardeña, 2008), although it was noted that the medium also gave all the readings a rating of low confidence which could indicate that they felt the environment was not conducive to making the necessary connection to obtain the relevant information. It is important to be wary of accepting such reasons at face value as it would always be possible to suggest that conditions are not conducive given current understanding of what this may mean.

Nevertheless, there are those that argue that certain mediums are able to accurately report specific information relating to a discarnate without any prior knowledge of the discarnate or sitter and in the absence of any feedback (Beischel, 2007), also that such information cannot be explained as a result of fraud or 'cold reading' (e.g., Beischel, 2019; Beischel, Boccuzzi, Biuso, & Rock, 2015; E. W. Kelly & Arcangel, 2011). For instance, Beischel and Schwartz (2007) using a rigorous triple-blinded approach found significantly more accurate whole-reading scores for readings intended for the sitter compared to those for a control, see Figure 11.2.

Such findings have led to the suggestion that 'some' mediums are able to relay accurate information under rigorous lab-based conditions (Rock & Storm, 2015). Indeed, a follow-up study incorporating two experimental reading sessions by Beischel, Boccuzzi et al. (2015) examined the accuracy of information reported by mediums who performed readings over the phone under blinded conditions. Subsequent comparisons of the accuracy and specificity of blinded target and decoy readings showed that the real readings were rated as significantly more accurate in both experiments (see Figure 11.3). Such findings have been suggested to provide evidence supporting the notion that mediums can receive and communicate anomalous information. Given that the experimental conditions eliminated the normal sensory sources for information transfer, Beischel, Boccuzzi et al. (2015) suggest that a non-local source was the most likely explanation.

Others agree they also point out that not all studies with rigorous methods have shown clear evidence supporting the accuracy of information provided by mediums (for a review see, Bastos Jr et al., 2015). To some extent this may be due to the heterogenous methodologies used (Aurelio et al., 2015). In part this may also be because mediums only have limited control over the specific individual that 'comes through' and that rather than calling up a particular individual they generally allow themselves to be open and receptive to whatever information, or whoever, comes through (Beischel, 2019). In addition, there is little in the way of any formal or consistent training and accreditation for those interested in becoming a medium. This is likely to influence the outcome of research because whilst some have argued that research should focus on mediums who have been screened, pre-tested, well trained and are experienced (see, Beischel, 2007),

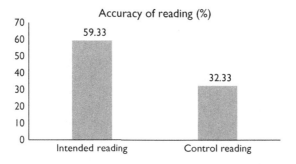

Figure 11.2 The mean accuracy (%) of readings intended for the sitter (left) and control readings (right) (adapted from Beischel & Schwartz, 2007).

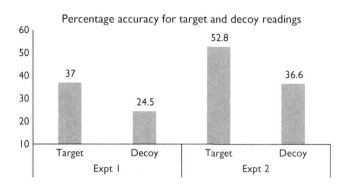

Figure 11.3 The percentage mean accuracy of blinded target (left column) and decoy (right column) readings for both experiment 1 (left panel) and experiment 2 (right panel) (adapted from Beischel, Boccuzzi, et al., 2015).

this may not always be the case. Nevertheless, the positive results reported by the more rigorous studies are sufficiently interesting to warrant further investigation.

Explanations

The three most common explanations for mediumship are fraud, either consciously or unconsciously, some form of super-psi and the possibility that it accurately represents a form of after death communication (Bastos Jr et al., 2015). It is true that the history of psi research, like many others, has experienced *some* cases of fraud (e.g., Kurtz, 1985; Markwick, 1985), though it should be noted that in most of these cases the deceptions came to light because researchers in the field of psi questioned the findings and made public their concerns (see, Roe, 2016a, 2016b, 2017). Furthermore, it should be made clear that the majority of those participating in psi research are sincere in what they do and the claims they make. Of course, sincerity is not a guarantee of scientific accuracy, though, as French and Stone (2014) note, there is no evidence that those who either participate in psi research or experience such phenomena are any less honest than those who do not. In fact, reflecting on the possible types of fraud across different areas of science Roe (2016b, p. 16) argues that the field of psi research 'is actually much *less* susceptible to fraud than other research areas'.

The second possibility is based on the notion that even when evidence for anomalous information reception by mediums emerges it is not possible to distinguish this from effects reliant on super psi (Beischel & Schwartz, 2007). Super psi refers to the idea that it is the psi ability of the medium, either through telepathy, precognition or even psychokinesis, to obtain any and all relevant information about the necessary deceased persons from the sitter (Braude, 1992). This is often seen as a more parsimonious interpretation suggesting that any effects produced by a medium are more *probably* the result of telepathy, or other aspects of psi, than the possibility of contact with discarnate entities (Bastos Jr et al., 2015). To an extent this is because the limits of psi are not clearly known or fully understood at this time. However, there is a problem with this idea in that it attempts to explain one unknown with reference to another and as such doesn't really explain anything. In addition, some have argued that it would be difficult if not impossible to test such a proposal as super psi is often seen to represent some form of omniscient or omnipotent capacity that cannot be falsified (Alvarado & Martinez-Taboas, 1983).

The final possibility is that mediumship is what it claims to be: a form of after death communication where a skilled medium can obtain and relay information from a discarnate entity. Such a proposal would provide clear evidence to support the survival of consciousness beyond physical death and have significant implications for the relationship between consciousness and the brain. Indeed, evidence from the more rigorous studies would certainly support such a view (Beischel, Boccuzzi, et al., 2015; Beischel & Schwartz, 2007; E. W. Kelly & Arcangel, 2011), though it is too early at this moment in time to reach a firm conclusion. Such findings need to be replicated by other laboratories, ideally using the same stringent procedures. Hence, there is no single explanation that at present can fully account for the data from mediumistic research.

Electronic voice phenomena (EVP)

The final line of enquiry into post death phenomena refers to an approach Beischel (2019) classifies as 'requested' in the sense that an experience may occur because of the experiencer engaging in a particular practice. In this instance it is attempting to communicate with the deceased via electronic equipment. *Electronic voice phenomena*, or EVP, refers to voices emerging from a recording when no voices were present during the initial recording process. Originally it may have involved tuning a radio between stations and recording the output on audiotape but with advancing technology now includes recording such alleged voices via telephones, televisions and computers (Barušs, 2001). They represent part of a wider range of phenomena grouped under the collective heading of *instrumental trans-communication* (ITC) which refers to attempts to communicate with entities beyond the current known reality (Barušs, 2001; Boccuzzi & Beischel, 2011; Laszlo, 2008). EVPs are interesting for several reasons. First, is the assumption that the voices are those of people who have died and as such the material has implications for the survival hypothesis. Second, some have suggested that EVPs may be the result of unconscious psychokinesis (PK) on the part of the individual making the recording, which again would bring the phenomenon within the remit of psi research. Furthermore, there have also been suggestions that the voices represent individuals from another planet, dimension or even from the past (see, Leary & Butler, 2015). Irrespective, the phenomenon represents a possible ADC experience, albeit one based on the use of technology, and as such it is worth briefly exploring the background history of EVP research.

History of EVP

Reports of anomalous voice phenomena began soon after the invention and use of radios, telephones and audio recording/playback equipment. One of the earliest reported events was that from Bayless (1959) who reported on audio recordings taken from a soundproofed closet containing a microphone and tape recorder. Over time various individuals sat in the closet and audio recordings were taken. Though the report clearly states that during the recording no sounds were heard, when the recordings were played back examples of human voices could be discerned. According to Leary and Butler (2015), at around the same time a Swedish amateur ornithologist by the name of Friedrich Jurgenson discovered strange unexplained voices on tape recordings he had made of birdsong while alone in the forest. Jurgenson wrote about these experiences, believing them to be voices of the dead, and this led to a spike in public interest, which included films and TV. After reading Jurgenson's book about EVPs Kontantin Raudive became convinced the voices were real and spent many years studying them. Raudive (1971) went on to claim that not only were such voices real but that they could be obtained using a microphone recording set up to record the output of one or more radios tuned between radio stations, generally referred to as the *radio-microphone method*. These ambiguous sounds became known at the time as 'Raudive voices'. Raudive (1971) also argued that recognising such utterances as words required intensive and concentrated listening. Unfortunately attempts to have independent observers identify the sounds recorded failed to show any clear effects as none were able to identify the sounds given by Raudive (Ellis, 1975). Others also noted that Raudive's work was often uncontrolled, and his interpretations often went beyond the data (Leary & Butler, 2015). Since then there have been few, if any, academically trained scientists willing (or able) to investigate this field, though some have suggested it is possible to characterise the different types of EVP.

Characteristics of EVP

An EVP is sound based, which makes it difficult to convey the nature and characteristics via the written word. However, selected websites listed at the end of the chapter provide the interested reader with an opportunity to listen to some audio samples of EVPs. Generally, EVPs have a short duration of around 1–5 seconds, and are between one and five words long. It is not clear why they are so short and the messages so abrupt. The quality of the voices and recordings also varies a great deal from the reasonably clear human type voice to whispers, hoarse rasping voices or pulsed speech. In his early work Raudive (1971) suggested that EVPs can be classified into three groups. The first, Class A, contain remarkably clear recordings of which there would be general agreement on the content. The second, Class B, may sound like voices but independent listeners may not always agree on the content. Finally, Class C refers to the less obvious, voice-like sounds which are difficult if not impossible to interpret. More recently, Leary and Butler (2015) have argued that EVPs can be classified in two ways. First are what they call *transform EVPs* which refer to voices or voice-like sounds. A key point is that these alleged voices are not heard at the time of the original recording. The second classification is called *live-voice EVPs* and refers to voice-like sounds which are heard at the time of the recording. Given the often vague and ambiguous sounds that form an EVP it should be no surprise that there is often disagreement about what a particular EVP is saying. For instance, Leary (2013) using a consensus style judgement found only 21% agreement on what an EVP clip contained. It has also been suggested that knowing what other people think an EVP clip contains influences your response (Leary & Butler, 2015).

Evidence

There are many interesting anecdotes and case reports of EVP phenomena. A particularly well-known case is that of the Italian Marcello Bacci's ability to speak to voices and conduct conversations through his radio. Bacci used a *Direct Radio Voice Method* (DRV) which involved attempting to obtain anomalous communications directly through the loudspeakers of radios, and such voices were frequently claimed to refer to listeners by name, respond to questions put to them and sometimes provide relevant and lengthy items of information. Interestingly, assessment of such claims has shown no evidence of fraud (see e.g., Laszlo, 2008; Richards, 2016). However, to date there have been only a few controlled empirical research studies exploring such a phenomenon.

For instance, Baruss (2001) attempted to document EVPs by having research assistants simulate interactions with discarnate entities while recording the output from two radios tuned between stations. This produced over 60 hours of recordings which they listened to for any evidence of anomalous voices or utterances. Unfortunately, there was no clear evidence in the recordings of any sounds that could be identified sufficiently clearly as voices. More recently Boccuzzi and Beischel (2011) examined the ability of people and a specialist software program to identify possible utterances from a range of audio samples. Unfortunately, about half of the participants tested reported hearing recognisable words in both the active (i.e., clips that were thought to contain utterances) and control (i.e., those that did not) sessions. Further analysis showed no evidence that individuals were able to correctly identify the presence of an utterance. In addition, when the active recordings were examined using specialist speech recognition software it failed to detect utterances that were reported by the person making the recording. This, they suggested, meant there was a high chance of someone reportedly hearing an utterance irrespective of whether one was there or not, also, that the recognition of such sounds tended to be highly subjective and that objective verification using specialist software did not match the subjective experience. A study by Cardoso (2012) that reportedly described a series of investigations into EVPs across a two-year period claimed to have produced a number of recordings with apparent anomalous voices. Unfortunately, the level of methodological rigour in these experiments was limited; in particular it was not made clear how each audio clip was rated or assessed and by how many, and whether they were blind to the study goals or not.

Given such findings it is not surprising that the conclusions offered by those that have looked into the phenomenon is that there is no clear evidence for EVPs (Baruss, 2001). However, Leary and Butler (2015) point out that the assumption that an EVP can simply be recorded at any time/place may not be accurate and that it may require a certain context and/or environment to elicit such an effect. Such a view is consistent with the notion that a unity of thought needs to be achieved in those attempting contact with the deceased for the electronic system to work (Locher & Harsch-Fischbach, 1997). These ideas are both interesting and potentially useful but they need to be empirically tested and supported before they can be accepted. Ideally, utilising the clear and rigorous protocols outlined by Boccuzzi and Beischel (2011).

Explanations of EVP

A number of potential explanations have been put forward to account for EVPs; these include contamination, radio interference, a form of auditory apophenia, psycho-kinesis and the possibility that they represent the communications from discarnate entities. As is often the case each view can offer some insights and may account for some aspects of the data but no single comprehensive theory has yet emerged.

Contamination

The simplest explanation is that the voices heard on an EVP clip are due to con-tamination, that is, someone present at the time of the recording uttered a word or sound which others either did not hear or did not remember hearing. For instance, it could simply be a growling stomach, or someone clearing their throat which is later 'misinterpreted' as a specific sound. Other potential artefacts include external en-vironmental noise which people at the time have habituated to, for instance, external noises such as a dog barking, birds singing, people passing nearby the recording lo-cation. Leary and Butler (2015) outlined some of the options open to researchers to deal with possible contamination, including employing multiple recording devices and clearly identifying on the recording any extraneous noises that are noticed.

Radio interference

Another obvious possibility is that EVPs are radio transmissions picked up by the recording equipment. However, Leary and Butler (2015) suggest that this is unlikely given the detection and processing requirements that would be involved. Also, they argue that signals from other sources such as baby monitors and mobile cellular phones employ different analogue-to-digital encoding protocols which would make it very unlikely for a digital recorder to detect such signals. In addition, EVPs have been recorded on instruments shielded against electromagnetic interference, including radio waves (MacRae, 2005). Leary and Butler (2015) also argue that the content of an EVP is distinctly different from the material broadcast on most radio stations. For instance, EVPs generally do not include songs or snippets of commercials, news broadcasts, weather forecasts or announcements.

Auditory pareidolia

Pareidolia is the psychological phenomenon of perceiving 'meaning' from vague and random stimuli, and includes visual as well as auditory sensations. For example, most people are familiar with the idea of seeing faces in the clouds or in other random elements. Similarly, auditory pareidolia involves interpreting random sounds as meaningful (Blom & Sommer, 2010). Given the wide range of possible processing parameters Nees and Phillips (2015) point out that anomalies are likely to occur in many recordings that may sound similar to human speech. Indeed, research has shown that when participants are played background noise that has been modulated to mimic voice like cadences but does not in fact contain any speech the number of participants reporting voices significantly increases (Butler, 2012). In addition, researchers have shown that simply suggesting that there may be paranormal events at play can shift people's perception of ambiguous stimuli. Specifically, Nees and Phillips (2015) found that priming participants by telling them that the audio files they were about to listen to may contain voices of ghosts led participants to report significantly more voices present compared to a control group who were simply told the recordings may contain voices in a noisy environment. However, it should be noted that whilst the paranormally primed group did report more instances of human voices there was no clear agreement among them in terms of the content of these perceived utterances. French and Stone (2014) suggest that this merely highlights the tendency of those who believe in psi and the paranormal to perceive meaning in randomness and assume it to be caused by an intentional agent. Hence, it is the top-down expectations and biases that lead some individuals to report illusory perceptions of voices in ambiguous auditory recordings. Of course, pareidolia may be able to account for some of the recordings, but it is unlikely to be able to account for all, in particular, when the voices heard stand out by virtue of their loudness/amplitude and other frequency characteristics.

Psychokinesis

One interesting suggestion, given that the language of the voices is often in the same language as those making the recording, is that the EVP is the result of a form of super psi PK (see, Braude, 1992). Unsurprisingly, it is the individual making the recordings who is often the most motivated to elicit or find an EVP and as such the suggestion is that, either through conscious intention or unconscious activation, the individual is able to alter the recording in a subtle way to produce the ambiguous sounds. Hence, the idea is that the electronic equipment used to record the material may be influenced by the researchers or interested parties which would be consistent with other claims regarding PK type effects. However, such a proposal is more anecdotal than empirical. For instance, the small PK effects seen in research using random event generators (see Chapter 6) suggests that such an idea may be possible, though given the complexity of the EVP phenomenon it is not necessarily probable.

Discarnate entities

A central assumption of early researchers was that the EVPs were the voices of discarnate entities. Some in fact claimed to have been addressed by name by deceased individuals whom they knew whilst alive (see e.g., Raudive, 1971). Hence, the voices could be accounted for by suggesting that they do in fact come from deceased individuals providing support for the survival hypothesis. However, such a proposal has little empirical support at this moment in time. In addition, it is not clear how it would be possible for a discarnate entity to influence such electronic equipment and/or why, if they can do so, the assumed messages are so vague and short.

Overview

This chapter examined three types of post death phenomena. The first related to the spontaneous ADC experiences which are commonly reported across all demographics and cultures and have a long history of occurring. Whilst there is no agreement on how such experiences should be classified, the sensed feeling of the presence of a deceased person was one of the most common. Along with this there are many types of sensory experience, including visual, auditory and olfactory. There does not seem to be anything unique or distinct about those that report such experiences as they come from all walks of life, socioeconomic and religious/spiritual groups, though it is often noted that women are more likely to talk about such experiences than men. In terms of the relationship with the deceased individual it is usually a family member, most commonly parents, that is felt or sensed. The precise frequency of occurrences is difficult to gauge as there is no single agreed upon method for assessing this and the fear of ridicule associated with making such claims may inhibit experients from coming forward to talk about their experiences. In terms of the impact these experiences can have this is generally positive and can lead to a reduced fear of death as well as help bring the grieving process to an end. In a small number of cases an ADC may have a negative impact on the individual but even when this does occur it has been suggested that it can ultimately have a beneficial outcome. Evidence for the various ADCs is invariably based on case studies and case reports which have known limitations and as such are often treated as providing only low levels of support. Attempts to account for ADC experiences have included neurological abnormalities, hallucinations and the possibility that contact with the deceased may be possible. However, at present there is insufficient data to clearly identify a single dominant account.

The second type of post death phenomena examined was the more active or facilitated process of having a medium relay information obtained from discarnate entities. Mediumship has a long and rich history from the séance room to the laboratory and is often classified into physical, trance and mental. Here the focus was on mental mediumship which revolves around the medium providing readings to a sitter regarding a specific discarnate. This has been investigated in the laboratory in two ways. First, researchers have spent time examining changes that occur in the brain of the medium during the reading process. This has suggested some possible differences but much more needs to be done to identify precisely why such differences might occur and what they mean. The second avenue explored the accuracy of anomalous information reception. Contemporary researchers are fully aware of the possible influence of Barnum type statements and the use of cold reading strategies and have developed rigorous methodological procedures to overcome these limitations. Though not always consistent such research has shown some very significant effects suggesting that some mediums may be able to accurately relay information about deceased individuals under controlled conditions. Accounting for such findings however is not easy. The idea that all such claims are the result of fraud does not stand up to any level of scrutiny. The problem with the super psi hypothesis is that, at present, it is difficult if not impossible to test and as such cannot shed any light on the situation. This leaves the possibility that mediums are really contacting the deceased and relaying their messages and information. Whilst the evidence supporting this idea is encouraging, more needs to be done to broaden the findings and replicate the effects.

The final aspect of post death phenomena examined related to EVPs. Although EVPs as a phenomenon have been around for some time very little empirical research has been conducted on them. Some have suggested they can be classified in terms of whether a voice, or voice-like sound, was heard when the recording took place or only afterwards when the recording is replayed. Again, there are case studies and anecdotal reports but these carry little weight in terms of empirical support. The very few research studies that have examined possible EVPs have not found any clear evidence to support the idea that they contain voices. However, given that so little research has been conducted in this area it is important to keep in mind that absence of evidence is not the same as evidence of absence. In addition, with technological developments, particularly in voice recognition software, it is possible that this area may benefit from future research utilising such software to provide more objective verification of whether EVPs contain voices or not. Overall, the findings from all three areas are more suggestive than conclusive. However, the suggestion they make is that consciousness may be a non-local phenomenon, not reliant solely on the brain, and able to survive physical death.

Reflective questions

Some questions that may prove helpful when reflecting on the material covered in this chapter.

- Why do you think so many people report ADCs?
- Have you ever experienced an ADC?
- If you had an ADC would you tell anyone?
- Why do you think there are different types of ADC?
- How would you assess the accuracy of information obtained from a medium?
- Have you ever visited a medium and been given accurate information?
- Do you think mediumship is something that should require specific training?
- Have you ever heard voices emerge from an electronic device with no known source?
- Is it possible to rule out super-psi as an explanation for any of these ADCs?

Websites

You may not be familiar with the sound of an EVP and as such it is a useful exercise to take the time to listen to some. The following websites contain a variety of EVPs with their alleged messages clarified to help you identify what may be there:

- https://www.evplondon.com/
- https://atransc.org/evp-online-listening-trials/

References

Albrecht, J., Werth, V. P., & Bigby, M. (2009). The role of case reports in evidence-based practice, with suggestions for improving their reporting. *Journal of the American Academy of Dermatology*, 60(3), 412–418.

Alvarado, C. S., & Martinez-Taboas, A. (1983). The super-psi hypothesis: A review. *Theta*, 11, 57–62.

Aurelio, M., Bastos, V., Bastos, P. R. H. O., Gonclves, L. M., Osorio, I. H. S. O., & Lucchetti, G. (2015). Mediumship: review of quantiative studies published in the 21st century. *Archives of Clinical Psychiatry*, *42*(5), 129–138.

Bara, M. M., & Cooper, C. (2017). *An interpretive phenomenological analysis of after-death communication in the bereavement process of professed sceptics.* Paper presented at the 60th Annual Convention of the Parapsychological Association, Athens, Greece.

Barbato, M., Blunden, C., Reid, K., Irwin, H., & Rodriquez, P. (1999). Parapsychological phenomena near the time of death. *Journal of Palliative Care*, *15*(2), 30–37.

Barušs, I. (2001). Failure to replicate electronic voice phenomenon. *Journal of Scientific Exploration*, *15*(3), 355–367.

Bastos Jr, M. A. V., Bastos, P. R. H. d. O., Gonçalves, L. M., Osório, I. H. S., & Lucchetti, G. (2015). Mediumship: Review of quantitatives studies published in the 21st century. *Archives of Clinical Psychiatry*, *42*(5), 129–138. doi: 10.1590/0101-60830000000063.

Bastos Jr, M. A. V., Bastos, P. R. H. d. O., Osório, I. H. S., Muass, K. A. R. C., Iandoli Jr, D., & Lucchetti, G. (2016). Frontal electroencephalographic (EEG) activity and mediumship: A comparative study between spiritist mediums and controls. *Archives of Clinical Psychiatry*, *43*(2), 20–26. doi: 10.1590/0101-60830000000076.

Bayless, R. (1959). Correspondence. *Journal of the American Society for Psychical Research*, *53*(1), 35–38.

Beischel, J. (2007). Contemporary methods used in laboratory-based mediumship research. *Journal of Parapsychology*, *71*, 37–68.

Beischel, J. (2014). Assisted after-death communication: A self-prescribed treatment for grief. *Journal of Near-Death Studies*, *32*(3), 161–165.

Beischel, J. (2019). Spontaneous, facilitated, assisted, and requested after-death communication experiences and their impact on grief. *Threshold: Journal of Interdisciplinary Consciousness Studies*, *3*(1), 1–32.

Beischel, J., Boccuzzi, M., Biuso, M., & Rock, A. J. (2015). Anomalous information reception by research mediums under blinded conditions II: Replication and extension. *Explore*, *11*(2), 136–142.

Beischel, J., Mosher, C., & Boccuzzi, M. (2015). The possible effects on bereavement of assisted after-death communication during readings with psychic mediums: A continuing bonds perspective. *OMEGA – Journal of Death and Dying*, *70*(2), 169–194. doi: 10.2190/OM.70.2.b.

Beischel, J., & Schwartz, G. E. (2007). Anomalous information reception by research mediums demonstrated using a novel triple-blind protocol. *Explore: The Journal of Science and Healing*, *3*(1), 23–27. doi: 10.1016/j.explore.2006.10.004.

Beischel, J., & Zingrone, N. L. (2015). Mental mediumship. In E. Cardena, J. Palmer, & D. Marcusson-Clavertz (Eds.), *Parapsychology: A handbook for the 21st century* (pp. 301–313). Jefferson, NC: McFarland & Company Inc.

Bennett, G., & Bennett, K. M. (2000). The presence of the dead: An empirical study. *Mortality*, *5*(2), 139–157.

Bennett, K. M., Hughes, G. M., & Smith, P. T. (2005). Psychological response to later life widowhood: Coping and the effects of gender. *OMEGA – Journal of Death and Dying*, *51*(1), 33–52.

Blom, J. D., & Sommer, I. E. (2010). Auditory hallucinations: Nomenclature and classification. *Cognitive and Behavioral Neurology*, *23*(1), 55–62.

Boccuzzi, M., & Beischel, J. (2011). Objective analyses of reported real-time audio instrumental transcommunication and matched control sessions: A pilot study. *Journal of Scientific Exploration*, *25*(2), 215–235.

Botkin, A. L. (2000). The induction of after-death communications utilizing eye-movement desensitization and reprocessing: A new discovery. *Journal of Near-Death Studies*, *18*(3), 181–209.

Braude, S. E. (1992). Survival or super-psi. *Journal of Scientific Exploration*, 6(2), 127–144.

Butler, T. (2012). Phantom voices. *Association TransCommunication*. Retrieved from Association TransCommunication website: https://atransc.org/phantom-voices/.

Cardoso, A. (2012). A two-year investigation of the allegedly anomalous electronic voices or EVP. *NeuroQuantology*, 10(3), 492–514.

Daggett, L. M. (2005). Continued encounters: The experience of after-death communication. *Journal of Holistic Nursing*, 23(2), 191–207.

Delorme, A., Beischel, J., Michel, L., Boccuzzi, M., Radin, D., & Mills, P. J. (2013). Electrocortical activity associated with subjective communication with the deceased. *Frontiers in Psychology*, 4, 1–10.

Devers, E. (1997). *Goodbye again*. Missouri: Andrews and McMeel.

Drewry, M. D. J. (2003). *Purported after-death communication and its role in the recovery of bereaved individuals: A phenomenological study*. Paper presented at the Proceedings of the Annual Conference of the Academy of Religion and Psychical Research.

Ellis, D. J. (1975). Listening to the 'Raudive voices'. *Journal of the Society for Psychical Research*, 48, 31–42.

Epstein, R., Kalus, C., & Berger, M. (2006). The continuing bond of the bereaved towards the deceased and adjustment to loss. *Mortality*, 11(3), 253–269.

French, C. C., & Stone, A. (2014). *Anomalistic psychology: Exploring paranormal belief and experience*. Hampshire, UK: Palgrave Macmillan.

Gardner, M. (1992). *On the wild side: The big bang, ESP, the Beast 666, levitation, rain-making, trance-channeling*. New York: Prometheus Books.

Gauld, A. (1977). Discarnate survival. In B. B. Wolman (Ed.), *Handbook of parapsychology* (pp. 577–630). New York: Van Nostrand Reinhold.

Gauld, A. (1982). *Mediumship and survival*. London: Heinemann.

Gauld, A. (2005). Survival. In J. Henry (Ed.), *Parapsychology: Research on exceptional experiences* (pp. 215–223). Hove, East Sussex: Routledge.

Greeley, A. M. (1987). Hallucinations among the widowed. *Sociology and Social Research*, 71(4), 258–265.

Grimby, A. (1998). Hallucinations following the loss of a spouse: Common and normal events among the elderly. *Journal of Clinical Geropsychology*, 4(1), 65–74.

Guggenheim, B., & Guggenheim, J. (1995). *Hello from heaven*. New York: Bantam.

Gurney, E., Myers, F. W. H., & Podmore, F. (1886). *Phantasms of the living*. London: Trubner.

Harris, K., & Alvarado, C. S. (2014). A review of qualitative mediumship research. In A. J. Rock (Ed.), *The survival hypothesis: Essays on mediumship* (pp. 196–219). Jefferson, NC: McFarland.

Harroldson, E. (1988). Survey of claimed encounters with the dead. *OMEGA – Journal of Death and Dying*, 19(2), 103–113.

Hastings, A. (1983). A counseling approach to parapsychological experience. *Journal of Transpersonal Psychology*, 15(2), 143–167.

Hodgson, R. (1898). *A further record of observations of certain phenomena of trance*. Paper presented at the Proceedings of the Society for Psychical Research.

Holden, J. M., Lankford, C., & Holmes, L. (2019). After-death communication and the biblical fruits of the spirit: An online survey. *Spirituality in Clinical Practice*, 6(1), 15–26. doi: 10.1037/scp0000161.

Holt, N. J., Simmonds-Moore, C., Luke, D., & French, C. C. (2012). *Anomalistic psychology*. New York, NY: Palgrave Macmillian.

Houck, J. A. (2005). The universal, multiple, and exclusive experiences of after-death communication. *Journal of Near-Death Studies*, 24(2), 117–127.

Houran, J., & Lange, R. (1997). Hallucinations that comfort: Contextual mediation of deathbed visions. *Perceptual and Motor Skills*, 84(Suppl. 3), 1491–1504.

Howitt, D. (2013). *Introduction to qualitative methods in psychology* (2nd edn). London: Pearson.

Irwin, H. J., & Watt, C. (2007). *An introduction to parapsychology* (5th edn). Jefferson, NC: McFarland & Co.

Jensen, C. G., & Cardeña, E. (2008). *A controlled long-distance test of a professional medium.* Paper presented at the 51st Annual Convention of the Parapsychological Association, University of Winchester, UK.

Kalish, R. A., & Reynolds, D. K. (1973). Phenomenological reality and post-death contact. *Journal for the Scientific Study of Religion, 12*(2), 209–221.

Keen, C., Murray, C., & Payne, S. (2013). Sensing the presence of the deceased: A narrative review. *Mental Health, Religion & Culture, 16*(4), 384–402.

Kelly, E. W., & Arcangel, D. (2011). An investigation of mediums who claim to give information about deceased persons. *The Journal of Nervous and Mental Disease, 199*(1), 11–17.

Kelly, R. E. (2002). Post mortem contact by fatal injury victims with emergency service workers at the scenes of their death. *Journal of Near-Death Studies, 21*(1), 25–33.

Klass, D. (1993). Solace and immortality: Bereaved parents' continuing bond with their children. *Death Studies, 17*(4), 343–368.

Klugman, C. M. (2006). Dead men talking: Evidence of post death contact and continuing bonds. *OMEGA – Journal of Death and Dying, 53*(3), 249–262.

Krippner, S. (2008). Learning from the spirits: Candomblé, Umbanda, and Kardecismo in Recife, Brazil. *Anthropology of Consciousness, 19*(1), 1–32.

Kurtz, P. (1985). Spiritualists, mediums and psychics: Some evidence of fraud. In P. A. Kurtz (Ed.), *A skeptic's handbook of parapsychology* (pp. 177–223). Buffalo, NY: Prometheus.

LaGrand, L. E. (2005). The nature and therapeutic implications of the extraordinary experiences of the bereaved. *Journal of Near-Death Studies, 21*(4), 3–20.

Laszlo, E. (2008). An unexplored domain of nonlocality: Toward a scientific explanation of instrumental transcommunication. *EXPLORE, 4*(5), 321–327.

Leary, M. R. (2013). A research study into the interpretation of EVP. *ATransC NewsJournal.* Available from: https://atransc.org/radiosweep-study2/.

Leary, M. R., & Butler, T. (2015). Electronic voice phenomena. In E. Cardena, J. Palmer, & D. Marcusson-Clavertz (Eds.), *Parapsychology: A handbook for the 21st century* (pp. 341–349). Jefferson, NC: McFarland.

Lindstrōm, T. C. (1995). Experiencing the presence of the dead: Discrepancies in 'the sensing experience' and their psychological concomitants. *OMEGA – Journal of Death and Dying, 31*(1), 11–21.

Locher, T., & Harsch-Fischbach, M. (1997). *Breakthroughs in technical spirit communication.* Boulder, CO: Continuing Life Research.

MacRae, A. (2005). Report of an electronic voice phenomenon experiment inside a double-screened room. *Journal of the Society for Psychical Research, 69*(4), 191–201.

Markwick, B. (1985). The establishment of data manipulation in the Soal-Shackleton experiments. In P. A. Kurtz (Ed.), *A sceptic's handbook of parapsychology* (pp. 287–312). Buffalo, NY: Prometheus.

Nees, M. A., & Phillips, C. (2015). Auditory pareidolia: Effects of contextual priming on perceptions of purportedly paranormal and ambiguous auditory stimuli. *Applied Cognitive Psychology, 29*(1), 129–134. doi: 10.1002/acp.3068.

Negro Jr, P. J., Palladino-Negro, P., & Louzã, M. R. (2002). Do religious mediumship dissociative experiences conform to the sociocognitive theory of dissociation? *Journal of Trauma & Dissociation, 3*(1), 51–73.

Normand, C. L., Silverman, P. R., & Nickman, S. L. (1996). Bereaved children's changing relationships with the deceased. In D. Klass, P. R. Silverman, & S. L. Nickman (Eds.), *Continuing bonds: New understandings of grief* (pp. 3–27). London: Taylor & Francis.

O'Keeffe, C., & Wiseman, R. (2005). Testing alleged mediumship: Methods and results. *British Journal of Psychology, 96*, 165–179.

Palmer, J. (1979). A community mail survey of psychic experiences. *Journal of the American Society for Psychical Research, 73*, 221–251.

Parker, J. S. (2005). Extraordinary experiences of the bereaved and adaptive outcomes of grief. *OMEGA – Journal of Death and Dying, 51*(4), 257–283.

Peres, J. F., Moreira-Almeida, A., Caixeta, L., Leao, F., & Newberg, A. (2012). Neuroimaging during trance state: A contribution to the study of dissociation. *PloS One, 7*(11), e49360. doi: 10.1371/journal.pone.0049360.

Persinger, M. A. (1983). Religious and mystical experiences as artifacts of temporal lobe function: A general hypothesis. *Perceptual and Motor Skills, 57*(3), 1255–1262.

Persinger, M. A. (1993). Vectorial cerebral hemisphericity as differential sources for the sensed presence, mystical experiences and religious conversions. *Perceptual and Motor Skills, 76*(3), 915–930.

Pierini, E. (2016). Embodied encounters: Ethnographic knowledge, emotion and senses in the Vale do Amanhecer; spirit mediumship. *Journal for the Study of Religious Experience, 2*(1), 25–49.

Raudive, K. (1971). *Breakthrough: An amazing experiment in electronic communication with the dead.* New York: Taplinger.

Rees, W. D. (1971). The hallucinations of widowhood. *British Medical Journal, 4*(5778), 37–41.

Richards, S. (2016). *'Anomalous voices re-visited': A summary of findings from a 14-month investigation into electronic voice phenomenon and instrumental trans-communication.* Paper presented at the 40th SPR International Annual Conference, 2–4 September, University of Leeds, UK.

Rock, A. J., & Storm, L. (2015). Testing telepathy in the medium/proxy-sitter dyad: A protocol focusing on the source-of-psi problem. *Journal of Scientific Exploration, 29*(4), 565–584.

Roe, C. A. (1996). Clients' influence in the selection of elements of a psychic reading. *The Journal of Parapsychology, 60*(1), 43–70.

Roe, C. A. (2016a). Is inconsistency our only consistent outcome? *Mindfield, 8*(2), 70–75.

Roe, C. A. (2016b). The problem of fraud in parapsychology. *Mindfield, 8*(1), 8–17.

Roe, C. A. (2017). Has parapsychology made progress? *Mindfield, 9*(2), 42–47.

Root, B. L., & Exline, J. J. (2014). The role of continuing bonds in coping with grief: Overview and future directions. *Death Studies, 38*(1), 1–8. doi: 10.1080/07481187.2012.712608

Ross, C. A., & Joshi, S. (1992). Paranormal experiences in the general population. *Journal of Nervous and Mental Disease, 180*(6), 357–361. doi: 10.1097/00005053-199206000-00004.

Roxburgh, E. C., & Roe, C. A. (2011). A survey of dissociation, boundary-thinness, and psychological well-being in spiritualist mental mediumship. *Journal of Parapsychology, 75*(2), 279–299.

Salter, W. H. (1950). *Trance mediumship: an introductory study of Mrs. Piper and Mrs. Leonard.* London: Society for Psychical Research.

Sanger, M. (2009). When clients sense the presence of loved ones who have died. *OMEGA – Journal of Death and Dying, 59*(1), 69–89. doi: 10.2190/OM.59.1.e.

Sidgwick, H., Sidgwick, E., & Johnson, A. (1894). Report on the census of hallucinations. *Proceedings of the Society for Psychical Research, 10*, 25–42.

Simon-Buller, S., Christopherson, V. A., & Jones, R. A. (1989). Correlates of sensing the presence of a deceased spouse. *OMEGA – Journal of Death and Dying, 19*(1), 21–30. doi: 10.2190/4QV9-186V-JXTC-4N0B.

Smith, J., & Dunn, E. V. (1977). Ghosts: Their appearance during bereavement. *Canadian Family Physician, 23*, 121–122.

Vandenbroucke, J. P. (1999). Case reports in an evidence-based world. *Journal of the Royal Society of Medicine, 92*(4), 159–163.

Wahbeh, H., & Radin, D. (2017). People reporting experiences of mediumship have higher dissociation symptom scores than non-mediums, but below thresholds for pathological dissociation. *F1000Research*, 6(1416). doi: 10.12688/f1000research.12019.3.

Wright, S. H. (1999). Paranormal contact with the dying: 14 contemporary death coincidences. *Journal of the Society for Psychical Research*, 63(857), 258–267.

Wright, S. H. (2006). Clues to the nature of the afterlife from after-death communication. *Journal of Spirituality & Paranormal Studies*, 29(3), 49–59.

Yamamoto, J., Okonogi, K., Iwasaki, T., & Yoshimura, S. (1969). Mourning in Japan. *American Journal of Psychiatry*, 125(12), 1660–1665.

Chapter 12

Implications for consciousness

This final chapter outlines some of the implications of psi research for consciousness. In order to do this, it begins by reflecting briefly on the evidence covered in the previous nine chapters. The essential take home message from this is that, when a broad view is taken that encompasses the various areas and findings, it is clearly evident that something strange is occurring. However, it is not clear yet precisely what this is, hence the term *Dark Cognition*. Nevertheless, given the range and variety of evidence covered in these chapters the continued sceptical rhetoric that there is either no evidence for psi, or that science in general should continue to ignore these findings, is simply untenable. Given that the range and diversity of findings supporting psi are both substantial and persistent, this in turn raises the question of how such effects may be accounted for in terms of consciousness. To explore this issue the chapter briefly examines current views on the nature of consciousness. It then outlines the dominant view that is currently accepted throughout the wider scientific field, that consciousness is solely the result of brain activity. However, it is clear when this view is used to try and account for the findings from psi-based research outlined in the previous chapters that it fails. Hence, there is a need for a paradigm shift in how consciousness is conceptualised. The shift outlined here is based on an emerging consensus that consciousness may be fundamental in nature and that an individual may interact with a wider *field of consciousness*. Exploration of this view shows that it is better able to account for the data from psi-based research. The chapter ends by exploring some of the implications of this new paradigm of consciousness.

Reflections on the evidence for psi

There can be no doubt that the field of psi research has come a long way since the inception of organisations such as the Society for Psychical Research and the Parapsychological Association. Indeed, some have argued that the field has demonstrated verifiable, concrete and useful contributions to science in general (Hovelmann, 2015). This is not to say that more cannot be done. It would of course be both useful and helpful if effect sizes and replicability could be improved. However, Cardeña (2015b) points out that in order to do this we would need to know much more about psi phenomena and related variables than we currently do, and even then it would not necessarily mean that the phenomena can be elicited when required. Nevertheless, it should be noted that the notion of *uncertainty* that those in the field of psi research have to face and deal with is not unique, as it is a common feature of many other scientific disciplines (Cardeña, 2015a).

The previous chapters have provided some coverage of a selected range of psi topics, including telepathy, remote staring effects, clairvoyance, remote viewing, precognition, psychokinesis, fields of consciousness, subtle energy healing, out of body experiences, near-death experiences and post death phenomena. In each of these areas, with the possible exception of out of body experiences, there is robust evidence of unusual or anomalous effects occurring. In many areas sufficient empirical studies have been conducted to allow for the use of meta-analytic approaches which provide a more comprehensive overview of the findings in a particular field. Each of these meta-analyses shows an often small but reliable and significant effect (e.g., Bem, Tressoldi, Rabeyron, & Duggan, 2015; Dogan, 2018; Duggan & Tressoldi, 2018; Honorton et al., 1990; Honorton & Ferrari, 1989; Milton, 1997; Mossbridge, Tressoldi, & Utts, 2012; Peters, 1999; Radin & Nelson, 2003; Roe, Sonnex, & Roxburgh, 2015; Schmidt, Schneider, Utts, & Walach, 2004; Storm et al., 2017; Storm, Tressoldi, & Di Risio, 2012). It is also interesting to note that the significant effects of psi reported in the various meta-analyses resemble, and at times exceed, those reported in the more acceptable areas of medicine and psychology (Richard, Bond Jr, & Stokes-Zoota, 2003; Tressoldi & Utts, 2015). Indeed the most recent review argues that the field of psi research has clearly demonstrated replicability and consistency of effects as well as cumulativeness (Cardeña, 2018). As such, if the findings from each of these fields of psi research are examined individually the results are both positive and encouraging. However, if the findings from these areas are taken together *en masse* it is simply incomprehensible that anyone could reach a conclusion arguing that there is no evidence for psi. Therefore, the continued objections regarding evidence of psi would seem to be based more on dogma and cultural acceptance than scientific evidence and reasoning. Indeed, some have argued that continuing to ignore the data on psi simply reflects a prejudicial attitude which is contrary to the very nature of science (Facco, Agrillo, & Greyson, 2015). Nevertheless, once the findings of psi are accepted this raises the question of how they can be accounted for.

Accounting for psi in terms of consciousness

To try to answer the question of how such findings may be accounted for in terms of human consciousness we need to briefly examine what is meant by consciousness. Following this, we can explore the currently accepted basis for consciousness and ask how such an approach can account for the findings of psi.

Defining consciousness

Possibly the only agreement there is in research on consciousness is the fact that there is no universally accepted notion of precisely what consciousness is (Williams, 2016), though most would agree that it involves aspects of awareness, self-awareness, subjective experience, knowing and understanding (e.g., Blackmore, 2003; Rose, 2006). A pragmatic definition offered by Searle (2008) is that it refers to the subjective awareness you have of yourself and your environment which begins when you wake each morning and ends each night when you fall asleep. Throughout this time an essential component of consciousness is its subjective and private nature. For instance, James (1890) pointed out early on that all people feel themselves to be conscious thinking individuals. Hence, the generally accepted view is that each person experiences their own consciousness but not that of another, no matter how close a relationship they may have. In addition, we conclude that others are conscious simply because they act in a manner that is similar to us and they can tell us they are conscious.

It is also worth reflecting for a moment on the idea that consciousness may not be a single state or construct. For example, researchers have distinguished between having something consciously in mind at a particular moment that can be reported or consciously experiencing a current event. The former is referred to as an aspect of *access consciousness* and the latter as *phenomenal consciousness* (Block, Flanagan, & Güzeldere, 1997). In addition, Searle (1997) notes that when we sleep we are often aware of our dreams and as such distinct or altered states of consciousness can occur. Some even suggest that each cortical system may be associated with a distinct aspect of consciousness. For example, Zeki (2001) uses the term *micro-consciousness* to refer to the possibility that each part of a system may have its own correlate of consciousness. Overall, it seems that consciousness refers to a range of possible states and types of experience rather than a simple single aspect of the self. In this way consciousness is more of an 'umbrella term' for a range of mental phenomena (see e.g., Blackmore, 2003). However, whilst there is much debate and discussion regarding the precise nature of consciousness the generally accepted view within mainstream science is that consciousness is directly related to the brain.

Consciousness is the brain

If an individual is asked to indicate where they think their consciousness resides many invariably point to the head to suggest that somewhere in this region is the basis for their sense of self. In part this may be because the major sensory inputs of vision, sound and touch are processed here. It also reflects the dominant view currently held in science which proposes that consciousness is a direct product of the brain. It is worth reflecting for a moment that this was not always the case. In fact, Aristotle put forward the *cardiac hypothesis* which suggested that the conscious mind resided in the heart region, because this was both warm and active. The brain was seen as nothing more than a radiator used to cool the blood. It was Plato who placed the conscious mind in the head, though he did this because that part of the body was deemed to be closer to heaven and not for any specific biological reason (Kolb, Whishaw, & Teskey, 2016).

Nevertheless, the proposal that consciousness is directly linked to the brain has remained the dominant view ever since. Hence, irrespective of how complex consciousness may be the central assumption of scientific materialism is that consciousness is identical with, or can be reduced to, the electrical impulses of the various neural networks of the brain (Beauregard, Trent, & Schwartz, 2018). Given this, each conscious experience is often perceived as emerging from the neural activity of the brain in response to internal processes and external sensory information (Tressoldi, Facco, & Lucangeli, 2016), in which case the human individual can be portrayed as a complex biochemical organism whose self-awareness is the result of these biochemical interactions. As such, when the organism dies its consciousness ceases to exist.

However, Chalmers (2013) has identified what he calls the *hard problem* of consciousness. This asks how we get from the objective activity of multiple networks of neurons to the subjective taste or experience of chocolate. Mainstream neuroscience has attempted to examine this by identifying and exploring specific neural correlates of consciousness (Crick & Koch, 2003). The assumption here is that by exploring how and why particular patterns of neural activity occur it will make the hard problem clearer. However, it would be fair to say that there are now an abundance of studies exploring and examining the various neural correlates of behaviour and cognition. Unfortunately, the hard problem of consciousness is still no clearer. Given this, it may be unsurprising that such a view also has difficulty accounting for the findings of psi.

Accounting for psi

Many have argued that models or theories which rely solely on the assumption that consciousness equates to brain activity have difficulty accounting for findings that suggest that the mind of an individual may not be limited to a precise space or time (Beauregard, 2014; Brabant, 2016; J. M. Schwartz, Stapp, & Beauregard, 2005). In particular, the findings from the field of *near-death experiences,* which suggests that rich conscious experiences may occur when the brain is either inactive or non-functioning, something that contemporary neuroscientific models would suggest is necessary for such experiences to occur, is difficult at best to account for using a materialist approach (van Lommel, 2004). Indeed, S. A. Schwartz (2018) argues that such a brain based account of consciousness is simply inconsistent with the available data. It is worth stressing at this point that the view of consciousness emerging as a result of brain activity is an *assumption* not an empirical fact. Furthermore, this assumption is based primarily on correlated activity between brain function and cognition or behaviour. Importantly, as most undergraduate students learn early on in their academic career, correlation does not equal causation. Hence, Brabant (2016), among many others, argues that the current view of consciousness as being solely an emergent phenomena of brain activity is certainly incomplete and very likely wrong (e.g., Beauregard et al., 2018; Facco, Lucangeli, & Tressoldi, 2017; S. A. Schwartz, 2018). However, this does not mean that the brain plays no part in conscious experience. As van Lommel (2004) argues, the many studies identifying clear associations between brain activity and cognition/behaviour show that the brain is in some way involved in these processes. Nevertheless, what such studies do *not* show is that the brain is producing these aspects of conscious behaviour. As such, there is a need for a paradigm shift.

A paradigm shift

It should not be the case that potential theories of consciousness avoid dealing with the findings related to psi simply because they are difficult to account for, ambiguous, complex and messy. In addition, where findings, such as those from across the various fields of psi, are either ignored or rejected a-priori then such decisions are based more on the beliefs of those responsible for such judgements than on science. Indeed, Facco et al. (2015) posit that this can lead to a *dogmatic drift,* where the currently accepted axioms and paradigms of science are prejudicially taken for truth, thus contradicting the very nature of science itself. In fact, the ability to check and change its axioms and paradigms, to question any accepted model, particularly when they prove to be incompatible with new findings, and attempt to understand all issues is a central strength of science and the scientific process. No theory or model, no matter how good, and no matter the professional credibility of the person proposing it should be allowed to stand if it cannot account for all the data. Hence, it is sometimes the case that in attempting to account for unusual data a paradigm shift is needed. A paradigm shift is often the result of scientists working within a particular paradigm that is no longer able to fully explain or account for the observed phenomena. Eventually, these anomalies accumulate making the current paradigm untenable which in turn can lead to a crisis. The crisis is overcome by a sudden revolution in thinking which involves a radical transformation in the way that science is then conducted. This marks the transition from the old paradigm to a new one that is more able to account for such findings (Kuhn, 1970). There are many examples in the history of science whereby a paradigm shift has produced a radical transformation in terms of what is viewed as accepted knowledge and understanding. Examples include the theories of relativity, evolution, plate tectonics and germ theory to name but a few. It should be noted that a possible paradigm shift does not mean that knowledge and understanding gained using the old paradigm should be rejected, simply that the anomalous findings indicate that the limits of such a paradigm have been reached (Facco et al., 2015). Just as the paradigm of Newtonian physics reached a limit when attempting to explain sub-atomic particles, this does not invalidate the findings of Newtonian physics, which are still used widely. It merely shows that the current paradigm has limits in terms of what it can explain. With regards to psi and consciousness many have argued that a shift needs to occur which gives serious consideration to two key points (e.g., Beauregard, 2014; Beauregard et al., 2018; Brabant, 2016; S. A. Schwartz, 2018). The first is that consciousness is not an emergent phenomenon but should be thought of as *fundamental*. Related to this is the idea that consciousness is not *solely* produced by the brain but may be interpreted, relayed or transmitted by the brain.

Consciousness is fundamental

The proposal that consciousness may be fundamental is a form of *panpsychism*. This is literally the view that mind (psyche) is found everywhere (pan) and is the doctrine that everything has a mind. This idea is not new; in fact it is an old idea originally put forward by the ancient Greeks, in particular Thales of Miletus and Plato. Since then there have been many great scholars who have taken this view seriously, including the philosopher Arthur Schopenhauer, and the father of American psychology William James; however it declined in popularity with the rise of positivism in the 20th century (see, Chalmers, 2015; Koch, 2014). The key point here is that rather than assuming consciousness is something that emerges from the underlying elements of physics, biology, chemistry and psychology, it is seen as operating at a more fundamental level (see Figure 12.1).

Hence, the idea is that this view sees conscious experience as a fundamental aspect or component of reality. That is, it is not a derivative of physical materialism but is primary (see, d'Espagnat, 2006). It is a view that has been around for some time,

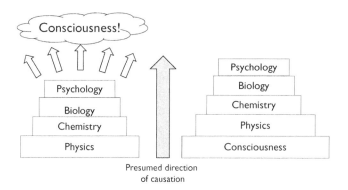

Figure 12.1 The current view of consciousness as an emergent property on the left, and the idea that consciousness be seen as fundamental on the right.

though it does now seem to be undergoing a resurgence of interest (e.g., Chalmers, 2019; Goff, 2017; Hameroff & Penrose, 1996b, 2014). Given our current limited understanding of what this fundamental level of consciousness may be researchers have come up with a variety of descriptors, including, but not limited to, *proto-consciousness* (Hameroff & Penrose, 2014), *mindful Universe* (Stapp, 2011), *self-aware Universe* (Goswami, 1995), *morphic field* (Sheldrake, 2015), *collective unconscious* (Jung, 1991), a non-local strata of *pure information* (Bohm, 2005), as well as a *zero dimension* (Byrne, 2018). It is important to note that these terms are at present simply descriptive labels for something that *may* exist. It is also worth keeping in mind that attempting to describe such an idea requires language but the language used is likely to influence, shape or restrict the thinking that follows, hence the need to keep a cautiously critical yet open mind when grappling with such complex ideas.

For the sake of simplicity, here the term *field of consciousness* will be used as it is both generic and non-specific, encapsulating some of the key ideas that are important. According to those proposing such an idea this fundamental field of consciousness represents a mind-like primordial substance, the physical laws of which are yet to be discerned (e.g., Chalmers, 2019; Goff, 2017; Hameroff & Penrose, 1996b, 2014). This field of consciousness is proposed to represent a fundamental level of reality, possessing the pre-cursors to individual consciousness as well as physical reality. It is thought to contain all information, possess holistic properties allowing it to operate in a non-local sense which means it can transcend the limitations of our space and time, and is self-organising with information constantly being added to it and retrieved from it (see, Brabant, 2016; Williams, 2016). For instance, Bohm (2005) has suggested that the physical world emerges from this hidden higher dimensional space which contains the source of all information enfolded within it (see also, Bohm & Hiley, 1993). Stapp (2011) has proposed something similar by positing an underlying reality of pure potential. Physical reality is then seen as something that unfolds or emerges from an interaction between physical processes and the pure potential of the underlying reality. It is important to point out that whatever this field of consciousness may be it is not likely to be conscious in the same way that a single human is conscious.

The key issue of relevance regarding this proposal for the field of psi research is the notion that consciousness may emerge as an interaction between the local brain of the individual and the wider field of consciousness. James (1890) was one of the early advocates of the position that the brain may play more of a *permissive* or transmissive role regarding consciousness. Since then many have continued to argue that localised consciousness is *related* to brain activity but not solely *reliant* upon it (e.g., Brabant, 2016; Tressoldi et al., 2016; van Lommel, 2004; Williams, 2016). The analogy often used to help explain this idea usually refers to the way an electromagnetic signal interacts with a television (TV) set to produce a moving image with soundtrack on a screen. The key point is that it is not the TV that is the *source* of the information portrayed on screen. It simply relays or transmits the incoming signal. However, instead of receiving electromagnetic signals the brain is capable of interacting with a higher dimensional or wider field of consciousness. In the same way that the stream of images and sounds presented by the TV are not generated within the set itself, some aspects of consciousness may not be uniquely generated within the individual brain itself. There is a need here to be cautiously precise in terms of the speculative suggestions put forward. This is because so little is currently known about consciousness that it would be a mistake at this early stage to rule out any ideas. Hence, it is not the suggestion that consciousness is *only* the result of a wider field interacting in some way with a localised individual. It may be that consciousness can be both: produced locally in a limited manner and more comprehensively when interacting with the wider field of consciousness. Again, this is a speculative idea but given the current limitations of what we know about consciousness it is important not to fall into the simplistic reasoning trap of thinking something needs to be 'either or' when in fact it may well be 'both and'. Hence, consciousness may result from *both* the interaction between the local individual *and* the wider field of consciousness. In this way, consistent with all neuroscience research, behaviour would clearly correlate with localised brain activity. However, consciousness could also be influenced by the information carried in the wider signal. It is this information which could offer a straightforward account for the findings relating to psi.

Accounting for psi

The suggestion is that the wider field of consciousness connects all things, all places and all times and it is this connectivity that not only allows for but may encourage non-local psi-type effects to emerge (see Figure 12.2).

As can be seen in Figure 12.2 the individuals on the right-hand side are linked, or connected via a wider field of consciousness that may be fundamental. This means that they would have access to a much wider range of information, which is shared and not reliant on any one individual. If this fundamental non-local view of consciousness is adopted then the findings from much, if not all, of psi research not only become more comprehensible but are exactly what would be expected. For example, telepathy would not be seen as the 'transfer' of information from one distant mind to another. Rather it could be viewed as the sharing of information between two linked aspects of mind via the wider field of consciousness. In a similar way clairvoyance and remote viewing could be accounted for in terms of accessing shared information from the wider field. As such, these processes may involve the individual focusing inwards

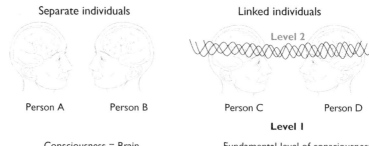

Figure 12.2 Two individuals. On the left, when viewed from the perspective that consciousness is solely the product of the brain these two individuals can be seen as distinct and separate. On the right, when viewed at the physical level (i.e., Level 1), they are also seen as distinct and separate entities. However, when the more fundamental level of consciousness is considered (i.e., Level 2) they are clearly linked.

at a deeper level rather than looking outwards. Such an approach could also account for precognition. For instance, Williams (2017) has suggested that precognition may be understood as the sensation and perception of current probabilities of future events from the wider field of consciousness. Hence, rather than perceiving future events the individual may be able to ascertain some information regarding the current probability of future events. If consciousness is fundamental and underpins all of reality then this would also suggest that mind and matter are not distinct (e.g., Bohm, 2005). As such, Beauregard (2014) argues that psychokinesis could be explained by the individual mind exploiting the intimate relationship between the information in the wider field and its link with physical reality. Possible changes in physical reality could be brought about by manipulating or attempting to influence the underlying information. This may explain the greater success of micro psychokinesis (PK) compared to macro PK as the information relating to the former may be more easily manipulated. The ability to exert a direct influence over physical events could also account for energy healing effects. The idea may also account for the patterns of findings relating to fields of consciousness. Where large groups of individuals gather together and meditate, their brain activity may become more coherent. This localised field of coherence may influence the wider field of consciousness which in turn sets up the potential for change at the normal level of reality. Finally, remaining with the TV set analogy, if the set is damaged or switched off the information presented will be degraded, or impaired in some way, and finally disappear completely. However, the signal still exists. In a similar way, if an individual suffers neurological damage or dies the wider aspect of consciousness can continue. This could offer an account for the reported experiences of those undergoing an OBE or NDE. Hence, as Tressoldi et al. (2016) point out, when the findings of psi are viewed from this perspective they are no longer seen as anomalous and difficult to account for. In fact, given such a model, such findings would be expected.

Interestingly, the idea that an individual can interact with a wider field of consciousness may also help to explain other areas of psychology that suggest psychological processes and/or experiences may transcend the assumed boundaries of space and time, such as those reported in spiritual and/or transpersonal encounters (see, Schwartz, 2015). In particular, the reported feelings of a connection with a greater whole and a timeless, space-less awareness. Such a view is also consistent with the idea that artists may at times be able to obtain a glimpse of this realm which helps to provide them with a unique insight into the nature of reality that is radically different from that of everyday life (see, Cardeña, Lynn, & Krippner, 2017). Others have also suggested that such an approach could account for the unusual behaviours exhibited by geniuses or prodigies. According to Brabant (2016) such gifted individuals may simply have access to a wider realm of information, which allows them to retrieve the correct answer or write out what is required without the need to think about it. All these ideas represent interesting possibilities; however, it is important not to fall into the trap of thinking that such a model is a panacea for all findings related to consciousness. There is no doubt that it provides a good account of various psi-type behaviours and certainly provides a more useful and accurate framework than the view that consciousness is simply an epiphenomenon of the brain. Nevertheless, it raises as many questions as it answers. For instance, if there is a wider non-material field of consciousness it raises the question of how a material-based individual would be able to interact with it.

Interacting with the field of consciousness

Ever since Descartes proposed the distinction between mind and body people have been asking how a non-material mind could interact with a material body. At the time Descartes put forward the idea Elisabeth, Princess of Bohemia, rejected the mind-body distinction based on the fact that it did not fit the mechanistic principles of the day (see Shapiro, 2013). However, today the idea that a physical device can access a non-physical field of information is synonymous with the pervasive use of tablets, phones and personal computers accessing the internet via a Wi-Fi signal. At this moment in time it is not possible to identify precisely where or how such a wider field of consciousness may interact with a physical person. Indeed, when taken at its most extreme, the view that consciousness is fundamental would imply that the material world is constructed from, or reliant upon, consciousness. This has led some to argue that there is no 'mind-body' distinction or problem because there is no separation between body and mind. The physical body is a part of the larger mind and as such the 'mind-body' problem simply dissolves (see, Gallimore, 2018; Meyer, 2018). Others have argued that the physical brain interacts with a wider field of consciousness and that it can do so in a number of ways.

First is an idea highlighted by van Lommel (2004) which suggests that deoxyribonucleic acid (DNA) may act as a sort of quantum antenna which is capable of interacting with a non-local hyperdimensional aspect of consciousness. In part this is based on the fact that throughout life the composition of an individual's body is undergoing continuous changes, as the cells of an individual's body grow, die and are replaced. The idea is that among all these changes DNA represents a stable and consistent aspect of the self which may act as an interface between the personal material body of the individual and the wider field of consciousness. A second possibility put forward by Lipton (2008) is that on the surface of cells in the human body are a range of personal self-receptors that may act as antennas interacting with signals from a wider field. A key point put forward by Lipton (2008) is that these receptors 'read a signal of self which does not exist within the cell but comes to it from the external environment' (p. 160). Returning to the analogy of the TV set the argument here is that the physical television set is equivalent to the biological cell and the TV aerial to the personal self-receptors on the surface of the cells. Hence, these receptors are capable of interacting with a wider field of consciousness. Both these approaches have been suggested to account for the strange thoughts and feelings reported by those who have undergone a major organ transplant, where it later becomes clear that such thoughts and feelings fit more closely with the character and consciousness of the donor (see e.g., Joshi, 2011; Matlock, 2019). A third possibility relates to the model of consciousness put forward by Hameroff and Penrose (2014). They argue that consciousness emerges from quantum events that take place in the skeletal structure of the neurons in the brain (Hameroff & Penrose, 1996a, 1996b), specifically, in parts of the neurons called microtubules which are tiny tube-like proteins that play a role in supporting the cell's structure and function. These microtubules are thought to operate in what is referred to as a quantum superposition. That is, they exist, or are able to represent, all possible states concurrently. They are also thought to work together simultaneously as they are entangled at a quantum level. It is this coherent collaboration of the microtubules that in turn leads to neural activity, which can be measured via the EEG, that gives rise to consciousness. In the model put forward by Hameroff and Penrose (2014), the quantum superposition of the microtubules in one neuron may be influenced by the synaptic inputs into that neuron, as well as possible quantum gravity effects, which end or collapse the superposition state and in turn may influence the activity of the neuron. However, a plausible alternative for ending or influencing the superposition states of the microtubules offered here is the interaction with a wider field of consciousness. Hence, it would be the interaction of the microtubules at a quantum level with the wider field of consciousness that would lead to the collapse of any superposition effects which in turn would lead to the neural activity assumed to underlie consciousness. In this way the wider field of consciousness may influence or effect the conscious experience of the individual. It should be made clear that the speculative extension to Hameroff and Penrose's (2014) model proposed here is not something they posit themselves; it is simply a plausible explanation for how a physical system may be influenced by and/or interact with a non-physical wider field of consciousness.

It is not possible at this moment in time to say which of these alternatives provides a more plausible account for the proposed interactions between a physical system and a non-physical wider field of consciousness. Indeed, given the current views of consciousness and our limited understanding of its causal mechanisms it would be foolhardy to restrict our thinking in any way. Hence, it may well be that a combination of one or more of these approaches better represents the reality of the situation. Furthermore, future research may shed light on new, unexpected or currently unknown areas of interest. Nevertheless, at present each of these ideas provides a plausible mechanism for how a physical individual could interact with a wider non-physical field of consciousness and this raises some interesting issues and implications.

Issues regarding the wider field of consciousness

The view put forward here is that consciousness occurs at *both* an individual level *and* at a more Cosmic fundamental level. Hence, consciousness is something that can work via the brain though need not be solely produced by it. Such aspects of consciousness are likely to be different though capable of working in coordination with one another, what Beauregard (2014) would refer to as an interaction between the local mind of the individual and the greater more fundamental level of mind of the Cosmos. Given this, a question that immediately springs to mind is how, if at all, would it be possible to discern between the idea that consciousness is solely the product of brain activity *alone* compared to the notion that the brain simply relays or transfers conscious information from a wider field. There are several lines of reasoning that may help to shed light on this point.

For instance, returning to the TV and signal metaphor, in such a set-up it would be possible to influence or alter what appears on the TV screen simply by blocking or interrupting the signal without the need to alter or damage the physical set. By influencing what is on the screen in this way it would be clear that it is the signal that is responsible for the final image on screen and not the TV set itself. However, at present there is little understanding of what the wider field of consciousness may be and such a lack of understanding means there is at present little or no possibility of influencing it. This need not always be the case. It may be that future research focusing on this issue can help to shed light on nature of the wider field.

In addition, some have suggested that an alternative view is to ask whether it is possible for an individual to have an experience that need not directly correlate with their brain activity (Kastrup, 2014). If consciousness is reliant on the activity of the brain alone then anyone reporting a rich and detailed conscious experience would be expected to show the pre-requisite pattern of complex and interactive brain activity. Individuals reporting such experiences without the pre-requisite brain activity would, according to Kastrup (2014), exclude the view that such a conscious experience is based on brain activity alone. Indeed, this is precisely what is reported in some instances of near-death experiences (see Chapter 10). Furthermore, research has also shown that the effects of psychedelic substances can often be associated with a reduction in brain activity despite the increased richness of the reported experiences (Kastrup, 2016). Such findings help to bolster the view that consciousness is not solely reliant on brain activity and leads the way to identifying the potential role of a wider field of consciousness.

A further issue to arise if the view of consciousness as an interaction between a local physical individual and a wider field is accepted regards the strength of the signal, or sensitivity of the individual to that signal. For instance, it may be that some individuals exhibit or maintain a stronger link and/or are more sensitive to the wider field of consciousness than others. According to Beauregard (2014) the strength of this link may be what accounts for psi. For example, greater connectivity between the individual's local level of consciousness and a wider field may lead to an expansion of consciousness with the individual experiencing non-physical domains of reality that are beyond this dimension of space and time. If this is the case then psi research could usefully explore potential techniques and approaches that may work to enhance the strength of the signal and/or sensitivity of the individual to this link. Indeed, much has already been done regarding this point. For instance, many of the positive findings within the domain of telepathy have been found when the receiver operates in sensory isolation, as in the ganzfeld paradigm (see Chapter 3). Such isolation may be required to enhance their sensitivity to the wider field. In a similar vein others have found that the long-term practice of meditation may be a useful way of enhancing the signal to noise ratio of the link between individual consciousness and the wider field. This is clearly evident in the research showing that long-term meditators are often better able to achieve altered states of consciousness which in turn facilitates the expression of psi (see e.g., Roney-Dougal & Solfvin, 2011; Schmidt, Han-Gue, Whittman, Ambach, & Kubel, 2018; Sedlmeier, 2018). A similar proposal has also been put forward by those exploring the psi potential of various psychedelic drugs (Luke & Spowers, 2018). These substances are often portrayed as providing a doorway to another realm that offers unique and potentially life changing insights. Such a view suggests that exposure to these wider realms can provide access to otherwise hidden levels of knowledge and understanding. Hence, future research may benefit from focusing on and developing ways in which the strength of the signal or sensitivity of the individual to that signal can be enhanced.

Implications of the wider field of consciousness

If, as argued here, consciousness is seen to be fundamental this in turn gives rise to a number of profound implications. First is the idea that all objects, material matter and particles contain some form of consciousness. These ideas are reflected in the view of *panpsychism* which proposes that mind (i.e., *psyche*) is literally everywhere (i.e., *pan*). Whether it is an electron, a table or a brain, all matter is seen as possessing or being based upon consciousness (Chalmers, 2015; Koch, 2014). Hence, consciousness is not a derivative of physical matter but is primary (see, d'Espagnat, 2006). Of course, not all objects will have the same form or level of consciousness and the distinctions between these levels is at present somewhat blurred by lack of knowledge and understanding. Nevertheless, some have suggested that the precise nature of consciousness for any object may to some extent depend on its level of complexity and interconnectedness (Tononi & Koch, 2015). For instance, a table with a low level of molecular complexity and interconnectedness would have a very basic level of consciousness compared to a highly complex brain with billions of interconnected neurons. Such ideas have even led some to suggest that the stars in the Cosmos may be conscious, which is evident in the speed with which they move (Matloff, 2016, 2017). Indeed, Vidal (2016) has suggested that the movement of binary stars satisfies some of the criteria used to classify an interactive system as a living organism.

Finally, and perhaps most importantly, is the idea that each individual is linked by, or part of the wider field of consciousness. Hence, rather than see themselves as isolated and separate both from each other and from the wider Cosmos, people should begin to see themselves and others as part of the same wider system. In a way, individuals need to begin looking at the world around them from a different level of perspective. Much in the same way that when viewed at the individual cellular level the brain can be seen to be made up of billions of discrete neurons: each neuron physically separate, alone and isolated, with no one neuron touching another. However, step back and look at the brain and you see a coherent organic whole. Such an idea may not appeal to all and for many it may require a distinct mind-shift in the way they view themselves, others and their relationships. Nevertheless, the idea that there is only one single mind in the Cosmos, of which each person is but a small aspect, is not new. For instance, Schrodinger (2018) stated that 'mind is by its very nature a *singulāre tantum*' (p. 134), that is, singular in nature, an idea that has been echoed down the ages by many other eminent scholars (e.g., James, Jung, Pauli, and Velmans; see Brabant, 2016). As Brabant (2016) points out, should this model of reality become accepted it would likely lead to dramatic changes in the way humans interact with one another and the world around them. Perhaps when we accept that we are not so different from our neighbour, and may in fact be connected in some meaningful and fundamental way, then, just perhaps, we may start to treat each other with the dignity and respect we each deserve.

Conclusion

Reflecting back on the topics covered in this book it is clear that there is a wide range of evidence for many of the different aspects of psi. Such findings have, perhaps un-surprisingly, led to claims that the field of psi has clearly demonstrated consistency and replicability of effects. Hence, the continued rhetorical arguments stating that no evidence for psi exists are simply untenable. This does not mean more cannot be done to confirm such effects and develop understanding of the underlying causes. Indeed, future research needs to build on these solid findings and move beyond the realm of continuing to produce and replicate effects in order to construct coherent theoretical models to help uncover why and when such effects would be expected to occur. Nevertheless, attempting to account for the effects of psi using the currently accepted model of consciousness simply highlights its limitations. The idea that consciousness is the result of brain activity *alone* fails to provide a coherent account of the data relating to psi. As such, the view that consciousness is solely reliant on brain function is at best incongruent with the data and at worst obsolete. Hence, there is a need for a paradigm shift. Here, it is argued that such a shift requires consciousness to be reframed from an epiphenomenon of biology to a view where consciousness should be seen as funda-mental. The idea that consciousness may be fundamental, connecting all things, all places and all times offers a clearer and more coherent account of the data relating to psi. Indeed, such findings would be expected and hence no longer viewed as anom-alous if such a view were accepted. Such an idea does raise some interesting questions regarding the nature of any interaction between a physical individual and the pro-posed fundamental field of consciousness. Furthermore, the view that individuals may be connected via a fundamental field of consciousness reveals some interesting and thought-provoking implications for the way people may see themselves and others.

At present, it would be fair to state that our understanding of psi and consciousness are far from complete. Nevertheless, all good scientists love a challenge and whilst the effects that emerge under the heading of dark cognition may be seen as anomalous and contentious now, there is no doubt that the findings from future research will help to illuminate the field, providing a greater and more comprehensive level of understanding.

Review questions

Some questions that may prove helpful when reflecting on the material covered in this chapter.

- Would you agree with the view that there is no evidence for psi?
- Has the evidence covered convinced you something unusual is occurring?

- What, if any, evidence do you find most compelling and why?
- How would you explain to someone you are conscious?
- How could you tell whether someone else is conscious or not?
- Do you think consciousness is static or fluid, changing over the years as the individual organism develops?
- Do you think you are the same conscious entity as you were 10 years ago?
- Do you think that consciousness is solely the product of the brain – why?
- Which approach do you think provides the best account for psi?
- What do you think some of the implications of this new model are?
- How would you feel if you knew that you are linked in a fundamental way to each and every other person on the planet?

References

Beauregard, M. (2014). The primordial psyche. *Journal of Consciousness Studies*, *21*(7–8), 132–157.

Beauregard, M., Trent, N. L., & Schwartz, G. E. (2018). Toward a postmaterialist psychology: Theory, research, and applications. *New Ideas in Psychology*, *50*, 21–33. doi: 10.1016/j.newideapsych.2018.02.004.

Bem, D. J., Tressoldi, P., Rabeyron, T., & Duggan, M. (2015). Feeling the future: A meta-analysis of 90 experiments on the anomalous anticipation of random future events. *F1000 Research*, *4*, 1–33. doi: 10.12688/f1000research.7177.2.

Blackmore, S. (2003). *Consciousness: An introduction*. Oxon, UK: Hodder Education.

Block, N. J., Flanagan, O. J., & Güzeldere, G. (1997). *The nature of consciousness: Philosophical debates*. Cambridge, MA: MIT Press.

Bohm, D. (2005). *Wholeness and the implicate order*. London: Routledge.

Bohm, D., & Hiley, J. (1993). *An undivided universe*. London: Routledge.

Brabant, O. (2016). More than meets the eye: Toward a post-materialist model of consciousness. *EXPLORE*, *12*(5), 347–354. doi: 10.1016/j.explore.2016.06.006.

Byrne, M. E. (2018). A basis for the non-local events of quantum mechanics and psi. *Journal of the Society for Psychical Research*, *82*(2), 65–80.

Cardeña, E. (2015a). On negative capability and parapsychology. In E. Cardeña, J. Palmer, & D. Marcusson-Clavertz (Eds.), *Parapsychology: A handbook for the 21st century* (pp. 399–403). Jefferson, NC: McFarland.

Cardeña, E. (2015b). The unbearable fear of psi: On scientific suppression in the 21st century. *Journal of Scientific Exploration*, *29*(4), 601–620.

Cardeña, E. (2018). The experimental evidence for parapsychological phenomena: A review. *American Psychologist*, *73*(5), 663–677. doi: 10.1037/amp0000236.

Cardeña, E., Lynn, S. J., & Krippner, S. (2017). The psychology of anomalous experience: A rediscovery. *Psychology of Consciousness: Theory, Research and Practice*, *4*(1), 4–22. doi: 10.1037/cns0000093.

Chalmers, D. (2013). How can we construct a science of consciousness? *Annals of the New York Academy of Sciences*, *1303*, 25–35. doi: 10.1111/nyas.12166.

Chalmers, D. (2015). Panpsychism and panprotopsychism. In T. Alter & Y. Nagasawa (Eds.), *Consciousness in the physical world: Perspectives on Russellian monism* (pp. 246–276). New York: Oxford University Press.

Chalmers, D. (2019). Idealism and the mind-body problem. In W. Seager (Ed.), *The Routledge handbook of panpsychism*. London: Routledge.

Crick, F., & Koch, C. (2003). A framework for consciousness. *Nature Neuroscience*, 6(2), 119–126. doi: 10.1038/nn0203-119.

d'Espagnat, B. (2006). *On physics and reality*. Princeton & Oxford: Princeton University Press.

Dogan, M. D. (2018). The effect of reiki on pain: A meta-analysis. *Complementary Therapies in Clinical Practice*, 31, 384–387. doi: 10.1016/j.ctcp.2018.02.020.

Duggan, M., & Tressoldi, P. (2018). Predictive physiological anticipation preceding seemingly unpredictable stimuli: An update of the Mossbridge et al. meta-analysis. *F1000 Research*, 407, 1–18. doi: 10.12688/f1000research.14330.2.

Facco, E., Agrillo, C., & Greyson, B. (2015). Epistemological implications of near-death experiences and other non-ordinary mental expressions: Moving beyond the concept of altered state of consciousness. *Medical Hypotheses*, 85(1), 85–93. doi: 10.1016/j.mehy.2015.04.004.

Facco, E., Lucangeli, D., & Tressoldi, P. (2017). On the science of consciousness: Epistemological reflections and clinical implications. *EXPLORE*, 13(3), 163–180. doi: 10.1016/j.explore.2017.02.007.

Gallimore, A. (2018). The neurobiology of conscious interaction with alternate realities and their inhabitants. In D. Luke & R. Spowers (Eds.), *DMT dialogues: Encounters with the spirit molecule* (pp. 175–204). Rochester, Vermont: Part Street Press.

Goff, P. (2017). *Consciousness and fundamental reality*. New York: OUP.

Goswami, A. (1995). *The self-aware universe: How consciousness creates the material world*. London: Penguin.

Hameroff, S., & Penrose, R. (1996a). Conscious events as orchestrated space-time selections. *Journal of Consciousness Studies*, 3(1), 36–53.

Hameroff, S., & Penrose, R. (1996b). Orchestrated reduction of quantum coherence in brain microtubules: A model for consciousness. *Mathematics and Computers in Simulation*, 40(3–4), 453–480.

Hameroff, S., & Penrose, R. (2014). Consciousness in the universe: A review of the 'Orch OR' theory. *Physics of Life Reviews*, 11(1), 39–78.

Honorton, C., Berger, R. E., Varvoglis, M., Quant, M., Derr, P., Schechter, E. I., & Ferrari, D. C. (1990). Psi communication in the ganzfeld: Experiments with an automated testing system and a comparison with a meta-analysis of earlier studies. *Journal of Parapsychology*, 54(2), 99–139.

Honorton, C., & Ferrari, D. C. (1989). Future telling: A meta-analysis of forced-choice precognition experiments, 1935–1987. *Journal of Parapsychology*, 53, 281–308.

Hovelmann, G. H. (2015). On the usefulness of parapsychology for science at large. In E. Cardena, J. Palmer, & D. Marcusson-Clavertz (Eds.), *Parapsychology: A handbook for the 21st century* (pp. 389–398). Jefferson, NC: McFarland.

James, W. (1890). *The principles of psychology*, Vol. 2. New York: Henry Holt and Company.

Joshi, S. (2011). Memory transference in organ transplant recipients. *Journal of New Approaches to Medicine and Health*, 19(1). Retrieved from https://www.namahjournal.com/doc/Actual/Memory-transference-in-organ-transplant-recipients-vol-19-iss-1.html.

Jung, C. G. (1991). *The collected works of C. G. Jung. Supplementary volume B: Psychology of the unconscious: A study of the transformations and symbolism of the libido* (B. M. Hinkle, trans.). Princeton: Princeton University Press.

Kastrup, B. (2014). *Why materialism is baloney: How true skeptics know there is no death and fathom answers from life, the universe and everything*. Winchester: Iff Books.

Kastrup, B. (2016). What neuroimaging of the psychedelic state tells us about the mind-body problem. *Journal of Cognition and Neuroethics*, 4(2), 1–9.

Koch, C. (2014). Ubiquitous minds. *Scientific American Mind*, 25(1), 26–29.

Kolb, B., Whishaw, I. Q., & Teskey, G. C. (2016). *An introduction to brain and behaviour* (Vol. 5). *New York*: Worth.

Kuhn, T. S. (1970). *The structure of scientific revolutions*. Chicago, IL: University of Chicago Press.

Lipton, B. H. (2008). *The biology of belief: Unleashing the power of consciousness, matter and miracles*. New York: Mountain of Love Productions.

Luke, D., & Spowers, R. (Eds.). (2018). *DMT dialogues: Encounters with the spirit molecule*. Rochester, VT: Park Street Press.

Matlock, J. G. (2019). *Signs of reincarnation: Exploring beliefs, cases, and theory*. London: Rowman & Littlefield Publishers.

Matloff, G. L. (2016). Can panpsychism become an observational science? *Journal of Consciousnes Exploration & Research*, 7(7), 524–543.

Matloff, G. L. (2017). Stellar consciousness: Can panpsychism emerge as an obervational science? *EdgeScience*, 29, 9–14.

Meyer, P. (2018). Concerning the nature of DMT entities and their relation to us. In D. Luke & R. Spowers (Eds.), *DMT dialogues: Encounters with the spirit molecule* (pp. 95–117). Rochester, VT: Part Street Press.

Milton, J. (1997). Meta-analysis of free-response ESP studies without altered states of consciousness. *Journal of Parapsychology*, 61, 279–319.

Mossbridge, J. A., Tressoldi, P., & Utts, J. (2012). Predictive physiological anticipation preceding seemingly unpredictable stimuli: A meta-analysis. *Frontiers in Psychology*, 3, 390. doi: 10.3389/fpsyg.2012.00390.

Peters, R. M. (1999). The effectiveness of Therapeutic Touch: A meta-analytic review. *Nursing Science Quarterly*, 12(1), 52–61.

Radin, D., & Nelson, L. D. (2003). Meta-analysis of mind-matter interaction experiments: 1959–2000. In W. Jonas & C. Crawford (Eds.), *Healing, intention and energy medicine*. London: Harcourt Health Sciences.

Richard, F. D., Bond Jr, , C. F., & Stokes-Zoota, J. J. (2003). One hundred years of social psychology quantitatively described. *Review of General Psychology*, 7(4), 331–363.

Roe, C. A., Sonnex, C., & Roxburgh, E. C. (2015). Two meta-analyses of noncontact healing studies. *Explore*, 11(1), 11–23. doi: 10.1016/j.explore.2014.10.001.

Roney-Dougal, S. M., & Solfvin, J. (2011). Exploring the relationship between Tibetan meditation attainment and precognition. *Journal of Scientific Exploration*, 25(1), 29–46.

Rose, D. (2006). *Consciousness: Philosophical, psychological and neural theories*. Oxford: Oxford University Press.

Schmidt, S., Han-Gue, J., Whittman, M., Ambach, W., & Kubel, S. (2018). Remote meditation support – a multimodal distant intention experiment. *Explore*. doi: 10.1016/j.explore.2018. 12.002.

Schmidt, S., Schneider, R., Utts, J., & Walach, H. (2004). Distant intentionality and the feeling of being stared at: Two meta-analyses. *British Journal of Psychology*, 95(2), 235–247.

Schrodinger, E. (2018). *What is life?: With mind and matter and autobiographical sketches (23rd printing edn)*. Cambridge: Cambridge University Press.

Schwartz, J. M., Stapp, H. P., & Beauregard, M. (2005). Quantum physics in neuroscience and psychology: A neurophysical model of mind–brain interaction. *Philosophical Transactions of the Royal Society B: Biological Sciences*, 360(1458), 1309–1327. doi: 10.1098/rstb. 2004.1598.

Schwartz, S. A. (2015). Six protocols, *neuroscience, and near death: An emerging paradigm incorporating nonlocal consciousness*. *Explore*, 11(4), 252–260.

Schwartz, S. A. (2018). Kuhn, consciousness, and paradigms. *EXPLORE*, 14(4), 254–261.

Searle, J. R. (1997). *The mystery of consciousness*. New York: New York Review of Books.

Searle, J. R. (2008). *Mind, language and society: Philosophy in the real world*. New York, NY: Basic Books.

Sedlmeier, P. (2018). Meditation and altered states of consciousness. *Journal of Consciousness Studies*, 25(11–12), 73–101.

Shapiro, L. C. (2013). Elisabeth, Princess of Bohemia. In E. N. Zalta (Ed.) *The Stanford encyclopaedia of philosophy*. Retrieved from https://plato.stanford.edu/entries/elisabeth-bohemia/.

Sheldrake, R. (2015). Psi in everyday life. In E. Cardena, J. Palmer, & D. Marcusson-Clavertz (Eds.), *Parapsychology: A handbook for the 21st century* (pp. 350–363). Jefferson, NC: McFarland & Company Inc.

Stapp, H. P. (2011). *Mindful universe: Quantum mechanics and the participating observer*. New York, NY: Springer Science & Business Media.

Storm, L., Sherwood, S. J., Roe, C. A., Tressoldi, P., Rock, A. J., & Di Risio, L. (2017). On the correspondence between dream content and target material under laboratory conditions: A meta-analysis of dream-ESP studies, 1966–2016. *International Journal of Dream Research*, 10(2), 120–140.

Storm, L., Tressoldi, P., & Di Risio, L. (2012). Meta-analysis of ESP studies, 1987–2010: Assessing the success of the forced-choice design in parapsychology. *Journal of Parapsychology*, 76(2), 243–273.

Tononi, G., & Koch, C. (2015). *Consciousness: here, there and everywhere? Philosophical Transactions of the Royal Society B: Biological Sciences*, 370(1668), 20140167.

Tressoldi, P., Facco, E., & Lucangeli, D. (2016). *Emergence of qualia from brain activity or from an interaction of proto-consciousness with the brain: Which one is the weirder? Available evidence and a research agenda*. Available at SSRN: https://ssrn.com/abstract=2765331.

Tressoldi, P., & Utts, J. (2015). Statistical guidelines for empirical studies. In E. Cardeña, J. Palmer, & D. Marcusson-Clavertz (Eds.), *Parapsychology: A handbook for the 21st century* (pp. 83–93). Jefferson, NC: McFarland.

van Lommel, P. (2004). About the continuity of our consciousness. *Advances in Experimental Medicine and Biology*, 550, 115–132.

Vidal, C. (2016). Stellivore extraterrestrials? Binary stars as living systems. *Acta Astronautica*, 128, 251–256.

Williams, G. (2016). What can consciousness anomalies tell us about quantum mechanics? *Journal of Scientific Exploration*, 30(3), 326–354.

Williams, G. (2017). Field effects, experimenter effects, and Bohm's implicate order. *Journal of Nonlocality*, 5(1), 1–42.

Zeki, S. (2001). Localization and globalization in conscious vision. *Annual Review of Neuroscience*, 24(1), 57–86.

Index

Page numbers in italics refer to figures.

Printed in Great Britain
by Amazon

23284512R00176